CW00336171

Queer Places

Retracing the Steps of LGBTQ people around the World

Pacific Time Zone

Alaska, Hawaii, Nevada, Oregon, Washington

7th edition

by

Elisa Rolle

Dedication

To my travelling companions, my mother Giuliana and my two best friends, Alessandra B. and Alessandra C., now you know why I was always searching for those old buildings.

Contents

Pacific Time Zone

United States of America have been named #1 out of 10 Gay-Friendly Countries in the World by Amerikanki, 2014.

Alaska

Alaska is ranked 26 out of 51 for % of same sex couples (0,476%), and is ranked 46 for # of same sex couples, 1.228. (US Census 2010)

99500

Anchorage

Anchorage, AK, has been named among the Queerest City in America by The Advocate, 2017

Anchorage, AK, has been named among the 8 Underrated Cities for LGBTQ Singles Around the World, 2021, Matador Network

LGBTQ friendly bookstore:
Ships, Shoes and Sealing Wax (#4, 513 W 7th Ave, Anchorage, AK **99501**) was a feminist bookstore active in the 1980s.
Anchorage Book Mart, 419 D St, Anchorage, AK **99501**, included in the Damron Address Book in 1980.

Theatre:
Cinema One, 324 W 4th Ave, Anchorage, AK **99501**, included in the Damron Address Book from 1974 to 1980.
Movie arcades & book stores on W 4th Ave & C St, Anchorage, AK **99501**, included in the Damron Address Book from 1974 to 1980.

Religious Building: Metropolitan Community Church, 602 W 10th Ave, Anchorage, AK **99501**, included in the Damron Address Book from 1977 to 1980.

Historic District: Park Strip at W 9th Ave & L St, Anchorage, AK **99501**, included in the Damron Address Book from 1976 to 1980.

Store: Penney's, 406 W 5th Ave, Anchorage, AK **99501**, included in the Damron Address Book from 1974 to 1980.

Club: Spartacus House, 120 W 4th Ave, Anchorage, AK **99501**, included in the Damron Address Book in 1979.

Restaurant/Bar:
A&D Rhytm Club, E 5th Ave & Eagle St, Anchorage, AK **99501**, included in the 1975 All Lavender International Gay Guide.
Alibi Club, 5th Ave, Anchorage, AK **99501**, included in the 1964 Directory.
Alley Cat Bar, 418 C St, Anchorage, AK **99501**, included in the 1964 and 1965 Guild Guide.

Included in the 1964 Directory. Included in the 1975 All Lavender International Gay Guide.
Bonfire Lounge, 111 W 5th Ave, Anchorage, AK **99501**, included in the Damron Address Book from 1971 to 1978. Later Jake's, included in the Damron Address Book from 1979 to 1980.
Chart Room and Top of the World at the Anchorage Westward Hotel, W 3rd Ave & F St,

Anchorage, AK **99501**, included in the 1975 All Lavender International Gay Guide.

Club Paris, 417 W 5th Ave, Anchorage, AK **99501**, included in the 1975 All Lavender International Gay Guide. As of 2023, it's still open.

Coffee Guitar, C St, Anchorage, AK **99501**, between 8th and 9th Ave, included in the 1975 All Lavender International Gay Guide.

The Crossroads, 4th Ave, Anchorage, AK **99501**, included in the 1964 Directory.

Disco Den, 122 E 4th Ave, Anchorage, AK **99501**, included in the Damron Address Book from 1979 to 1980.

Five Fifteen Club or Five-One-Five Club or 515 Club, 515 W 4th Ave, Anchorage, AK **99501**, included in the 1964 and 1965 Guild Guide. Included in the 1964 Directory. Included in the Damron Address Book from 1966 to 1970. Included in the 1975 All Lavender International Gay Guide.

Gay 90's, 4th Ave, Anchorage, AK **99501**, included in the 1964 Directory.

Golden Nugget, 225 E 5th Ave, Anchorage, AK **99501**, included in the Damron Address Book from 1966 to 1972. Included in the 1975 All Lavender International Gay Guide. Later Village Lounge and Disco, active in the 1980s. Included in the Damron Address Book in 1980. It is now the Kodiak Bar & Grill, also a gay entertainment venue with drag shows.

Gordo's Cocktail Lounge, 1411 Gambell St, Anchorage, AK **99501**, included in the Damron Address Book in 1973.

Hal's Place, 618 Gambell St, Anchorage, AK **99501**, included in the Damron Address Book in 1980.

The Highland Fling, 4th Ave, Anchorage, AK **99501**, included in the 1964 Directory.

Hi Hat Club, 4th Ave & C St, Anchorage, AK **99501**, included in the 1964 Directory. Included in the 1975 All Lavender International Gay Guide.

Hunter Bar, 4th Ave & C St, Anchorage, AK **99501**, included in the 1964 Directory. Included in the 1975 All Lavender International Gay Guide.

Last Chance, W 5th Ave & G St, Anchorage, AK **99501**, included in the 1964 Directory.

Mad Myrna's (530 E 5th Ave, Anchorage, AK **99501**) has been named among the Amazing Gay Bars Around The World To Visit Before You Die, by BuzzFeed, 2019. Named among the Greatest Gay Bars in the World by Out.com, 2013.

Mays Café, 4th Ave & C St, Anchorage, AK **99501**, included in the 1975 All Lavender International Gay Guide.

Montana Club, 222 W 4th Ave, Anchorage, AK **99501**, included in the 1964 Directory. Included in the 1965 Guild Guide. Included in the 1975 All Lavender International Gay Guide.

Ole and Joe's, 4th Ave, Anchorage, AK **99501**, included in the 1964 Directory.

Pal Joe Cocktail Lounge, 1911 E 5th Ave, Anchorage, AK **99501**, included in the 1964 and 1965 Guild Guide.

Rendezvous, 612 E 4th Ave, Anchorage, AK **99501**, and 531 E 5th Ave, Anchorage, AK **99501**, included in the Damron Address Book from 1975 to 1978.

Scandinavian Club, 307 W 4th Ave, Anchorage, AK **99501**, included in the 1964 and 1965 Guild Guide.

Trade Winds Bar, 239 W 4th Ave, Anchorage, AK **99501**, included in the 1964 and 1965 Guild Guide.

Accommodation:

City Garden B&B (1352 W 10th Ave, Anchorage, AK **99501**), LGBTQ owned. GLD, Gay Lesbian Directory

Open since 1964, Hotel Captain Cook (939 W 5th Ave, Anchorage, AK **99501**), LGBTQ friendly, is a luxury Anchorage hotel with a history of impeccable service and welcoming hospitality. Enjoy total comfort and elegance, as well as true attention to detail for a notable stay. The perfect place to relax and unwind, this award-winning, four-star downtown hotel boasts delicious dining and a legendary 10,000 bottle wine cellar. Experience the natural beauty of Alaska and return to total comfort at Hotel Captain Cook. Hotel Captain Cook features 546 guestrooms, 4 on-site restaurants, a 24-hour business center, 14 different meeting spaces, and lobby shops of women's and men's clothing, fine jewelry, gifts, art galleries sundries, a barbershop, and beauty salon. The Athletic Club features fitness facilities and classes, an indoor pool, sauna, steam room, and Jacuzzi. The hotel is located in central downtown, three blocks from the Egan Convention Center in Anchorage. Hotel Captain Cook, a member of Historic Hotels of America since 2016, dates back to 1964.

Copper Whale Inn (440 L St, Anchorage, AK **99501**), gay owned. With easy access to attractions, shopping, galleries and the Anchorage Museum.

A Wildflower Inn (1239 I St, Anchorage, AK **99501**), gay owned. Walk to shops, restaurants, parks, bars, trails, etc.

Anchorage Mahogany Manor B&B (204 E 15th Ave, Anchorage, AK **99501**), LGBTQ friendly.

Earth B&B (1001 W 12th Ave, Anchorage, AK **99501**), LGBTQ owned.

Restaurant/Bar: Winter Palace, Jewel Lake Rd & Raspberry Rd, Anchorage, AK **99502**, included in the Damron Address Book in 1975.

Accommodation: Jewel Lake B&B (8125 Jewel Lake Rd, Anchorage, AK **99502**), gay owned. Great year-round location just minutes from the International Airport.

Store: Love Boutique, 2621 Spenard Rd, Anchorage, AK **99503**, included in the Damron Address Book in 1980.

Accommodation:
Hampton Inn Anchorage (4301 Credit Union Dr, Anchorage, AK **99503**), LGBTQ friendly.
Hilton Garden Inn (4555 Union Square Dr, Anchorage, AK **99503**), LGBTQ friendly.
Hyatt House Anchorage (5141 Business Park Blvd, Anchorage, AK **99503**). This 144 room hotel with its central location in midtown Anchorage offers their guest free Wi-Fi, free breakfast, heated indoor pool, free public computers in the commons and meeting and event space. Part of World Rainbow Hotels (WRH), Lesbian and Gay Welcoming Hotels.

Restaurant/Bar: Olive Garden Italian, 1186 North Muldoon Road, Anchorage, AK **99504**

Accommodation: Alaska House of Jade B&B (3800 Delwood Pl, Anchorage, AK **99504**), LGBTQ friendly.

Cheney Lake B&B (6333 Colgate Dr, Anchorage, AK **99504**) Included in Inn Places 1999, Gay & Lesbian Accommodations Worldwide. Gay friendly. As of 2021 it's closed.

Restaurant/Bar: The Jet, Fort Richardson, Anchorage, AK **99505**, included in the 1964 Directory.

LGBTQ friendly bookstore: Alaska Women's Bookstore, 2470 E Tudor Rd, Anchorage, AK **99507**, active in 1990.

Restaurant/Bar: Cattleman's, 3471 E Tudor Rd, Anchorage, AK **99507**, included in the Damron Address Book from 1976 to 1980.

Accommodation: Aurora Winds, An Exceptional B&B Resort (7501 Upper O'Malley Rd, Anchorage, AK **99507**) Included in Inn Places 1999, Gay & Lesbian Accommodations Worldwide. Gay and Lesbian. As of 2021 it's closed.

LGBTQ Center: Alaska Gay Community Center, 838 E 8th Ave, Anchorage, AK **99508**, included in the Damron Address Book in 1979. The first Alaska Gay Community Center was on 837 I Street, behind a bakery called the Bread Factory. After eviction, it moved into a building on 5th Avenue, just west of the Egan Convention Center, in a building which no longer exists. At the end of June 1983, the AGLRC closed its physical facility due to inability to continue paying rent. Shortly thereafter, the board of directors renamed the organization Identity, Inc. — the name it's held ever since. Identity did its work for nearly two decades without a physical office until it opened the Gay and Lesbian Community Center of Alaska (GLCCA) on Northern Lights in 2001 (moving to its present location on E. 5th Avenue a few years later).

Store: Fred Myers Dept. Store T-Room, 1000 E Northern Lights Blvd, Anchorage, AK **99508**, included in the Damron Address Book in 1980.

Religious Building: Metropolitan Community Church, 1413 Norene St, Anchorage, AK **99508**, included in the Damron Address Book in 1976.

Accommodation:
Camai B&B (3838 Westminster Way, Anchorage, AK **99508**), LGBTQ friendly.

Lake Hood Inn (4702 Lake Spenard Dr, Anchorage, AK **99509**), LGBTQ friendly.

Restaurant/Bar:

Olive Garden Italian, 800 E Dimond Blvd Suite # 160, Anchorage, AK **99515**

Accommodation:
A Rabbit Creek B&B (4540 Rabbit Creek Rd, Anchorage, AK **99516**), LGBTQ friendly.
Aawesome Retreat B&B (16528 Kings Way Dr, Anchorage, AK **99516**), LGBTQ friendly. GLD, Gay Lesbian Directory
Alaskan Leopard B&B (16136 Sandpiper Dr, Anchorage, AK **99516**), gay friendly. Luxury mountaintop B&B with spectacular views of the entire area, Mt McKinley, and the Kenai peninsula.
Alaska's North Country Castle B&B (14600 Joanne Cir, Anchorage, AK **99516**), gay friendly. Sunny, warm, Victorian home. Quiet, forested acreage. Sparkling Chugach Mountains and

Cook Inlet views. Moose watching from gazebo-style breakfast nook, & four decks. Voted Best in Alaska 2004, Inn Traveler Magazine. Featured on cover of Arrington's B&B Journal.
Microtel Inn & Suites by Wyndham Anchorage Airport (5205 Northwood Dr, Anchorage, AK **99517**). Affordable Comfort will help make the most of your Alaska vacation. Located a 10-minute drive from Ted Stevens International Airport with free shuttle service available. Modern rooms. Part of World Rainbow Hotels (WRH), Lesbian and Gay Welcoming Hotels.

Restaurant/Bar:

Oasis, Seward Hwy, Bird Creek, AK **99540**, included in the Damron Address Book from 1968 to 1970.

World Heritage List: Wrangell-St. Elias National Park & Preserve (Richardson Hwy, Copper Center, AK **99573**)

Attractions: Christmas Chute (Anchorage, AK **99587**) has been named among the Most difficult ski slopes in the world.

Accommodation:

Ma Johnson's Hotel (101 Kennicott Avenue, McCarthy, AK **99588**), LGBTQ friendly.

99600

Restaurant/Bar:
Alice's Champagne Palace (195 E Pioneer Ave, Homer, AK **99603**), LGBTQ friendly
Cafe Cups (162 W Pioneer Ave, Homer, AK **99603**), LGBTQ friendly

Little Mermaid Bistro (4246 Homer Spit Rd, Homer, AK **99603**), LGBTQ friendly
Two Sisters Bakery (233 E Bunnell Ave, Homer, AK **99603**), LGBTQ friendly

Accommodation:
Alaska's Sadie Cove Wilderness Lodge (In Kachemak Bay State Park, Box 2265, Homer, AK

99603), gay friendly. A peaceful resort where private parties of 8 or more have the entire lodge to themselves.

Bay Avenue B&B Inn (7941, 1393 Bay Ave, Homer, AK **99603**), gay friendly.
Brigitte's Bavarian B&B (59800 Tern Ct, Homer, AK **99603**), gay friendly. GLD, Gay Lesbian Directory

Tutka Bay Lodge (Kenai Peninsula Borough, Homer, AK **99603**), LGBTQ friendly, has its own cooking school run by talented chef-owner Kirsten Dixon.

Oldest Building in the State: Russian-American Company Magazin Erskine House, 101 E Marine Way, Kodiak, AK **99615**. Now known as the Baranov Museum, the Magazin Erskine House can be traced to the Russian colonization of Alaska. It was built in 1808 and used as a storage facility for the Russian-American Company. Today, it's a National Historic Landmark and a remnant of Kodiak's history as the first permanent Russian settlement and territory in North America.

Oldest Bar in the State: B&B Bar, 326 Shelikof St, Kodiak, AK **99615**. The B&B Bar was moved piece by piece by horse and buggy to Kodiak. Open since 1906, it's has a low-key, welcoming reputation as a place regulars gather for beer specials and pool.

Accommodation:
Alaska Garden Gate B&B (950 Snodgrass Dr, Palmer, AK **99645**), LGBTQ owned. B&B in Palmer just north of Anchorage - gateway to Hatcher Pass, glaciers, hiking and wildlife.

Renfro's Lakeside Retreat (27177 Seward Hwy, Seward, AK **99664**), LGBTQ friendly.
Serenity by the Sea Cabins (P.O.Box 145, 14000 Shady Ln, Seward, AK **99664**), LGBTQ friendly.
Alaska Red Fish Lodge (32815 Eldorado Way, Sterling, AK **99672**), LGBTQ friendly.

Store: Operating since 1921, Nagley's General Store, 13650 E Main St, Talkeetna, AK **99676**, has certainly earned its slogan, Established Before Most of You Were Born. For over a century it has been a focal point of the community, who helped rebuild it after the site was destroyed by fire in 1997. Today, Nagley's is still a firm favorite with the people of Talkeetna for its Kaladi Brothers coffees and hand-scooped ice cream cones. It's also famous for its long lineage of store cats, with Aurora currently prowling the place. This historic log building was nearly lost in the 1997 fire, but the community helped rebuild the store. (It was originally founded at the height of the early XX century Alaska gold rush.) Nagley's General Store has groceries, coffee and sandwiches, but is perhaps most popular for the generations of cats that have greeted customers since the 1970s. Named among the Most charming general stores in every US state, 2018, by Love Food. Named among the 25 Old-Fashioned General Stores Across America, 2022, by Taste of Home.

Whittier

Toward the end of WWII, roughly a quarter of Americans lived in multigenerational households—a trend that's making a comeback among millennials. But even if your house is getting fuller these days, it's nothing compared with Whittier, AK **99693**. The vast majority of the town's 200 residents live together in the 14-story Begich Towers, according to The California Sunday Magazine. Named among the 25 Tiny Towns to Visit for a Glimpse at How We Used to Live, by Bob Vila, Tried, True, Trustworthy Home Advice.

99700

Store:

Bently Mall, 32 College Rd, Fairbanks, AK **99701**, included in the Damron Address Book in 1980.

Gavora Mall, 250 3rd St, Fairbanks, AK **99701**, included in the Damron Address Book in 1980.

Theatre: Cinema Two, Steese Hwy, Fairbanks, AK **99701**, included in the Damron Address Book from 1976 to 1980.

Historic District: State Of Alaska Fairbanks Regional Office Building, 675 7th Ave, Fairbanks, AK **99701**, included in the Damron Address Book from 1976 to 1980.

School: University of Alaska, 613 Cushman St, Fairbanks, AK **99701**, Library, Constitution Hall, Gym & Wood Ctr., included in the Damron Address Book from 1976 to 1980.

Restaurant/Bar:
The Cottage Bar, 510 2nd Ave, Fairbanks, AK **99701**, near Lacy, included in the 1964 and 1965 Guild Guide. Included in the 1964 Directory. Included in the Damron Address Book from 1969 to 1970. Included in the 1975 All Lavender International Gay Guide.

Crystal Room, Fairbanks, AK **99701**, included in the 1964 Directory.

Tommy's Elbow Room, 410 2nd Ave, Fairbanks, AK **99701**, included in the 1964 Directory. Included in the Damron Address Book from 1971 to 1978.

Flame Lounge, Fairbanks, AK **99701**, included in the 1964 Directory.

Fox Lounge, 500 1st Ave, Fairbanks, AK **99701**, included in the Damron Address Book in 1975.

The Polaris Cocktail lounge, Polaris Building, 125 Lacey St, Fairbanks, AK **99701**, included in the 1964 Guild Guide. Included in the 1964 Directory.

Upstairs Club, next to Cinema Two, Steese Hwy, Fairbanks, AK **99701**, included in the Damron Address Book in 1980.

Accommodation:
All Seasons B&B Inn (763 7th Ave, Fairbanks, AK **99701**), LGBTQ friendly.

Fairbanks Hotel (517 3rd Ave, Fairbanks, AK **99701**) included in Inn Places 1999, Gay & Lesbian Accommodations Worldwide. Gay friendly, women owned and women operated. As of 2021 it's closed.

Dale and Jo View Suites (3260 Craft Rd, Fairbanks, AK **99708**), LGBTQ friendly.

Blue Loon Club, Fairbanks

Restaurant/Bar: *The Blue Loon is an entertainment complex featuring LGBTQ events. It was home to the touring LGBTQ entertainment troupe, KlonDykes, Queens, and Company from 1997 through 2003.*

Address: 2999 George Parks Hwy, Fairbanks, AK 99709

Blue Loon Club, Fairbanks

As of May 2016, The Blue Loon is up for sale. The Loon's owner, Adam Wool, listed the Fairbanks institution for a reported sale price of $750,000. Located just west of Fairbanks on the Parks Highway, the Blue Loon serves as one of the Fairbanks area's largest venues. The business routinely hosts concerts and other shows in addition to its everyday roles as a nightclub, restaurant and movie theater. The Blue Loon first opened in the early 1990s, but Wool has owned and operated it for the last 19 years.

Accommodation:
Aurora Ice Hotel (17600 Chena Hot Springs Rd, Fairbanks, AK **99712**) has been named among the Most beautiful ice hotels in the world, 2019.

Nenana

Nenana, AK **99760**. For more than 100 years, competitors in the Nenana Ice Classic have been betting on the exact time when the more-than-a-meter-deep layer of ice on the Tanana River will break in spring. According to Climate Central, placing your bet is easy: Just guess a date and time, then wait until a tripod on the ice, which is connected to a clock, shifts when the ice breaks. Although the rules of the game have remained unchanged over the years, thanks to technological advancements the organizers can now keep a webcam trained on the river so anyone who really wants to watch ice melt can do so. Named among the 25 Tiny Towns to Visit for a Glimpse at How We Used to Live, by Bob Vila, Tried, True, Trustworthy Home Advice.

99800

Juneau

Southeast Alaska Gay and Lesbian Association

The Southeast Alaska Gay and Lesbian Alliance (SEAGLA) works to provide a supporting social network for gay, lesbian, bisexual, transgender, and queer people in Southeast Alaska.

Address:
120 2nd St, Juneau, AK 99801
2nd Floor, 2 Marine Way, Juneau, AK 99801

Downtown Juneau, Creative Commons Licenses, via Wikimedia Commons

Place

In the early 1980's a group of like-minded friends realized there was a need for social opportunity for the Gay, Lesbian and Bi-sexual people of Juneau. The friends took turns hosting house parties or monthly potlucks and in some cases, actual dance parties were held in a host's garage. During the Gay Pride month of June one of the biggest events was billed as the annual solstice party. With a big bon fire crackling in the back yard, and dance music playing in the garage, it was a really fun place to go, have a beer and dance with a same sex partner without fear or discrimination that was very common place at that point in history. The Southeast Alaska Gay and Lesbian Association hosted events in the back room of the Silverbow Bakery (120 2nd St, Juneau, AK) in the 1980s and 1990s and then was located on the second floor of Merchant's Wharf (2 Marine Way, Juneau, AK) in the 1990s. The Merchants Wharf - T-Rooms have been included in the Damron Address Book in 1980.

Historic District: Federal and State Office Building, 333 Willoughby Ave, Juneau, AK **99801**, included in the Damron Address Book in 1980.

Restaurant/Bar:

Crystal Saloon, 418 S Franklin St, Juneau, AK **99801**, included in the Damron Address Book in 1980.

Latch String Bar at Barnahof Hotel, 127 N Franklin St, Juneau, AK **99801**, included in the Damron Address Book from 1974 to 1980.
Pomeri, Main St, Juneau, AK **99801**, included in the 1964 Directory.

Accommodation:
Alaska's Capital Inn B&B (113 5th Street Stairs, Juneau, AK **99801**), LGBTQ friendly.
The Historic Silverbow Inn (120 2nd St, Juneau, AK **99801**), LGBTQ friendly.

Pearson's Pond Luxury Inn & Adventure Spa (4541 Sawa Cir Ste #1, Juneau, AK **99801**), LGBTQ friendly.

World Heritage List: Glacier Bay (1 Park Rd, Gustavus, AK **99826**)

Accommodation:
Glacier Bay Cottage Vacation Rental (1251 Gustavus Rd, Gustavus, AK **99826**), LGBTQ friendly. Located in Gustavus, AK, the gateway to Glacier Bay National Park.

The Guardhouse Boardinghouse (15 Seward Dr., Haines, AK **99827**), LGBTQ owned.
Alaska Ocean View B&B Inn (1101 Edgecumbe Dr, Sitka, AK **99835**), LGBTQ friendly.

Oldest Restaurant in the State: The Historic Skagway Inn, 1897, Seafood, 655 Broadway, Skagway, AK **99840**. What people say: Reviewers on TripAdvisor like the Skagway Inn's historic feel and big portions of local seafood. One reviewer called the food very tasty and plentiful and deemed the bread pudding some of the best I have had in a long time.

99900

Restaurant/Bar:

Frontier Bar, Main St, Ketchikan, AK **99901**, included in the Damron Address Book in 1980.

Hawaii

Hawaii is ranked 9 out of 51 for % of same sex couples (0,711%), and is ranked 38 for # of same sex couples, 3.239. (US Census 2010)

In 1993, the Hawaii Supreme Court ruled that the state's ban on same-sex marriage might violate the state constitution's equal rights amendment (since women were prohibited from doing something—marry a woman—that men were allowed to do).

Hawaii Rainbow Chamber of Commerce: http://www.hirainbowchamber.org/

Hawaii has been named among the 8 LGBT-friendly destinations based on the colors of the Pride Flag, by Orbitz, 2016

96700

Ohau

Ohau (**96701**) has been named among the Highest waves in the world, 2019

Restaurant/Bar:
Ben & Jerry's, 99-500 Salt Lake Blvd, Aiea, HI **96701**

Ben & Jerry's, 98-1005 Moanalua Road #K8, Aiea, HI **96701**

Accommodation:
Mahina Kai Ocean Villa (4933 Aliomanu Rd, Anahola, HI **96703**), gay owned. Walk across the street to the beach from this ocean-view villa on Kauai's tropical North Shore.

Oldest Restaurant in the State: Hotel Manago, 1917, American, 82-6155 Hawai'i Belt Rd, Captain Cook, HI **96704**. What people say: The restaurant averages 4.5 stars out of 5 on Yelp, where customers like its low cost (all entrees are $19 or less) and lack of pretension (it's super basic but so worth it). They also love The Hotel Manago restaurant's signature pork chops.

Accommodation:
Aloha Guest House (84-4780 Mamalahoa Hwy, Captain Cook, HI **96704**), LGBTQ friendly.
Hale Aloha Guest Ranch (84-4780 Mamalahoa Hwy, Captain Cook, HI **96704**) included in Inn Places 1999, Gay & Lesbian Accommodations Worldwide. Gay, Lesbian and gay operated. As of 2021 it's closed.
Horizon Guest House (86-3992 Mamalahoa Hwy, Captain Cook, HI **96704**), gay owned. Casually elegant private resort on 40 acres, spectacular 20 mile panoramic ocean views.
Ka'awa Loa (82-5990 Napoopoo Rd., Captain Cook, Big Island / South Kona, HI **96704**), LGBTQ owned. 5-acre coffee farm and guesthouse conveniently located in South Kona.
Luana Inn B&B (82-5856 Lower Nāpo'opo'o Rd, Captain Cook, HI **96704**), gay friendly. New, upscale B&B overlooking Kealakekua Bay
Puhala Hale, 88-1547 Puhala Ave, Captain Cook, HI **96704**, GLD, Gay Lesbian Directory
Rainbow Plantation B&B, PO Box 122, Captain Cook, HI **96704**, GLD, Gay Lesbian Directory

Rick's Hut, Milolii Beach, HI **96704**, GLD, Gay Lesbian Directory
South Kona Hideaway (83-5399 Middle Keei Rd, Captain Cook, HI **96704**), LGBTQ owned.
Marriott Ihilani Resort and Spa at Ko Olina (92-1001 Olani St, Kapolei, HI **96707**), LGBTQ friendly.
The Cliff's Edge B&B & Guest House (Haiku, HI **96708**), gay friendly. Experience privacy and romance on this oceanfront estate.
Golden Bamboo Ranch (422 Kaupakalua Rd, Haiku, HI **96708**) included in Inn Places 1999, Gay & Lesbian Accommodations Worldwide. Gay friendly, gay owned and gay operated. As of 2021 it's closed.
Haiku Anuenue B&B (544 Kaiapa Pl, Haiku, HI **96708**), LGBTQ friendly.
Haiku Plantation Inn, 555 Haiku Road, Haiku, HI **96708**, GLD, Gay Lesbian Directory
Halfway to Hana (13710 Hana Hwy, Haiku, HI **96708**) included in Inn Places 1999, Gay & Lesbian Accommodations Worldwide. Gay friendly.

Huelo Point Flower Farm (222 Door of Faith Rd, Haiku, HI **96708**), 2-acre oceanfront estate on Maui's Northshore on a sea cliff providing dramatic views of Waipio Bay. Included in Inn Places 1999, Gay & Lesbian Accommodations Worldwide. Gay friendly, gay owned and gay operated.

Maui Ocean Breezes (240 N Holokai Rd, Haiku, HI **96708**), gay friendly. Fully equipped, private cottages and studio with great ocean views. GLD, Gay Lesbian Directory
Maui Retreat (610 Huelo Rd, Haiku, HI **96708**), LGBTQ friendly.

Store: Founded in 1910 on the Hawaiian island of Maui, the Hasegawa General Store, 5165 Hana Hwy, Hana, HI **96713**, was immortalized in song by legendary American composer Paul Weston, who was mesmerized by the wonderful variety of merchandise...spread out there before your eyes. Indeed, variety is the spice of life here. At this ultra-kooky general store you'll never be short of fresh local produce, gallons of mayonnaise, CDs from Hawaiian musicians, books on island culture and philosophy, or Maui's largest selection of pareaus (sarongs). Named among the Most charming general stores in every US state, 2018, by Love Food.

Other non-queer residents: Charles Augustus Lindbergh (1902-1974), 40990 Hana Hwy, Hana, HI **96713**, from the 1960s to 1974.

Accommodation:
Travaasa Hana (5031 Hana Hwy, Hana, HI **96713**), LGBTQ friendly.

Ala'aina Ocean Vista (184 Hana Hwy, Hana, HI **96713**), LGBTQ friendly.

World Heritage List: Hawaii Volcanoes National Park: Ola'a Forest Tract (Volcano, HI **96718**)

Big Island

Big Island has been named among the Best places in the world to snorkel, 2019

Park: Lawns in front of Court House, 777 Kilauea Ave, Hilo, HI **96720**, included in the Damron Address Book in 1980.

Restaurant/Bar:
City Tavern, 55 Haili St, Hilo, HI **96720**, included in the Damron Address Book from 1977 to 1980.

Hilo Travelodge Bar, 121 Banyan Dr, Hilo, HI **96720**, included in the Damron Address Book from 1973 to 1980.

Accommodation:
Following a $30 million renovation, the Grand Naniloa Hotel Hilo (93 Banyan Dr, Hilo, HI **96720**) debuted on November 10, 2016 as the first hotel on the Big Island of Hawaii for DoubleTree by Hilton, one of Hilton's 13 market-leading brands. The Grand Naniloa Hotel Hilo, a DoubleTree by Hilton is located on 70 acres of stunning and lush oceanfront property, with magnificent views of Hilo Bay and the Mauna Kea Volcano. The hotel's 320 fully-refurbished guestrooms and suites provide upscale, contemporary lodging for vacationers exploring the charms of Hilo and nearby attractions, such as stunning waterfalls, Volcanoes National Park, and snorkeling or surfing off the beautiful bay and ocean coasts. Resort amenities include daily complimentary golf on Hilo's only 9-hole course, adjacent to the hotel, on-site restaurant, lobby bar, bayside wedding gazebo, meeting space, fitness center, and local entertainment in the Willie K. Crown Room concert hall. Grand Naniloa Hotel Hilo, a DoubleTree by Hilton, a member of Historic Hotels of America since 2016, dates back to 1939.
Hilo Bay Hale (301 Ponahawai St, Hilo, Big Island, South Hilo, HI **96720**), gay owned. Enjoy views of Hilo Town and magical koi ponds from your private lanai (deck) in this beautifully restored 1912 home in downtown hilo. Walk to everything, no need for a car.

Castle Hilo Hawaiian Hotel (71 Banyan Dr, Hilo, HI **96720**), LGBTQ friendly.

The Bay House (42 Pukihae St, Hilo, HI **96720**), LGBTQ friendly.

Wild Ginger Inn (100 Puueo St, Hilo, HI **96720**), LGBTQ friendly.

Emeraldview Guesthouse, 272 Kaiulani St, Hilo, HI **96720**. Waterfall river view from your own deck, 35 minute drive to Volcanoes National Park.

The Inn at Kulaniapia Falls (100 Kulaniapia Dr, Hilo, HI **96721**), LGBTQ friendly.

Club Wyndham Bali Hai Villas (4970 Pepelani Loop, Princeville, HI **96722**). Located on Kaweonui Point and opposite 2 golf courses, this upscale, all-suites resort surrounded by waterfalls and palm trees is a 12-minute walk from Queen's Bath salt water spa. Part of World Rainbow Hotels (WRH), Lesbian and Gay Welcoming Hotels.

Club Wyndham Ka Eo Kai (3970 Wyllie Rd, Princeville, HI **96722**) is 1.5 miles from the Queen's Bath tide pool and 4.2 miles from Hanalei Bay. The suites offer free Wi-Fi, flat-screen TV's with premium channels and separate living areas. Part of World Rainbow Hotels (WRH), Lesbian and Gay Welcoming Hotels.

Club Wyndham Shearwater (3730 Kamehameha Rd, Princeville, HI **96722**) is 4.1 miles from Hanalei Bay and 9.5 miles from Haena State Park. Part of World Rainbow

Restaurant/Bar:

Accommodation:

Restaurant/Bar:
Swiss Chalet Restaurant, 52 Oneawa St, Kailua, HI **96734**, included in the 1964 and 1965 Guild Guide. Included in the 1964 Directory. Included

Accommodation:
Hawaii's Hidden Hideaway B&B, 1369 Mokolea Dr, Kailua, Oahu, HI **96734**

Kimos's Beach House (481 Kawailoa Rd # A1, Kailua, HI **96734**), LGBTQ friendly.

A Tropic Paradise (43 Laiki Pl, Kailua, HI **96734**) included in Inn Places 1999, Gay & Lesbian Accommodations Worldwide. Gay friendly and gay owned. As of 2021 it's closed.

Hilton Waikoloa Village (69-425 Waikoloa Beach Dr, Waikoloa Village, HI **96738**), TAG Approved LGBTQ friendly accommodation.

Hotels (WRH), Lesbian and Gay Welcoming Hotels.

Kauai Tiki Tower (3920 Wyllie Rd, Princeville, HI **96722**), LGBTQ friendly. GLD, Gay Lesbian Directory

Princeville Resort (5520 Ka Haku Rd, Princeville, HI **96722**), LGBTQ friendly.

Sealodge Sunrise Vacation Rental Condo (3700 Kamehameha Rd, Princeville, HI **96722**), LGBTQ owned.

The Westin Princeville Ocean Resort Villas (3838 Wyllie Rd, Princeville, HI **96722**), LGBTQ friendly.

Hale Hualalai B&B (74-4968 Mamalahoa Hwy, Holualoa, HI **96725**), LGBTQ friendly. Hale Hualalai is a luxury B&B in Kona, HI. B&B suites overlooking Kailua Kona on the Big Island of Hawaii. Up in the coffee belt, at the 1300' elevation makes for fabulous views and sunsets. Enjoy the slow paced, relaxing style on 4 acres of coffee, tropical fruit & flowers

Holualoa Inn (76-5932 Mamalahoa Hwy, Holualoa, HI **96725**), LGBTQ friendly.

Horizon Guest House, POB 268, Honaunau, HI **96726**, GLD, Gay Lesbian Directory

Hamakua Hideaway Cliff House (Honokaa, HI **96727**), LGBTQ friendly. GLD, Gay Lesbian Directory

Waianuhea B&B (45-3503 Kahana Dr, Honokaa, HI **96727**), gay friendly. Tropical Hawaiian B&B just outside Waimea on Hawaii's north shore.

Turtle Bay Resort (57-091 Kamehameha Hwy, Kahuku, HI **96731**), gay friendly.

Bistro Casanova, 33 Lono Avenue, Kahului, HI **96732**, GLD, Gay Lesbian Directory

Maui Beach Hotel, a LITE hotel (170 W Kaahumanu Ave, Kahului, HI **96732**), TAG Approved LGBTQ friendly accommodation.

in the Damron Address Book from 1965 to 1969. Included in the 1975 All Lavender International Gay Guide.

Aston Shores at Waikoloa (69-1035 Keana Pl, Waikoloa Village, HI **96738**), TAG Approved LGBTQ friendly accommodation.

Aston Waikoloa Colony Villas (69-1022 Keana Pl, Waikoloa Village, HI **96738**), TAG Approved LGBTQ friendly accommodation.

Outrigger Fairway Villas (69-200 Pohakulana Pl, Waikoloa Village, HI **96738**), LGBTQ friendly.

Paniolo Greens Resort (68-1745 Waikoloa Rd, Waikoloa Village, HI **96738**). Located on the Kohala Coast, offers easy access to the Big Island's northern ranch Kuleana highlands. World Rainbow Hotels (WRH), Lesbian and

Waikoloa Beach Marriott Resort & Spa (69-275 Waikoloa Beach Dr, Waikoloa Beach, HI **96738**), LGBTQ friendly.

Kona

Kona has been named among the Best places in the world for scuba diving, 2019

LGBTQ friendly bookstore:

Kona Stories Book Store (78-6831 Alii Dr #142, Kailua, HI **96740**), lesbian owned.
Kona Bay Books, 74-5487 Kaiwi St, Kailua-Kona, HI **96740**, 56 Queer-Owned Bookstores to Support, by Oprah Daily, 2021

Restaurant/Bar:

Kona Steak House, Kailua-Kona, HI **96740**, included in the Damron Address Book from 1974 to 1978.

Accommodation:

Aston Kona by the Sea (75-6106 Alii Dr, Kailua-Kona, HI **96740**), TAG Approved LGBTQ friendly accommodation.

Castle Kona Bali Kai (76-6246 Alii Dr, Kailua-Kona, HI **96740**), LGBTQ friendly.

Castle Kona Reef (75-5888 Alii Dr, Kailua-Kona, HI **96740**), LGBTQ friendly.

Club Wyndham Kona Hawaiian Resort (75-5961 Ali'i Drive, Kailua-Kona, HI **96740**). This all-condo seaside resort, set overlooking Kahalu'u Bay, is 1.2 miles from Hulihee Palace and 4 miles from Kahalu'u Beach Park. Part of World Rainbow Hotels (WRH), Lesbian and Gay Welcoming Hotels.

Club Wyndham Mauna Loa Village (78-7190 Kaleiopapa St, Kailua-Kona, HI **96740**). This resort hotel is 2 miles from Kahaluu Beach Park and 7 miles from the Kona Coffee Living History Farm. Part of World Rainbow Hotels (WRH), Lesbian and Gay Welcoming Hotels.

Makaloa Villa at the Four Seasons Resort, 72-100 Ka'upulehu Drive, Kailua-Kona, HI **96740**, has been named among the 25 of the world's most expensive hotel rooms ($18,000/night). A one-story bungalow nestled right beside the Pacific Ocean, the Four Seasons Resort Hualalai's Makaloa Villa is a luxurious way to take in paradise. The resort sits on the northwest part of the Big Island, and the three-bedroom, 3,885-square-foot villa has window walls in its living room, dining room, and office to take in the breathtaking sights such as tropical gardens, the Waiakauhi Pond and, of course, the Hawaiian sunset over the ocean. The Makaloa Villa has its own hot tub, private pool, outdoor lava-rock showers, and a hammock; each guest also gets a lei upon arrival at the resort recently voted the Best Hotel in America by U.S. News & World Report.

Hawaiian Oasis B&B (74-4958 Kiwi St, Kailua-Kona, HI **96740**), LGBTQ friendly.

Holua Resort At Mauna Loa Village (78-7190 Kaleiopapa St, Kailua-Kona, HI **96740**) offers villas furnished with modern amenities, including full kitchens. Guests can enjoy private lanais or patios, DVD players, free Wi-Fi along with on-site laundry. World Rainbow Hotels (WRH), Lesbian and Gay Welcoming Hotels, GLD, Gay Lesbian Directory.

Honu Kai B&B (74-1529 Hao Kuni St, Kailua-Kona, HI **96740**), gay friendly. Plantation home on 1.3 acres, with luxury linens and high-end furnishings. GLD, Gay Lesbian Directory.

King Kamehameha's Kona Beach Hotel (75-5660 Palani Rd, Kailua-Kona, HI **96740**), LGBTQ friendly.

Kona Coast Resort (78-6842 Alii Dr, Kailua-Kona, HI **96740**), gay friendly. Sitting on 21 acres of lush, tropical gardens amidst the panoramic backdrop of Hawaii's Kona Coast, the Kona Coast Resort on Hawaii's Big Island offers spectacular views of palm trees and calm waters. World Rainbow Hotels (WRH), Lesbian and Gay Welcoming Hotels, GLD, Gay Lesbian Directory.

Nancy's Hideaway (73-1530 Uanani Pl, Kailua-Kona, HI **96740**), gay friendly. Enjoy all that the Big Island has to offer from your own private cottage or studio tucked away on 3 tropical acres with ocean views. GLD, Gay Lesbian Directory.

Oceanfront Condo Kailua-Kona, 75-5782 Alii Drive #303, Kailua-Kona, HI **96740**, GLD, Gay Lesbian Directory.

Oceanfront Condo Retreat, 76-6268 Alii Drive #404, Kailua-Kona, HI **96740**, GLD, Gay Lesbian Directory.

Outrigger Keauhou Beach Resort (78-6740 Alii Dr, Kailua-Kona, HI **96740**), LGBTQ friendly.

Outrigger Royal Sea Cliff (75-6040 Alii Dr, Kailua-Kona, HI **96740**), LGBTQ friendly.
Royal Kona Resort (75-5852 Alii Dr, Kailua-Kona, HI **96740**), LGBTQ friendly.
Royal Sea Cliff Kona by Outrigger (75-6040 Alii Dr, Kailua-Kona, HI **96740**). This condo hotel is 1.7 miles from Hulihee Palace royal museum, 3.3 miles from Kahaluu Beach Park and 3.6 miles from Old Kona Airport State Recreation Area. Part of World Rainbow Hotels (WRH), Lesbian and Gay Welcoming Hotels.
Hale Kua Kauai B&B (4896E Kua Rd, Kalaheo, HI **96741**), gay friendly. On Kauai's sunny south shore, minutes to Poipu Beach, short drive to Lihue, Kapa, and the lush north shore of Kauai.

Attractions: Waihilau Falls (Waimea, HI **96743**) has been named among the Most beautiful waterfalls in the world, 2019.

Other non-queer residents: Cornwell House, 62-2145A Ouli St, Waimea, HI **96743**, designed by Frank Lloyd Wright in 1995.

Attractions: In Hawaii, Pu'ukohola Heiau National Historic Site (62-3601 Kawaihae Rd, Waimea, HI **96743**) contains the history of Kamehameha I, the Hawaiian king who built a kingdom from nothing in the late XVIII century. Visitors can tour the ruins of an ancient temple. Among the 50 most popular historic sites in America, 2022.

Accommodation:
The Mauna Kea Beach Hotel (62-100 Mauna Kea Beach Dr, Waimea, HI **96743**), LGBTQ friendly, is an international destination resort, upholding a timeless tradition of luxury and aloha. The resort was developed by legendary venture capitalist Laurance S. Rockefeller, after he spotted the crystal clear waters and white sands of Kauna'oa Bay and was inspired to create a great hotel that reflected the spirit of this special place. With thoughtful sensitivity to the dramatic natural surroundings, Rockefeller's team of experts created a stunning mid-century modern design, that in the 1960s was far ahead of its time. As a crowning touch, he installed a 1,600-piece collection of museum-quality Asian and Oceanic art and artifacts throughout the hotel - the first hotel to install art in this manner. Guest amenities at the 252-room resort include an award-winning 18-hole golf course, 11-court seaside tennis club, a beach club, island dining, homes, and villas. The resort was lauded soon after opening, and in 1966, received the Honor Award from the American Institute of Architects and added to its most significant 150 buildings lists. Fortune named it among the Ten Best Buildings of 1966 and Esquire named it one of the Three greatest hotels in the world in 1967. While remaining firmly committed to honoring the hotel's stunning mid-century modern architecture, Mauna Kea has made extensive improvements over the years, of course to guestrooms, but so much more. Most recently, renovations have been completed in public areas, in multiple restaurant dining venues, and the hotel has added new meeting and ballroom space to remain competitive in the luxury hotel marketplace. Mauna Kea Beach Hotel, a member of Historic Hotels of America since 2016, dates back to the 1965.
Mauna Lani Bay Hotel and Bungalows (68-1400 Mauna Lani Dr, Waimea, HI **96743**), LGBTQ friendly.
The Fairmont Orchid, Hawaii (1 N Kaniku Dr, Waimea, HI **96743**), LGBTQ friendly.
Jacaranda Inn (65-1444 Kawaihae Rd, Waimea, HI **96743**), gay friendly. The Jacaranda Inn offers restful, romantic accommodations at an historic ranch estate on Hawaii's Big Island.

Restaurant/Bar:
Kaneohe Rice Bowl, 46-014 Kamehameha Hwy, Kaneohe, HI **96744**, included in the Damron Address Book from 1965 to 1970.

Accommodation:
Ali'i Bluffs Windward B&B (46-251 Ikiiki St, Kaneohe, HI **96744**), gay owned. On the windward side of Oahu, just 20 minutes from Honolulu.

Paradise Bay Resort (47-039 Lihikai Dr, Kaneohe, HI **96744**), LGBTQ friendly.
Hale Kipa 'O Pele (74-381 Kealakehe Pkwy # J, Kailua-Kona, HI **96745**) included in Inn Places

Religious Building: Kathryn Hulme (1900-1981) was an American author and memoirist most noted for her novel The Nun's Story. She is also the author of Wild Place, a description of her experiences as the UNRRA Director of the Polish Displaced Persons (DP) camp at Wildflecken, Germany, after WWII. At Wildflecken Hulme met a Belgian nurse and former nun named Marie Louise Habets (1905-1986), who became her lifelong companion. The Nun's Story is a slightly fictionalized biographical account of Habets' life as a nun. In 1960, Hulme and Habets moved to Kauai, where Hulme continued to write, with Habets's support and assistance. They grew tropical fruits, bred dogs, rode horses, had friends to stay, gave talks, and socialised among the other Kauai expats. Marie Louise Habets and Kathryn Hulme are both buried at Kauai. A mass was held at St Catherine Church (5021 Kawaihau Rd, Kapaa, HI **96746**)

Cemetery: Carlos Almaraz (1941–1989) was a Mexican-American artist and an early proponent of the Chicano street arts movement. Almaraz was married to Elsa Flores, Chicana activist and photographer. Together, the pair produced California Dreamscape. He exhibited his work at the Jan Turner Gallery starting in the mid-1980s in Los Angeles through his passing. Carlos Almaraz died in 1989 of AIDS-related causes. He is remembered as an artist who used his talent to bring critical attention to the early Chicano Art Movement, as well as a supporter of Cesar Chávez and the UFW. His work continues to enjoy popularity. In 1992 the Los Angeles County Museum of Art honored him with a tribute featuring 28 of his drawings and prints donated by his widow. He is buried at St Catherine Cemetery (2071 Kuhio Hwy, Kapa'a, HI **96746**).

Beach: Queen Pond BA (Bare Ass) Beach, Wailua, Kapa'a, HI **96746**, West side of Kauai, included in the Damron Address Book from 1975 to 1979.

Attractions: Nā Pali Coast State Wilderness Park (Kapa'a, HI **96746**) has been named among the beautiful natural landscapes in the world, 2019.

Restaurant/Bar:

Casa Nostra, center of Hotel row, Wailua, Kapa'a, HI **96746**, included in the Damron Address Book from 1974 to 1978.

Accommodation:
17 Palms Kauai Vacation Cottages (414 Wailua Kai St, Kapa'a, HI **96746**), gay owned. 17 Palms Kauai is a vacation rental in a garden setting named by Conde Nast Traveler Magazine as one of the 20 perfect places to stay in Hawaii.
Aloha Kauai B&B (156 Lihau St, Kapa'a, HI **96746**) included in Inn Places 1999, Gay & Lesbian Accommodations Worldwide. Gay and Lesbian. As of 2021 it's closed.
Aston Aloha Beach Hotel (3-5920 Kuhio Hwy, Kapa'a, HI **96746**), LGBTQ friendly.

Aston Islander on the Beach (440 Aleka Pl, Kapa'a, HI **96746**), TAG Approved LGBTQ friendly accommodation.
Fern Grotto Inn (4561 Kuamoo Rd, Kapa'a, HI **96746**), gay friendly. Surrounded by state park land on all sides we are situated a Block from the Beach in Hawaii's largest coconut grove.
Hale Kahawai (185 Kahawai Pl, Kapa'a, HI **96746**) included in Inn Places 1999, Gay & Lesbian Accommodations Worldwide. Gay and Lesbian. As of 2021 it's closed.
Kauai Coast Resort at the Beachboy (Kaua'i, 520 Aleka Loop, Kapa'a, HI **96746**) is located on the shores of Kauai's Royal Coconut Coast. The

property features oceanfront resort suits. This resort features studios, one and two bedroom suites. World Rainbow Hotels (WRH), Lesbian and Gay Welcoming Hotels, GLD, Gay Lesbian Directory

Mohala Ke Ola B&B Retreat (5663 Ohelo Rd, Kapa'a, HI 96746) included in Inn Places 1999, Gay & Lesbian Accommodations Worldwide. Gay friendly. It's now Secret Falls Retreat.

Outrigger at Lae nani (410 Papaloa Rd, Kapa'a, HI 96746), LGBTQ friendly.

Outrigger Waipouli Beach Resort & Spa (4-820 Kuhio Hwy, Kapa'a, HI 96746), LGBTQ friendly. Plantation Hale Suites (525 Aleka Loop, Kapa'a, HI 96746), TAG Approved LGBTQ friendly accommodation.

Royal Drive Cottages (147 Royal Dr, Kapa'a, HI 96746) included in Inn Places 1999, Gay & Lesbian Accommodations Worldwide. Gay, Lesbian, lesbian owned and lesbian operated. As of 2021 it's closed.

Attractions:

Pu'uka'oku Falls (Kaunakakai, HI 96748) has been named among the Highest waterfalls in the world, 2019.

Olo'upena Falls (HI 96748) has been named among the Highest waterfalls in the world, 2019.

Accommodation:

Aqua Hotel Molokai (1300 Kamehameha V Hwy, Kaunakakai, HI 96748), LGBTQ friendly.

Rainbow Plantation (6327 Mamalahoa Hwy, Kealakekua, HI 96750), gay friendly. Tropical, secluded, natural retreat on a Coffee Macadamia Plantation. Centrally located above Kealakekua Bay

Kauai Harbor House (8948 Kaumualii Hwy, Kekaha, HI 96752), LGBTQ friendly.

Queer Architects: Bruce Dunbar House, 5400 Makena Rd, Kihei, HI 96753, Designed by Arthur Erickson with Nick Milkovich (1988).

Restaurant/Bar:

Ambrosia Martini Lounge, 1913-H, S Kihei Rd, Kihei, HI 96753

Cafe La Plage (2395 S Kihei Rd, Kihei, HI 96753), gay owned.

Accommodation:

Aloha Pualani (15 Wailana Pl, Kihei, HI 96753), LGBTQ friendly.

Andaz Maui At Wailea Resort - A Concept By Hyatt (3550 Wailea Alanui Dr, Wailea, HI 96753), TAG Approved LGBTQ friendly accommodation.

Aston at the Maui Banyan (2575 S Kihei Rd, Kihei, HI 96753), TAG Approved LGBTQ friendly accommodation.

Aston Maui Hill Resort (2881 S Kihei Rd, Kihei, HI 96753), TAG Approved LGBTQ friendly accommodation.

Aston Maui Lu Resort (575 S Kihei Rd, Kihei, HI 96753), LGBTQ friendly.

Dreams Come True on Maui (3259 Akala Dr, Kihei, HI 96753), LGBTQ friendly.

The Fairmont Kea Lani Maui (4100 Wailea Alanui Dr, Wailea-Makena, HI 96753), LGBTQ friendly.

Four Seasons Resort Maui at Wailea (3900 Wailea Alanui Dr, Kihei, HI 96753), LGBTQ friendly.

The Girls Island Properties (Coldwell Baker Island Properties, 3750 Wailea Alanui Dr B35, Kihei, HI 96753), ran by a lesbian couple, Caron Barrett and Deborah Vial.

Grand Wailea Resort Hotel & Spa, The Waldorf Astoria Collection (3850 Wailea Alanui Dr, Wailea, HI 96753), LGBTQ friendly. Named among the Most beautiful spas in the world, 2019.

Hale Kai O Kihei Vacation Rental Condo (1279 S Kihei Rd # 107, Kihei, HI 96753), gay owned. Great ocean views from your private lanai.

Kamaole Sands (2695 S Kihei Rd, Kihei, HI 96753), LGBTQ friendly.

Kihei Ali'I Kai (2387 S. Kihei Rd, Unit #B-301, Kihei, HI 96753), gay friendly. Elegant South Maui complex close to the beach.

Kihei Park Shore (2037 S Kihei Rd, Kihei, HI 96753), LGBTQ friendly.

Makena Beach and Golf Resort (5415 Makena Alanui, Kihei, HI 96753), LGBTQ friendly.

Maui Oceanfront Inn (2980 S Kihei Rd, Kihei, HI 96753), LGBTQ friendly.

Maui Sunseeker Honeymoons (551 South Kihei Rd, Kihei, Maui, HI 96753), gay owned. Hawaii is the number one destination for US and Canadian honeymoon couples, both straight and gay, for very good reason. GLD, Gay Lesbian Directory

Maui Surfside Condo (3*), 715 South Kihei Rd, #118, Kihei, Maui, HI **96753**

Maui What a Wonderful World B&B (2828 Umalu Pl, Kihei, HI **96753**), LGBTQ friendly.

Outrigger Palms at Wailea (3200 Wailea Alanui Dr, Wailea, HI **96753**), LGBTQ friendly.

Pineapple Inn Maui (3170 Akala Dr, Kihei, HI **96753**), gay owned. Close to Wailea Beach, shopping, and world class restaurants, resorts and golf courses.

Ra Amuru, 2575 South Kihei Rd, Kihei, Maui, HI **96753**

Take Me 2 Maui Condo, 25 Wailana Place, #103, Kihei, Maui, HI **96753**, GLD, Gay Lesbian Directory

Two Mermaids (2840 Umalu Pl, Kihei, HI **96753**), LGBTQ friendly.

Wailea Beach Marriott Resort & Spa (3700 Wailea Alanui Dr, Kihei, HI **96753**), TAG Approved LGBTQ friendly accommodation.

Wailea Beach Villas Resort (3800 Wailea Alanui Dr, Kihei, HI **96753**), LGBTQ friendly.

Hotel Wailea, Relais & Châteaux (555 Kaukahi St, Wailea, HI **96753**), gay friendly and TAG Approved LGBTQ friendly accommodation. Escape the ordinary at the beautiful Hotel Wailea Maui, a haven for rejuvenation and spiritual transformation.

Twin Hearts (4300 Wailapa Rd, Kilauea, HI **96754**), LGBTQ friendly.

Allerton Garden, Kauai

We sail together: *The former Hawaiian Royal tropical estate, located on the island of Kaua'i in Hawaii is now called the Allerton Garden. After John Gregg Allerton's death it became part of the National Tropical Botanical Garden, with public tours.*

Address: 4425 Lawai Rd, Koloa, HI 96756

Allerton Garden, Kauai - Allerton house, Creative Commons Licenses, via Wikimedia Commons

Place

Allerton Garden, also known as Lāwa'i-kai, is a botanical garden, originally created by Robert Allerton and John Gregg Allerton, located on the south shore of Kauai. The garden covers an 80-acre (320,000 m2) area and is situated beside the Lāwaʻi Bay, in a valley transected by the Lāwaʻi Stream. It is one of the five gardens of the non-profit National Tropical Botanical Garden. Queen Emma of Hawaii resided above this valley for a short interval, and a modest house that was perhaps her residence has subsequently been moved to the valley floor and renovated. The entire valley, including what is now the adjacent McBryde Garden, was purchased by the McBryde family in the late XIX century for a sugarcane plantation.

Life

Who: Robert Henry Allerton (March 20, 1873 – 1964) and John Gregg (1899–1986) Robert Allerton, who had a lifelong passion for garden design, sculpture, and landscape architecture had already expressed it at The Farms estate and sculpture gardens in Illinois (now Robert Allerton Park). His adopted son John Gregg Allerton had studied architecture at the University of Illinois in the 1920s. In 1938 they came to Hawaii and purchased a relatively small portion of Queen Emma's plantation for a residence and gardens. They quickly began designing the landscape master plan and individual gardens, incorporating Hawaiian and new plants they had acquired from tropical Asia and other Pacific Islands, built landscape elements, and sculptures from The Farms. Allerton would later join a group of individuals and organizations who were pushing for the establishment of a tropical botanical garden on US soil. In his final year before he died, Allerton was able to witness the charter being granted and the creation of the Pacific Tropical Botanical Garden (now National Tropical Botanical Garden). John Gregg Allerton maintained the garden until his death in 1986, and left it in truSt In the early 1990s, management was assumed by the National Tropical Botanical Garden and the garden was named after its founding fathers. Robert Allerton and John Gregg Allerton's ashes were scattered on Kawai Bay, Kauai.

Accommodation:
Grand Hyatt Kauai Resort And Spa (1571 Poipu Rd, Koloa, HI 96756), TAG Approved LGBTQ friendly accommodation.
Aston at Poipu Kai (1775 Poipu Rd, Koloa, HI 96756), TAG Approved LGBTQ friendly accommodation.
Poipu Plantation Inn & Vacation Rental Suites (1792 Pe'e Rd, Koloa, HI 96756), TAG Approved LGBTQ friendly accommodation.

Sheraton Kauai Resort (2440 Hoonani Rd, Koloa, HI 96756), LGBTQ friendly.
Castle Makahuena at Poipu (1661 Pe'e Rd, Koloa, HI 96756), LGBTQ friendly.
Castle Poipu Shores (1775 Pe'e Rd, Koloa, HI 96756), LGBTQ friendly.
Outrigger Kiahuna Plantation (2253 Poipu Rd, Koloa, HI 96756), LGBTQ friendly.

Historic District: Front St, Lahaina, HI 96761, along Seawall or Beach Walk, included in the Damron Address Book from 1979 to 1980.

Restaurant/Bar:
Betty's Beach Café (505 Front St #120, Lahaina, HI 96761), gay owned.

Alex's Hole in the Wall, Wahie Ln & Front St, Lahaina, HI 96761, included in the Damron Address Book in 1979.
Maui Bell, Lahaina, HI 96761, included in the Damron Address Book from 1975 to 1976.

Accommodation:
Aston Kaanapali Shores (3445 Lower Honoapiilani Rd, Lahaina, HI 96761), TAG Approved LGBTQ friendly accommodation.

Aston Mahana at Kaanapali (110 Kaanapali Shores Pl, Lahaina, HI 96761), TAG Approved LGBTQ friendly accommodation.

Aston Maui Kaanapali Villas (45 Kai Ala Dr, Lahaina, HI **96761**), gay friendly and TAG Approved LGBTQ friendly accommodation. Fine condominium resort amidst 11 acres of beautiful gardens, perfectly located in the heart of the Kaanapali Resort area.

Aston Paki Maui (3615 Lower Honoapiilani Rd, Lahaina, HI **96761**), LGBTQ friendly.

Aston at Papakea Resort (3543 Lower Honoapiilani Rd, Lahaina, HI **96761**), TAG Approved LGBTQ friendly accommodation.

Aston at The Whaler on Kaanapali Beach (2481 Kaanapali Pkwy, Lahaina, HI **96761**), TAG Approved LGBTQ friendly accommodation.

Garden Gate Inn - Long Term Rentals, 67 Kaniau Road, Lahaina, HI **96761**, GLD, Gay Lesbian Directory

Hyatt Regency Maui Resort And Spa (200 Nohea Kai Dr, Lahaina, HI **96761**), TAG Approved LGBTQ friendly accommodation, is a luxurious hotel offering elegant accommodation and a range of exceptional services and gorgeous views for a taste of paradise. Part of World Rainbow Hotels (WRH), Lesbian and Gay Welcoming Hotels.

Ka'anapali Beach Hotel (2525 Kaanapali Pkwy, Lahaina, HI **96761**), TAG Approved LGBTQ friendly accommodation.

Kaanapali Maui at the Eldorado by Outrigger (2661 Kekaa Dr, Lahaina, HI **96761**), TAG Approved LGBTQ friendly accommodation.

The Kapalua Villas (300 Kapalua Dr, Lahaina, HI **96761**), LGBTQ friendly.

Lahaina Inn (127 Lahainaluna Rd, Lahaina, HI **96761**), LGBTQ friendly.

Marriott Vac Club Ocean Club I (100 Nohea Kai Dr, Lahaina, HI **96761**), LGBTQ friendly.

Maui Tropical Sunsets (4435 Lower Honoapiilani Rd, Lahaina, HI **96761**), LGBTQ owned, GLD, Gay Lesbian Directory

Outrigger Aina Nalu (660 Waine'e St, Lahaina, HI **96761**), LGBTQ friendly.

Outrigger Napili Shores (5315 Lower Honoapiilani Rd, Lahaina, HI **96761**), LGBTQ friendly.

Built by George Alan Freeland and a hui of local businessmen, the Pioneer Inn (658 Wharf St, Lahaina, HI **96761**), an historic Maui hotel, captures the ambiance of Maui's plantation days and is the focal point of Lahaina. Although the exterior faithfully preserves this gem of plantation architecture, inside and around the grounds, visitors will enjoy updated accommodations and facilities. The Pioneer Inn guests are surrounded by constant reminders of Hawaii's special beauty and will find the Inn's staff as hospitable and warm as an island trade wind. This 34-room Hawaiian hotel, located at the water's edge on Lahaina Harbor (once the whaling capital of the Pacific), features an outdoor pool and complimentary WiFi. Visitors who dine at the Grill & Bar can enjoy great harbor views with their meals. The lush, tropical courtyard has a gazebo and is the perfect backdrop for a destination Hawaii wedding or celebration. The Inn's convenient location means guests won't have to go far to enjoy whale watching, scuba diving, snorkeling, world class fishing, yacht and submarine cruises, and para-sailing. The Pioneer Inn is a contributing building in the Lahaina Historic District. This historic district in Lahaina, Hawaii, on the west side of the island of Maui, was declared a National Historic Landmark in 1962. The Inn is the oldest hotel on Maui and the oldest in continuous operation in the state of Hawaii. It celebrated its 100th year anniversary on December 8, 2001. Pioneer Inn, a member of Historic Hotels of America since 2016, dates back to 1901.

The Plantation Inn (174 Lahainaluna Rd, Lahaina, HI **96761**), TAG Approved LGBTQ friendly accommodation.

The Ritz-Carlton (1 Ritz Carlton Dr, Kapalua, HI **96761**), LGBTQ friendly.

Royal Kahana Maui by Outrigger (4365 Lower Honoapiilani Rd, Lahaina, HI **96761**), TAG Approved LGBTQ friendly accommodation.

Royal Lahaina Resort (2780 Kekaa Dr, Lahaina, HI **96761**), LGBTQ friendly.

Sheraton Maui Resort & Spa (2605 Kaanapali Pkwy, Lahaina, HI **96761**), LGBTQ friendly.

The Westin Ka'anapali Ocean Resort Villas (6 Kai Ala Dr, Lahaina, HI **96761**), TAG Approved LGBTQ friendly accommodation.

The Westin Maui Resort & Spa (2365 Kaanapali Pkwy, Lahaina, HI **96761**), LGBTQ friendly.

The Whaler on Kaanapali Beach (2481 Kaanapali Pkwy, Lahaina, HI **96761**), LGBTQ friendly.

Four Seasons Resort Lanai at Koele (1, Keomoku Highway, Lanai City, HI **96763**), TAG Approved LGBTQ friendly accommodation.

Four Seasons Resort Lanai at Manele Bay (1 Manele Bay Rd, Lanai City, HI **96763**), LGBTQ friendly.

Hotel Lanai (828 Lanai Ave, Lanai City, HI **96763**), LGBTQ friendly.

Restaurant/Bar:
Club Jetty, near Kauai Surf Hotel, 3610 Rice St, Lihue, HI **96766**, included in the Damron Address Book from 1977 to 1980.

Kentucky Fried Chicken, Lihue, HI **96766**, included in the Damron Address Book from 1979 to 1980.

Our House, below entrance to Kauai Surf Hotel, 3610 Rice St, Lihue, HI **96766**, included in the Damron Address Book from 1979 to 1980.

Accommodation:

Kauai Beach Resort (4331 Kauai Beach Dr, Lihue, HI **96766**), gay friendly and TAG Approved LGBTQ friendly accommodation. Escape to paradise at the Kauai Beach Resort, a breathtaking oceanfront resort on a 3-mile beach on Kauai's eastern Coconut Coast.

Castle Kaha Lani Resort (4460 Nehe Rd, Lihue, HI **96766**), LGBTQ friendly.

Kauai Surf Hotel, 3610 Rice St, Lihue, HI **96766**. Later Kauai Marriott Resort, LGBTQ friendly. It's now Royal Sonesta Kaua'i Resort Lihue. Included in the Damron Address Book from 1965 to 1969.

Aloha Cottage Vacation Rental (Olinda Rd, Makawao, HI **96768**), lesbian owned. A one-of-a-kind vacation cottage designed for romance, style, charm and seclusion.

The Banyan Tree House (3265 Baldwin Ave, Makawao, HI **96768**), gay friendly. Enjoy plantation living unique to upcountry Maui.

Hale Ho'okipa Inn, 32 Pakani Place, Makwawao, HI **96768**, GLD, Gay Lesbian Directory

Hawi Hideaway Vacation Rental Cottage (333 Hoopalua Dr, Makawao, HI **96768**), gay owned. In oldest district of Hawaii, new cottage, 1,000 sq ft. Full kitchen, bath, two patios with Maui Views.

Maliko Retreat Vacation Rental Cottage (365 Kaluanui Rd, Makawao, HI **96768**), gay friendly. Breathtaking ocean view, seasonal waterfall view. Fully equipped kitchen. Completely private.

Kaluakoi Villas (1121 Kalua Koi Rd, Maunaloa, HI **96770**), LGBTQ friendly.

Volcano Men's Retreat (11-2888 Hibiscus Street, Mountain View, HI **96771**), gay owned. Volcano Men's Retreat is nestled among eight acres of our private Ohia forest, near Volcanoes National Park. This peaceful and intimate retreat is of Polynesian inspired design, but with upscale amenities. Enjoy your own personal bungalow, or mingle with other quests in our common lounge and dinning areas or in our 6 man spa.

Kalaekilohana, Big Island

Accommodation: *Kenny Joyce and Kilohana Domingo built this B&B from the ground up, and their love for the building and the grounds shows in every detail. Unique opportunities to work with Hawaiian artists combined with the rich country elegance.* LGBTQ owned

Address: 94-2152 South Point Rd, Na`alehu, Big Island, HI, 96772

Kalaekilohana

The Kalaekilohana won a Keep It Hawai'i award from the Hawai'i Tourism Authority only a year after it opened in 2006. Kalaekilohana offers classes in lei making, lauhala weaving and other Native Hawaiian crafts, plus free weekly Hawaiian-language gatherings and kanikapila (music jams). Kilohana, who is half-Hawaiian, grew up in Kealakekua, where his father worked as a Greenwell Ranch hand. At 13 he attended Kamehameha Schools in Honolulu, where he joined Robert Cazimero's hula halau. Later, during graduate school at UH Manoa, he studied Hawaiian language and traditional arts. Originally from the Chicago area, Joyce moved to Ka'u in 1987. I came with no survival tools in terms of local culture, he says, but I received thousands of lessons along the way. He's also the chef, whose home-cooked breakfasts feature local ingredients, including Ka'u's delicious tomatoes, honey and coffee.

House: Pat Rocco (1934—2018) was an entertainer, photographer, and an activist who appeared on radio and on television; performed, produced and directed for the stage; photographed, produced, and directed motion pictures; participated, organized and documented the struggle for equal rights for gays and lesbians in Southern California and in Hawaii; provided emergency shelter and job training for the homeless, and was with his partner, David Kirk Ghee (known as David Kirk), since 1972. They lived at 12-7007 Ka'Ehukai St, Pāhoa, HI **96778**. Pasquale Vincent Serrapica grew up in Brooklyn until he and his family relocated to California in 1946. As a child Pat loved to entertain his family and friends by singing, as a teenager he was featured twice weekly for two years on a Pasadena radio station, KWKW. After completing high school at home for his unwillingness to renounce his homosexuality, Pat attended colleges and worked at a defense plant in Monrovia, California. While working he meet a local Youth for Christ director, Chuck Leviston; after a second meeting, Pat left college to sing for Youth for Christ. During this time Pat recorded an album of devotion music for Cornerstone Records. In 1954, theatrical programs document his adoption of the stage name, Pat Rocco; in 1966 he officially changed his name. For the remainder of the 1950s Rocco sang on stage in musicals, toured with country with Marge and Gower Champion, and appeared as a member of the Top Twenty on the Tennessee Ernie Ford Show. Also during this period Rocco began to photograph theatrical performances. In June of 1960 he left the stage to become the owner and operator of a motion picture theater in Moorpark, California and later district manager for three motion picture theaters and a skating rink. In 1962, Rocco returned to the stage as managing director and went on to produce and direct several stage shows and musicals until the late 1960s. In 1967, he answered an advertisement to shoot still photographs of nude male models, Rocco soon realized the potential of this enterprise and began shooting his own motion pictures. Named after an earlier business, Bizarre Production sold photographs and short non-explicit erotic motion pictures by mail-order. The Park Theater near McArthur Park in Los Angeles expressed interest in showing Rocco's motion picture along others of gay interest to the general public. After the success of the first program the Park Theater sought more programs of short motion pictures. Rocco later added Bizarre News Films to his programs, capturing local protests and interviews on film. His motion pictures attracted an audience of like minded individuals that appreciated the beauty of the human form and Rocco's positive depiction of gay intimacy. In appreciation of his films Dick Winters and others formed The Society of Pat Rocco Enlightened Enthusiasts (SPREE). SPREE met monthly for nine and half years (1968-1978) as a primarily gay male theatrical company and social organization. During this time Bizarre Productions cease to exist as the industry turned to more explicit depictions of sex, however Rocco continued to photograph events and protests in Southern California for a number of gay newspapers. He became increasing involved in the struggle for equal rights for the gays and lesbians in the community and through the Democratic Party. Rocco campaigned for the resumption of the Christopher Street West (CSW) pride parade, developed and championed the idea of an accompanying festival, and the participation of a float from the gay and lesbian community in the annual Santa Claus Lane Parade in Hollywood. Rocco also organized events to raise money for those arrested at the Mark IV Slave Auction and to pay tribute to Councilman Harvey Milk and Mayor George Moscone. He collaborated in organizing and participated in numerous organizations and events in Southern California. As Rocco worked in the community he became aware of the need for emergency housing for gay, lesbian, and transgendered individuals in Los Angeles. Through the auspices of the United States Mission, Rocco branded his own emergency housing program, Hudson House, that rewarded industry, provided meals, and later job training to those in need. Rocco operated Hudson Houses in Los Angeles, San Diego, San Francisco, and Hawaii. In 2015, Rocco and his partner retired to Hawaii where they continued to be active in the community and in the struggle for equal rights for LGBTQ people.

Accommodation:
Absolute Paradise B&B (12-118 Kipuka St, Pahoa, Big Island, Puna, HI **96778**), gay owned. Puna, Big Island, Hawaii, Beautiful B&B located a short 5 minute walk to a clothing-optional black sand beach, close to Pahoa and Hilo.
Aloha Ocean Guesthouse, 14-4791 Kumuloulu Road, Pahoa, HI **96778**, GLD, Gay Lesbian Directory

The Bali Cottage at Kehena Beach (12-7198 Kalapana Kapoho Beach Road, Pāhoa, HI **96778**), LGBTQ friendly. Only 65 yds from Kehena Black sand Beach. GLD, Gay Lesbian Directory
Coconut Cottage B&B (13-1139 Leilani Ave, Pāhoa, HI **96778**), gay owned. 1940's Hawaii is yours to experience among our one acre of lush tropical paradise.

Gay Hawaii B&B (12-110 Ala Iki St, Pāhoa, HI **96778**), gay owned. Basking on Gay Hawaii B&Bs sunny deck, hiking to active lava flow nearby, relaxing to ocean sounds, showering outdoors, swimming with dolphins, walking to Cafe & Kava Bar, Wednesday Farmer's Market with Hawaiian music culture and arts. Suntaning on secluded black sand beaches. Naked Gay volleyball. modeling or drawing at artists' gathering. Snorkeling/ scuba with manta rays.

Hale Kai Olinolino, 12-105 Mapuana Ave, Pahoa, HI **96778**, GLD, Gay Lesbian Directory

Hale Kukui Ola, 12169 Mapuana, Pahoa, Big Island, Puna, HI **96778**, GLD, Gay Lesbian Directory

Hale Lalala, 12-112 Ala Iki, Pahoa, Big Island, Puna, HI **96778**

Hale Mohalu (13-698 Kamaili Rd, Pāhoa, HI **96778**), gay owned. Located on the rugged and picturesque Puna Coast of the Big Island, Hale Mohalu, the House of Rest and Relaxation, is situated on 22 landscaped acres in the lush and verdant District of Puna. The designer appointed main residence commands sweeping views to the east, where the sun rises from the Pacific Ocean.

Hale Ohai (12-183 Kipuka St, Pāhoa, HI **96778**), LGBTQ owned.

Hali Ka Ikena Nani, 12-7848 Ainaua Place, Kalapana, HI **96778**, GLD, Gay Lesbian Directory

Hawaii Lalala GuestHouse or Oceanfront Bali Hut, 12-112 Ala Iki RR2 #4857, Kalapana, HI **96778**, GLD, Gay Lesbian Directory

Isle of You Farm & Naturist Retreat (13-790 Kamaili Rd, Pāhoa, HI **96778**), LGBTQ owned. GLD, Gay Lesbian Directory

Kalani Oceanside Retreat (12-6860 Kalapana-Kapoho Rd, Pahoa, Big Island, Puna, HI **96778**), 120 acres on the Big Island's tropical coast focused on natural beauty,health and tropical relaxation. Included in Inn Places 1999, Gay & Lesbian Accommodations Worldwide. Gay and Lesbian. GLD, Gay Lesbian Directory

Kehena Beach Getaway (12-7036 Ka'iwa St, Pāhoa, HI **96778**), gay owned. This two story modern house sits on a lava flow from 1955. Two terrific rooms. One is called Maluhia which means Peace and the other room is known as Moena or Resting Place.

Kehena Honey House, 12-7244 Kii Nani St, Pahoa, HI **96778**, GLD, Gay Lesbian Directory

The Kimos' Ohanas, 13-3545 Maile St, Pahoa, Big Island, HI **96778**. A relaxing private B&B located on 2 acres in the Puna District of Hawaii. Offering 2 suites with their own entrances and a separate Ohana with 2 rooms which can be reserved separately or individually. A separate lounge area and screened lanai where a gourmet breakfast is served.

Mahi Oli'Oli, 13-653 Pohoiki Road, Pahoa, HI **96778**, GLD, Gay Lesbian Directory

Paradise Cliffs Vacation Rental, P.O. Box 939, Pahoa, HI **96778**, GLD, Gay Lesbian Directory

Rainbow Dreams Cottage, 13-6412 Kalapana Kapoho Beach Rd, Opihikao, Big Island, Puna, HI **96778**

Volcano Rainforest Retreat, 11-3832 12th St., P.O. Box 957, Volcano, HI **96778**, GLD, Gay Lesbian Directory

Restaurant/Bar:

E-Z Café, 89 Hana Hwy, Paia, HI **96779**, included in the Damron Address Book from 1979 to 1980.

Accommodation:

Spyglass House Oceanfront Inn (44 Kulani Pl, Paia, HI **96779**), LGBTQ friendly.

World Heritage List: Hawaii Volcanoes National Park: Mauna Loa and Kilauea Volcanoes ('Ainapō, HI **96785**)

Accommodation:
Aloha Junction B&B (19-4037 Olapalapa Rd, Volcano, HI **96785**), LGBTQ friendly. GLD, Gay Lesbian Directory

The Artist Cottage at Volcano Garden Arts (19-3834 Old Volcano Rd, Volcano, HI **96785**), gay owned. Lovingly restored private one bedroom redwood cottage set on a lush 3-acre artist's estate.

At The Crater's Edge (11-3802 12th St, Volcano, HI **96785**), gay owned. Next to Hawaii Volcanoes National Park, modern cedar/glass architect-designed house.

Crater Rim Cabin (99-267 Hawaii Belt Rd, Volcano, HI **96785**), gay owned. Situated at the edge of the fern-ohia forest on the boundary of Hawaii Volcanoes National Park. Your own private one bedroom cabin with full living room, kitchen and bath.

Hale KupuKupu (19-4292 Wright Rd., Volcano, Big Island, HI **96785**), gay owned. Hale KupuKupu is constructed from old growth redwood planks in the single wall design traditional to the islands during the plantation period of the 1930s and 40's. Hale KupuKupu offers a quiet and tranquil experience, reminiscent of a lifestyle from an era gone-by. The outside surroundings of the house provide natural beauty and unmatched privacy.
Hale Ohia Cottage (11-3968 Hale Ohia Rd, Volcano, HI **96785**), LGBTQ owned.
Kulana Artist Sanctuary, POB 190, Volcano, HI **96785**, GLD, Gay Lesbian Directory
Lotus Garden Cottages (19-4245 Kekoa Nui Blvd, Volcano, HI **96785**), LGBTQ friendly.

Volcano Forest Inn, 19-4024 Old Volcano Rd, Volcano, Big Island, Puna, HI **96785**
Volcano Inn (11-3832 2nd St, Volcano, HI **96785**), LGBTQ friendly.
Volcano Mist Cottage (11-3932 9th St, Volcano, HI **96785**), gay friendly. A luxury cottage in the Mauna Loa Estates, just a mile from Volcanoes National Park.
Volcano Rainforest Retreat B&B (11-3832 12th St, Volcano, HI **96785**), LGBTQ friendly.
Volcano Village Lodge (19-4183 Kawailehua Road, Volcano, HI **96785**), gay friendly. Distinctive lodges with a seamless blend of natural beauty and worldly comfort.

Other non-queer residents: The King Kamehameha Golf Club, 2500 Honoapiilani Hwy, Wailuku, HI **96793**, designed by Frank Lloyd Wright in 1993.

Restaurant/Bar:

Taro Patch, 131 N Market St, Wailuku, HI **96793**, included in the Damron Address Book from 1977 to 1979.

Accommodation:

'Aha Iki Beach House (186 Lower Waiehu Beach Rd, Wailuku, HI **96793**) included in Inn Places 1999, Gay & Lesbian Accommodations Worldwide. Gay, Lesbian, gay owned and gay operated. As of 2021 it's closed.
Alohalani's Guest House (193 Lower Waiehu Beach Rd, Wailuku, HI **96793**) included in Inn Places 1999, Gay & Lesbian Accommodations Worldwide. Women, lesbian owned and lesbian operated. As of 2021 it's closed.
Maui Dreamin, 70 Hauoli Street, Maalaea Village, HI **96793**, GLD, Gay Lesbian Directory

Waimanalo Beach Bungalow (41-10 Wailea St, Waimanalo, HI **96795**), gay friendly. 3 houses from the beach, surrounded by the lush Ko olau Mountains.
Waimea Plantation Cottages (9400 Kaumualii Hwy, Waimea, HI **96796**), TAG Approved LGBTQ friendly accommodation. Private seaside cottages set admidst a 27-acre coconut grove are reminiscent of the way Hawaii used to be. Each historic cottage has been fully restored with modern amenities and conveniences. Part of World Rainbow Hotels (WRH), Lesbian and Gay Welcoming Hotels.

96800

Honolulu

The Honolulu LGBTQ community truly embodies the aloha spirit — one of love, friendship, and acceptance. In fact, same-sex and bisexual relationships have been present and widely accepted in Hawaiian culture dating back to ancient times. The term aikāne defines such relationships in the Hawaiian language, and māhū refers to a third gender alongside male and female.
Honolulu has been named among the Most beautiful skylines in the world, 2019

Ala Moana Boulevard

Restaurant/Bar: Liberty House, 1450 Ala Moana Blvd, Honolulu, HI **96815**, Ala Moana Shopping Center, included in the 1975 All Lavender International Gay Guide.

Beach: Ala Moana Beach & Park, 1605 Ala Moana Park Dr, Honolulu, HI **96815**, included in the Damron Address Book from 1974 to 1980. Included in the 1975 All Lavender International Gay Guide.

Accommodation: Aqua Equus Hotel (1696 Ala Moana Blvd, Honolulu, HI **96815**), gay friendly. An intimate boutique hotel featuring Ralph Lauren-inspired rooms located 1 block from the beach.

Restaurant/Bar:
Yours 'n' Mine, 1700 Ala Moana Blvd, Honolulu, HI **96815**, included in the Damron Address Book in 1979. Later Bob & Tony's Steak House, included in the Damron Address Book in 1980.
Red Lobster, 1765 Ala Moana Blvd, Honolulu, HI **96815**

Accommodation:
The Modern Honolulu (1775 Ala Moana Blvd, Honolulu, HI **96815**), TAG Approved LGBTQ friendly accommodation.
Ilikai Hotel & Luxury Suites (1777 Ala Moana Blvd, Honolulu, HI **96815**), TAG Approved LGBTQ friendly accommodation. It's now Waikiki Marina Resort. Just 2 minutes from the world famous beach, Waikiki Marina Resort provides beautifully decorated rooms, an outdoor Swimming pool, Spa and wellness centre and gym. World Rainbow Hotels (WRH), Lesbian and Gay Welcoming Hotels, GLD, Gay Lesbian Directory
Grand Waikikian Suites by Hilton (1811 Ala Moana Blvd, Honolulu, HI **96815**), LGBTQ friendly.
Ramada Plaza Waikiki (1830 Ala Moana Blvd, Honolulu, HI **96815**), LGBTQ friendly.
Aqua Palms Waikiki (1850 Ala Moana Blvd, Honolulu, HI **96815**), gay friendly and TAG Approved LGBTQ friendly accommodation. AAA 3-Diamond contemporary boutique hotel located 1 block to the beach and across from the Hilton Hawaiian Village.

Atkinson Drive

Accommodation: Ala Moana Hotel (410 Atkinson Dr, Honolulu, HI **96814**), TAG Approved LGBTQ friendly accommodation.

Restaurant/Bar: The Cocktail Center, 435 Atkinson Dr, Honolulu, HI **96814**, near Central YMCA, included in the Damron Address Book from 1970 to 1980. Included in the 1975 All Lavender International Gay Guide.

Auahi Street

House: Franklin Lucas Bolt (1908-1966) was born in Virginia. The first record we have of him is dated April 21, 1910 when he was just three years old. The US Federal Census has no record of parents at his home in Hiawassim, Pulaski, VA. Instead he lived with a cousin, a seamstress for a private family, by the name of Ellen Kemp. Ellen was 37 years old, had married within the year (although her husband was also not present) and had never had children of her own. Frank was the illegitimate second child of Alice Matilda Bolt (1887-1920) and John Jackson (born about 1880). Frank's father never claimed him so Alice gave both her children the Bolt name. She did not keep either child. Ellen Kemp, as well as her parents, were born in Virginia suggesting that the Bolt family had probably been in the state for some time. Also in the household was 16-year-old Mollie Childress who is listed as companion to Ellen. Such a relationship status is unheard of in a Federal Census record and was not one of the authorized relationships given to the enumerators to use. Mollie was also born in Virginia, was unemployed and was not attending school. She most likely helped around the house and with the raising of Frank. In 1920 Frank is living in Pine Creek, Carroll, VA. He is no longer living with family, but is now the 12 year old servant of a 49 year old man named Charles Dorvane (the last name is difficult to read in the original record). Charles is listed as a widow, and although Frank is noted as his servant under relationship, the occupation for both was given as teamster. Although only 12 years old, Frank did not attend school that year and it seems that he did not receive a formal education during his childhood. By 1930 he was in the army and a member of Battery E, Ld. Coast Artillary and living at Fort Sherman in Cristobal, Panama Canal Zone. In the fall of 1932, when Frank was 24, he was arrested by the Military Police for a homosexual act which was listed as sodomy in his criminal record. The military classified anything untoward as sodomy so it is unlikely that the act was meant in the truest sense because Frank was incarcerated with more than 50 other soldiers who had the same offense. According to the warden's notebook for Alcatraz, Frank's five year sentence began in 1933 in Honolulu. He arrived in Alcatraz from USADB Pacific Branch on June 19, 1934 with a parole hearing date of September 25, 1934. His minimum sentence was scheduled to end September 3, 1936 and his maximum date was January 23, 1938. He had no detainers and no prior criminal record. On May 10, 1936, four months before the end of his minimum sentence, he was transferred to USP McNeil Island in Washington State. He had been at the countries most maximum security prison for just one month shy of 2 full years. Frank has the prestigious honor of being inmate #1 for Alcatraz Island, the first ever prisoner of the official national maximum security prison. Immediately after his release on September 3, 1936 he headed back to San Francisco and back on to Honolulu, Hawaii. He is listed with a third class ticket on the ship SS President Hoover which set sail from San Francisco on September 10, 1936 and arrived in Honolulu on September 14. He gave the Territory of Hawaii as his permanent residence. Within two months he got a job as a stevedore at the largest employer in Hawaii - Castle & Cook, which owned controlling interests in Dole Pineapple, Hawaiian Pineapple, Hawaiian Tuna, Standard Fruit and Steamship Company (Bananas), Hawaiian Oil Company (cooking oil) and Royal Hawaiian Macadamia Nut Company. They occupied most of the docks in the major Hawaiian cities and employed over 25,000 people. Today, they are in real estate and resort management and employ over 100,000 people. In 1940, Frank Lucas Bolt married Rachel Lahela Kekoa and they raised their family in Hawaii. Their first child Virginia was born 4 months later. They were married for 26 years and had 9 children. By 1942 he was living at 627 Auahi St, Honolulu, HI **96813**, just one block from the port where cruise ships now enter at Honolulu, and was working as a stevedore for C&CT. He continued here until at least 1949 and in 1951 was living in Maili. His social security was listed as being issued in Hawaii before 1951 so perhaps he returned to that state. He is buried at Sunset Memorial Park (848 4th St, Pearl City, HI **96782**).

Beach Walk

Accommodation:
Embassy Suites Hotel - Waikiki Beach Walk (201 Beach Walk, Honolulu, HI **96815**), LGBTQ friendly.
Outrigger Regency on Beach Walk (255 Beach Walk, Honolulu, HI **96815**), LGBTQ friendly.

Beretania Street

Restaurant/Bar: Question Mark, 43 S Beretania St, Honolulu, HI **96813**, included in the Damron Address Book from 1972 to 1980.

Queer Artists: *The Honolulu Museum of Art (formerly the Honolulu Academy of Arts) is an art museum in Honolulu. The museum is largest of its kind in the state, and was founded in 1922 by Anna Rice Cooke. The museum has one of the largest single collections of Asian and Pan-Pacific art in the US, and since its official opening on April 8, 1927, its collections have grown to more than 50,000 works of art.*

Address: 900 S Beretania St, Honolulu, HI 96814

Notable queer elements:

John Singer Sargent (1856-1925). Mrs. Thomas Lincoln Manson, Jr., (painting, 1890).
Malvina Hoffman (1885-1966). Shankar, (sculpture, 1933), Mongolian Archer, (sculpture).
Thomas Eakins (1844-1916). William Rush and his Model, (painting, 1907-08).

Bethel Street

Theatre: Hawaii Theatre, 1130 Bethel Street, Honolulu, HI **96813**, included in the 1975 All Lavender International Gay Guide. The Hawaii Theatre opened September 6, 1922. This former 1,776 capacity vaudeville and movie palace struggled through the 1960's and 1970's and finally closed in the late-1970's. On 23rd November 1979 the Hawaii Theatre was added to the National Register of Historic Places. When it reopened in 1996, the theatre received awards from both the National Trust for Historic Preservation and the League of Historic American Theaters. $30 million dollars and 10 years later, the Hawaii Theatre is once again The Pride of the Pacific. Although it primarily hosts live entertainment events, the Hawaii Theatre still has a projection screen and digital projection system which can be used to screen films. This most commonly happens for special screenings during the Hawaii International Film Festival.

Bishop Street

Accommodation: Aston at the Executive Centre Hotel (1088 Bishop St, Honolulu, HI **96813**), TAG Approved LGBTQ friendly accommodation.

Cartwright Road

Accommodation: Ewa Hotel Waikiki (2555 Cartwright Rd, Honolulu, HI **96815**), TAG Approved LGBTQ friendly accommodation.

Diamond Head Road

Beach: Diamond Head Beach or B.A. (Bare Ass) Beach, 3300 Diamond Head Rd, Honolulu, HI **96815**, below Coast Guard Lighthouse, included in the Damron Address Book from 1974 to 1980. Included in the 1975 All Lavender International Gay Guide.

House: Nesta Obermer (1896-1984) was made an Officer of the British Empire for her war-time broadcasts from England to the US. In 1936 Gluck painted a double profile portrait to commemorate her marriage to the writer and socialite Nesta Obermer, entitled Medallion, but she referred to it as YouWe. This work was intended to comment on the social divisions and difficulties of leading a lesbian life at that time. As Obermer recalled some sixty years later, running away, about which Gluck was obsessional, was the biggest thing in her life, and she not only told every new acquaintance about tis at once, but put it clearly in a biographical sketch which she completed, had typed out, and xeroxed and distributed lavishly. Medallion was inspired by a night in 1936 when Gluck and Nesta attended a Fritz Busch production of Mozart's Don Giovanni. According to Gluck's biographer Diana Souhami, They sat together in the third row and felt the intensity of the music fused them both into one person and matched their love. It was later used as the cover of a Virago Press edition of The Well of Loneliness. Nesta Obermer moved to Haway in 1948 where she earned the reputation as The Master Voice in recognition of her tape recordings of books of world literature for the blind. At first she spend six years at the Royal Hawaiian Hotel, and then bought a home at 3635 Diamond Head Rd, Honolulu, HI **96816**. She, with her husband Seymour Obermer (died 1957), gave devoted directorship to the Heritage Craft Schools for Crippled Children in England. Obermer gave support to Amnesty International, the Yehudi Menuhin School in Surrey, England and the Royal Society for Prevention of Cruelty to Animals. She also played an active role in politics as a speaker for England's Conservative Party. She was always a strong booster of youth and learning, giving countless private – and usually anonymous – grants to individuals for the pursuit of their education and the realization of their talents. In 1969 Obermer moved back to Europe; she bought a house near Lausanne, Switzeland. She spent springs in Addis Ababa, Ethiopia, and South Africa.

Dudoit Lane

Restaurant/Bar: Golden Panther, 1913 Dudoit Ln, Honolulu, HI **96815**, included in the Damron Address Book in 1968. Later Pink Panther, included in the Damron Address Book in 1969.

Ena Road

Restaurant/Bar: Fox Cinema Club, 478 Ena Rd, Honolulu, HI **96815**, included in the Damron Address Book in 1977. Later Lavender Fox, included in the Damron Address Book in 1978.

Fort DeRussy Boulevard

Beach: Fort DeRussy Beach, Fort DeRussy Blvd, Honolulu, HI 96815, included in the 1975 All Lavender International Gay Guide.

Fort Street

Theatre: Princess Theatre, 1236 Fort St, Honolulu, HI **96813**, included in the 1975 All Lavender International Gay Guide. The Princess Theatre opened on November 8, 1922 seating 1,600. It was located on Fort Street just off the Pali Highway. The Princess Theatre ran first run fare until a remodel in 1958. It was re-done to accommodate three-strip Cinerama which ran from 7/22/58 through 5/24/58. It had a curved screen that measured 62 feet by 23 feet. After the three-strip, it reverted back to regular first run films. In 1962 Cinerama returned to Honolulu, first in the three-strip process then in the 70mm format to the Cinerama Theatre (Pawaa Theatre). The Princess Theatre struggled along until 1968 when it closed and a short time later was demolished.

House: Yonemitsu Arashiro (1923-1992) was a fashion designer who worked in the San Francisco of the 1960s. Yonemitsu Arashiro was born in Kekaha, Kaui, the son of Kenneth Arashiro. In the 1940s the family lived at 3021 Hinano St, Honolulu, HI **96815**, and he worked for Sunny Sundstrom, Kau Kau Korner. In the 1950s Morris Graves was not faring very well in his love life. He had been involved with Yonemitsu (Yone) Arashiro, who fell hopelessly in love with him but was taken aback at Graves' contradictory nature. Yone lived with Graves from about 1947 to 1952. The extant letters between the two men reveal a chronology of hopeful, romantic love, followed by Yone's desperate attempt to resign himself to a hopeless loss of the idea of romantic love. In a letter dated November 13, 1952, he wrote to Graves: You are building your life with one justifiable selfishness. My downfall is that I need someone to love and share the hopes and dreams that belong to nowhere, no other, or even anywhere. A selfish love for two people, for their inner self alone. If I must walk this life alone, I would do so. I cannot comply or try to discharge this inner feeling. So, I am going to resign myself to a solitary life & live another kind of life void of all emotional ties. In 1953 Yone Arashiro opened Yone SF, a bead store (originally called Sueko, after his sister), in North Beach, San Francisco. Arashiro and his partner since 1956, Hermon Baker, a former theater set and lighting designer who conceived and built the shop's interior, lived upstairs above the shop, becoming neighborhood fixtures and befriending the likes of Ruth Asawa, Imogen Cunningham and Janice Joplin. They welcomed anyone that needed a place to feel free to express their creativity, and became known as the gentlemen bead sellers. Yone designed very special clothing for unusual people. Known for adorning his designs with beads and jewelry, his passion for beads soon took over. Yone San Francisco became the first real bead store where customers could see, handle and select loose beads from one cent to $125 for an antique Venetian bead more than 100 years old. Some of the leading people in beads and bead design today came around. Beads were new, but bead lovers knew what to do with them. Yone SF was a gold mine for beads of every size, shape, color and material. An awesome inventory of 8,000 to 10,000 separate types of beads, Yone and Hermon Baker together created a world-class collection of beautiful beads. The shop has been packed up and is in storage as the complex process to move the collection into the virtual world continues. Hermon passed away in 2020 at the grand old age of 97, but his spirit is still deeply felt by his niece and nephew who have taken over day-to-day operations.

Accommodation: Hawaii Prince Hotel Waikiki (100 Holomoana St, Honolulu, HI **96815**), LGBTQ friendly.

Oldest Bar in the State: Smith's Union Bar, 19 N Hotel St, Honolulu, HI **96817**. Self-described as having a colorful group of patrons, Smith's Union Bar in Honolulu is a classic dive where people come for conviviality rather than artisanal drinks. Opened since 1935, it was at home in an old red light district popular with sailors.

Theatre:
Risque Theatre & Spa, 32 N Hotel St, Honolulu, HI **96817**, included in the Damron Address Book from 1979 to 1980.
Baron Theatre, 63 N Hotel St, Honolulu, HI **96817**, included in the Damron Address Book in 1974.

Restaurant/Bar:
Loraine's, 110 N Hotel St, Honolulu, HI **96817**, included in the Damron Address Book from 1979 to 1980.
Glades, 152 N Hotel St, Honolulu, HI **96817**, included in the Damron Address Book from 1965 to 1980. Included in the 1975 All Lavender International Gay Guide.

Accommodation: Armed Forces YMCA, 250 S Hotel St, Honolulu, HI **96817**, included in the 1975 All Lavender International Gay Guide.

Iwilei Road

Accommodation: Gay Vacations Hawaii, 680 Iwilei Road, Honolulu, HI **96817**, GLD, Gay Lesbian Directory

Ka'iulani Avenue

Accommodation:
Sheraton Princess Kaiulani (120 Ka'iulani Ave, Honolulu, HI **96815**), TAG Approved LGBTQ friendly accommodation.
OHANA Waikiki East by Outrigger (150 Ka'iulani Ave, Honolulu, HI **96815**). Part of World Rainbow Hotels (WRH), Lesbian and Gay Welcoming Hotels.

Kahala Avenue

Accommodation: The Kahala Hotel & Resort, 5000 Kahala Ave, Honolulu, HI **96816**, TAG Approved LGBTQ friendly accommodation. Part of World Rainbow Hotels (WRH), Lesbian and Gay Welcoming Hotels. Part of The Leading Hotels of the World.

Kalakaua Avenue

Historic District: Kalakaua Ave, Honolulu, HI **96815**, included in the Damron Address Book from 1973 to 1980.

Restaurant/Bar:
Coco's, Kalakaua Ave & Kapiolani Blvd, Honolulu, HI **96826**, included in the Damron Address Book from 1974 to 1980.
Hideout, 1735 Kalakaua Ave, Honolulu, HI **96815**, included in the Damron Address Book in 1973.
Forbidden City, 1736 Kalakaua Ave, Honolulu, HI **96815**, included in the Damron Address Book in 1965.
La Coq D'Or, 1900 Kalakaua Ave, Honolulu, HI **96815**, included in the 1964 Directory. Later Betty Reilly's, included in the Damron Address Book from 1965 to 1968. Later Gay Nineties Cabaret, included in the Damron Address Book from 1973 to 1977.
Cesar's, 1911 Kalakaua Ave, Honolulu, HI **96815**, included in the Damron Address Book in 1973.
Tiki Torch, 1944 Kalakaua Ave, Honolulu, HI **96815**, included in the 1975 All Lavender International Gay Guide.

Accommodation: Luana Waikiki Hotel & Suites (2045 Kalakaua Ave, Honolulu, HI **96815**), TAG Approved LGBTQ friendly accommodation.

Restaurant/Bar:
The Mask, 2060 Kalakaua Ave, Honolulu, HI **96815**, included in the 1964 Directory.
Wagon Wheel, 2070 Kalakaua Ave, Honolulu, HI **96815**, included in the Swasarnt Neft's Gay Guides for 1949 and 1950. Included in the 1964 and 1965 Guild Guide. Included in the Damron Address Book from 1965 to 1970. Included in the 1975 All Lavender International Gay Guide.

Queer Architects: Canlis's Charcoal Broiler Restaurant at Waikiki Beach alterations, 2100 Kalakaua Ave, Honolulu, HI **96815**, designed by Roland Terry (1980). Included in the 1964 and 1965 Guild Guide.

LGBTQ friendly bookstore:
Peep-O-Rama Screening Room, 2146 Kalakaua Ave, Honolulu, HI **96815**, included in the Damron Address Book in 1980.
Screening Room, 2162 Kalakaua Ave, Honolulu, HI **96815**, included in the Damron Address Book in 1979. Later Adult Book Stores, included in the Damron Address Book in 1980.

Restaurant/Bar:
Prime Rib, 2223 Kalakaua Ave, Honolulu, HI **96815**, included in the 1964 Directory. Later the Gourmet, included in the 1965 Guild Guide.
Attic, 2254 Kalakaua Ave, Honolulu, HI **96815**, included in the Damron Address Book from 1971 to 1972.

Accommodation:
Sheraton - Waikiki Beach, 2255 Kalakaua Ave, Honolulu, HI **96815**, included in the Damron Address Book from 1977 to 1979. As of 2022, it's still open. TAG Approved LGBTQ friendly accommodation.
From its opening in 1927, The Royal Hawaiian, a Luxury Collection Resort (2259 Kalakaua Ave, Honolulu, HI **96815**), TAG Approved LGBTQ friendly accommodation, has been recognized as an icon of luxury resort travel. Known to the world as The Pink Palace of the Pacific, The Royal Hawaiian is a lifestyle destination, mirroring the quiet confidence and impeccable standards expected by discerning travelers. Creating a connection to our rich Hawaiian culture, it is a place quite unlike any other...welcoming, yet exclusive...relaxing, yet invigorating...contemporary, yet steeped in timeless glamour. Located on the picture-perfect Waikiki beachfront, the resort's Spanish-Moorish façade lies between a tropical garden oasis and the gentle waters of the Pacific. A sprawling collection of coconut grove gardens and intimate pools, replete with quiet alcoves and bubbling spas, await and just beyond, billowing cabanas invite guests' every indulgence poolside and oceanside, along with a cadre of attendants ready to service every request. The Royal Hawaiian is an exclusive enclave of elegance and tranquility and each of the 528 guestrooms and suites encapsulates extraordinary accommodation experiences, effortlessly weaving modern comfort, indigenous accents, and refined luxury. In the Mailani Tower, each newly renovated room provides an intimate lanai for a private vantage point of the translucent Pacific Ocean. As a testament to its rich history, the resort offers guests a complimentary tour of its historic royal grounds. Discover something new each day at The Royal Hawaiian, a Luxury Collection Resort and partake in various cultural activities such as Hawaiian quilting, lei making, kukui nut bracelet making, lauhala basket making, 'Aha'aina, an oceanfront Luau, and more. The resort also offers guests the opportunity to enjoy traditional ocean sporting activities such as surfing, outrigger canoeing, snorkeling expeditions, scuba diving, catamaran sailing, and dolphin encounters. It has been said that The Royal Hawaiian, a Luxury Collection Resort is the place where the world first fell in love with Hawai'i. Now, 88 years later, following multimillion dollar renovations and the opening of the reimagined Mailani Tower, a new romance has sparked. Come and discover the legend for what it was and what it is. A piece of paradise awaits. The Royal Hawaiian, A Luxury Collection Resort, a member of Historic Hotels of America since 2011, dates back to 1927.
Waikiki Beachcomber By Outrigger (2300 Kalakaua Ave, Honolulu, HI **96815**), TAG Approved LGBTQ friendly accommodation. Part of World Rainbow Hotels (WRH), Lesbian and Gay Welcoming Hotels.

Historic District: International Market Place, 2330 Kalakaua Ave, Honolulu, HI **96815**, included in the Damron Address Book from 1973 to 1974.

Accommodation:
Outrigger Waikiki on the Beach (2335 Kalakaua Ave, Honolulu, HI **96815**), LGBTQ friendly.
Known as The First Lady of Waikiki, Moana Surfrider, A Westin Resort & Spa (2365 Kalakaua Ave, Honolulu, HI **96815**), TAG Approved LGBTQ friendly accommodation, has remained a premier destination for an ultimate luxury vacation since it first opened on March 11, 1901. Ideally situated on a prime section of pristine Waikiki beach, the resort offers a true Hawaiian experience with the extravagance of elegant accommodations. Boasting 793 thoughtfully-appointed guestrooms and suites, the relaxing, historic Moana Lani Spa, a variety of refined dining establishments, and elegant meeting spaces, Moana Surfrider, A Westin Resort & Spa is a legendary landmark with contemporary amenities and unparalleled service and hospitality. Moana Surfrider, A Westin Resort & Spa, a charter member of Historic Hotels of America since 1989, dates back to 1901.
Hyatt Regency Waikiki Beach Resort&Spa (2424 Kalakaua Ave, Honolulu, HI **96815**), TAG Approved LGBTQ friendly accommodation.

The Waikiki Tavern and Inn

Restaurant/Bar:
The Waikiki Tavern and Inn, 2437 Kalākaua Ave, Honolulu, HI **96815**, on the makai (ocean) side of Waikiki's Kalakaua Avenue was built in 1928 and demolished around 1962. Included in the Swasarnt Neft's Gay Guides for 1949 and 1950. The Waikiki Beach Center is on the site today.
Hofbrau, 2448 Kalakaua Ave, Honolulu, HI **96815**, included in the Damron Address Book from 1965 to 1970. Included in the 1975 All Lavender International Gay Guide.

Accommodation: ESPACIO The Jewel of Waikiki, 2452 N Kalakaua Avenue, Honolulu, HI **96815**. Part of The Leading Hotels of the World.

Beach: Kūhiō Beach, 2453 Kalakaua Ave, Honolulu, HI **96815**, included in the Damron Address Book from 1974 to 1980.

Accommodation:
Aston Waikiki Circle Hotel (2464 Kalakaua Ave, Honolulu, HI **96815**), gay friendly and TAG Approved LGBTQ friendly accommodation. Just across the street from the world-famous beach.
Aston Waikiki Beach Tower 2470 Kalākaua Ave, Honolulu, HI **96815**), TAG Approved LGBTQ friendly accommodation. Travellers' Choice Awards, 2022 Best of the Best Hotel in the US, by Tripadvisor.com

De Swamp, 2478 Kalakaua Ave, Honolulu, HI **96815**, included in the from 1965 to 1966.

Alohilani Resort Waikiki Beach (2490 Kalakaua Ave, Honolulu, HI **96815**), . Nearly every room of the Alohilani Hotel offers ocean and Diamond Head Views from private lanais. And if you are visiting in October, the fifth-floor pool deck hosts the annual Lei Magazine Pride Pool Party, during which you can join hundreds from the Honolulu LGBTQ community for festivities. Outside of this event, The hotels Swell Pool and Bar has a great cocktail list, saltwater infinity pool, and cabanas for a chill but luxurious lounging experience. And weekly Sunday pool parties are open and welcome to all.
Waikiki Beach Marriott Resort & Spa (2552 Kalakaua Ave, Honolulu, HI **96815**), .
Aston Waikiki Beach Hotel (2570 Kalakaua Ave, Honolulu, HI **96815**), .

LuLu's Waikiki, 2586 Kalakaua Ave, Honolulu, HI **96815**. Conveniently located right next door to Hula's Bar & Lei Stand, Lulu's is an LGBTQ-friendly restaurant and bar featuring basic American fare with an island twist. Order the Aloha Burger with pineapple, teriyaki sauce, and grilled onions or opt for the Adulting Mac n' Cheese with bacon crumbles for a true indulgence — you won't be disappointed. The restaurant turns into a nightclub on Monday night for industry night, and locals from all around the island congregate for dancing and drink specials until 2:00 AM.

Park Shore Waikiki Hotel (2586 Kalakaua Ave, Honolulu, HI **96815**), and . Park Shore Waikiki is situated on the glistening white sand of Waikiki Beach. Discover this perfectly located Waikiki Beach hotel overlooking Diamond Head and the pristine expanses of Kapiolani Park.

Kapiolani Park Beach, 2686 Kalakaua Ave, Honolulu, HI **96815**, included in the from 1973 to 1980.
Queen's Surf Beach, 2699 Kalakaua Ave, Honolulu, HI **96815**, included in the from 1973 to 1980.

Queen's Surf Club, 2709 Kalakaua Ave, Honolulu, HI **96815**, included in the from 1965 to 1970. Included in the .

Lotus Honolulu at Diamond Head (2885 Kalakaua Ave, Honolulu, HI **96815**), . Experience the tranquil side of Waikiki, a peaceful retreat uniquely located along the exclusive Gold Coast. Part of .

Kahala Hilton, 5000 Kahala Ave, Honolulu, HI **96816**, designed by Roland Terry (1962)

Kalaniana'ole Highway

Mr. and Mrs. Dick Hadley Residence, 2633 Kalaniana'ole Hwy, Honolulu, HI **96821**, designed by Roland Terry (1974)

Hanauma Bay, 7455 Kalaniana'ole Hwy, Honolulu, HI 96825, included in the .

Kalia Road

Accommodation: Halekulani, 2199 Kalia Road, Honolulu, HI **96815**. Part of The Leading Hotels of the World.

Kalia Road

Accommodation:
As Waikiki's only true destination resort, Hilton Hawaiian Village Waikiki Beach Resort (2005 Kalia Rd, Honolulu, HI **96815**) offers the perfect mix of exceptional resort accommodations and classic Hawaiian hospitality. Originally developed by industrialist Henry J. Kaiser in 1955 as the Kaiser Hawaiian Village Hotel, this historic Honolulu hotel affords the widest stretch of white sand on Waikiki, a serene beachfront lagoon, lush tropical gardens and cascading waterfalls, majestic views of Diamond Head and romantic seaside sunsets. Stay in a variety of thoughtfully-appointed guestrooms and suites, including accommodations in the iconic Rainbow Tower, enjoy a diverse selection of dining, not to mention the vibrant Waikiki Starlight Luau experience, and uncover the resort's five exceptional pools, waterslides, and the beachfront Super Pool—the largest in Waikiki—where every Friday night it becomes the stage for a celebration of Hawaiian culture ending with a spectacular fireworks show. In addition, Hilton Hawaiian Village stands as the premier meeting center of the Pacific with more than 150,000 sq ft of flexible indoor and outdoor function space, ensuring an inspired and seamless event. Fun Facts: One of the beach front towers, the Ali'i Tower has been the home-away-from-home for presidents, heads of state, movie stars and entertainers. All of the last 7 U.S. presidents have been stayed in the presidential suite. This was Elvis' favorite hotel in Waikiki and Michael Jackson stayed here on his last U.S. Tour. Hilton Hawaiian Village, a member of Historic Hotels of America since 2015, dates back to 1957.
Castle Waikiki Shore (2161 Kalia Rd, Honolulu, HI **96815**), LGBTQ friendly.
Outrigger Reef on the Beach (2169 Kalia Rd, Honolulu, HI **96815**), LGBTQ friendly.
Halekulani (2199 Kalia Rd, Honolulu, HI **96815**), LGBTQ friendly.

Kamakee Street

Restaurant/Bar: Ben & Jerry's, 310 Kamakee St, Honolulu, HI **96814**

Kānekapōlei Street

Accommodation: Aqua Aloha Surf Waikiki Hotel (444 Kānekapōlei St, Honolulu, HI **96815**), gay friendly and TAG Approved LGBTQ friendly accommodation. One of Waikiki's most popular hotels is now transformed as a boutique hotel located 2 blocks from the beach.

Kapahulu Avenue

Restaurant/Bar:
Little Dipper Cocktail Lounge or The Clouds, 124 Kapahulu Ave, Honolulu, HI **96815**, included in the 1964 and 1965 Guild Guide. Included in the 1964 Directory. Included in the Damron Address Book from 1965 to 1968. Later Apartment Cabaret, included in the Damron Address Book from 1970 to 1974. Also Fernbody's, included in the Damron Address Book in 1970. Later Clouds Hotel, included in the 1975 All Lavender International Gay Guide. Later Blow Hole Cabaret, included in the Damron Address Book from 1976 to 1980.
Hula's Bar and Lei Stand (134 Kapahulu Ave, Honolulu, HI **96815**) has been named among the Greatest Gay Bars in the World by Out.com, 2013. It has been named among The 25 Best LGBTQ Bars and Nightclubs in the US, 2019, Matador Network. Known as the gathering place for explorers, this friendly gay bar is a welcoming destination for everyone. The long windows open to a gentle Waikiki breeze and stellar view of the Pacific for an oceanfront dining experience. In the evening, live music, a large dance floor, and drink specials keep the aloha spirit flowing. Be sure to check the site for upcoming events. including weekly catamaran cruises.

Accommodation:
Waikiki Grand Hotel (134 Kapahulu Ave, Honolulu, HI **96815**), gay friendly. The Waikiki Grand offers a selection of moderately priced, non-smoking hotel rooms, some with kitchenettes.

The newly renovated Queen Kapiolani Hotel (150 Kapahulu Ave, Honolulu, HI **96815**) is located at the edge of Waikiki within walking distance to Kapiolani Park, Waikiki Beach with unobstructed views of Diamond Head. Part of World Rainbow Hotels (WRH), Lesbian and Gay Welcoming Hotels.

Restaurant/Bar:
Blazing Saddles, 404 Kapahulu Ave, Honolulu, HI **96815**. Cowboy boots are more than welcome at Blazing Saddles, Hawaii's only LGBTQ western dance club. Blazing Saddles prides itself on being a non-profit organization committed to providing a safe, fun, and friendly environment where all are welcome. There's no cover charge, but donations are gratefully accepted. Each night is filled with live music, refreshments, and dancing. Go early for free dance lessons starting at 6:30 PM.
Yappy's Cocktail Lounge, 435 Kapahulu Ave, Honolulu, HI **96815**, included in the 1964 Directory. Included in the Damron Address Book from 1965 to 1970.

Ke'eaumoku Street

Club: The Island Club Baths, 825 Ke'eaumoku St, Honolulu, HI **96814**, included in the 1971 Homosexual National Classified Directory. Included in the Damron Address Book from 1973 to 1975.

Kekau Place

House: Abigail Kinoiki Kekaulike Kawānanakoa (born 1926), sometimes called Kekau, is a member of the House of Kawānanakoa. She is referred to by many as a princess, a common honorary bestowed to descendants of titled subjects of the Kingdom of Hawaii or important figures in Hawaiian history, although she holds no official title or role in the Hawaiian state government. She lives at 420 Kekau Pl, Honolulu, HI **96817**. She was the only child of Lydia Liliuokalani Kawānanakoa, born during her marriage with William Jeremiah Ellerbrock. At the age of six, she was legally adopted by her grandmother, Princess Abigail Campbell Kawānanakoa, in the Hawaiian tradition of hānai with the intention that she remain a direct heir to a possible restoration of the kingdom. As Lili'uokalani's great grand niece, she is considered by some to be heir apparent should restoration of the monarchy occur. Kawānanakoa was educated at Punahou School in Honolulu, the Shanghai American School in Shanghai from 1938 to 1939, and Notre Dame High School in Belmont, CA, from which she graduated in 1943. She attended Dominican College in San Rafael, California from 1943 to 1944, and studied at the University of Hawaii in 1945. Kawānanakoa is an expert horsewoman and owner of ranches in Hawaii, California, and Washington State. She is a 20-year cumulative breeder of AQHA quarter horses. Due to her support of the equine medicine program at Colorado State University, she was awarded an honorary degree. Kawānanakoa has been active in various causes for the preservation of native Hawaiian culture, including the restoration of 'Iolani Palace. She was heiress to the largest stake in the estate of her great-grandfather, James Campbell, a XIX-century industrialist from Ireland. When the estate was converted into a corporation in 2007, her share was estimated to be about US$250 million. In 2013 Kawānanakoa requested to be buried in a new crypt at the Royal Mausoleum of Hawaii at Mauna 'Ala directly adjacent to the Wyllie Tomb. The request was approved by the State Land Board on April 26, 2013, but the decision has become controversial in the Hawaiian community. On 1 October 2017, Kawānanakoa married Veronica Gail Worth, in Honolulu. The couple were married in a ceremony performed at the home of Justice Steven Levinson.

King Street

Theatre: King Theatre, 55 S King Street, Honolulu, HI **96813**, included in the **1975 All Lavender International Gay Guide**. The King Theatre was opened December 15, 1935 with Robert McWade in Cappy Ricks Returns plus a Fanchon Marco revue on the stage. Seating was provided for 876. The King Theatre was later twinned and was closed on March 11, 1986. It was demolished and a multi-story car park was built on the site.

Iolani Palace

House: *The 'Iolani Palace was the royal residence of the rulers of the Kingdom of Hawai'i beginning with Kamehameha III under the Kamehameha Dynasty (1845) and ending with Queen Lili'uokalani (1893) under the Kalākaua Dynasty, founded by her brother, King David Kalākaua. It is located in the capitol district of downtown Honolulu. After the monarchy was overthrown in 1893, the building was used as the capitol building for the Provisional Government, Republic, Territory, and State of Hawai'i until 1969. The palace was restored and opened to the public as a museum in 1978. 'Iolani Palace is the only royal palace on US soil. Abigail Kinoiki Kekaulike Kawānanakoa (born 1926) is a member of the House of Kawānanakoa. Kawānanakoa was the president of the Friends of 'Iolani Palace from 1971 to 1998, succeeding her mother, who founded the organization. In June 1992, Kawānanakoa pleaded with activists to hold further sovereignty demonstrations away from the palace after 32 demonstrators attempted to enter the building. The palace was built by her great-grand uncle, King David Kalākaua. She has been active in various causes for the preservation of native Hawaiian culture, including the restoration of 'Iolani Palace.*

Address: 364 S King St, Honolulu, HI 96813
National Register of Historic Places: 66000293, 1966

'Iolani Palace, Creative Commons Licenses, via Wikimedia Commons

By the time David Kalākaua assumed the throne, the original 'Iolani Palace was in poor condition, suffering from ground termite damage. He ordered the old palace to be razed. Kalākaua was the first monarch to travel around the world and like Kamehameha V, he dreamed of a royal palace befitting the monarch of a modern state. While visiting Europe, Kalākaua took note of the customs and traditions practiced by his contemporaries where he decided that incorporating their elements would help legitimize his kingdom through their eyes; this included the building of a new palace inspired by these European grand palaces. Thus, he commissioned the construction of a new 'Iolani Palace, directly across the street from Ali'iōlani Hale, to become the official palace of the Hawaiian monarchy. Three architects, Thomas J. Baker, Charles J. Wall, and Isaac Moore, contributed to the design; of these, Baker designed the structure, while Wall and Moore offered other details. The cornerstone was laid December 31, 1879 during the administration of Minister of the Interior Samuel Gardner Wilder. It was built of brick with concrete facing. The building was completed in November 1882 and cost over $340,000 — a vast fortune at the time ($9,546,966 in 2021 dollars). It measures about 140 feet (43 m) by 100 feet (30 m), and rises two stories over a raised basement to 54 feet (16 m) high. It has four corner towers and two in the center rising to 76 feet (23 m). On February 12, 1883, a formal European-style coronation ceremony was held, even though Kalākaua had reigned for nine years. The coronation pavilion officially known as Keliiponi Hale was later moved to the southwest corner of the grounds and converted to a bandstand for the Royal Hawaiian Band. 'Iolani Palace features architecture seen nowhere else in the world. This unique style is known as American Florentine. On the first floor a grand hall faces a staircase of koa wood. Ornamental plaster decorates the interior. The throne room (southeast corner), the blue meeting room, and the dining room adjoin the hall. The blue room included a large 1848 portrait of King Louis Philippe of France and a koa wood piano where Lili'uokalani played her compositions for guests.

Upstairs are the private library and bedrooms of the Hawaiian monarchs. It served as the official residence of the Hawaiian monarch until the 1893 overthrow of the Kingdom of Hawai'i. Therein not only Lili'uokalani, but, Queen Kapi'olani and other royal retainers were evicted from the palace after the overthrow.

Oldest Building in the State: Ka Hale Lā'au, 553 S King St, Honolulu, HI **96813**. Ka Hale Lā'au was a pre-cut wooden frame structure designed in New England with little consideration for the Hawaiian climate, but it nonetheless housed missionaries for about 60 years. The home was shipped to Hawaii from Boston in 1820, traveling around Cape Horn to reach its destination. For six decades, it was a communal home for missionary families as well as island visitors and boarders.

Hawaiian Mission Houses Historic Site and Archives

House: *Annie Montague Alexander was born in Honolulu during the Kingdom of Hawaii in what is now the Mission Houses Museum.*

Address: 553 S King St, Honolulu, HI 96813

Hawaiian Mission Houses Historic Site and Archives, Creative Commons Licenses, via Wikimedia Commons

Place

The Hawaiian Mission Houses Historic Site and Archives Honolulu, HI, was established in 1920 by the Hawaiian Mission Children's Society, a private, non-profit organization and genealogical society, on the 100th anniversary of the arrival of the first Christian missionaries in Hawai'i. In 1962, the Mission Houses, together with Kawaiaha'o Church, both built by those early missionaries, were designated a U.S.

National Historic Landmark (NHL) under the combined name Kawaiahao Church and Mission Houses. In 1966 all the NHLs were included in the National Register of Historic Places. The Hawaiian Mission Houses Historic Site and Archives collects, preserves, interprets, and exhibits documents, artifacts, and other records of Hawaii's missionary period from about 1820 to 1863. It interprets its historic site and collections and makes these collections available for research, educational purposes, and public enjoyment. The archive's collection holds over 3,000 Hawaiian, Western, and Pacific artifacts, and more than 12,000 books, manuscripts, original letters, diaries, journals, illustrations and Hawaiian church records. The historic site and archive is open Tuesday through Saturday from 10:00 a.m. to 4:00 p.m. The general admission charge is $12, with discounts for students, seniors, and the military. The evolution of Mission House architecture illustrates the progressive adaptation of missionaries from New England to the climate, culture, and building materials they encountered in the Sandwich Islands. The materials to build the Oldest Frame House (Ka Hale Lāʻau the wood house) arrived by ship around Cape Horn from Boston in 1821. They had already been measured and cut, ready to assemble into a frame house suitable for the climate of New England: with small windows to help keep the heat inside and short eaves so as not to risk cracking under a load of snow. Though principally occupied by the seven members of Daniel Chamberlain's family, it often housed as many as five other missionary families, along with occasional ailing sailors or orphans. The small parlor served as a schoolhouse, and the basement served as the dining hall. The cookhouse was a separate building. The Chamberlain House (Ka Hale Kamalani) was built in 1831 from materials procured locally: coral blocks cut from reefs offshore and lumber salvaged from ships. Designed by the mission's quartermaster, Levi Chamberlain, to hold supplies as well as people, it had two stories, an attic, and a cellar. The windows are larger, more numerous, and shuttered against the sun. The building now serves as the main exhibition hall for the Museum. In 1841, a covered porch and balcony were added to the frame house, and an extra bedroom was built next door out of coral blocks. Both additions show further adaptation to an indoor-outdoor lifestyle appropriate to the climate. The extra coral building later became the mission's Print House (Ka Hale Paʻi) and now serves as a museum exhibit to show how the missionaries and native Hawaiians worked together to produce the first materials printed in the Hawaiian language.

Life

Who: Annie Montague Alexander (December 29, 1867 - September 10, 1950)
Annie Alexander was an American philanthropist and paleontological collector. She established the University of California Museum of Paleontology (UCMP), Museum of Vertebrate Zoology (MVZ), and financed their collections as well as a series of paleontological expeditions to the western United States at the turn of the 20th century. She took part in many of these expeditions, gathering a significant collection of fossils and exotic game animals in her own right. Annie Montague Alexander was born December 29, 1867, in Honolulu during the Kingdom of Hawaii in what is now the Mission Houses Museum. She was the granddaughter of New England missionaries in Maui, part of the Kingdom of Hawaii. Her father Samuel Thomas Alexander and her uncle Henry Perrine Baldwin were founders of Alexander & Baldwin. Her mother Martha Cooke was daughter of Amos Starr Cooke, the founder of Castle & Cooke. These were two of the Big Five corporations that started as sugar

cane plantation owners and then dominated the economy of the Territory of Hawaii. Her cousins included Henry Alexander Baldwin and Clarence Hyde Cooke who carried on the family businesses, Charles Montague Cooke, Jr. who studied snails (malacology), and architect Charles William Dickey. She attended Punahou School for one year, but in 1882 her family moved to Oakland, California, to get medical attention for her grandfather, and she enrolled in Oakland High School. In 1886 she attended Lasell Seminary for Young Women in Auburndale, MA. In 1888 she traveled with her family to Paris and studied painting. She returned to Oakland and trained briefly as a nurse, but enjoyed being outside instead. Her father left the business to others and took Annie on a bicycle trip through Europe in 1893, and sailed through the Pacific in 1896. In 1899 she went camping in Oregon and then went with her father to Bermuda. Alexander first became fascinated with paleontology in 1900 while attending a lecture by Professor John C. Merriam at the University of California, Berkeley. She offered to underwrite the entire cost of his upcoming expeditions. She took part in Merriam's 1901 expedition to Fossil Lake in Oregon, and his 1902 and 1903 expeditions to Mount Shasta in northern California. In 1904, Alexander left on a trip with her father and Thomas L. Gulick, son of missionary Peter Johnson Gulick and younger brother of John Thomas Gulick who was an early developer of theories of evolution. The men were looking forward to hunting big game in Africa, while Annie was collecting fossils and taking pictures. Gulick became ill and died August 15, 1904, in Kijabe, Kenya. On September 8 the Alexanders reached Victoria Falls. The next day they crossed the Zambezi river and climbed down the canyon for a better view. While she was preparing to take a picture, Samuel was hit by a boulder tossed down from workers above that crushed his foot. The foot was amputated and her father was buried at the Old Drift cemetery after dying a day later on September 10, 1904. In 1905 she financed and took part in the Saurian Expedition to the West Humboldt Range in Nevada. The expedition discovered many of the finest specimens of ichthyosaur. From April to August 1907 Alexander financed and led a trip to Alaska; the expedition to southeastern Alaska included Alexander, Joseph S. Dixon, Chase Littlejohn, Frank Stephens and Kate Stephens. From 1908 she collaborated continuously in the field with her companion Louise Kellogg. She proposed a Natural History Museum at the University of California, offering to support its research and collections. In 1908 she helped finance the newly established Museum of Vertebrate Zoology after the state fell short in its appropriations. At her request, Joseph Grinnell served as its first director until his death in 1939. In 1920 when Merriam left the University to become president of the Carnegie Institution, the paleontology department was merged with the geology department, displeasing both Merriam and Alexander. She subsequently helped establish the UCMP and created an endowment for its funding. She also helped finance much of the work of William Diller Matthew and his protégé George Gaylord Simpson. Alexander shared her life with Kellogg for forty-two years. By all accounts, it was a devoted Boston marriage. Among other activities, the two ran a working farm together; their asparagus was sold nationwide. Alexander continued to finance expeditions and perform field work throughout her life, celebrating her 80th birthday while in the Sierra de la Laguna mountains. She died of a stroke on September 10, 1950, and her ashes were buried at Kawaiaha'o Church (957 Punchbowl St, Honolulu, HI **96813**), overlooking her childhood home on Maui. At least seventeen species of plants and animals honor

Alexander in their scientific names (such as Hydrotherosaurus alexandrae), and several others are named after Kellogg. Lake Alexander in Alaska is named for her.

Koa Avenue

Restaurant/Bar:
Wang Chung's Karaoke Bar (2424 Koa Ave, Honolulu, HI 96815), has been named among the Amazing Gay Bars Around The World To Visit Before You Die, by BuzzFeed, 2019. Wang Chung's is a close-knit Waikiki gay bar tucked into the back of the Stay Hotel lobby. This lively hideaway's menu is full of creative cocktails, pizzas, and comforting bites, and its famous Sunday drag brunches guarantee a good time. And for those who wish to show off their vocal abilities, the mic is always passed around for daily karaoke. Seashore Condo in Waikiki (2450 Koa Ave # 26, Honolulu, HI 96815), LGBTQ friendly.

Kūhiō Avenue

Accommodation:
Ambassador Hotel Waikiki (2040 Kūhiō Ave, Honolulu, HI 96815), TAG Approved LGBTQ friendly accommodation.
Holiday Inn Express Waikiki (2058 Kūhiō Ave, Honolulu, HI 96815), TAG Approved LGBTQ friendly accommodation.

Restaurant/Bar:
Hamburger Mary's, 2109 Kūhiō Ave., Honolulu, HI 96815, included in the Damron Address Book in 1980. Also Sweet Al's Donut Shop, included in the Damron Address Book in 1980.
Hula's Bar & Lei Stand, 2130 Kūhiō Ave., Honolulu, HI 96815, included in the Damron Address Book from 1977 to 1980.

Accommodation: OHANA Waikiki Malia (2211 Kuhio Ave, Honolulu, HI 96815). Part of World Rainbow Hotels (WRH), Lesbian and Gay Welcoming Hotels.

Restaurant/Bar: House of Charles, 2260 Kūhiō Ave., Honolulu, HI 96815, included in the Damron Address Book in 1975.

Club: Roxy Baths, 2270 Kūhiō Ave., Honolulu, HI 96815, included in the Damron Address Book in 1979. Later Club Honolulu Baths, included in the Damron Address Book in 1980.

Accommodation:
The Laylow, Autograph Collection (2299 Kuhio Ave, Honolulu, HI 96815), gay friendly. Stunning boutique hotel featuring spacious rooms with a hip decor located 1 block to the beach and next to the International Marketplace. Mid-century modern meets Hawaiian charm at The Laylow, Autograph Collection, a welcoming and LGBTQ-friendly hotel in the heart of Waikiki. Here all guests receive a gift basket chock-full of local kine snacks and a pair of Laylow's signature slippas upon arrival, a true sign of Hawaiian hospitality. Before heading out on the town, sip flower-adorned craft cocktails at the bar, a place to see and be seen in Waikiki.
Hilton Garden Inn Waikiki Beach (2330 Kūhiō Ave, Honolulu, HI 96815), TAG Approved LGBTQ friendly accommodation.
Aqua Bamboo Waikiki Hotel (2425 Kūhiō Ave, Honolulu, HI 96815), gay friendly and TAG Approved LGBTQ friendly accommodation. An intimate, Southeast Asian-inspired boutique hotel located 1 1/2 Waikiki Beach.
Aqua Pacific Monarch Hotel (2427 Kūhiō Ave, Honolulu, HI 96815), TAG Approved LGBTQ friendly accommodation.
ResortQuest Pacific Monarch (2427 Kuhio Ave, Honolulu, HI 96815), LGBTQ friendly.
Hilton Waikiki Beach (2500 Kūhiō Ave, Honolulu, HI 96815), TAG Approved LGBTQ friendly accommodation. A partner of the International LGBTQ Travel Association since 2010, Hilton hotels are known to be welcoming to LGBTQ travelers. This hotel is famous for its panoramic views and quintessential Hawaiian hospitality, warmly greeting travelers of all kinds. Located just one block from the

beach and steps from many iconic gay bars in Waikiki, the hotel serves as the perfect launchpad for any big gay vacation. For those who enjoy a late-night snack after a night out, the classic all-day and all-night diner M.A.C 24/7 is all-too conveniently located off of the lobby.

Kulamanu Place

Jim Nabors House

House: *Jim Nabors' Diamond Head estate was on the market in 2018 for $15M.*

Address: 215 Kulamanu Pl, Honolulu, HI 96816

Jim Nabors House

Place

The oceanfront Hawaii estate belonging to Jim Nabors, known best for playing Gomer Pyle on The Andy Griffith Show and Gomer Pyle: USMC in the 1960s, was on the market for $14.88 million. The 5,877-square-foot house sits on a 25,059-square-foot lot east of Diamond Head and about three parcels from the Shangri La, the five-acre estate that once belonged to heiress Doris Duke and is now a museum of Islamic art. The Nabors house has five bedrooms and six baths, including a one-bedroom, one-bath guest suite tucked under the main living floor, adjacent to the pool and lanai. Patricia Choi of the Choi Group at Hawaii Life said Nabors, who died in November at age 87, bought the home in the 1970s, after leaving Hollywood. I knew him for a long time, wonderful person, absolutely kind, knowledgeable and one of the greatest people you'd ever meet, she said. The house was built in 1950, and Choi acknowledges that the land, one of the larger oceanfront lots in the Diamond Head area with 170 linear feet of ocean frontage, is more valuable than the structure. Choi said the property, even though next to a public access spot, is very private. Nabors was able to maintain his privacy and yet he could also swim and surf, she said.

Who: James Thurston Nabors (June 12, 1930 – November 30, 2017)

Jim Nabors was an American actor, singer, and comedian. He was born and raised in Sylacauga, AL, but he moved to southern California because of his asthma. He was discovered by Andy Griffith while working at a Santa Monica nightclub, and he later joined The Andy Griffith Show as Gomer Pyle. The character proved popular, and Nabors was given his own spin-off show, Gomer Pyle, U.S.M.C. Nabors was known for his portrayal of Gomer Pyle, although he became a popular guest on variety shows which showcased his rich baritone singing voice in the 1960s and 1970s, including two specials of his own in 1969 and 1974. He subsequently recorded numerous albums and singles, most of them containing romantic ballads. Nabors was also known for singing Back Home Again in Indiana prior to the start of the Indianapolis 500, held annually over the Memorial Day weekend. He sang the unofficial Indiana anthem almost every year from 1972 to 2014, except for occasional absences due to illness or scheduling conflicts. Nabors began vacationing in Hawaii in the 1960s, and in 1976, moved from Bel Air, CA, to Honolulu, HI. For 25 years, he owned a macadamia plantation on Maui before selling it to the National Tropical Botanical Garden, a conservationist organization, though he still retained farming rights to the land and owned a second home on the property. Nabors married his partner of 38 years, Stan Cadwallader, at Seattle, Washington's Fairmont Olympic Hotel on January 15, 2013, a month after same-sex marriage became legal in Washington. They had met in the 1970s, when Cadwallader was a fireman in Honolulu, and began dating in 1975. Although he had been closeted before this, his sexual orientation was not completely secret; for instance, Nabors brought his then-boyfriend Cadwallader along to his Indy 500 performance in 1978. A longstanding rumor maintains that Nabors married Rock Hudson in the early 1970s, shortly before Nabors began his relationship with Cadwallader. According to Hudson, the story originated with a group of middle-aged homosexuals who live in Huntington Beach, who sent out joke invitations for their annual get-together. One year, the group invited its members to witness the marriage of Rock Hudson and Jim Nabors, at which Hudson would take the surname of Nabors' most famous character, Gomer Pyle, becoming Rock Pyle. The rumor was spread by those who failed to get the joke, and because Nabors was still closeted at the time and Hudson never publicly admitted to being gay (despite widespread suspicion that he was), the two never spoke to each other again. Nabors died at his Honolulu, Hawaii, home on November 30, 2017, aged 87. The US Marine Corps released a statement on Nabors: Semper Fi, Gomer Pyle. Rest in peace Jim Nabors, one of the few to ever be named an Honorary Marine.

Lauula Street

Restaurant/Bar: In Between, 2155 Lauula St, Honolulu, HI **96815**. For an intimate bar experience, pull up one of a dozen or so seats at In Between. Referred to as the friendliest gay bar in Waikiki, this no-frills hideaway bar features happy hour until 8:00 PM. Bartender Sabrina's rotating selection of dessert shots are delicious and include creations such as apple butterbeer and orange creamsicle.

Lewers Street

Restaurant/Bar: Yard House, 226 Lewers St, I148, Honolulu, HI **96815**

Accommodation: Club Wyndham at Waikiki Beach Walk (227 Lewers St, Honolulu, HI **96815**). This resort is a 2-minute walk from Royal Hawaiian Centre, and 2.6 miles from Honolulu Museum of Art. Part of World Rainbow Hotels (WRH), Lesbian and Gay Welcoming Hotels.

Club: Surf Baths, 307 Lewers St, Honolulu, HI **96815**, included in the Damron Address Book from 1975 to 1977. Later Steam Works, included in the Damron Address Book from 1978 to 1980.

Restaurant/Bar: Embers, 311 Lewers St, Honolulu, HI **96815**, included in the Damron Address Book from 1965 to 1968.

Accommodation: Aqua Oasis Hotel (320 Lewers St, Honolulu, HI **96815**), TAG Approved LGBTQ friendly accommodation. Escape to Waikiki where days are spent relaxing at white sand beaches and nights filled with amazing cuisine from around the world and vibrant nightlife. Part of World Rainbow Hotels (WRH), Lesbian and Gay Welcoming Hotels.

Restaurant/Bar:
Bacchus Waikiki, 408 Lewers St, Honolulu, HI **96815**. This casual, natural-wood-adorned gay bar hosts myriad community events, including monthly catamaran cruises, trivia, live music, and other entertainment in a setting where respect and inclusion are championed. Don't miss nightly drink specials such as $4 Margarita Mondays, Wednesday Airport Double $3 doubles, and Flirty Friday's two-for-one happy hour from 5:00 to 8:00 PM.
Four Twelve, 412 Lewers St, Honolulu, HI **96815**, included in the Damron Address Book in 1974. Later Red Bamboo, included in the Damron Address Book in 1979.

Accommodation:
Surfjack Hotel & Swim Club, 412 Lewers St, Honolulu, HI **96815**, TAG Approved LGBTQ friendly accommodation, is a 7 minutes' walk from the beach. The hotel is 5 minutes' drive from Waikiki Beach and 15 minutes' drive to Diamond Head State Monument. Part of World Rainbow Hotels (WRH), Lesbian and Gay Welcoming Hotels. Featuring the iconic Wish You Were Here pool, the Surfjack Boutique Hotel and Swim Club is a favorite hotel for both visitors and stay-cationers alike. Even if you don't happen to have a room, come lounge at the weekend pool parties, gay-friendly and welcoming to all.
Coconut Waikiki Hotel (450 Lewers St, Honolulu, HI **96815**). Located across from the Ala Wai Canal, this gay-friendly boutique hotel offers fabulous views, a choice of modern guestrooms and first-class services. Part of World Rainbow Hotels (WRH), Lesbian and Gay Welcoming Hotels.

Maunakea Street

Restaurant/Bar: French Quarter, 1112 Maunakea St, Honolulu, HI **96817**, included in the Damron Address Book from 1965 to 1970.

Theatre: Roosevelt Theatre, 1152 Maunakea Street, Honolulu, HI **96817**, included in the 1975 All Lavender International Gay Guide. Built in downtown Honolulu as the Asahi Gekijo (Asahi Theater), where sumo and other athletic events were held, along with plays. It opened as the Roosevelt Theatre on September 28, 1934 and was operated by Franklin Theatres. It was taken over by Royal Theatres in 1938. In 1959 it became one of Chinatown's adult film venues and was renamed Rex Theatre on June 20, 1970, eventually shutting down as a theatre for good. The Hong Fa Market is now in its place.

McCully Street

Restaurant/Bar: Stuffed Tomato or Tomato Cabaret, 240 McCully St, Honolulu, HI **96815**, included in the Damron Address Book from 1975 to 1980.

Nāhua Street

Accommodation: Pearl Hotel Waikiki (415 Nāhua St, Honolulu, HI **96815**), TAG Approved LGBTQ friendly accommodation.

Nohonani Street

Accommodation: White Sands Hotel (431 Nohonani St, Honolulu, HI **96815**), TAG Approved LGBTQ friendly accommodation.

Nuuanu Avenue

Restaurant/Bar: Vic's Club, 1112 Nuuanu Ave, Honolulu, HI **96817**, included in the Damron Address Book in 1980.

Ōhua Avenue

Accommodation:
Aston at the Waikiki Banyan (201 'Ōhua Ave, Honolulu, HI **96815**), TAG Approved LGBTQ friendly accommodation.
C.I.M.Y. Hawaii (201 'Ōhua Ave, Honolulu, HI **96815**), LGBTQ friendly.

Other non-queer residents: Robert Louis Stevenson (1850-1894), Robert Louis Stevenson Grass House (3016 Oahu Ave, Honolulu, HI **96822**), In 1893.

Olohana Street

Accommodation: Club Wyndham Royal Garden at Waikiki (440 'Olohana St, Honolulu, HI **96815**). This resort is 0.8 miles from Waikiki Beach, 1.2 miles from Ala Wai Golf Course and 2.6 miles from Diamond Head. The rooms offer free Wi-Fi, flat-screen TV's and DVD players and kitchenettes. Part of World Rainbow Hotels (WRH), Lesbian and Gay Welcoming Hotels.

Pali Highway

Religious Building: Metropolitan Community Church, 2500 Pali Hwy, Honolulu, HI **96817**, included in the Damron Address Book from 1974 to 1980.

Paoakalani Avenue

Accommodation:
Aqua Hotel Renew (129 Paoakalani Ave, Honolulu, HI **96815**). Honolulu's first true designer boutique hotel, is an intimate getaway located just steps to Waikiki Beach. Part of World Rainbow Hotels (WRH), Lesbian and Gay Welcoming Hotels.
Hyatt Place Waikiki Beach (175 Paoakalani Ave, Honolulu, HI **96815**), TAG Approved LGBTQ friendly accommodation, has been named among the Best Gay-Friendly Hotels in the World by Amerikanki, 2014. Just a few minutes from Waikiki Beach, the Hyatt Place Waikiki Beach is a well-endowed 4-star hotel with stellar views of both the ocean and surrounding island sure to please any traveller. Part of World Rainbow Hotels (WRH), Lesbian and Gay Welcoming Hotels.
Aston Waikiki Sunset (229 Paoakalani Ave, Honolulu, HI **96815**), TAG Approved LGBTQ friendly accommodation.

Shangri La

House: *The Shangri La Museum of Islamic Art, Culture & Design is housed in the former home of Doris Duke near Diamond Head just outside Honolulu, HI. It is now owned and operated as a public museum of the arts and cultures of the Islamic world by the Doris Duke Foundation for Islamic Art (DDFIA). Guided tours depart from the Honolulu Museum of Art, which operates the tours in co-operation with DDFIA.*

Address: 4055 Pāpū Cir, Honolulu, HI 96816

Shangri La, Creative Commons Licenses, via Wikimedia Commons

Place

Construction of Shangri La took place from 1936 to 1938, after Doris Duke's 1935 honeymoon which took her through the Islamic world. For nearly 60 years, Duke commissioned and collected artworks for the space, eventually forming a collection of over 4,000 objects. The structure was designed by Marion Sims Wyeth. An artistic reflection of the construction of Shangri La can be found in Kiana Davenport's novel Song of the Exile. The building was opened to the public as a museum, the Shangri La Museum for Islamic Art, Design & Culture, in 2002. The Shangri La Museum for Islamic Art, Design & Culture displays a wide-ranging collection of art, furnishings, and built-in architectural elements from Iran, Morocco, Turkey, Spain, Syria, Egypt, and India - among others. Gilt and painted ceilings from Morocco, vivid ceramics from Iran (including the only complete lusterware Ilkhanid mihrab in North America), painted wooden interiors from Syria, pierced metalwork and vibrant textiles from

Spain to India (including a magnificent pair of shaped carpets, made for the Mughal emperor) are among the many highlights. Its multiple buildings on the campus also include The Playhouse (a reduced-scale version of the XVII century Chehel Sotoun in Esfahan, Iran, now used for public programs and artist residencies). The outdoor landscaping has a number of gardens, including a formal Mughal garden inspired by the Shalimar Gardens, as well as terraced water features, a Hawaiian fishpond, tropical gardens and a waterfall, and fabulous vistas of the Pacific Ocean. The museum also hosts two visual artists per year for onsite exhibitions, workshops, and/or lectures. Recently-featured artists have included Hayv Kahraman, Faig Ahmed, Bahia Shehab, and Reem Bassous.

Pauahi Street

Restaurant/Bar: Scarlet Honolulu, 80 S Pauahi St, Honolulu, HI **96813**. Scarlet is the quintessential hub of Honolulu's LGBTQ community and the epitome of the welcoming culture of the islands. Locals say there is truly never a bad night at Scarlet. With shows every Friday and Saturday night, renowned queens and kings take the stage for the Fresh Fish Drag Revue and beats that keep clubgoers dancing until the wee hours of the morning.

Pensacola Street

Cemetery: The Rev. Mineo Katagiri (1919-2005) was a leader in the United Church of Christ and strong advocate for minority and LGBT rights. He was an avid golfer who sometimes used golf outings as part of his ministry; he died as a result of a fall on the 18th hole of the San Geronimo Golf Course in Marin County, said his daughter, Iao Katagiri. The Rev. Katagiri's career was marked by public service, outreach to ethnic communities and opposition to discrimination based on ethnicity or sexual orientation. Born of Japanese ancestry in Haleiwa, HI, he graduated from the University of Hawaii in 1941 and received his theological degree from Union Theological Seminary in New York City in 1944. He was ordained in 1945 and encountered postwar discrimination against Japanese Americans. He was a minister in several churches in Hawaii and Ohio and also taught at Doshisha University in Kyoto after WWII. He moved to Seattle in 1959, serving as campus minister for the University of Washington and metropolitan minister for the University Congregational Church. In 1969, he founded the Asian Coalition for Equality. He also started the First Avenue Service Center on Seattle's Skid Road and was founding director of the Office of Economic Opportunity for King County. His work in Washington earned him appointments to the former state Council on Higher Education and the Governor's Advisory Committee on Urban Affairs. He moved to New York City in 1970 as director of mission priorities for the United Church of Christ. As head of the church's Northern California Conference from 1975 to his retirement in 1984, he helped establish or strengthen churches in ethnic communities, such as the First Filipino-American United Church of Christ in San Bruno. He lived in San Francisco and was a trustee emeritus at the Pacific School of Religion in Berkeley at the time of his death. He was survived by his wife of 61 years, Nobu Sasai Katagiri. He is buried at Makiki Cemetery (1630 Pensacola St, Honolulu, HI **96822**).

Portlock Road

Other non-queer residents: Henry John Kaiser (1882-1967), 525 Portlock Rd, Honolulu, HI **96825**, from 1959 to 1967.

Queen Emma Square

Religious Builing: Edmond L. Browning (1929-2016), as the presiding bishop in the US, welcomed women into the hierarchy of the Episcopal Church, supported a role for gay and lesbian congregants, and lobbied aggressively for civil rights and against the nuclear arms race. He consecrated the church's first female bishop (the Rt. Rev. Barbara C. Harris of the Diocese of Massachusetts in 1989); brokered a compromise with the worldwide Anglican Communion, based in Britain, that allowed individual dioceses to decide whether to ordain women; and commissioned a report that similarly left it to the discretion of local dioceses to ordain gay Episcopalians. He also opposed apartheid in South Africa and supported legal abortions. He argued against Israel's treatment of the Palestinians, maintaining that they had become victims of oppression. He received bachelor of arts, bachelor of divinity and doctor of divinity degrees from the University of the South in Sewanee, TN, and was ordained a priest in 1955. He was the first bishop of Okinawa and later the bishop of Hawaii. He is buried in The Cathedral of St. Andrew, 229 Queen Emma Square, Honolulu, HI **96813**.

Richards Street

Queer Architects: YWCA Laniakea, 1040 Richards St, Honolulu, HI **96813**, Designed by Julia Morgan (1925-26).

Round Top Drive

House: Richard Chamberlain (born 1934) is an American actor who built a career in television, film, and theater playing romantic heterosexual roles. Deeply closeted for most of his life, he at last publicly acknowledged his homosexuality in his 2003 memoir Shattered Love. Chamberlain, born in Los Angeles, grew up in Beverly Hills, but, he says, on the wrong side of the now-vanished streetcar tracks in a city whose name is synonymous with affluence. Although the Chamberlains were not rich, they were reasonably comfortable financially. Emotional comfort was a far rarer commodity in the household. Chamberlain's father was an alcoholic who terrorized his wife and two sons with psychological rather than physical violence. In his memoir Chamberlain describes consistent feelings of inadequacy and failure to live up to his father's expectations. Chamberlain entered Pomona College in 1952, intending to major in art, but he soon began appearing in the drama program's plays, enjoying enough success that he decided to pursue an acting career after graduating. His plans were briefly interrupted when he was drafted and served two years in the army. Upon his return to civilian life he enrolled in acting classes, in one of which he met a young man who became his first love. Because of the homophobia prevalent in the late 1950s, the pair were careful to keep the year-long affair as secret as possible. Chamberlain made his movie debut in the forgettable The Secret of the Purple Reef (1960, directed by William Witney) and filmed a pilot for a proposed television series that never materialized. Shortly thereafter, however, he won the title role in the NBC drama Dr. Kildare, which began its immensely successful five-year run in 1961 and established the handsome Chamberlain as a romantic leading man, the object of desire of both men and women. When Dr. Kildare ended, Chamberlain declined offers of other television series to work in theater and film. This led him to England, where he lived for four and a half years. A highlight of his British sojourn was the opportunity to play Hamlet at the Birmingham Repertory Theatre in 1968. Chamberlain's movie career has included an eclectic mix of projects. His roles in Bryan Forbes's The Madwoman of Chaillot (1969) and Ken Russell's The Music Lovers (1971), in which he played Pyotr Ilich Tchaikovsky, are generally considered among his best, earning critical accolades. He also appeared in Irwin Allen's disaster films The Towering Inferno (1974) and The Swarm (1978) and Richard Lester's The Three Musketeers (1974), among others. Chamberlain was involved romantically with actor Wesley Eure in the early 1970s. In the late 1970s and 1980s Chamberlain reigned on television as the king of the mini-series, starring in Centennial (1978, based on the novel by James Michener and directed by Harry Falk, Paul Krasny, Bernard McEveety, and Virgil Vogel), Shogun (1980, based on James Clavell's novel and directed by Jerry London), and the phenomenally successful adaptation of Colleen McCullough's The Thorn Birds (1983, directed by Stan Margulies). Around 110 million television viewers watched the tale of Father Ralph de Bricassart's doomed love for Meggie, an Australian sheep rancher, putting The Thorn Birds among the highest-rated mini-series in the history of television. The mini-series also solidified Chamberlain's status as a mysterious heart-throb for legions of female fans. When cable television began drawing an ever increasing share of the audience, the major networks moved away from producing costly mini-series. Chamberlain returned to the theater, where he undertook such mature roles as Henry Higgins in a 1994 Broadway revival of Alan Jay Lerner and Frederick Loewe's My Fair Lady and Baron von Trapp in a national tour of Richard Rodgers and Oscar Hammerstein's The Sound of Music in 1999. When Chamberlain publicly acknowledged that he is gay in his 2003 memoir Shattered Love, the news came as a shock to virtually no one. That he chose at the age of 68 finally to speak of his sexuality was considerably more surprising. Although the tabloids had outed him in the early 1990s, and his homosexuality was an open secret in much of the theatrical and television community, as well as the subject of gossip in the gay male community, throughout his career he had refused to comment on the topic because, he stated later, of his own selfrejection as a gay man. He also feared that coming out might jeopardize his job prospects, which was certainly a valid concern when he was starting out in the early 1960s. Even today many gay male actors wonder if they can be accepted in romantic heterosexual roles if they are openly gay. When Chamberlain finally revealed the worst kept secret in Hollywood, however, he found his fans supportive, positive, and friendly. In his memoir Chamberlain writes of his search for inner peace and of his relationship with producer/director Martin Rabbett, his partner from the mid-1970s to 2010. The couple made their home at 3711 Round Top Dr, Honolulu, HI **96822**, since Rabbett grew up in Hawaii. The two worked together on various professional projects over the years. One of the most recent was a July 2003 production of Timothy Findley's The Stillborn Lover at the Berkshire Repertory Theater in Stockbridge, Massachusetts. Rabbett directed the play, in which Chamberlain starred as an ambassador who reveals to his family that he is gay. Critic Malcolm Johnson observed that Chamberlain brought a deep reserve and quiet dignity to the role, perhaps reflecting both his many years of reticence and his newfound self-acceptance. The couple split amicably in 2010, with Chamberlain moving to Los Angeles. In a 2014 interview, Chamberlain said that while he and Rabbett were no longer intimately involved, they remained close friends.

Royal Hawaiian Avenue

Accommodation: Courtyard by Marriott Waikiki Beach (400 Royal Hawaiian Ave, Honolulu, HI **96815**), TAG Approved LGBTQ friendly accommodation.

Royal Place

Queer Architects: Craig Cullinan and Nina Neal Dodge House, 4375 Royal Pl, Honolulu, HI **96816**, designed by John Elgin Woolf (1966)

Rycroft Street

Accommodation: Pagoda Hotel (1525 Rycroft St, Honolulu, HI **96814**), TAG Approved LGBTQ friendly accommodation.

Saratoga Road

Restaurant/Bar: BLT Steak, Trump International Tower, 223 Saratoga Rd, Honolulu, HI **96815**

Accommodation: Trump International Hotel Waikiki, 223 Saratoga Rd, Honolulu, HI **96815**, Travellers' Choice Awards, 2022 Best of the Best Hotel in the US, by Tripadvisor.com

Seaside Avenue

Accommodation:
The stylish Shoreline Hotel Waikiki (342 Seaside Ave, Honolulu, HI **96815**) is a modern boutique hotel, only minutes from the beach and offering gay-friendly accommodation and first-class services. Part of World Rainbow Hotels (WRH), Lesbian and Gay Welcoming Hotels.
Hyatt Centric Waikiki Beach (349 Seaside Ave, Honolulu, HI **96815**), TAG Approved LGBTQ friendly accommodation. Part of World Rainbow Hotels (WRH), Lesbian and Gay Welcoming Hotels. Home of Gay Island Guide's monthly Super Slyde Pool Party, the fun never stops at Hyatt Centric. Floor-to-ceiling windows in each room offer views of iconic Waikiki Beach amongst contemporary decor. The lounge pool features private cabanas and a tapas-style eatery for small bites between play. And this LGBTQ-friendly hotel is a proud partner of Honolulu PRIDE Festival.
Waikiki Place, 364 Seaside Ave, Honolulu, Oahu, HI **96815**, GLD, Gay Lesbian Directory
Aqua Island Colony Hotel (435 Seaside Ave, Honolulu, HI **96815**), gay friendly. The tallest hotel in Waikiki with commanding views of the Pacific Ocean and majestic Koolau Mountains, 2 blocks from the beach.
Aqua Skyline Hotel at Island Colony (445 Seaside Ave, Honolulu, HI **96815**), TAG Approved LGBTQ friendly accommodation. The General Manager and many of the front line staff are LGBTQ members at this ultimate gay hotel, a proud partner of many LGBTQ organizations in Honolulu. For gay travelers, being located walking distance from many of the most popular LGBTQ bars and restaurants means no boredom will ensue. Rooms come complete with kitchenettes for a home-away-from-home feel.

Uluniu Avenue

Restaurant/Bar: Governor's Coffee House, 117 Uluniu Ave, Honolulu, HI **96815**, included in the Damron Address Book in 1973.

University Avenue

Women's Word Bookstore 1820 University Ave, Honolulu, HI **96822**) was a feminist bookstore active in the 1980s.

Waialae Avenue

Restaurant/Bar: Sierra Madre, 3574 Waialae Ave, Honolulu, HI **96816**, included in the 1975 All Lavender International Gay Guide.

Waikiki Beach

Beach: Waikiki Beach (Honolulu, HI **96815**) has been named among the Most beautiful beaches in the world, 2019. Between Queen's Surf Club and Kapiolani Park Beach House, included in the 1975 All Lavender International Gay Guide.

Wasp Boulevard

World Heritage List: Papahānaumokuākea (1845 Wasp Blvd Building 176, Honolulu, HI **96818**)

18th Avenue

Find a grave

We sail together: Charles Bell (1935–1995) was an American Photorealist known primarily for his large scale still lifes. Bell was born and raised in Tulsa, OK, where he graduated from Will Rogers High School in 1953. He earned a Bachelor of Business Administration degree from the University of Oklahoma in 1957, then served for two years in the US Navy as a lieutenant. Bell died in Manhattan, New York of AIDS-related lymphoma on April 1, 1995. His partner of 26 years, interior designer Willard Ching (1942-1992), had died of AIDS three years earlier. Ching was born in Honolulu and was founder of Will Ching Planning & Design. He was former national director of the Institute of Business Designers and twice president of the National Council for Interior Design Qualification. He was also vice president of Contract Interior Design Standards governing board; and was an honorary member of the International Society of Interior Designers. Projects on which he worked included the New York City police headquartes, Westinghouse Nuclear Center in Pennsylvania and Lum Yip Kee offices in Honolulu. Both Bell and Ching are buried at Diamond Head Memorial Park (529 18th Ave, Honolulu, HI **96816**), Plot: Flowers Urn Gar. A-4 (Bell) and Plot: Peace#7-BH-4 (Ching)

Restaurant/Bar:
Continental Travelodge Lounge, Tumon Beach, Tamuning, **96913**, Guam, included in the Damron Address Book in 1978.

Salon del Mar Lounge, Tumon Beach, Tamuning, **96913**, Guam, included in the Damron Address Book in 1978.

Nevada

State bordering with: New York, Pennsylvania, Delaware.
Nevada is ranked 11 out of 51 for % of same sex couples (0,710%), and is ranked 47 for # of same sex couples, 714. (US Census 2010)
The Gay & Lesbian Chamber of Commerce of Nevada: http://www.glccnv.org/

89000

Henderson

Henderson, NV 89002, has been named among the Queerest City in America by The Advocate, 2017

Boulder Dam Hotel, 1305 Arizona St, Boulder City, NV 89005, by Elisa Rolle (own work)

Tried for You (Food): Southwest Diner, 761 Nevada Hwy, Boulder City, NV 89005

Lake Las Vegas, by Elisa Rolle (own work)

Queer Architects: Lake Las Vegas, 101 Montelago Blvd, Henderson, NV **89011**, Designed by David M. Schwarz (1998).

Accommodation: Aston MonteLago Village Resort (30 Strada Di Villaggio, Henderson, NV **89011**), LGBTQ friendly.	Westin Lake Las Vegas Resort & Spa (101 Montelago Blvd, Henderson, NV **89011**), LGBTQ friendly.

Cemetery: Tony Curtis (1925–2010) was an American film actor whose career spanned six decades but who achieved the height of his popularity in the 1950s and early 1960s. He acted in more than 100 films in roles covering a wide range of genres, from light comedy to serious drama. In his later years, Curtis made numerous television appearances. Curtis gave what could arguably be called his best performance in the comedy Some Like It Hot (1959). Critic David Thomson called it an outrageous film, and an American Film Institute survey voted it the funniest American film ever made. The film co-starred Jack Lemmon and Marilyn Monroe, and was directed by Billy Wilder. On July 8, 2010, Curtis, who suffered from chronic obstructive pulmonary disease (COPD), was hospitalized in Las Vegas after suffering an asthma attack during a book-signing engagement in Henderson, Nevada, where he lived. Curtis died at his Henderson home on September 29, 2010, of cardiac arreSt His remains were interred at Palm Memorial Park Cemetery (Westridge Dr, Henderson, NV **89012**), on October 4, 2010.

Restaurant/Bar: Olive Garden Italian, 4400 E Sunset Rd, Henderson, NV **89014**	Red Lobster, 570 Marks St, Henderson, NV **89014** Ben & Jerry's, 1301 W Sunset Rd, Henderson, NV **89014**
Accommodation:	Edgewater Casino Resort (2020 S Casino Dr, Laughlin, NV **89029**), LGBTQ friendly.

Walking Box Ranch, Searchlight

House: *Walking Box Ranch, 7 mi (11 km) west of Searchlight, NV, in the Mojave Desert, was founded in 1931 by Rex Bell and Clara Bow as a working 400,000 acres (160,000 ha) ranch. Bow lived here from 1931 to 1945. The ranch includes four buildings and is owned by the Bureau of Land Management (BLM).*

Address: Ykl Ranch Rd, Searchlight, NV 89046
National Register of Historic Places: 08001392, 2009

YKL Ranch, Creative Commons Licenses, via Wikimedia Commons

Place

Over the years, Rex and Clara Bell entertained many notable Hollywood figures, including Clark Gable, Carole Lombard, Errol Flynn, and Lionel Barrymore. The Walking Box Ranch was purchased by Bell from the Rock Springs Cattle Company. The company owned 1,000,000 acres (400,000 ha) in the Mojave Desert. The Nature Conservancy purchased 151,331 acres (61,241 ha) of land that surrounded the Walking Box Ranch in June 1994. The Walking Box Ranch was purchased by Las Vegas Gaming Investments in 2000 for $950,000.

Accommodation:
Built in 1907, the Mizpah Hotel (100 N Main St, Tonopah, NV **89049**) was known to be called the Grand Old Lady for its elegant service, comfort, and amenities. Supported by 18 inches of solid granite walls, the five-story hotel was the tallest building in Nevada until 1929 and featured the first electric elevator west of the Mississippi. With its modern luxuries and charming opulence, the Mizpah Hotel was known throughout the United States and drew luminaries and notable clientele. Through the shifting economic tides, the many hands of investors, and over a century of dramatic seasons in the high Nevada desert, the Mizpah Hotel is once again a place of timeless elegance, exceptional guest service, luxurious comfort and amenities. The Mizpah Hotel is an elegant retreat into Nevada's past, to include a full service restaurant and upscale lobby bar. Chosen by Nevada Magazine as the Best Hotel in Rural Nevada, the hotel is centrally located in the heart of Nevada on highway 95, halfway between Las Vegas and Reno, and within easy walking distance to the award-winning Tonopah Historic Mining Park and the Tonopah Convention Center. Mizpah Hotel, a member of Historic Hotels of America since 2013, dates back to 1907.

Restaurant/Bar:

Ben & Jerry's, 2225 Village Walk Dr, Henderson, NV **89052**

Layers Bakery Café, 665 S. Green Valley Pkwy., Suite 100, Henderson, NV **89052**, GLD, Gay Lesbian Directory

Shake Shack, 2225 Village Walk Dr #191, Henderson, NV **89052**

89100

Las Vegas

Las Vegas, NV, has been named among the Gayest Cities in America by The Advocate, 2011

Las Vegas, NV, has been named among the Gayest Cities in America by The Advocate, 2014

Las Vegas, NV, has been named among the Best Gay Honeymoon Destinations by Amerikanki, 2014.

Las Vegas, NV, has been named among the LGBTQ vacations you must take before you die, by Orbitz, 2016

Las Vegas, NV, has been named among the Top LGBT-friendly cities by ellgeeBE, 2018

Las Vegas, NV, has been named among the Top Lesbian Vacation Destinations by Lesbian Business Community, 2019.

Las Vegas, NV, has been named among the Best cities for nightlife in the world, 2019

Las Vegas, NV, has been named among the Funniest cities in the world, 2019

Almond Tree Lane

Religious Building: After an unsuccessful beginning in Las Vegas in 1974, the Metropolitan Community Church (MCC) re-established itself in 1979 at 1140 Almond Tree Ln #302, Las Vegas, NV **89104**. Throughout the 1980s, MCC served as the meeting place for numerous community organizations, sponsoring marriages, concerts, and auctions, as well as the first LGBTQ community bookstore, and was among the first in the community to provide help for people with HIV and AIDS.

Arville Road

Restaurant/Bar: Charlie's Las Vegas, 5012 Arville Rd, Las Vegas, NV **89118**, GLD, Gay Lesbian Directory

Bledsoe Lane

Religious Building: The American Eastern Orthodox Church, St George Monastery (1580 Bledsoe Ln, Las Vegas, NV **89110**) included in the 1971 Homosexual National Classified Directory.

Bonneville Avenue

The Lou Ruvo Center for Brain Health, Creative Commons Licenses, via Wikimedia Commons

Attractions: The Lou Ruvo Center for Brain Health (LRCBH, 888 West Bonneville Ave, Las Vegas, NV **89106**), officially the Cleveland Clinic Lou Ruvo Center for Brain Health, opened on May 21, 2010, in Las Vegas, Nevada. It is operated by the Cleveland Clinic and was designed by Frank Gehry.

Boulder Highway

Restaurant/Bar:
Four Mile Bar, 3642 Boulder Hwy, Las Vegas, NV **89121**, included in the Damron Address Book in 1977.
Italian Village, 4000 Boulder Hwy, Las Vegas, NV **89121**, included in the Damron Address Book from 1977 to 1979.

California Avenue

Club: Manhattan Health Spa at Manhattan Hotel, 15 E California Ave, Las Vegas, NV **89104**, included in the Damron Address Book in 1980.

Casino Center Boulevard

Club: Las Vegas Spa, 1130 S Casino Center Blvd, Las Vegas, NV **89104**, included in the Damron Address Book in 1979. Also Manhattan Hotel, included in the Damron Address Book from 1977 to 1978.

Centennial Center Boulevard

Restaurant/Bar: Olive Garden Italian, 6191 Centennial Center Blvd, Las Vegas, NV **89149**

Charleston Boulevard

Restaurant/Bar: The Back Door, 1415 E Charleston Blvd, Las Vegas, NV **89104**, included in the Damron Address Book in 1980. As of 2022 it's still open.

Store: Old Memories Antique Shop, 1431 E Charleston Blvd no 8, Las Vegas, NV **89104**, included in the Damron Address Book in 1976.

Restaurant/Bar: Sixteen-Ten, 1610 E Charleston Blvd, Las Vegas, NV **89104**, included in the Damron Address Book from 1977 to 1980.

Club: The Charleston Men's Health Club was open briefly around 1980 at 2120 E Charleston Blvd, Las Vegas, NV **89104**, in the Crestwood Shopping Center, where there were several porno theater/bookstores, many of which catered to gay men. The Crestwood Shopping Center at Eastern Avenue and Charleston Boulevard in 1973 was renamed the Adult Center for its collection of pornographic businesses. The Talk of the Town Bookstore and movie arcade, opened in September 1970, was the first adult business in Las Vegas to openly advertise its gay merchandise in the commercial press.

LGBTQ friendly bookstore: Talk of the Town Book Store, 2232 E Charleston Blvd, Las Vegas, NV **89104**, included in the Damron Address Book from 1977 to 1980.

Restaurant/Bar:
Olive Garden Italian, 10800 W Charleston Blvd, Las Vegas, NV **89135**
Yard House, 11011 W Charleston Blvd, Las Vegas, NV **89135**

Cheyenne Avenue

Restaurant/Bar: Olive Garden Italian, 6850 W Cheyenne Ave, Las Vegas, NV **89108**

Convention Center Drive

Accommodation:
Royal Resort (99 Convention Center Dr, Las Vegas, NV **89109**). A mile from the Las Vegas Convention Centre, this straightforward hotel is less than a block from the Strip. Standard rooms offer free Wi-Fi, mini fridges, coffeemakers, and TV's. Part of World Rainbow Hotels (WRH), Lesbian and Gay Welcoming Hotels.
Las Vegas Marriott (325 Convention Center Dr, Las Vegas, NV **89109**), LGBTQ friendly.

Dean Martin Drive

Accommodation: Hampton Inn Tropicana (4975 Dean Martin Dr, Las Vegas, NV **89118**), TAG Approved LGBTQ friendly accommodation.

Decatur Boulevard

Restaurant/Bar:
Red Lobster, 200 S Decatur Blvd, Las Vegas, NV **89107**
Olive Garden Italian, 1361 S Decatur Blvd, Las Vegas, NV **89102**

Accommodation: Hilton Vacation Club Desert Retreat Las Vegas, 5165 S Decatur Blvd, Las Vegas, NV **89118**, LGBTQ friendly.

Desert Inn Road

Restaurant/Bar: In 1983 Marge Jacques resurrected her notorious gay bar, Le Café as Disco Le Café Bar and Restaurant in the old Country Rebel Steakhouse (2710 E Desert Inn Rd, Las Vegas, NV **89121**). Her partners in this venture were noted casino designer Don Schmitt, entertainer Breck Wall, and businessman Warren Fulbright. Disco Le Café had its grand opening on October 20, 1983. The nightclub came alive at night with drag, Punk, and New Wave shows, while the restaurant side hosted meetings of groups and organizations both straight and gay. The rooms were decorated with paintings by performer/designer Joey Skilbred, while a huge fireplace kept the foyer and restaurant warm. The menu featured dishes named after famous gay people such as James Dean Hot Cakes and the Bessie Smith Platter. For awhile some of the glamour that had made the first Le Café world famous was reborn at Disco Le Café. But Disco Le Café died a quick death. Its East Desert Inn location worked against it because it was too remote from the Paradise Road/Naples area known as the Fruit Loop; Marge was aiming for a high-end clientele that didn't exist in Las Vegas then; and the bar owners in the Fruit Loop, angry with Marge's competition, spread rumors that the cops were following gay people from the Fruit Loop on their way to Disco Le Café and ticketing them on trumped-up DUIs. It was an effective lie which, taken with the other factors working against Marge, killed the bar. On April 13, 1984, the Women's Concerns Group of Nevadans for Human Rights arrived at Le Café for their monthly meeting only to find the doors locked. Le Café, closed the day before, had passed into history.

Duke Ellington Way

Accommodation: Desert Rose Resort (5051 Duke Ellington Way, Las Vegas, NV **89119**)'s 1km pristine beach, and its idyllic 40,000m² natural lagoon with golden sands. World Rainbow Hotels (WRH), Lesbian and Gay Welcoming Hotels, GLD, Gay Lesbian Directory

Fashion Show Drive

Accommodation: Trump Las Vegas (2000 Fashion Show Dr, Las Vegas, NV **89109**), LGBTQ friendly.

Flaming Road

Accommodation:
The Westin Las Vegas Hotel & Spa (160 E Flamingo Rd, Las Vegas, NV **89109**), TAG Approved LGBTQ friendly accommodation.
The Platinum Hotel & Spa (211 E Flamingo Rd, Las Vegas, NV **89169**), Wisconsin LGBT Chamber of Commerce member and TAG Approved LGBTQ friendly accommodation.

Restaurant/Bar: Lotus of Siam, 620 E Flamingo Rd, Las Vegas, NV **89119**

LGBTQ friendly bookstore: Bookworm, 1350 E Flamingo Rd, Las Vegas, NV **89119**, included in the Damron Address Book in 1980.

Restaurant/Bar:
The Garage, 1487 E Flamingo Rd, Las Vegas, NV **89119**
Olive Garden Italian, 1545 E Flamingo Rd, Las Vegas, NV **89119**
Hamburger Mary's, 1700 E Flamingo Rd, Las Vegas, NV **89119**
Red Lobster, 2325 E Flamingo Rd, Las Vegas, NV **89119**

Accommodation:
In the entertainment capital of the world, Brazilian-themed Rio All-Suite Hotel and Casino (3700 W Flamingo Rd, Las Vegas, NV **89103**) stands tall against the skyline with its signature purple and red glass exterior. Part of World Rainbow Hotels (WRH), Lesbian and Gay Welcoming Hotels.
Palms Casino Resort (4321 W Flamingo Rd, Las Vegas, NV **89103**) has been named among the Most expensive hotels in the world, 2019.

Freemont Street

Historic District: Fremont St, Las Vegas, NV **89101**, McDonald's to Union Plaza, included in the Damron Address Book from 1976 to 1980.

Restaurant/Bar:
Las Vegas' Kit Kat Club, at the intersection of Fremont St & Charleston Blvd, Las Vegas, NV **89104**, hosted drag reviews as early as 1943. Noted as Nevada's Gayest Night Club, the Kit Kat was declared out-of-bounds for eager soldiers stationed at the nearby Las Vegas Army Airfield.

Heart Attack Grill (450 Fremont St #130, Las Vegas, NV **89101**) has been named among the Craziest restaurants in the world, 2019.

Krave Massive (450 Fremont St #370, Las Vegas, NV **89101**) has been named among the Greatest Gay Bars in the World by Out.com, 2013.

Theatre: Gay bookstore/theaters began opening in Las Vegas in the 1960s–1970s. Among the first of these was the Flick, which opened at 719 Fremont St, Las Vegas, NV **89101**, on November 8, 1969, with Andy Warhol's I, A Man. The manager was John Turnquist. The Flick advertised itself as Las Vegas' first Experimental Art Theatre. By 1977, the Flick was all gay, with such features as Wonderful World of Guys and Boys in the Round.

The Green Shack

Restaurant/Bar: *It was the community of female impersonators, like Billy Richards, who first built a bridge between the straight and queer communities. In 1938, Richards played the Fremont Tavern and the Green Shack restaurant and nightclub, where he was noted as The Entertainment Sensation of the World!*

Address: 2504 Fremont St, Las Vegas, NV 89104
National Register of Historic Places: 94000552, 1994

The Green Shack, Creative Commons Licenses, via Wikimedia Commons

The Green Shack was a restaurant located on Fremont Street. It was opened by Mattie Jones and was famous for its fried chicken. Opened in 1929 and known as the Colorado when it opened on Christmas Eve 1929, the Green Shack had previously been the Swanky Club. With the addition of an old Union Pacific Railroad barracks for expansion, it was renamed Green Shack in 1932. The green paint on the addition was the source of the new name. The Green Shack closed in May 1999 by Jim and Barbara McCormick who were the owners, and was demolished several years later. When it closed, the Green Shack was the oldest restaurant in Las Vegas.

Grand Central Parkway

Restaurant/Bar: Shake Shack, 905 S Grand Central Pkwy #1700, Las Vegas, NV **89106**

Harmon Avenue

AIDS Memorial: UNLV Rod Lee Bigelow Health Sciences, southwest corner (Las Vegas, NV **89154**), Las Vegas AIDS Memorial Garden, since 17 May 1998.

Accommodation:
The Signature at MGM Grand (145 E Harmon Ave, Las Vegas, NV **89109**), The Gay & Lesbian Chamber of Commerce of Nevada member.

Club Wyndham Grand Desert (265 E Harmon Ave, Las Vegas, NV **89169**). This all-suite hotel offers views of the Las Vegas skyline and Desert Mountains. It is a mile from both the Las Vegas Strip and McCarran International Airport. Part of World Rainbow Hotels (WRH), Lesbian and Gay Welcoming Hotels.
Alexis Park Resort Hotel (375 E Harmon Ave, Las Vegas, NV **89169**), TAG Approved LGBTQ friendly accommodation.
Vdara Hotel & Spa (2600 W Harmon Ave, Las Vegas, NV **89158**), The Gay & Lesbian Chamber of Commerce of Nevada member and TAG Approved LGBTQ friendly accommodation.

Highland Drive

Club: The Camp David bathhouse opened on January 20, 1980, at 2631 Highland Dr, Las Vegas, NV **89109**. Even though staff gave out free condoms and safe-sex literature early in the AIDS epidemic, Las Vegas authorities frequently raided and harassed the place. Camp David closed in June 1986.

Hughes Center Drive

Accommodation: Residence Inn by Marriott Las Vegas Hughes Center (370 Hughes Center Dr, Las Vegas, NV **89169**), TAG Approved LGBTQ friendly accommodation.

Restaurant/Bar: Bahama Breeze, 375 Hughes Center Dr, Las Vegas, NV **89109**

Lake Mead Boulevard

Restaurant/Bar: Levi Club Discotheque, 810 E Lake Mead Blvd, North Las Vegas, NV **89030**, included in the Damron Address Book in 1971.

Theatre: In 2000, Center Stage, Inc., Las Vegas' first queer theatre group, produced Hidden: A Gender, the city's first transgender play, which run at the West Las Vegas Library Theatre (951 W Lake Mead Blvd, Las Vegas, NV **89106**). Among those starring were former Nevada state senator Lori Brown, who wrote the legislation repealing Nevada's sodomy law in 1993, and tireless transgender advocate Jane Heenan.

Las Vegas Boulevard

Cemetery: When Nevada Supreme Court chief justice Frank McNamee (1905-1968) was beaten senseless in 1965 by Philipe Denning, a young man he picked up for sex at Lake Tahoe, the case was covered up and never went to public trial in order to prevent embarrassing the state. McNamee died without justice in 1968, and Denning was paroled four months later. McNamee is buried at Woodlawn Cemetery (1500 N Las Vegas Blvd, Las Vegas, NV **89101**).

Accommodation:
King's Rest Motel, 526 S Las Vegas Blvd, Las Vegas, NV **89101**, included in the Damron Address Book from 1974 to 1976.
Royal Motel, 615 S Las Vegas Blvd, Las Vegas, NV **89101**, included in the Damron Address Book from 1974 to 1977.

Restaurant/Bar: The Verdict's Inn, 801 S. Las Vegas Blvd, Las Vegas, NV **89101**, GLD, Gay Lesbian Directory

Theatre: In September 1972, the former Phil's Strip Theatre, located in an alley behind 1304 S Las Vegas Blvd, Las Vegas, NV **89104**, became the Gaiety Theatre and was the first such all-gay venue in town. Included in the Damron Address Book from 1974 to 1977. Kenny Kerr was the first female impersonator whose performances became a Las Vegas entertainment tradition. Kerr's Boylesque opened at the Silver Slipper Casino's Gaiety Theatre on Friday, May 13, 1977. Kerr became one of the queer community's most ardent advocates and paved the way for such later female impersonation productions as Frank Marino's An Evening at La Cage.

Stratosphere, by Elisa Rolle (own work)

Tried for You (Food): Stratosphere, 2000 Las Vegas Blvd S, Las Vegas, NV 89104

Theatre: Transgender entertainer Christine Jorgensen first performed at the Sahara Hotel and Casino (2535 S Las Vegas Blvd, Las Vegas, NV **89109**) in 1953 and again in November 1955 at the Silver Slipper Casino (3120 S Las Vegas Blvd, Las Vegas, NV **89109**). The Silver Slipper operated from September 1950 to November 29, 1988. The building was designed by architect Martin Stern, Jr. The casino was known for its rotating slipper that sat atop the casino. The casino was purchased for $70 million on June 23, 1988 by Margaret Elardi, who by this time owned the Frontier next door. It was demolished several months later and turned into a parking lot for the Frontier until its closing and demolition in 2007. In 2009, the Silver Slipper sign was restored and is now part of a display of vintage signs in the median along Las Vegas Boulevard North.

Tried for You (Sleep): Circus Circus Hotel & Resort, 2880 S Las Vegas Blvd, Las Vegas, NV 89109

Accommodation: Circus Circus Hotel & Resort (2880 S Las Vegas Blvd, Las Vegas, NV **89109**), The Gay & Lesbian Chamber of Commerce of Nevada member. Transgender entertainer Jennifer Fox played the Gay 90s nightclub in North Las Vegas in 1970 and, in 1972, starred in producer Ann Corio's famous Best of Burlesque at Circus Circus Hotel and Casino, which ran for 22 weeks.

Theatre: On September 18, 1985, An Evening at La Cage opened at the Riviera Hotel (2901 S Las Vegas Blvd, Las Vegas, NV **89109**). Frank Marino became principal in the show shortly after it opened and, like Kenny Kerr before him, became one of the Las Vegas queer community's greatest boosters. Riviera (colloquially, the Riv) operated from April 1955 to May 2015. It was last owned by the Las Vegas Convention and Visitors Authority, which decided to demolish it to make way for the Las Vegas Global Business District.

Wynn, 3131 S Las Vegas Blvd, Las Vegas, NV 89109, by Elisa Rolle (own work)

Accommodation: Wynn Las Vegas (3131 S Las Vegas Blvd, Las Vegas, NV **89109**), TAG Approved LGBTQ friendly accommodation.

Wynn, by Elisa Rolle (own work)

Wynn, by Elisa Rolle (own work)

Accommodation: Howard Robard Hughes (1905-1976) lived at the Desert Inn (3145 Las Vegas Blvd S, Las Vegas, NV **89109**), from 1966 to 1970.

Restaurant/Bar:
Throughout the 1940s, female impersonators performed in small clubs along the Las Vegas Strip and the Boulder Highway. Famed impersonator Lucian appeared at El Rancho Rio nightspot (3183 Las Vegas Blvd S, Las Vegas, NV **89109**) in 1949.
The Capital Grille, 3200 S Las Vegas Blvd, Las Vegas, NV **89109**
Maggiano's Little Italy, 3200 S Las Vegas Blvd, Las Vegas, NV **89109**

Treasure Island (3300 S Las Vegas Blvd, Las Vegas, NV **89109**), .

The Venetian, 3355 S Las Vegas Blvd, Las Vegas, NV 89109, by Elisa Rolle (own work)

The Venetian, 3355 S Las Vegas Blvd, Las Vegas, NV **89109**

The Venetian, by Elisa Rolle (own work)

The Venetian, by Elisa Rolle (own work)

The Mirage, 3400 S Las Vegas Blvd, Las Vegas, NV 89109, by Elisa Rolle (own work)

Accommodation: The Mirage (3400 S Las Vegas Blvd, Las Vegas, NV **89109**), The Gay & Lesbian Chamber of Commerce of Nevada member.

Restaurant/Bar:
Ben & Jerry's, 3411 S Las Vegas Blvd, Las Vegas, NV **89109**
Ben & Jerry's, 3475 S Las Vegas Blvd, Las Vegas, NV **89109**

Accommodation: Gay-friendly Harrah's Las Vegas (3475 S Las Vegas Blvd, Las Vegas, NV **89109**) is located centrally on the world famous Las Vegas Strip offering upscale amenities and good times. Bright lights and entertainment await. Part of World Rainbow Hotels (WRH), Lesbian and Gay Welcoming Hotels.

Restaurant/Bar: Sushi Roku (3500 S Las Vegas Blvd, Ste T-18, Las Vegas, NV **89109**), Los Angeles Gay & Lesbian Chamber of Commerce member.

Queer Architects: The Linq, 3545 S Las Vegas Blvd, Las Vegas, NV **89109**, Designed by David M. Schwarz (2013). The Linq Hotel and Casino is located in the centre of the Las Vegas Strip. The Colosseum Shops at Caesars Palace is 200 yards away and Bellagio Foundations are only 650 yards. Part of World Rainbow Hotels (WRH), Lesbian and Gay Welcoming Hotels.

Restaurant/Bar: Yard House, 3545 S Las Vegas Blvd, Las Vegas, NV **89109**

Flamingo Las Vegas Hotel & Casino, 3555 S Las Vegas Blvd, Las Vegas, NV 89109, by Elisa Rolle (own work)

Accommodation: Flamingo Hotel & Casino (3555 S Las Vegas Blvd, Las Vegas, NV **89109**). Howard Robard Hughes (1905-1976) lived here from 1965 to 1966. A full-service spa, outdoor Caribbean-style pool with waterfalls, a state-of-the-art gym and a casino combine to make up the amenities in this stylish fully-equipped hotel located on The Strip. Part of World Rainbow Hotels (WRH), Lesbian and Gay Welcoming Hotels.

Caesars Palace, by Elisa Rolle (own work)

Payard Patisserie & Bistro, 3570 S Las Vegas Blvd, Las Vegas, NV **89109**

Taking its cue from the opulence of Rome, Caesars Palace (3570 S Las Vegas Blvd, Las Vegas, NV **89109**) is an all-in-one hotel featuring everything you could possibly imagine from a fully-equipped spa to a 4000-seater theatre. Part of World Rainbow Hotels (WRH), Lesbian and Gay Welcoming Hotels. Other non-queer residents: Joe Louis (1914-1981), in the 1970s.
The world's first ever Nobu Hotel at Caesars Palace (3570 Las Vegas Blvd S, Las Vegas, NV **89109**) is a luxury infused, celebrity-driven exhibition. Immerse yourself in luxury that emerges at every turn, every texture, and every amenity. Part of World Rainbow Hotels (WRH), Lesbian and Gay Welcoming Hotels.
The Cromwell Las Vegas Hotel & Casino (3595 S Las Vegas Blvd, Las Vegas, NV **89109**) is one of the only upscale, intimate hotels in Las Vegas. Chic suites and sophisticated rooms feature a contemporary design aesthetic and deluxe amenities. Part of World Rainbow Hotels (WRH), Lesbian and Gay Welcoming Hotels.

Caesars Palace, by Elisa Rolle (own work)

Bellagio Hotel and Casino, by Elisa Rolle (own work)

Tried for You (Food): The Buffet at Bellagio, 3600 S Las Vegas Blvd, Las Vegas, NV 89109

Tried for You (Sleep): Bellagio Hotel and Casino, 3600 S Las Vegas Blvd, Las Vegas, NV 89109

Accommodation: Bellagio Hotel and Casino (3600 S Las Vegas Blvd, Las Vegas, NV **89109**), The Gay & Lesbian Chamber of Commerce of Nevada member.

Bellagio Hotel and Casino, by Elisa Rolle (own work)

Bellagio Hotel and Casino, by Elisa Rolle (own work)

Bellagio Hotel and Casino, by Elisa Rolle (own work)

Bellagio Hotel and Casino, by Elisa Rolle (own work)

Bellagio Hotel and Casino, by Elisa Rolle (own work)

Bellagio Hotel and Casino, by Elisa Rolle (own work)

Ben & Jerry's, 3627 S Las Vegas Blvd Suite 900, Las Vegas, NV **89109**
BLT Steak, Bally's Hotel & Casino, 3645 S Las Vegas Blvd, Las Vegas, NV **89109**

Bally's Las Vegas Hotel & Casino (3645 S Las Vegas Blvd, Las Vegas, NV **89109**). While it captures the feel of Old Vegas, these rooms have upgraded room amenities like flat-screen TVs, docking stations and pillow-top beds. Stay in the stylish Jubilee rooms. Part of World Rainbow Hotels (WRH), Lesbian and Gay Welcoming Hotels.

Paris Las Vegas, by Elisa Rolle (own work)

Accommodation: Paris Las Vegas (3655 S Las Vegas Blvd, Las Vegas, NV **89109**). Experience all the passion and romance of Paris in Las Vegas. The luxurious Paris Las Vegas transports the ultimate in European sophistication to the entertainment capital of the world. Part of World Rainbow Hotels (WRH), Lesbian and Gay Welcoming Hotels.

Paris Las Vegas, by Elisa Rolle (own work)

Ben & Jerry's, 3663 S Las Vegas Blvd Suite #520, Las Vegas, NV **89109**
KittyBar Lesbian Nightclub, 3663 Las Vegas Blvd S, Las Vegas, NV **89109**, GLD, Gay Lesbian Directory

Planet Hollywood Resort & Casino, by Elisa Rolle (own work)

Accommodation: Planet Hollywood Resort & Casino (3667 S Las Vegas Blvd, Las Vegas, NV **89109**) is located on the Las Vegas Strip, the Las Vegas Convention Centre is 8 minutes' drive away. Part of World Rainbow Hotels (WRH), Lesbian and Gay Welcoming Hotels.

Restaurant/Bar: The Chandelier (Levels 1, 1.5 and 2, The Boulevard Tower, 3708 S Las Vegas Blvd, Las Vegas, NV **89109**) has been named among the Most beautiful and special bars in the world, 2019.

Accommodation:
The Cosmopolitan of Las Vegas (3708 S Las Vegas Blvd, Las Vegas, NV **89109**), LGBTQ friendly.
ARIA Resort & Casino (3730 S Las Vegas Blvd, Las Vegas, NV **89158**), The Gay & Lesbian Chamber of Commerce of Nevada member.

Restaurant/Bar: Alibi Room, 3733 S Las Vegas Blvd, Las Vegas, NV **89109**, included in the Damron Address Book from 1978 to 1979.

Accommodation:
Polo Towers (3745 S Las Vegas Blvd, Las Vegas, NV **89109**), LGBTQ friendly.
Mandarin Oriental (3752 S Las Vegas Blvd, Las Vegas, NV **89158**), LGBTQ friendly. Named among the Most beautiful spas in the world, 2019.
Park MGM (3770 S Las Vegas Blvd, Las Vegas, NV **89109**), The Gay & Lesbian Chamber of Commerce of Nevada member.

Monte Carlo, 3772 S Las Vegas Blvd, Las Vegas, NV 89109, by Elisa Rolle (own work)

NoMad (3772 S Las Vegas Blvd, Las Vegas, NV **89109**), The Gay & Lesbian Chamber of Commerce of Nevada member.

Monte Carlo, by Elisa Rolle (own work)

Shake Shack, 3780 S Las Vegas Blvd, Las Vegas, NV **89109**

New York-New York Hotel & Casino, 3790 S Las Vegas Blvd, Las Vegas, NV 89109, by Elisa Rolle (own work)

Accommodation: New York-New York Hotel & Casino (3790 S Las Vegas Blvd, Las Vegas, NV **89109**), The Gay & Lesbian Chamber of Commerce of Nevada member.

New York-New York Hotel & Casino, by Elisa Rolle (own work)

New York-New York Hotel & Casino, by Elisa Rolle (own work)

Shake Shack, 3790 S Las Vegas Blvd, Las Vegas, NV **89109**
Hakkasan Las Vegas Nightclub (3799 S Las Vegas Blvd, Las Vegas, NV **89109**) has been named among the Most beautiful discos in the world, 2019.
Joel Robuchon at MGM Grand, 3799 S Las Vegas Blvd, Las Vegas, NV **89109**

MGM Grand (3799 S Las Vegas Blvd, Las Vegas, NV **89109**), LGBTQ friendly and The Gay & Lesbian Chamber of Commerce of Nevada member.
The Tropicana, 3801 S Las Vegas Blvd, Las Vegas, NV **89109**, LGBTQ friendly, was decorated in 1970 by Tom Douglas. Tom Douglas (1896-1978) was a dark-haired silent screen actor, at Fox in the 1920's. He was an actor, known for Guilty or Not Guilty (1932), Broken Lullaby (1932) and Blinkeyes (1926). Tom Douglas was born in Louisville, KY. In the hearts of many, Tom Douglas would hold a special place. George Cukor would remember La Belle Epoque as much for Tom Douglas' ethereal beauty as Edmund Goulding's rowdy revelries. Douglas had actually made his first film in 1922, playing with Dorothy Gish in The Country Flapper for D.W. Griffith. But the Kentucky-born teenager found his niche on the London stage, wowing British audiences as the American boy in Merton of the Movies. He followed that success with a string of hits in England, among them Fata Morgana and Young Woodley, written expressly for him by the gay playwright John Van Druten, who fell hard for the pretty young actor. In his memoir, Emlyn Williams, too, would admit to being smitten with Douglas: With his short nose and wide soft mouth that seemed not to know its potency, he cast a spell over his own sex, as often as not in unexpected quarters. In 1926 Cecil Beaton was invited to a party at British Vogue editors Madge Garland and Dorothy Todd's homse where he met socialites like actor Tom Douglas, Elizabeth Ponsonby and Cynthia Noble (Lady Gladwyn). At the party Freddie Ashton performed campy, shy-making imitations of various ballet dancers and Queen Alexandra, the sort of thing one is ashamed of and only does in one's bedroom in front of large mirrors when one is rather excited and worked up. By the time Douglas returned to Hollywood, playing The Boy in the mystery The Phantom of Crestwood in 1932, his fabled beauty had started to fade, partly due to his fast-and-furious high living among the Cukor-Haines-Goulding circle. Stardom demanded not just ambition and talent but eternal youth: Douglas would wisely opt for interior decoration after a Monogram quickie, West of Singapore, in 1933. He'd remain a popular star in the gay subculture, however, frequently popping up in the letters and stories of many. Douglas died in 1978 in Cuernavaca, Mexico.

Excalibur Hotel & Casino, 3850 S Las Vegas Blvd, Las Vegas, NV 89109, by Elisa Rolle (own work)

Accommodation: Excalibur Hotel & Casino (3850 S Las Vegas Blvd, Las Vegas, NV **89109**), The Gay & Lesbian Chamber of Commerce of Nevada member.

Luxor Hotel & Casino, 3900 S Las Vegas Blvd, Las Vegas, NV 89119, by Elisa Rolle (own work)

Accommodation:
Luxor Hotel & Casino (3900 S Las Vegas Blvd, Las Vegas, NV **89119**), **LGBTQ friendly** and The Gay & Lesbian Chamber of Commerce of Nevada member. Named among the Largest pyramids in the world.
Delano (3940 S Las Vegas Blvd, Las Vegas, NV **89119**), The Gay & Lesbian Chamber of Commerce of Nevada member.

Mandalay Bay, 3950 S Las Vegas Blvd, Las Vegas, NV 89119, by Elisa Rolle (own work)

Restaurant/Bar: Border Grill Mandalay Bay (3950 S Las Vegas Blvd, Las Vegas, NV **89119**), lesbian owned by Susan Feniger. Named among the Top 10 Lesbian-Owned Companies by Curve Magazine, 2010. Top LGBTQIA+ Owned and Operated Restaurants in America, OpenTable 2021

Accommodation:
Mandalay Bay (3950 S Las Vegas Blvd, Las Vegas, NV **89119**), The Gay & Lesbian Chamber of Commerce of Nevada member.
Casa Malaga Motel, 4615 S Las Vegas Blvd, Las Vegas, NV **89119**, included in the Damron Address Book in 1980.

Restaurant/Bar: Yard House, 6593 S Las Vegas Blvd B-161, Las Vegas, NV **89119**

Accommodation: WorldMark Las Vegas – Boulevard (8601 S Las Vegas Blvd, Las Vegas, NV **89123**) is 4.9 miles from McCarran International Airport and 6.1 miles from the Las Vegas Strip. Part of World Rainbow Hotels (WRH), Lesbian and Gay Welcoming Hotels.

Main Street

Club: Las Vegas bathhouses were places where gay men could make anonymous sexual connections. Vegas Club Baths, opened in May 1971 as the Sir Gay Men's Spa at 1413 S Main St, Las Vegas, NV **89104**, advertised private rooms, steam rooms, a movie room, and offered a 2 people for the price of 1 deal on Mondays. Included in the Damron Address Book from 1973 to 1976.

Restaurant/Bar:
Confederacy, 1511 S Main St, Las Vegas, NV **89104**, included in the Damron Address Book in 1977.
Driftwood Lounge, 4231 S Main St, Las Vegas, NV **89104**, included in the 1975 All Lavender International Gay Guide.

Maryland Parkway

Restaurant/Bar: Paymon's Mediterranean Cafe Maryland Pkwy, 4147 S. Maryland Pkwy, Las Vegas, V

89119, GLD, Gay Lesbian Directory

Queer Architects: Greenspun Hall, Greenspun College of Urban Affairs, University of Nevada, Las Vegas, 4609-4725 S Maryland Pkwy, Las Vegas, NV **89119**, Designed by Robert A.M. Stern with Graham S. Wyatt (2008)

Club: Those who used to frequent the old Camelot Health Spa (5090 Maryland Pkwy, Las Vegas, NV **89119**) would recall the old attendant who kept the pool, spa and sauna areas really clean. The white mustachioed man would get down on his knees and scrub the drains while towel-clad patrons walked about the clothing-optional pool areas. Few of them even knew his name. Claude Howard (1905-1998) was the spa's owner and a multimillionaire philanthropist who during his lifetime gave away as much as $20 million to local institutions including colleges, hospitals, police departments and area charities. Claude I. Howard grew up in an orphanage and made his fortune by building more than 4,000 apartments in Southern Nevada. Camelot Health Spas had several Las Vegas locations in the 1970s and '80s. Howard's many contributions to the community include: countless gifts to UNLV, which named its public safety building after him; $6 million to the University of Nevada Medical School, including $1 million for construction of the school's family medical center in Reno; a building worth $2 million to the Community College of Southern Nevada's Charleston Boulevard Campus; a building to the city of North Las Vegas that became its justice court; $300,000 for the Metropolitan Police Department to buy a helicopter and tens of thousands of dollars more for computer equipment for Metro's records bureau; $300,000 to renovate the pediatrics wing at the University Medical Center, then Southern Nevada Memorial Hospital; a cash gift that enabled Child Haven to expand its campus for abused and neglected children; cash to purchase the North Las Vegas Police Department's radio system and renovate its jail; cash to build a jail and police substation in Laughlin. As long as I make money, I'll give it away, Howard said in a brief public statement in 1986. Publicity shy, he rarely gave interviews. Also, because many of Howard's gifts were given anonymously, the full scope of his generosity to the Las Vegas community may never be learned.

Naples Drive

Restaurant/Bar: FreeZone (610 E Naples Dr, Las Vegas, NV **89119**), LGBTQ friendly.

Nellis Boulevard

Restaurant/Bar:
Dylan's Sports Pub, 40 N Nellis Blvd, Las Vegas, NV **89110**, corner of Charleston, was for three decades Max and Marie's, then Maxine's then Maxie's, run by a Maxine Perron (1923-2018), who was a pioneer in the local gay and lesbian community. Included in the Damron Address Book from 1965 to 1980. Included in the 1975 All Lavender International Gay Guide. Maxine ran a bar for what they termed queers, said Mrs. Morgan, interviewed by Nevada State Museum Director Dennis McBride, the author of Out of the Neon Closet. And they all stated that she was reputed to be a lesbian. She was willing in later years to take all the accolades that the gay community was willing to give her, says McBride. But do not out her, even though the idea of Maxine being closeted is ridiculous, and it always was ridiculous. Maxine's opened about 1950 on the eastern outskirts of Las Vegas. A raucous bar with donkey baseball games staged in the surrounding desert, it was often isolated by flash floods during monsoon season. Maxine's closed in January 1989.
Olive Garden Italian, 80 N Nellis Blvd, Las Vegas, NV **89110**

Oval Park Drive

Restaurant/Bar: Shake Shack, 10975 Oval Park Dr, Las Vegas, NV **89135**

Paradise Road

Gay Village

Paradise, NV **89119** is ranked 25 out of 25 among US Mid-size cities (Population between 100.000 and 250.000) for % of same sex couples (0,952%), and is ranked 10 for # of same sex couples, 857. (US Census 2010)

Accommodation:
SpringHill Suites by Marriott Las Vegas Convention Center (2989 Paradise Rd, Las Vegas, NV **89109**), TAG Approved LGBTQ friendly accommodation.
Residence Inn by Marriott Las Vegas Convention Center (3225 Paradise Rd, Las Vegas, NV **89109**), TAG Approved LGBTQ friendly accommodation.
Courtyard by Marriott Las Vegas Convention Center (3275 Paradise Rd, Las Vegas, NV **89109**), TAG Approved LGBTQ friendly accommodation.
Renaissance Las Vegas Hotel (3400 Paradise Rd, Las Vegas, NV **89169**), TAG Approved LGBTQ friendly accommodation.
Embassy Suites Convention Center Las Vegas (3600 Paradise Rd, Las Vegas, NV **89169**), LGBTQ friendly.
Candlewood Suites (4034 Paradise Rd, Las Vegas, NV **89169**), LGBTQ friendly.

Restaurant/Bar: Prelude, 4310 Paradise Rd, Las Vegas, NV **89109**, included in the Damron Address Book in 1980.

Accommodation:
Hard Rock Hotel, 4455 Paradise Rd, Las Vegas, NV **89169**, Designed by Franklin D. Israel (1987).
Hyatt Place Las Vegas (4520 Paradise Rd, Las Vegas, NV **89169**), TAG Approved LGBTQ friendly accommodation.

Restaurant/Bar: Studio 4, 4605 Paradise Rd, Las Vegas, NV **89169**, included in the Damron Address Book in 1980. Later the Village Station. Las Vegas queer bars were often raided and harassed by local authorities. The Village Station was closed in November 1980 after a sting operation conducted by the Las Vegas Metropolitan Police Department found men hugging and kissing in blatant physical contact. The bar reopened on April 1, 1981, as Gipsy.

LGBTQ friendly bookstore:

In 1987 Rob Schlegel, publisher of the Bohemian Bugle and one of the community's greatest activists, opened Bright Pink Literature, the city's first specifically commercial LGBT bookstore. On December 11, 1987 Schlegel opened Bright Pink in a small office space connected to the Body Shop bar at 4610 Paradise Rd, Suite 202-A, Las Vegas, NV **89169**. Schlegel came up with the name Bright Pink Literature and its pink triangle logo as an homage to the book, The Men With the Pink Triangle, about Nazi persecution of gay men. Bright Pink's location next to the Body Shop, however, was problematic: patrons wandering in from the bar spilled their drinks on the merchandise, and cigarette smoke turned the books and t-shirts yellow. Schlegel moved Bright Pink in July 1988 to Paradise Plaza at 4640 Paradise Rd, Las Vegas, NV **89169**, next to the Buffalo bar. Schlegel had been there only a month when the Gipsy nightclub across the street burned down, which robbed the Bohemian Bugle of its biggest advertiser. It was saved by real estate investor Ed Uehling, who gave Schlegel $5,000 to keep the bookstore - and the renamed Las Vegas Bugle -- going. When Uehling and his lover, Marlon Tinana, bought the Gelo's nightclub shopping center across the street from Paradise Plaza, Schlegel moved Bright Pink into the storefront where R&R Assordid Sundries had been. In 1990, Schlegel moved the bookstore into more spacious quarters in a renovated cinderblock duplex behind the Gelo's shopping center. In association with Bright Pink Literature, Schlegel established a gay and lesbian film festival he named Bright Pink Cinema, which debuted on April 20, 1991 and ran for six weeks at the Metropolitan Community Church. Among the films Schlegel presented were many which have become classics of LGBT cinema: Before Stonewall; Billy Turner's Secret; Fun Down There; and the gay African-American documentaryTongues Untied. After Bright Pink Cinema, Las Vegas would not have another LGBT film festival until the annual Neonfest, first presented in 2004. The more successful Bright Pink Literature grew, however, the more of a target it became for the straight community. When Schlegel agreed to sell the book Las Vegas Post Mortem--a sensational exposé about the Las Vegas Metropolitan Police Department -- Metro cops began harassing Bright Pink's patrons and threatened Schlegel. In August 1991 Bright Pink moved out of its spacious duplex and into a much smaller storefront around the corner at 4640 Paradise Rd #15, Las Vegas, NV **89169**. Schlegel decided to sell it to Marlon Tinana and Wes Miller, who had moved to Las Vegas from Ohio in 1990. Tinana and Miller expanded the shop, added gifts and videos, and enhanced the book and magazine inventory with the help of Raul Mangubat, whom the two met at the March on Washington in April 1993 and who moved to Las Vegas from New York to run the bookstore. By 1995, Miller had become sole owner. When Wes Miller and Marlon Tinana took over Bright Pink Literature, they changed the name to Get Booked in honor of Wes Miller's 1992 arrest in a Las Vegas Metropolitan Police sting operation that targeted gay men along Paradise Road.

In the years before Stonewall, gay literature was unavailable in Nevada outside porn shops, and there were few commercial bookstores willing to stock such material. The first establishment in Las Vegas to offer LGBT merchandise and to advertise openly as a gay shop, was R&R Assordid Sundries. R&R opened February 14, 1984 at 4637 Paradise Rd, Las Vegas, NV **89119**, next door to Gelo's nightclub, then closed in November 1985. R&R was ahead of its time, was more gift shop than book store, and was not much patronized by the Las Vegas gay community. Opening at the outset of the AIDS epidemic in Nevada didn't help. It would be several years before the chain bookstores in town such as B. Dalton, Waldenbooks, and, later, Barnes & Noble and Borders, began stocking gay sections.

Bright Pink Literature, 4640 Paradise Rd, #10, Las Vegas, NV **89109**, active in 1990.

The longest-lived LGBT bookstore in Nevada is Get Booked, located in the Paradise Plaza shopping center (4640 Paradise Rd #15, Las Vegas, NV **89169**) on the corner of Paradise Road and East Naples Drive, an area known as the Fruit Loop for its cluster of gay businesses. Get Booked has survived for more than 20 years. Part of that reason is that, as gay author Michael Thomas Ford has pointed out, There's more to be found in a gay bookstore than just something nice to read. Just walking into a gay bookstore can be an act of liberation, and such shops often serve as welcoming space for the queer community in otherwise hostile environments.

Restaurant/Bars

Le Café opened originally as the Club Black Magic on August 18, 1954 at 4817 or 4917 Paradise Rd, Las Vegas, NV **89169**, on the southwest corner of Tropicana Avenue, then known as Bond Road. Included in the Damron Address Book from 1971 to 1980. The Black Magic was the most popular jazz club in Las Vegas throughout the 1950s and '60s. In November 1968 Camille Castro, a stylish and flamboyant European lesbian, opened Le Bistro French restaurant in the Black Magic, known by then as the Club de

Paris. Camille had owned La Manche a Gigot restaurant on the Isle St. Louis in Paris among whose famous clientele were two well-known Las Vegans: Dunes Hotel owner Major Riddle and Line Renaud, star of the Dunes' Casino de Paris production. Camille was also associated with a celebrated Parisian lesbian bar called the Crazy Horse and she came to Las Vegas from Paris as the lighting engineer when Caesars Palace imported a show called the Crazy Horse Revue. When the revue went down, Camille, bankrolled by Riddle, stayed on to open her restaurant. Club de Paris and Le Bistro held their grand opening on January 10, 1969 and quickly became a favorite hangout for Las Vegas' gay community, particularly the show crowd from the Strip. Betty Grable, a Las Vegas resident at the time, often hosted parties at Le Bistro, and the cast of Boys in the Band, performing at Caesars Palace during the summer of 1969, gathered at Le Bistro. Las Vegas food critic Fedora Bontempi frequently reviewed Le Bistro in her column in Panoramamagazine noting that it was the first and the only authentic French restaurant in Las Vegas. By late 1969 both Le Bistro and the Club de Paris were failing when Marge Jacques became interested in running the bar. Marge had worked as a cocktail waitress at the Sands Hotel and was at the Golden Nugget during the late 1960s when Las Vegas was forced to integrate the casino industry first by hiring black dealers, then by hiring women dealers and she had been in the forefront of both fights. Marge obtained a liquor license, bought the Club de Paris, changed the name to Le Café, and held a grand opening on January 16, 1970. Marge's club was unique because she opened it publicly as a gay bar, which had never been done in Las Vegas before. Both Maxine's and the Red Barn, two other gay bars operating at the time, were low-key and closeted—but Le Café was gay out loud. The club's motto, printed on matchbooks and t-shirts, was Glitter and Be Gay at Le Café! a motto which perfectly reflected 1970s gay disco glamour. The club's reputation spread around the world and throughout the 1970s Le Café was frequented by such entertainers as Liberace, Joan Rivers, Shirley Maclaine, Rip Taylor and Paul Lynde, Bobbie Gentry, Debbie Reynolds, Sammy Davis, Jr.—even Milton Berle. It was through Marge Jacques and Le Café that the Las Vegas gay community first found its voice. Gay Notes from Le Caféwas the first gay publication in Las Vegas. Openly gay herself, Marge appeared on a local NBC television news show in 1976, taped in the living room of her own house, and she was the contact for a two-part Las Vegas Review-Journal series on gay people in Las Vegas in 1977. It was Marge and friends and employees from Le Café who founded the first Las Vegas chapter of the National Organization for Women in 1971 and who wrested control of the Clark County Democratic Party from the Mormon Church in the mid-1970s. Marge was in demand as a lecturer on gay people and gay life and addressed groups at the University of Nevada, Las Vegas and Nellis Air Force Base. But the good times ended on August 24, 1978 when Le Café was torched. It was never determined beyond doubt who burned Marge's club, although rumor in the gay community had it that she was burned out by the owner of a bar down the street at 4310 Paradise Road called Prelude. That owner was Camille Castro, who had sold Le Bistro to Marge, left the country, then returned in 1975 to open a new bar and disco in direct competition with Le Café. There were rumors, too, that Marge had burned her own club, although at the time of the fire she had failed to update her insurance and lost everything. A second fire on May 5, 1979 completely gutted the empty building. For the next five years Marge operated a number of other gay bars in Las Vegas including the Other Place at 5410 Paradise Road and the Village Station, which became the Gipsy in 1981.

Other Place, 5410 Paradise Rd, Las Vegas, NV **89119**, included in the from 1979 to 1980.

Promenade Place

Queer Architects: Donald W. Reynold's Discovery Children's Museum, 360 Promenade Place, Las Vegas, NV **89106**, Designed by David M. Schwarz (2013).

Rainbow Boulevard

Gay Village

Enterprise, NV **89139** is ranked 22 out of 25 among US Mid-size cities (Population between 100.000 and 250.000) for % of same sex couples (0,972%), and is ranked 22 for # of same sex couples, 387. (US Census 2010)

Restaurant/Bar: All Natural Emporium, 1725 S. Rainbow #16-127, Las Vegas, NV **89146**, GLD, Gay Lesbian Directory

Accommodation: Courtyard Las Vegas Summerlin (1901 N Rainbow Blvd, Las Vegas, NV **89108**), LGBTQ friendly.

Rampart Boulevard

Accommodation: JW Marriott Las Vegas Resort & Spa (221 N Rampart Blvd, Las Vegas, NV **89145**), TAG Approved LGBTQ friendly accommodation.

Sahara Avenue

LGBTQ Center: The Gay and Lesbian Community Center of Southern Nevada opened at 912 E Sahara Ave, Las Vegas, NV **89104**, on September 7, 1993. Within a few months, the center was providing meeting space for community groups, HIV testing, and public programs. The Gay and Lesbian Community Center of Southern Nevada's years were difficult, and it nearly shut down several times. In 1996, community advocate Dan Hinkley and others who wanted to save the center formed a group called Looking Forward to run board candidates who would professionalize the center. Looking Forward was successful in rescuing the community center and Hinkley became executive director. The center outgrew its first small building and, in 2002, moved into new digs in the Commercial Center at 953 E Sahara Ave, Las Vegas, NV **89104**. As the Las Vegas gay community found its political voice, the center became more important. Center executive director Candice Nichols and her board established a successful capital campaign called Opening New Doors to raise funds for a new building. On April 6, 2013, the center dedicated its new home at 401 S Maryland Pkwy, Las Vegas, NV **89101**, named for the late Robert Rob Forbuss, community activist and philanthropist.

Club: On September 9, 1996, the Apollo Spa and Health Club was opened in The Historic Commercial Center District (953 E Sahara Avenue e11a, Las Vegas, NV **89104**) by German expatriate Torsten Reineck. When Andrew Cunanan shot Gianni Versace to death in Miami on July 15, 1997, authorities in Las Vegas connected Reineck to the crime.

Restaurant/Bar: Badlands Saloon, 953 E Sahara Ave #22B, Las Vegas, NV **89104**.

Accommodation: Artisan Hotel Boutique (1501 W Sahara Ave, Las Vegas, NV **89102**), LGBTQ friendly.

Restaurant/Bar:
The Phoenix Bar & Lounge, 4213 W Sahara Ave, Las Vegas, NV **89102**. It has been named among The 25 Best LGBTQ Bars and Nightclubs in the US, 2019, Matador Network. With a giant phoenix painted over its doors, The Phoenix in Las Vegas, Nevada, immediately creates a unique ambiance for its patrons. Once inside, guests are greeted with a spacious bar — complete with a lounge area that doubles as a dance floor, pool tables, and an outdoor patio that's inviting and secluded enough for conversation over cocktails. In addition to sipping mixed drinks on the dance floor, guests can play Super Smash Bros. and Mario Kart on the massive projected screen located centrally in the bar. At the end of the day, The Phoenix appeals to older audiences in search of a true LGBTQ dive bar — and the younger Grindr generation who would rather dance and play video games all night long.
Paymon's Mediterranean Cafe – Sahara, 8380 W. Sahara Ave, Las Vegas, NV **89117**, GLD, Gay Lesbian Directory

Sphere, by Elisa Rolle (own work)

Theatre: Sphere, 255 Sands Ave, Las Vegas, NV 89169, is a music and entertainment arena in Paradise, NV, east of the Las Vegas Strip. Designed by Populous, the spherical project was announced by the Madison Square Garden Company in 2018, known then as the MSG Sphere. The 18,600-seat auditorium is being marketed for its immersive video and audio capabilities, which include a 16K resolution wraparound interior LED screen, speakers with beamforming and wave field synthesis technologies, and 4D physical effects. The venue's exterior also features 580,000 sq ft (54,000 m2) of LED displays. The Sphere measures 366 feet (112 m) high and 516 feet (157 m) wide in diameter. Construction was underway in 2019, with the opening initially scheduled for 2021. Construction was suspended for several months in 2020, due to supply disruptions caused by the COVID-19 pandemic. The Sphere opened on September 29, 2023, with Irish rock band U2 beginning a 36-show residency called U2:UV Achtung Baby Live at Sphere. Director Darren Aronofsky's docu-film Postcard from Earth opened on October 6, 2023.

Sphere, by Elisa Rolle (own work)

Sphere, by Elisa Rolle (own work)

Seminole Circle

Other non-queer residents: Joe Louis (1914-1981), 3333 Seminole Cir, Las Vegas, NV **89169**, from 1970 to 1981.

Shadow Lane

Hospital: Dr. Lisa Bechtel was the medical director of the UMC Wellness Center (701 Shadow Ln, Las Vegas, NV **89106**). Her wife was Ann Occhi. Bechtel was one of the first physicians in Las Vegas to treat AIDS patients. She was honored by the ACLU as Humanitarian of the Year and by the Gay and Lesbian Community Center at its first Honorarium in 1994. Bechtel died on May 10, 1994 of AIDS contracted from an accidental needle prick.

Stewart Avenue

Attractions: The Mob Museum (300 Stewart Ave, Las Vegas, NV **89101**) has been named among the Strangest museums in the world, 2019.

Symphony Park Avenue

Queer Architects: Reynolds Hall (2012) and Boman Pavilion (2012), The Smith Center for the Performing Arts, 1409, 361 Symphony Park Avenue, Las Vegas, NV **89106**, Designed by David M. Schwarz.

Tanager Way

Accommodation: Featherdanse (6384 Tanager Way, Las Vegas, NV **89103**), LGBTQ friendly.

Tierra Hope Court

Accommodation: Jewel Manor Estate, 8816 Tierra Hope Ct, Las Vegas, NV **89143**, GLD, Gay Lesbian Directory

Tropicana Avenue

Accommodation: Hooters Casino Hotel (115 E Tropicana Ave, Las Vegas, NV **89109**), LGBTQ friendly.

Restaurant/Bar:
The Red Barn at the Tropicana Hotel, began its existence in the late 1950s as an antique store inside the Tropicana Hotel at 1317 E Tropicana Ave, Las Vegas, NV **89119**. Included in the 1971 Homosexual National Classified Directory. Included in the Damron Address Book from 1968 to 1980. Included in the 1975 All Lavender International Gay Guide. In the early 1960s, new owners converted it into a bar that became popular due to its proximity to the new university on Maryland Parkway. By the end of the decade, the bar had become a favorite entertainment spot for Las Vegas' emerging gay community. The Red Barn closed in 1988 and owner Claude Howard donated its classic cocktail glass sign to the Allied Arts Council which installed it in downtown Las Vegas, on Fremont Street, as part of a free outdoor gallery overseen by The Neon Museum. After closing permanently on March 31, 1988, the abandoned bar burned to the ground on September 11 that year.

Carluccio's Tivoli Gardens (1775 E Tropicana Ave #16, Las Vegas, NV **89119**) was an Italian restaurant in Las Vegas. The restaurant was designed by Liberace (1919-1987) who owned the restaurant as Liberace's Tivoli Gardens. It was located adjacent to the Liberace museum that he opened in 1979, just 8 years before his death due to complications related to AIDS. Until it was open, the restaurant maintained the decor designed by Liberace. The Ghost of Liberace is said to haunt the Tivoli Gardens. His image can sometimes be seen peaking into the banquet room in the back of the restaurant from outside through the windows.

Accommodation: WorldMark Tropicana (5275 W Tropicana Ave, Las Vegas, NV **89103**). Next to Charlie Frias Park in Spring Valley, this condo is 4 miles from McCarran International Airport and within 3 miles of the Las Vegas Strip. Part of World Rainbow Hotels (WRH), Lesbian and Gay Welcoming Hotels.

Twain Avenue

Accommodation: Club Wyndham Desert Blue (3200 W Twain Ave, Las Vegas, NV **89103**) is 1 mile from the Las Vegas Strip and 6 miles from McCarran International Airport. Part of World Rainbow Hotels (WRH), Lesbian and Gay Welcoming Hotels.

Washington Avenue

Oldest Building in the State and Oldest Building in America: Old Las Vegas Mormon Fort, 1855, 500 E Washington Ave, Las Vegas, NV **89101**. The oldest building in Las Vegas is not a casino of some sort. It is an 150-square-foot adobe fort constructed by Mormon colonists. The property, in downtown Las Vegas, is now surrounded by a public park.

Park: Fantasy Park, 1401 E Washington Ave, Las Vegas, NV **89101**, included in the Damron Address Book from 1976 to 1980.

Westwood Drive

Blue Moon Hotel, 2651 Westwood Drive, Las Vegas, NV **89109**, GLD, Gay Lesbian Directory

3rd-6th Street

Restaurant/Bar:
Lady Luck, 206 N 3rd St, Las Vegas, NV **89101**, included in the Damron Address Book from 1979 to 1980. Bastille on 3rd, 1402 S 3rd St, Las Vegas, NV **89104**.

Accommodation: Star Motel, 1418 S 3rd St, Las Vegas, NV **89104**, included in the Damron Address Book from 1979 to 1980.

Restaurant/Bar:
Snick's, 1402 S 4th St, Las Vegas, NV **89104**, included in the Damron Address Book from 1979 to 1980. Bronze Cafe Downtown (124 S 6th St Suite 160, Las Vegas, NV **89101**), LGBTQ owned. Supports LGBTQIA+ Community and Causes. Originally located inside The Gay & Lesbian Community Center of Southern Nevada from 2013-2017, Bronze Cafe has deep ties within the local LGBTQ scene. It's bacon sammich is named The LGBTQ and stands for lemon, greens, bacon, tomato, q-cumber.

89300

Attractions: Prometeus (Wheeler Peak, NV **89311**) has been named among the Oldest trees in the world.

Accommodation:	Silver Jack Inn & Lectrolux Café, 10 Main Street, Baker, NV **89311**, LGBTQ owned. GLD, Gay Lesbian Directory

89400

Oldest Bar in the State: Genoa Bar, 2282 Main St, Genoa, NV **89411**. Hollywood has showed its love repeatedly for this former gentleman's saloon built in 1853. The Genoa Bar is so authentic it still uses electric lamps from around 1900 and has a lone wood stove to keep warm. Since it's the only source of heat, the locals often bring in firewood when I'm getting low, the owner says.

Restaurant/Bar:	Olive Garden Italian, 1481 E Lincoln Way, Sparks, NV **89434**

Virginia City

Piper-Beeb Mansion

House: *The Piper–Beebe House is a historic Italianate house. It was an 1876 work of Virginia City builder/architect A.F. MacKay, the only one of his works in Virginia City that survives. It was built after the Great Fire of 1875 that destroyed much of the city.*

Address: 2 A St, Virginia City, NV 89440

National Register of Historic Places: 93000684, 1993

The Piper–Beebe House, Creative Commons Licenses, via Wikimedia Commons

Place

A. F. Mackay designed and built several buildings in Virginia City, but the Piper-Beebe House is the only one that remains. Built after the Great Fire of 1875, this house is representative of the elaborate homes built for mine superintendents and wealthy businessmen. The Italianate style found strong favor following the fire, as Virginia City sought to rebuild and present itself in a grand fashion. The Italianate style, exemplified by a vertical design orientation, heavy cornice brackets and elaborate turned wooden decorative treatments, was the height of fashion on the west coast during the 1870s and the Piper-Beebe house would feel quite at home on a fashionable Victorian street in San Francisco. The home was occupied by Mackay and his family until the mid-1880s. It was later owned by Edward Piper, operator of the nearby Piper's Opera House and son of its founder John Piper. After Edward Piper's death in 1907, his widow Lavinia married Dan Connors, a bare-fisted prizefighter who came to Nevada as a sportswriter in 1897 to cover the famous Fitzsimmons-Corbett fight which took place in Carson City. After his marriage to Lavinia, Connors took over the management of the opera house, and in 1911 he introduced silent films to Virginia City. In 1949, the house was purchased by Charles Clegg and Lucius Beebe, revivers of the Territorial Enterprise, the original newspaper of the Comstock. Beebe and Clegg were two of the leading figures in the artistic community that established itself in Virginia City during WWII. Together they operated the Enterprise as a weekly paper and published numerous books on the Comstock and railroad history.

Territorial Enterprise, Creative Commons Licenses, via Wikimedia Commons

Life

Who: Charles Myron Clegg Jr. (June 29, 1916 – August 25, 1979) and Lucius Morris Beebe (December 9, 1902 – February 4, 1966)

Charles Clegg was an American author, photographer, and railroad historian. Clegg is primarily remembered as the lifelong companion of famed railroad author Lucius Beebe, and was a co-author of many of Beebe's best-known books. Born into an old New England family, Clegg grew up in Rhode Island, and during his early years developed strong interests in railroads, electronics, and photography. In 1940, Clegg met Beebe while both were house guests at the Washington, D.C. home of Evalyn Walsh McLean. The two soon became inseparable, developing a personal and professional relationship that continued for the rest of Beebe's life. The pair initially lived in New York City, where Beebe was a columnist for the New York Herald Tribune and both men were prominent in café society circles. They moved in 1950 to Virginia City, NV, a tiny community that had once been a fabled mining boomtown. There, they reactivated and began publishing the Territorial Enterprise, a XIX century newspaper that had once been the employer of Mark Twain. Beebe and Clegg shared a renovated the Piper mansion, and also owned a private railroad car, redone in a Victorian Baroque style. The pair traveled extensively, and remained prominent in social circles. Clegg and Beebe sold the Territorial Enterprise in 1961, and purchased a home in suburban San Francisco. They continued the writing, photography, and travel that had marked their lives until Beebe's death from a heart attack in 1966. Beebe left the bulk of his $2 million estate to Clegg (with provision for T-Bone Towser II, their Newfoundland). Clegg committed suicide in 1979, on the day that he reached the precise age at which Beebe had died.

Accommodation: B Street House B&B (58 B St, Virginia City, NV 89440), LGBTQ friendly.

Cobb Mansion B&B (18 S. A St, Virginia City, NV 89440), LGBTQ owned. GLD, Gay Lesbian Directory

Oldest Restaurant in the State: The Martin Hotel, 1898, Basque/American, 94 W Railroad St, Winnemucca, NV 89445. What people say: The Martin serves its food family style, but in reviews on TripAdvisor, customers are divided about how well it represents the cuisine of France and Spain's Basque region. Ask about spiciness if that is a factor for you, and be prepared that everything has tons of garlic, one warns.

Restaurant/Bar: Back Door, Round Hill Mall, US-50, Zephyr Cove, NV 89448, included in the Damron Address Book from 1977 to 1980.

Pine Cone Bar at Sahara Hotel, now Hard Rock Hotel & Casino Lake Tahoe, 50 US-50, Stateline, NV 89449, included in the Damron Address Book in 1975.

Accommodation: Harrahs Lake Tahoe Resort (15 US-50, Stateline, NV 89449). A 5-minute walk from Tahoe's main ski gondola, this upscale casino hotel is also a 12-minute walk from Edgewood Tahoe Golf Course. Part of World Rainbow Hotels (WRH), Lesbian and Gay Welcoming Hotels.

Harveys Lake Tahoe (18 US-50, Stateline, NV 89449). Part of World Rainbow Hotels (WRH), Lesbian and Gay Welcoming Hotels. Horizon Casino Resort, 50 US-50, Stateline, NV 89449, LGBTQ friendly. It's now Hard Rock Hotel & Casino Lake Tahoe.

Restaurant/Bar:

Village Pub, Incline Village Shopping Center, Incline Village, NV 89451, included in the Damron Address Book in 1977.

Accommodation:

Hyatt Regency Lake Tahoe Resort (111 Country Club Dr, Incline Village, NV 89451), LGBTQ friendly.

89500

LGBTQ Archives: Baker Archives, 350 S Center St, #350, Reno, NV 89501, active in 1990.

Restaurant/Bar: Bad Dolly's (210 W Commercial Row, Reno, NV 89501) was a lesbian bar active in the 1990s. Calvi's, 73 N Sierra St, Reno, NV 89501, included in the Damron Address Book in 1977.

Jade Room, 214 W Commercial Row, Reno, NV 89501, included in the Damron Address Book from 1973 to 1978. Paul's Lounge, 132 West St, Reno, NV 89501, included in the Damron Address Book from 1977 to 1980.

Prime Rib Room, 300 N Virginia St, Reno, NV **89501**, included in the Damron Address Book in 1975.

Accommodation:
Circus Circus (500 N Sierra St, Reno, NV **89501**), LGBTQ friendly.
Courtyard by Marriott Reno (1 Ballpark Ln, Reno, NV **89501**), LGBTQ friendly.
Harrah's Hotel Casino (219 N Center St, Reno, NV **89501**) is a complete destination with everything you want for fun, with seven mouth-watering restaurants and a 60,000 sq. ft. casino. Part of World Rainbow Hotels (WRH), Lesbian and Gay Welcoming Hotels. As of 2021 it's closed.

Silver Legacy Resort Casino (407 N Virginia St, Reno, NV **89501**), LGBTQ friendly.
Sands Regency Hotel and Casino (345 N Arlington Ave, Reno, NV **89501**), LGBTQ friendly.
Whitney Peak Hotel (255 N Virginia St, Reno, NV **89501**), TAG Approved LGBTQ friendly accommodation. Part of World Rainbow Hotels (WRH), Lesbian and Gay Welcoming Hotels.

Restaurant/Bar:
Pop's Club 99, 999 or 1099 S Virginia St, Reno, NV **89502**, included in the Damron Address Book from 1973 to 1980.
Pacific Bar, 1278 S Virginia St, Reno, NV **89502**, included in the Damron Address Book from

1972 to 1973. Later Exchange, included in the Damron Address Book in 1980.
Knights of Malta, Reno, NV **89502**, included in the Damron Address Book from 1977 to 1980.
Olive Garden Italian, 4900 S Virginia St, Reno, NV **89502**

Accommodation:
Peppermill Reno (2707 S Virginia St, Reno, NV **89502**), TAG Approved LGBTQ friendly accommodation.

Reno Tahoe, 4001 S. Virginia St, Reno, NV **89502**, GLD, Gay Lesbian Directory

Club: The Club Baths, 1030 W 2nd St, Reno, NV **89503**, at Keystone Ave, included in the 1965 Guild Guide. Included in the Damron Address Book from 1965 to 1980. Included in the 1975 All Lavender International Gay Guide.

Restaurant/Bar:
Beto's Taqueria, 575 W 5th St, Reno, NV **89503**

Park: Idlewild Park, 2055 Idlewild Dr, Reno, NV **89509**, included in the Damron Address Book from 1978 to 1980.

LGBTQ friendly bookstore: Virginia St. Adult Book Store, 961 S Virginia St, Reno, NV **89509**, included in the Damron Address Book in 1980.

Restaurant/Bar:
Red Lobster, 5015 Kietzke Ln, Reno, NV **89511**
Jim's Reno Bar, 424 E 4th St, Reno, NV **89512**, included in the Damron Address Book from 1965 to 1973. Included in the 1975 All Lavender International Gay Guide.
Midway Bar, 722 E 4th St, Reno, NV **89512**. On November 26, 1944, twenty-four-year-old LaDell McKay robbed and murdered Robert Leslie Flindt (1906–1944), was convicted of first-degree murder, and was sentenced to death. Claiming gay panic, McKay said Flindt made a pass at him and, blind with anger, he beat Flindt to death. Robbery was only an afterthought. Both the Nevada and US Supreme Courts turned down McKay's appeals. Robert Leslie Flindt was born in Manchester Township, Freeborn County, MN, to Edward Henry Flindt (1873-1950) and Anna Teresa Hartwig (1880-1955). He lived in Freeborn, MN, in 1906 and in a lodging house in Minneapolis, Hennepin, MN, in 1940. A Reno garage man, he died from head injuries which police say were inflicted on him early on November 26, 1944, morning by Ladell Mackay, of Tooele, UT. According to police, Mackay, who was booked under the alias of Lloyd Patrick, admitted having beat up Flindt and robbing him of

between S200 and $250 so he could do a bit of gambling and eat. Mackay also admitted that he was AWOL from Lemoore army air field in California. The police also said that he had served a term in the Utah state prison on a second degree burglary charge prior to his entry into the army. An autopsy, conducted at the direction of Coroner Harry Dunseath, found that Flindt's death was caused by a cerebral hemorrhage due to contusion of the brain. Kenneth Petsch, companion of Mackay, was being held by the police as a material witness. The two were taken into custody a short time after the discovery of Flindt's body. After questioning, Petsch was allowed to go but was rearrested. According to Chief Fletcher, the death of Flindt occurred following a meeting at the Midway Bar. Lee Mmoi, proprietor of the Midway, insisted that there had been no trouble in the bar. Instead, he stated that Flindt, Bart Kerr, a local butcher, and Kerr's brother in law and sister, Mr. and Mrs. Frank Rowe, were at the bar talking with him when Mackay and Petsch entered. Mackay appeared to be under the influence of liquor, according to Miner. When they asked for a drink he refused to serve them. Petsch then asked Kerr to help him get Mackay to his rooms in the Gallery, a rooming house half a block away. Kerr, not wanting to leave his party, refused, according to Miner. Then Petsch asked Flindt to assist him. The latter agreed and the three men walked out of the place. According to Miner, Mackay and Petsch returned to the bar in about half an hour. When asked by Kerr where Flindt was, they gave an evasive answer. Mackay appeared so drunk that Miner poured a glass of cold water on him. The way he jumped up and yelled at me I knew he was not drunk. stated Miner. Then I ordered them out of the place. According to Kerr the absence of Flindt did not arouse any suspicion as he often left the Midway and returned to his garage to work and where he had a cot on which he often slept when on late jobs. What I want to emphasize, stated Miner, is that Flindt was not drunk when he left the Midway, as he had only been there a short time and had only taken one glass of beer. Neither were the other two connected with Kerr and his party. According to police investigation, when Mackay, Petsch and Flindt left the Midway, they walked down Fourth street about four blocks. Then Flindt was attacked and beaten over the head. After being robbed his body, they say, was dragged behind a fence. Flindt, who was well thought of in Reno, was born in Albert Lea, MN. He graduated from the high school there and attended college in Winabego, MN. For a time he worked in the Freeborn county bank as a teller and was prominent in boy scout work. After working in several Minnesota banks he came to Reno in 1940 and worked for the Bureau of Mines at the University of Nevada. In 1942 he took over his brother's garage, filling station and trucking business. He was a member of the Elks.

Phil's Copper Club, 1303 E 4th St, Reno, NV 89512, included in the Damron Address Book in 1974.

Rainbow Room, 2081 E 4th St, Reno, NV 89512, included in the Damron Address Book in 1971.

Accommodation:
Club Lakeridge Resort (6028 Plumas St, Reno, NV 89519) is located in the South Reno area of Reno (NV). The hotel is close to Lake Ridge Golf Course, Bartley Ranch Park, Reno Town Mall.

Part of World Rainbow Hotels (WRH), Lesbian and Gay Welcoming Hotels.
Residence Inn (9845 Gateway Dr, Reno, NV 89521), LGBTQ friendly.

Club: Dave's VIP Club or Dave's Baths, 3001 W 4th St, Reno, NV 89523, on US-40 West, included in the Damron Address Book from 1966 to 1980. Included in the 1975 All Lavender International Gay Guide. Also Dave's Westside Motel, included in the 1965 Guild Guide. Included in the Damron Address Book from 1965 to 1977. Included in the 1975 All Lavender International Gay Guide. Later Blue Cactus Nightclub and Bar, a lesbian bar active from 2001 to 2004.

Restaurant/Bar:
4th Street Bistro (3065 W 4th St, Reno, NV 89523), lesbian owned by chef Natalie Sellars and her longtime partner Carol Wilson. Supports LGBTQIA+ Community and Causes.
Roughrider, 7350 W 4th St, Reno, NV 89523, included in the Damron Address Book in 1978.

Later Mahone's, included in the Damron Address Book in 1980.
Sunnyside Bar, 8100 W 4th St, Reno, NV 89523, included in the Damron Address Book from 1969 to 1971.

The Trapp, 5201 W 4th St, Reno, NV **89523**, included in the Damron Address Book from 1973 to 1980.

Accommodation:
Stagecoach Inn, 7350 W 4th St, Reno, NV **89523**, included in the Damron Address Book from 1969 to 1971.
Wildflower Village B&B (4395-4275 W 4th St, Reno, NV **89523**), gay friendly. Quiet, quaint and comfortable, Wildflower is a unique experience; with B&B superb breakfasts, studios, hostel rooms, apartments, B&B rooms, wedding chapel, gift shop, art galleries, an art house for classes and retreats, Penske Truck Rentals and Moving Supplies plus a coffee shop.
Grand Sierra Resort Casino (2500 E 2nd St, Reno, NV **89595**), LGBTQ friendly.

89700

Restaurant/Bar:
Olive Garden Italian, 4253 S Carson St, Carson City, NV **89701**

House: Samuel Langhorne (Mark Twain) Clemens (1835-1910) lived at 502 N Division St, Carson City, NV **89703**, from 1863 to 1864.

Restaurant/Bar:
J.J.W.'s, 4750 US-50, Carson City, NV **89706**, included in the Damron Address Book in 1979.

89800

Store: Anacabe's-Elko General Merchandise, 416 Idaho St, Elko, NV **89801**, has been a center of Elko's trade for around 80 years. Even Bing Crosby was a patron of the store. Although the store sells a wide range of products like flashlights, knives and Nevada souvenirs, it's primarily a clothing outlet. Footwear fans will certainly be impressed; there are over 200 different types of shoes on display. They also sell high-visibility jackets, cowboy hats, and everything Carhartt. Named among the Most charming general stores in every US state, 2018, by Love Food.

Oregon

State bordering with: Washington, Idaho, Nevada, California.
Oregon is ranked 5 out of 51 for % of same sex couples (0,775%), and is ranked 18 for # of same sex couples, 11.773. (US Census 2010)

97000

Store: Penzey's Spices, 3831 SW 117th Ave, Beaverton, OR **97005**, Ste F. They have some of the best spices & seasonings, many salt-free, and they're LGBT+ allies.

Restaurant/Bar:
Olive Garden Italian, 11650 SW Canyon Rd, Beaverton, OR **97005**

Olive Garden Italian, 8700 SE Sunnyside Rd, Clackamas, OR **97015**

Park: Rooster Rock State Park, Corbett, OR **97019**, B.A. (Bare Ass) Beach, east end, 30 mi. E. of Portland, included in the Damron Address Book from 1972 to 1980. One nude beach is along the Columbia: Rooster Rock, or Cock Rock, as it's known. For a while, Tom says, the cops were harassing gays at Rooster Rock, but now everyone knows we're there, and they leave us alone. Edmund White, States of Desire (1980).

Accommodation:
An architectural gem atop a natural wonder, Timberline Lodge (27500 E Timberline Road, Government Camp, OR **97028**) is an acclaimed ski lodge and mountain retreat on the south slope of Mt. Hood, standing 6,000 feet above sea level. Boasting a rustic elegance, Timberline Lodge is a beautiful mountain-top resort affording exceptional service and enchanting accommodations. Hand-built in 1938, using regional materials and resources, including local stone and timber, Timberline Lodge was declared a National Historic Landmark in 1977. Embracing and celebrating the regional themes: wildlife, Native American, and pioneer, the lodge's original structure, architectural details, and decorations remain unyielding, attesting to its authenticity of the Pacific Northwest style. Inviting a gracious warmth, Timberline Lodge is a historic luxury hotel featuring comfortable guestrooms and suites, refined and sustainable dining, a world-class ski and snowboarding facility, thoughtfully-appointed event spaces, and, most of all, distinguished hospitality. Surrounded by lush forest with stunning views of the Cascade Mountain Range, Timberline Lodge is a truly unique destination for recreational travel and leisure. Timberline Lodge, a charter member of Historic Hotels of America since 1989, dates back to 1937.

Restaurant/Bar:

Red Lobster, 240 NW Burnside Rd, Gresham, OR **97030**

Queer Architects: Wendy Willow House, 3239 Cascade Ave, Hood River, OR **97031**, designed by John H. Howe in 1986.

Other non-queer residents: William Ashely (Billy) Sunday (1862-1935), Sunday Ranch (3024 Sunday Dr, Hood River, OR **97031**), from 1910 to 1935.

Restaurant/Bar:
Solstice Wood Fire Pizza, Bar & Catering, 501 Portway Ave, Hood River, OR **97031**
Broder Øst, 102 Oak St #100, Hood River, OR **97031**

Whiskey Tango, 112 Oak St, Hood River, OR **97031**
The River City Saloon, 207 Cascade Ave, Hood River, OR **97031**

Accommodation:
Hood River Hotel, 102 Oak St, Hood River, OR **97031**

Sakura Ridge - The Farm and Lodge (5601 York Hill Rd #8662, Hood River, OR **97031**), LGBTQ friendly.

Restaurant/Bar:

Olive Garden Italian, 6355 Meadows Rd, Lake Oswego, OR **97035**

Accommodation:
Mt Hood Hamlet B&B (6741 OR-35, Mt Hood, OR **97041**), LGBTQ friendly.

Old Parkdale Inn B&B (4932 Baseline Dr, Mt Hood, OR **97041**), gay friendly. Three romantic and artistically decorated rooms, nestled at the foot of Mt Hood.

Oldest Building in the State: Molalla Log House, 16750 S Brockway Rd, Oregon City, OR **97045**. The Molalla Log House predates the famous Lewis and Clark Expedition of 1804. It is thought by some to be the work of Russian settlers who were sent to Oregon's Willamette Valley by Catherine the Great. The 18-foot-wide structure, dating to 1799, is unlike any pioneer construction seen in Oregon from that period in history.

Accommodation:

Scappoose Creek Inn (53758 W Lane Rd, Scappoose, OR **97056**), lesbian owned.

Store: A popular spot for cyclists to stop for lunch at the gateway to the Columbia River Gorge, the Troutdale General Store, 289 E Historic Columbia River Hwy, Troutdale, OR **97060**, also offers made-in-Oregon specialties, and holiday decor items are sold year-round. Community Cook Tawny Nelson of North Plains, Oregon, says her family liked browsing the gifts and toys, both modern and retro. Next time I'm going to try a milkshake and go on a weekend when they have smoked salmon chowder! Named among the 25 Old-Fashioned General Stores Across America, 2022, by Taste of Home.

Accommodation:

Whispering Woods Resort, 67800 East Nicklaus Way, Welches, OR **97067**, GLD, Gay Lesbian Directory

Restaurant/Bar:

Olive Garden Italian, 2330 SE Burnside Rd, Gresham, OR **97080**

Accommodation:
Forest Springs B&B (3680 SW Towle Ave, Gresham, OR **97080**), gay owned. Next to over 1,000 acres of forested open space, just a short

drive from Portland. GLD, Gay Lesbian Directory

AIDS Memorial: Lincoln Memorial Park, right of the Funeral Home (11801 SE Mt Scott Blvd, Portland, OR **97086**), Darcelle XV AIDS Memorial, since 25 August 2017, without names. The memorial is named in honor of Darcelle XV, a legendary performer and tireless advocate for AIDS awareness and support in Oregon. This monument serves as way to honor all Oregonians who have lost their life to AIDS. Also, to appreciate those who have cared for impacted individuals. The red ribbon symbolizes solidarity with those who live with AIDS and the memorial's base is shaped like the outline of Oregon state. The memorial was designed by Cal Christensen and won the 1st place 2017 design award of the American Institute of

Commemorative Art (AICA) in the category Public Monuments. Patrick Kelly (1953-1993) was a dancer and dance writer. A member of the corps de ballet of companies in Portland, San Francisco, and Cleveland. He also performed as the ballerina Doris Videnya in the all-male Ballets Trockadero de Monte Carlo. His companion was Richard Dworkin, who at once was also percussionist and partner of Michael Callen. Born in Portland, where he began his dance training and received a degree in nursing from Oregon Health Services University, Kelly wrote about dance for New York Native and Dance Magazine. He worked as a psychiatric nurse and supervisor at St Vincent's Hospital in Manhattan. He was the founder and president of the Village Dive Club and Diving for Life, a national scuba-diving organization active in AIDS support services. He is buried at Lincoln Memorial Park Cemetery.

Store: Penzey's Spices, 11211 SE 82nd Ave, Happy Valley, OR **97086**, #D. They have some of the best spices & seasonings, many salt-free, and they're LGBT+ allies.

97100

Accommodation:	Ocean Point Inn & Spa (79819 Ocean Point Rd, Arch Cape, OR **97102**), LGBTQ owned. GLD, Gay Lesbian Directory

Astoria

Instead of heading to the popular queer haven of Portland, drive instead to Astoria, Oregon, a city located on Oregon's northern coast. Aside from its beautiful coastal scenery, the town of Astoria has a lively LGBTQ community and a generally welcoming and friendly atmosphere. While you're passing through Astoria, make sure to pay a visit to one of its many local breweries and coffee shops, including gay-owned Astoria Coffee House & Bistro. Then, after a heavy dose of caffeine, you'll be ready to hit the road again or just take in the stunning views of the rugged coastline. Astoria, OR, has been named among The Best Places To Stop on Your LGBTQ-Friendly US Road Trip, 2019, Matador Network

House: Meriwether Lewis (1774-1809) lived at Fort Clatsop (92345 Fort Clatsop Rd, Astoria, OR **97103**), from 1805 to 1806 (demolished).

Restaurant/Bar:	Liberty Theater, 1203 Commercial St, Astoria, OR **97103**
Fort George Brewery, 1483 Duane St, Astoria, OR **97103**	Astoria Coffee House & Bistro (243 11th St #4114, Astoria, OR **97103**), gay owned.
Buoy Beer Company, 1 8th St, Astoria, OR **97103**	Street 14 Café, 1410 Commercial St, Astoria, OR **97103**
Frite & Scoop, 175 14th St, Astoria, OR **97103**	
Coffee Girl, 100 39th St, Astoria, OR **97103**	

Accommodation:	Cannery Pier Hotel, 10 Basin St, Astoria, OR **97103**
Commodore Hotel, 258 14th St, Astoria, OR **97103**	
Norblad Hotel, 443 14th St, Astoria, OR **97103**	

Beach: Cannon Beach, OR **97110**, included in the Damron Address Book in 1980.

Accommodation:

Cannon Beach Hotel (1116 S Hemlock St, Cannon Beach, OR **97110**), LGBTQ friendly.	The Courtyard (964 S Hemlock St, Cannon Beach, OR **97110**), LGBTQ friendly.

Attractions: Haystack Rock (US-101, Cannon Beach, OR **97110**) has been named among the Highest stacks in the world.

Accommodation:	Sandlake Country Inn (8505 Galloway Rd, Cloverdale, OR **97112**), LGBTQ friendly. GLD, Gay Lesbian Directory

Cemetery: Johnnie Ray (1927–1990) was an American singer, songwriter, and pianiSt Extremely popular for most of the 1950s, Ray has been cited by critics as a major precursor of what would become rock and roll, for his jazz and blues-influenced music and his animated stage personality. Tony Bennett credits Ray as being the true father of rock and roll. In 1951, when Ray was obscure and not yet signed to a record label, he was arrested in Detroit for accosting and soliciting an undercover vice squad police officer in the restroom of the Stone Theatre, a burlesque house. When he appeared in court, he pleaded guilty. He paid a fine and was released. Because of his obscurity at the time, the Detroit newspapers did not report the story. After his sudden rise to fame the following year, rumors about his sexuality began to spread. Despite her knowledge of the solicitation arrest, Marilyn Morrison, daughter of the owner of West Hollywood's Mocambo nightclub, married Ray at the peak of his American fame. The couple separated in 1953 and divorced in 1954. Several writers have noted that the Ray-Morrison marriage occurred under false pretenses, and that Ray had a long-term relationship with his manager, Bill Franklin. A biography of Ray points out, however, that Franklin was 13 years younger than Ray and that both their personal and business relationships began in 1963, many years after the Ray-Morrison divorce. In 1959, Ray was arrested again in Detroit for soliciting an undercover officer at the Brass Rail, a bar that was described many years later by one biographer as a haven for musicians and by another biographer as a gay bar. Ray went to trial following this second arrest and was found not guilty. Two years after his death, several friends shared with biographer Jonny Whiteside their knowledge of his homosexuality. Johnnie Ray was born January 10, 1927, in Hopewell, OR, to parents Elmer Ray and Hazel Simkins. Along with older sister Elma, Ray spent part of his childhood on a farm in Dallas, OR and attended grade school there. The family later moved to Portland, OR, where Ray attended high school. On February 24, 1990, he died of liver failure at Cedars-Sinai in Los Angeles. He is buried at Hopewell Cemetery (12475 SE Finn Ln, Dayton, OR **97114**).

Accommodation: Dundee Manor (8380 NE Worden Hill Rd., Dundee, OR **97115**), gay owned. Destination for wine lovers to a location truly ment for those who appreciate. Romance and the	absolute best hosts and cuisine in the PNW. Location/location. Up the hill and over the top. Voted 5 stars with Trip Advisor #1 in Dundee.

Cemetery: Jeff Gates (1954-1991) was in the Nicaraguan revolution and joined ACT UP New York after coming out as a gay man. He is buried at Forest View Cemetery (1161 SW Pacific Ave, Forest Grove, OR **97116**).

Accommodation:

Courtyard Portland Hillsboro (3050 NW Stucki Pl, Hillsboro, OR **97124**), LGBTQ friendly.	TownePlace Suites Portland Hillsboro (6550 NE Brighton St, Hillsboro, OR **97124**), LGBTQ friendly.

House: Mark Morrisroe (1959-1989) was an American performance artist and photographer. He is known for his performances and photographs, which were germane in the development of the punk scene in Boston in the 1970s and the art world boom of the mid to late 1980s in New York City. By the time of his death he had created some 2,000 pieces of work. He attended the School of the Museum of Fine Arts, Boston, where he made friends with several soon-to-be-well-known artists. His boyfriend in Boston was Johnathan Pierson, who later changed his name to Jack Pierson. He graduated from the Museum School with honors receiving the coveted 5th Year Award. While attending, he performed as a drag character of his own creation, Sweet Raspberry, and co-founded a zine called Dirt Magazine with his friend Lynelle White, distributing it in Boston nightclubs. This zine was composed of fake news and gossip about celebrities, bands and other famous people, mostly from Boston. Morrisroe died aged 30, in Jersey City, NJ from complications of AIDS. His ashes are scattered in McMinnville, OR on the farm of his last boyfriend, Ramsey McPhillips (13351 SW McPhillips Rd, McMinnville, OR **97128**). His fame has increased steadily since his death. He is considered a member of the New England School of Photography and his work is found in many important collections including that of the Whitney and MOCA of Los Angeles. The estate of Mark Morrisroe (Collection Ringier) is currently located at the Fotomuseum Winterthur.

Accommodation: Oregon Wine Cottage (515 NW Birch St, McMinnville, OR **97128**), LGBTQ friendly. Spindrift Inn (114 Laneda Ave, Manzanita, OR **97130**), gay friendly. Only one block from the 6 mile Manzanita Beach, Spindrift Inn retains the quaint charm of yesteryear while providing all the modern conveniences. Family owned and operated since 1946, the cozy atmosphere, private hidden garden and affordable rooms are within easy walking distance to shops and restaurants.

Store: Patricia Green Cellars (15225 NE North Valley Rd, Newberg, OR **97132**) is dedicated fully and solely to displaying the nature of Pinot Noir that is derived from where it is grown.

Other non-queer residents: Herbert Clark Hoover (1874-1964), Hoover-Minthorn House Museum (115 S River St, Newberg, OR **97132**), from 1884 to 1889.

Cemetery: Keith L. Davis (1954-1987) was a graphic designer who worked at the magazine Artforum. He was deeply involved with the East Village gallery scene in the early 1980s, collecting artists' work and inviting them use the equipment and supplies in his home and at Artforum. He and David Wojnarowicz were close friends, and they traveled together. An interview he taped with Wojnarowicz, as well as Davis's will, can be found in the Wojnarowicz Papers. He died of complications related to AIDS in 1987 and is buried at Valley View Memorial Park (Newberg, OR **97132**).

Accommodation:	The Getaway Oceanfront Lodging (621 S Pacific St, Rockaway Beach, OR **97136**), LGBTQ friendly.

House: James Beard (1903-1985) was born in Portland, OR in 1903 to Elizabeth and John Beard. His mother operated the Gladstone Hotel, and his father worked at the city's customs house. The family vacationed on the Pacific coast in Gearhart, OR, where Beard was exposed to Pacific Northwest cuisine. After spending many summers in Gearhart, Beard and his mother bought the smallest house in the seaside village, a cottage built in 1922 (498 E St, Gearhart, OR **97138**). Restored to its original character, this charming cottage is located close to the beach on a large lot in West Gearhart. Beautifully landscaped, there is a garden/tool shed and playhouse included. Last sold in April 2012 for 327,500$. James Beard died of heart failure on January 21, 1985 at his home in New York City at age 81. He was cremated and his ashes scattered over the beach in Gearhart, OR.

Beach: T-Room beneath turn-around on Seaside Beach, 229-299 S Promenade, Seaside, OR **97138**, included in the Damron Address Book from 1978 to 1980.

Accommodation: Gearhart Ocean Innm 67 N Cottage Ave, Gearhart, OR **97138**, GLD, Gay Lesbian Directory	Hillcrest Inn (118 N Columbia St, Seaside, OR **97138**), gay friendly. Guest lodging with Cape Cod ambience offers cottages, spa-rooms, mini-suites and the traditional.

Cemetery: Joey Skilbred (1946-1996), whose stage name was Jocelyn Somers, was one of Las Vegas'most beloved impersonators. Skilbred began performing in Las Vegas in the early 1970s and eventually joined the troupes of Kenny Kerr's Boylesque and Frank Marino's An Evening at La Cage. Skilbred died in 1996 and is buried at Pleasant View Cemetery (14250 SW Westfall Rd, Sherwood, OR **97140**).

Beach: Cannon Beach, OR **97145**, included in the Damron Address Book from 1978 to 1979.

Accommodation:	Old Wheeler Hotel (0555, 495 US-101, Wheeler, OR **97147**), LGBTQ friendly.

97200

Portland

Portland, OR, is ranked 6 out of 25 among US Large cities (Population above 250.000) for % of same sex couples (1,925%), and is ranked 6 for # of same sex couples, 4.784. (US Census 2010)

Portland, OR, is ranked 3 out of 18 among US cities for Percentage of Same-Sex Couple Households, 2017

Portland Area Business Association: http://www.paba.com/

Portland, OR, has been named among the Gayest Cities in America by The Advocate, 2012

Portland, OR, has been named among the Most Lesbianish Cities in America by Jezebel, A supposedly Feminist Website, 2012

Portland, OR, has been named among the Gayest Cities in America by The Advocate, 2014

Portland, OR, has been named among the great Lesbian-friendly destinations by Pink Triangle Press (dailyxtra.com), 2015

Portland, OR, has been named among the 10 Dreamy Lesbian Holidays To Inspire Your Travels This Summer by Queer In the World, 2018

Portland, OR, has been named among the Top LGBT-friendly cities by ellgeeBE, 2018

Portland, OR, has been named among the Featured Cities by Wanderful Homesharing, 2018

Portland, OR, has been named among the Top Lesbian Vacation Destinations by Lesbian Business Community, 2019

Alberta Street

Accommodation: Traveller's House, 710 N Alberta St, Portland, OR **97217**. Hip social hostel centrally located with access to great nightlife, microbreweries, and food options. The hostel is a walking distance to Historic Mississippi, Alberta Arts, and Williams Districts; and has exceptional public transit connecting you to all of Portland. These neighborhoods are what make Portland weirdly awesome and different from other cities that only have nightlife in the downtown area. Friendly staff will help guide you in your Portland travels. The hostel's small size sets it apart from the big hosteling international chains in Portland.

Restaurant/Bar:
Tin Shed Garden Café (1438 NE Alberta St, Portland, OR **97211**), lesbian owned.
Back To Eden Bakery (2215-2217 NE Alberta St, Portland, OR **97211**), Portland Area Business Association member.
Natural Selection (3033 NE Alberta St, Portland, OR **97211**) has been named among the Best destinations for vegans in the world.

Albina Avenue

Restaurant/Bar: Sweedeedee, 5202 N Albina Ave, Portland, OR **97217**

Alder Street

Restaurant/Bar: Portland Youth Alliance, 615 SE Alder St, Portland, OR **97214**, included in the Damron Address Book in 1976.

Accommodation: Cherokee Rose Inn (2924 SE Alder St, Portland, OR **97214**) has been named among the Best destinations for vegans in the world.

Restaurant/Bar:
Other Inn, 242 SW Alder St, Portland, OR **97204**, included in the Damron Address Book from 1968 to 1980. Included in the 1975 All Lavender International Gay Guide.
Second Foundation Social Club, 258 SW Alder St, Portland, OR **97205**, included in the Damron Address Book in 1974.

Archives: Located at 610 SW Alder St, Portland, OR **97205** (National Register of Historic Places: 1991), the Selling Building was built in 1910. Early tenants of the building were physicians and dentists, including psychologist J. Allen Gilbert who, in 1917, treated Dr. Alan Hart (nee Alberta Lucille Hart) for sexual inversion. Despite categorizing Hart's condition as pathological and abnormal, Dr. Gilbert eventually supported Hart's transition, including their choice to undergo a hysterectomy and adopt male attire. Dr. Hart's given name was Lucille; he was raised in Albany, OR, and did not seek medical or psychological treatment until 26 years of age, but it is clear from Dr. Gilbert's notes and Hart's own writings that he rejected the feminine identity from a young age. Although his gender transition and medical career were unique successes for the time period, Hart endured the prejudiced attacks of others while struggling with his own identity. Preferring to dress in men's clothes, Hart was outed several times and was forced to move from one location to another. According to Dr. Gilbert, the primary barrier in curing Hart's condition was his own negative attitude toward women; despite numerous romantic engagements, including two marriages, he is quoted as loathing the female type of mind. Although Dr. Hart was the victim of rumors and hounding throughout his medical career, he became a leader in the research and treatment of tuberculosis. He later became a successful novelist, writing about prejudice and other social ills in stories that closely mirrored his own life experiences.

Accommodation:
Dossier (750 SW Alder St, Portland, OR **97205**) is inspired by things that are timeless. Part of World Rainbow Hotels (WRH), Lesbian and Gay Welcoming Hotels.
Woodlark (813 SW Alder St, Portland, OR **97205**). Part of World Rainbow Hotels (WRH), Lesbian and Gay Welcoming Hotels.

Ankeny Street

Restaurant/Bar: Chocolate Moose, 211 SW Ankeny St, Portland, OR **97204**, included in the Damron Address Book from 1974 to 1977.

Barbur Boulevard

Accommodation: Portland Rose Motel, 8920 SW Barbur Blvd, Portland, OR **97219**, included in the Damron Address Book from 1974 to 1975.

Beech Street

Store: She Bop (909 N Beech St suite a, Portland, OR **97227**) is a female-friendly sex toy boutique that hosts an array of non-toxic toys, as well as ongoing classes and workshops you can sign up for (many fill up fast!),

Belmont Street

Restaurant/Bar:
Bare Bones Café, 2900 SE Belmont St, Portland, OR **97214**, is a low-noise level kinda place where the screen door smacks open, the food goes great with your coffee and there happens to be a just-as-cool adjacent bar, Bare Bones Bar.
A favorite go-to food cart is Fish Box (in the Good Food Here carts, 4262 SE Belmont St, Portland, OR **97215**), serves up a to-die-for Ahi tuna melt, and their salmon tacos are bomb dot com.

Broadway

LGBTQ friendly bookstore: A Woman's Place Bookstore, 1431 NE Broadway, Portland, OR **97232**, active in 1990.

Restaurant/Bar: Judy's (1431 NE Broadway St, Portland, OR **97232**) was a lesbian bar active from 1983 to 1985.

LGBTQ friendly bookstore: Broadway Books, 1714 NE Broadway, Portland, OR **97232**, **56 Queer-Owned Bookstores to Support**, by Oprah Daily, 2021.

Store: Asha Integrative Wellness (2100 NE Broadway St #225, Portland, OR **97232**) is wonderful for acupuncture, massage, reiki and so on. You are visiting Portland, so don't forget to hydrate with some kombucha and take a disco nap before you venture into the night.

The Embers Avenue, Creative Commons Licenses, via Wikimedia Commons

Restaurant/Bar: The Embers Avenue, 110 NW Broadway, Portland, OR **97209**

Stag PDX, Creative Commons Licenses, via Wikimedia Commons

Restaurant/Bar: Stag PDX, 317 NW Broadway, Portland, OR **97209**

The Benson

Accommodation: *The Benson is located in the heart of downtown Portland in the middle of many attractions. It is only a few minutes walking distance to attractions such as the Alder Street food carts, the Pioneer Square Courthouse, and many great coffee shops and restaurants. The Benson Hotel Bar has been included in the* Damron Address Book *from 1965 to 1977.* TAG Approved LGBTQ friendly accommodation.

Address: 309 SW Broadway, Portland, OR 97205

The Benson

Since opening this downtown Portland Hotel in 1913, The Benson has been a hidden gem. Built by the millionaire innovator Simon Benson, this fabled, European-style hotel was built to put Portland on the international map. Featuring Italian marble floors, Austrian crystal chandeliers, and Circassian walnut wood from the imperial forests of Russia. As the last of its kind, no other hotel in the region comes close to the quintessential elegance, amenities and charm of The Benson. For more than 100 years, the hotel's staff has welcomed celebrities, CEOs, dignitaries and a majority of US presidents.

Accommodation:
Hotel Lucia (400 SW Broadway, Portland, OR **97205**), TAG Approved LGBTQ friendly accommodation, has been named among the Best LGBT-friendly hotels by CNN Travel, 2019. Oregon's main metropolis is one of America's most progressive. It's also such a residential city that its hotels are predominantly clustered downtown. That includes Hotel Lucia, part of the LGBTQ friendly Provenance Hotels portfolio. The boutique property occupies a landmarked high rise that's now positively brimming with designer charm: think a stellar photography collection, daily craft-brew happy hours, free bike rentals and uniquely Portland amenities (like discounts on locally-made goods). Part of World Rainbow Hotels (WRH), Lesbian and Gay Welcoming Hotels.

Kimpton Hotel Vintage, 422 SW Broadway, Portland, OR **97205**. Celebrate Willamette Valley wines in an urban-chic environment in the heart of PDX. As The Trevor Project's Premier National Hotel Partner, Kimpton Hotels are involved on local and national levels hosting fundraisers across America. In 2022, when you made a reservation, they donated $10 per night to The Trevor Project, plus you got 15% off our Best Flexible Rate.

Queer Architects: Encore Restaurant remodel, 512 SW Broadway, Portland, OR **97205**, designed by Roland Terry (1959)

Accommodation: The Heathman Hotel (1001 SW Broadway, Portland, OR **97205**), a Portland cultural fixture since the day it opened in 1927, recently completed a renovation that has polished this treasured jewel, renewed its luster, reaffirmed its illustrious past, and readied it for a bright new future. The restoration included the 151 cozy guestrooms and public spaces. Lighter, brighter, and more contemporary, the design is nonetheless rooted in the building's unique history and pays homage to the hotel's role as muse to generations of guests. The Heathman Hotel has been a Portland touchstone for travelers in the past and continues to serve as a welcome respite for friends and neighbors right here at home and visitors from around the globe. The Heathman Hotel is a downtown landmark, built in the late 1920s in the popular Italian Renaissance style. Then, as now, the hotel was a popular center of cultural activity. Its dramatic public spaces have been renovated in grand Art Deco style and provide the perfect backdrop for the hotel's extensive collection of artwork. A prominent supporter of the city's cultural and fine arts community, it is adjacent to the Portland Center for the Performing Arts and is attached to the Arlene Schnitzer Concert Hall. The hotel's ties to the arts run deep and for years it has sponsored Give to the Arts, Even in Your Sleep, a program which donates a portion of the hotel's weekend revenue to local arts organizations. Many of the hotel's guest rooms feature views of the Traveler's Song mural, a 9-foot high work by artist Henk Pander that was commissioned to adorn the interior wall of the attached concert hall. As the only hotel in the city's designated Cultural District, the Heathman is truly a place where service is still an art. The Heathman Hotel, a member of Historic Hotels of America since 1991, dates back to 1927.

Restaurant/Bar: Nineteenth Hole, 1002 SW Broadway, Portland, OR **97205**, included in the Damron Address Book in 1965. Later Beefeater, included in the Damron Address Book from 1968 to 1969.

Burnside Street

Gay Village
Burnside Triangle, Burnside St, Portland, OR **97209**

LGBTQ friendly bookstore: US Adult Bookstore & Arcade, 628 E Burnside St, Portland, OR **97214**, included in the Damron Address Book from 1979 to 1980.

Accommodation:
Jupiter Hotel Portland (800 E Burnside St, Portland, OR **97214**), TAG Approved LGBTQ friendly accommodation. GLD, Gay Lesbian Directory
Jupiter NEXT (900 E Burnside St, Portland, OR **97214**), LGBTQ friendly.

LGBTQ friendly bookstore: A Woman's Place Bookstore, 706 SE Grand Ave, Portland, OR **97214**, 2349 SE Ankeny St, Portland, OR **97214**, and 1533 E Burnside St, Portland, OR **97214**, was a feminist bookstore active in the 1980s. Included in the Damron Address Book from 1976 to 1978.

Restaurant/Bar: Doug Fir Lounge, 830 E Burnside St, Portland, OR **97214**

Accommodation: Old St. George Hotel, 118 W Burnside St, Portland, OR **97209**, included in the Damron Address Book from 1977 to 1979.

Restaurant/Bar:
Tash's, 316 W Burnside St, Portland, OR **97209**, included in the Damron Address Book from 1974 to 1975.
Rising Moon, 413 W Burnside St, Portland, OR **97209**, included in the Damron Address Book from 1978 to 1980.
Purple Cat, 625 W Burnside St, Portland, OR **97209**, included in the Damron Address Book from 1970 to 1972. Included in the 1975 All Lavender International Gay Guide.

LGBTQ friendly bookstore: Powell's City of Books (1005 W Burnside St, Portland, OR **97209**) is one of those things you just do when you come to Portland. Get a Stumptown Coffee at their little coffee shop inside, and then get lost for hours finding rare, old, forgotten and newly coveted books, or just huff the air for the sheer smell of it all. (Pro tip: The buzz in Powell's is like Disney. Weekends are busiest, so if you're trying to beat the crowd, always pick a weekday.)

Restaurant/Bar: Mentioned in 1964 Vice Squad reports as a lesbian hangout frequented by women who dress like men, act like men, and are believed to be from areas outside Portland, the Milwaukee Tavern (1535 W Burnside St, Portland, OR **97209**) was owned by Edna Jordal, who employed only women. It was active in the 1960s. Konnie's Korner, 1650 W Burnside St, Portland, OR **97209**, included in the Damron Address Book in 1979. J&J Tavern, 1719 W Burnside St, Portland, OR **97209**, included in the Damron Address Book in 1980.

Cedar Street

House: Leo Bersani (1931–2022) was an American academic, known for his contributions to French literary criticism and queer theory. He was known for his 1987 essay Is the Rectum a Grave? and his 1995 book Homos. Bersani's parter Sam Geraci, who, he met in 1994 and married in 2014, was a constant support to him. They lived at 2384 SW Cedar St, Portland, OR **97205**. Bersani was born in the Bronx. He studied at Harvard University, graduating in 1952 with a bachelor's in Romance languages, and with a Ph.D. in comparative literature in 1958. He was awarded a Guggenhein Fellowiship in French Literature in 1967. He taught at Wellesley College and Rutgers University before joining University of California, Berkeley in 1972, where he'd remain for the rest of his career, assuming emeritus status in 1996. He was elected a Fellow of the American Academy of Arts and Sciences in 1992.

Clackamas Street

Accommodation: Sullivan's Gulch B&B (1744 NE Clackamas St, Portland, OR **97232**) included in Inn Places 1999, Gay & Lesbian Accommodations Worldwide. Gay and Lesbian. As of 2021 it's closed.

Clay Street

Accommodation: Hotel Zags (515 SW Clay St, Portland, OR **97201**) is the oasis of the Fountain District, a hidden gem in downtown Portland. Zen out in our lush courtyard featuring a living wall, or get wild in our game room, The Colosseum. Part of World Rainbow Hotels (WRH), Lesbian and Gay Welcoming Hotels.

Corbett Avenue

Accommodation: Bellaterra B&B (3935 SW Corbett Ave, Portland, OR **97239**), gay friendly. A recently-restored 1893 home in close-in SW Portland Inspired by diverse cultures and natural settings, each suite is furnished with antiques, its own stone- or glass-tiled bath, and a theme designed to spark the sense of being in a chosen place or time.

Couch Street

The Silverado, Creative Commons Licenses, via Wikimedia Commons

Restaurant/Bar: The Silverado Bar (610 NW Couch St, Portland, OR **97209**) has been named among the Greatest Gay Bars in the World by Out.com, 2013.

Davis Street

Gay Village

Old Town, NW Davis St, Portland, OR **97209**

CC Slaughters, Creative Commons Licenses, via Wikimedia Commons

Restaurant/Bar: CC Slaughters Nightclub and Lounge (219 NW Davis St, Portland, OR **97209**) has been named among the Greatest Gay Bars in the World by Out.com, 2013.

Division Street

Store: Rudy's Barbershop (3005 SE Division St, Portland, OR **97202**) is an old-fashion-meets-modern hair salon where the motto is simple: We cut heads Rudy's supports the It Gets Better campaign.

Accommodation: Bluebird Guesthouse (3517 SE Division St, Portland, OR **97202**), **LGBTQ friendly**.

Restaurant/Bar:
Varsity Tavern, SE 35th Pl & SE Division St, Portland, OR **97202**, included in the **Damron Address Book** in 1980.
Egyptian Club (3701 SE Division St, Portland, OR **97202**) was a lesbian bar active from 1995 to 2010.

Store: New Rose Tattoo (4823 SE Division St, Portland, OR **97206**) is a **LGBTQ friendly**, **LGBTQ owned** ink parlor that will make your Portland stay a trip to remember.

Everett Street

Accommodation: Oakwood Portland Pearl District (1155 NW Everett St, Portland, OR **97209**) is located in Portland. The nearest airport is Portland International Airport, which is 6.2 miles from the property. Part of **World Rainbow Hotels (WRH), Lesbian and Gay Welcoming Hotels**.

Flanders Street

Club: Finnish Steam Baths, 304 NW Flanders St, Portland, OR **97209**, included in the 1975 All Lavender International Gay Guide.

Accommodation: Portland International Guesthouse (2185 NW Flanders St, Portland, OR **97210**), gay owned. European-style accommodations in the heart of Portland's Northwest district.

Foster Road

Restaurant/Bar: Hot Patata, 5842 SE Foster Rd, Portland, OR **97206**, included in the Damron Address Book in 1980.

Fremont Street

Store: Rerun (707 NE Fremont St, Portland, OR **97212**) is a consignment shop with all kinds of treasures.

Gladstone Street

Restaurant/Bar: Ship Ahoy Tavern, 2889 SE Gladstone St, Portland, OR **97202**, included in the 1964 and 1965 Guild Guide.

Glisan Street

Accommodation: Tiny Digs Hotel (2646 NE Glisan St #2318, Portland, OR **97232**), lesbian owned.

Theatre: Tom Kat Theatre, 425 NW Glisan St, Portland, OR **97209**, included in the Damron Address Book from 1974 to 1980.

Restaurant/Bar: Byways Café (1212 NW Glisan St, Portland, OR **97209**), lesbian owned.

Grand Avenue

Accommodation: Hotel Eastlund (1021 NE Grand Ave, Portland, OR **97232**), TAG Approved LGBTQ friendly accommodation, is a luxury Gay-Welcoming boutique hotel in downtown Portland's Eastside. Part of World Rainbow Hotels (WRH), Lesbian and Gay Welcoming Hotels.

Store: The tomboy headquarters of LGBTQ owned Wildfang (1230 SE Grand Ave, Portland, OR **97214**) is situated right here in Portland where you can score some dapper duds, or just pick out where Tegan and Sara carved their initials on the wall.

Greenburg Road

Restaurant/Bar: Red Lobster, 10330 SW Greenburg Rd, Tigard, OR **97223**

Greenwood Road

Queer Architects: Mr. T. T. Denison residence guest house addition, 2206 S Greenwood Rd, Portland, OR **97219**, designed by Roland Terry (1954)

Hall Street

1423 SW Hall, Portland, Google Maps 2016

House: For lengthy periods between 1926 and 1936 Marie Equi (1872–1952) invited the WWI leader Elizabeth Gurley Flynn to live with her and help care for Equi's daughter. Flynn suffered serious health problems, including exhaustion from overwork and depression from political setbacks. Equi, Flynn, and Equi's daughter lived at 1423 SW Hall St, Portland, OR **97201**, in Portland's westside neighborhood—Gander Ridge of Goose Hollow. In 1930 Equi suffered a heart attack, sold her medical practice, and asked Flynn to assist her for several more years. Finally Flynn retreated to the East and resumed her work. She became a national leader of the Communist Party USA. Equi died on July 13, 1952, and is buried at Wilhelm Portland Memorial in twin tombstones alongside Harriet who had died on May 26, 1927.

Hamilton Court

Accommodation: River's Edge Hotel (0455 SW Hamilton Ct, Portland, OR **97239**), TAG Approved LGBTQ friendly accommodation. Located on the edge of the Willamette River in Portland's modern South Waterfront District, the Rivers Edge Hotel and Spa offers relaxing spa services in a scenic location. Part of World Rainbow Hotels (WRH), Lesbian and Gay Welcoming Hotels.

Hancock Street

House: Alan L. Hart (1890–1962) was an American physician, radiologist, tuberculosis researcher, writer and noveliSt He was, in 1917–18, one of the first trans men to undergo hysterectomy and gonadectomy in the US, and lived the rest of his life as a man. In 1917, as Alberta Lucille Hart, he obtained a doctor of medicine degree from the University of Oregon Medical Department in Portland (now Oregon Health & Science University). During this time he boarded at 3610 NE Hancock St, Portland, OR **97212**.

Harbor Way

Kimpton RiverPlace Hotel, 1510 S Harbor Way, Portland, OR **97201**. Boutique charm and laid-back luxury in a tranquil riverside location close to downtown Portland. As The Trevor Project's Premier National Hotel Partner, Kimpton Hotels are involved on local and national levels hosting fundraisers across America. In 2022, when you made a reservation, they donated $10 per night to The Trevor Project, plus you got 15% off our Best Flexible Rate.

Harrison Street

Queer Architects: Lovejoy Fountain, SW Harrison St & Southwest 3rd Avenue, Portland, OR **97214**, Designed by Charles Moore.

Harvey Milk Street

Restaurant/Bar: Victoria's Nephew, 212 SW Harvey Milk St, Portland, OR **97204**, included in the Damron Address Book from 1977 to 1979.

Accommodation: Hi-Lo Hotel (320 SW Harvey Milk St, Portland, OR **97204**) is an excellent, trendy, gay-friendly hotel in the heart of Portland, Oregon, aimed at foodies, artists, young professionals and savvy business travellers. Part of World Rainbow Hotels (WRH), Lesbian and Gay Welcoming Hotels.

LGBTQ friendly bookstore: Random Strands, next door to Riptide, 933 SW Harvey Milk St, Portland, OR **97205**, included in the Damron Address Book in 1973.

Restaurant/Bar:
Riptide, 933 SW Harvey Milk St, Portland, OR **97205**, opened in June 1965 as one of the first gay bars on Stark Street. City pressure resulted in its closure in 1969. It re-opened in November 1970 as Roman's Riptide. Included in the Damron Address Book from 1972 to 1973.
Roman's Lounge, 949 SW Harvey Milk St, Portland, OR **97205**, included in the Damron Address Book in 1974.
Rhondee, 1014 SW Harvey Milk St, Portland, OR **97205**, included in the Damron Address Book from 1978 to 1980.

Accommodation: Ace Hotel Portland (1022 SW Harvey Milk St, Portland, OR **97205**, National Register of Historic Places), where cool music acts like Holly Miranda have performed in the lobby, occupies the former Clyde Hotel in downtown Portland. In its former incarnation, the hotel's lobby served as the setting for a scene from the film Drugstore Cowboy by Gus Van Sant.

Restaurant/Bar: Red Cap Garage, 1035 SW Harvey Milk St, Portland, OR **97205**

Scandals, Creative Commons Licenses, via Wikimedia Commons

Restaurant/Bar:
Scandals, 1125 SW Harvey Milk St, Portland, OR **97205**
Roxy Hearts, 1211 SW Harvey Milk St, Portland, OR **97205**, included in the Damron Address Book from 1979 to 1980.
Kachina Lounge, 1217 SW Harvey Milk St, Portland, OR **97205**, included in the Damron Address Book from 1979 to 1980.

Hawthorne Boulevard

Accommodation: Hawthorne Hostel (3031 SE Hawthorne Blvd, Portland, OR **97214**), LGBTQ friendly.

Restaurant/Bar: Dingo's (4612 SE Hawthorne Blvd, Portland, OR **97215**) was a lesbian bar active from 2000 to 2013.

Hayden Island Drive

Accommodation: Jantzen Beach RV Park (1503 N Hayden Island Dr, Portland, OR **97217**), LGBTQ friendly.

Hoyt Street

Restaurant/Bar: Barbary Coast Nite Club and Hoyt Hotel Coffee Shop at Hoyt Hotel, 614 NW Hoyt St, Portland, OR **97209**, included in the Damron Address Book from 1972 to 1973.

International Way

Accommodation: Go Africa Adventures, 4160 SE International Way, Suite #D106, Portland, OR **97222**, GLD, Gay Lesbian Directory

House: Waldo Rasmussen (1928-2013) joined the Museum of Modern Art staff in 1954. He was appointed the director of the Department of Circulating Exhibitions in 1962, and then director of the International Program in 1969. He organized the first exhibitions of modern American art to be seen overseas. At his retirement in 1994, in an oral interview, he commented on the LGBT legacy at MOMA, The number of distinguished homosexuals at the Museum...is a very distinguished group, beginning, after all, with Philip Johnson, but also the culture of homophobia: The contribution gay men have made to the Museum has been very important, and there was a time in...probably in the late 1940s, there was an attack on the Museum for the number of gay men and lesbian women on the staff, and that this was coloring the program. Waldo Rasmussen, 1994. In the 1940s Waldo Rasmussen's family lived at 4264 N Juneau St, Portland, OR **97203**. A native of Tekoa, WA, whose father was a Native American, Waldo worked at the Portland Art Museum while he was at Reed, where he earned a BA in general literature and graduated Phi Beta Kappa. He attended graduate school at the Institute of Fine Arts in New York and then joined the Museum of Modern Art, where he worked on the preparation and circulation of traveling exhibitions and became director of the department of circulating exhibitions in 1962. The experience, he said, made me understand what it felt like to see exhibitions and original works of art for the first time after having seen them in reproductions only— away from the center. It's shaped the way I've always worked. When the International Program became an independent department in 1969, Waldo was appointed to direct it. He organized the first exhibitions of modern American art to be sent abroad, an experience that he cited among the high points of his career. His landmark exhibition was Two Decades of American Paintings 1945–65 and American Abstract Expressionists, and he assembled the most extensive survey of modern Latin American art in the exhibition Latin American Artists of the Twentieth Century. He retired in 1994. In addition to his work in art, he enjoyed classical music, dance and theatre performances, and film. Waldo and Gail Marie (Geraldine) Preston were married in 1953 and had a son and daughter. Waldo Rasmussen died on August 15, 2013, in New York City, from complications of Alzheimer's disease. Waldo was survived by his life companion and spouse, John Dowling. At Rasmussen's death, Dowling published a simple obituaty in the New York Time: ASMUSSEN--Waldo. Sept. 16, 1928 - Aug. 15, 2013 In loving memory of Waldo, always with me. John Dowling.

House: Deborah Betron is the Principal Broker at Bridgetown Realty. Once founded, Bridgetown Realty ended up operating for five years without making any money. Although founded in 1979, it was not until the 1990s that Betron saw her business surge. She lives at 16262 SE Katie Ct, Portland, OR **97267**.

Restaurant/Bar:
Florida Room, 435 N Killingsworth St, Portland, OR **97217**
Blend Coffee, 2710 N Killingsworth St, Portland, OR **97217**

LGBTQ friendly bookstore: One of the only 13 self-described feminist bookstores still in existence today in the US and Canada is In Other Words (14 NE Killingsworth St, Portland, OR **97211**). In Other Words was founded in 1993 by Johanna Brenner, Kathryn Tetrick and Catherine Sameh. It is a non-profit, volunteer-run, feminist community center with a mission to inspire and cultivate feminist communities and nurture social justice. Its bookstore serves as a lending library and a venue for feminist events. It's also where the feminist bookstore sketches are filmed for the TV show Portlandia. 50 Queer Bookstores Which You Need to Visit this Pride Month, by BookRiot, 2018.

Lincoln Street

Religious Building: Eastwood Community Church, 3950 SE Lincoln St, Portland, OR **97214**, included in the Damron Address Book from 1977 to 1979.

Lombard Street

Eagle Portland, Creative Commons Licenses, via Wikimedia Commons

Restaurant/Bar: Eagle Portland, 835 N Lombard St, Portland, OR **97217**

Main Street

Restaurant/Bar: Cellar, 2210 SW Main St, Portland, OR **97205**, included in the Damron Address Book in 1971.

Martin Luther King Jr Boulevard

Restaurant/Bar: Local Lounge, 3536 NE Martin Luther King Jr Blvd, Portland, OR **97212**

Mill Street

Restaurant/Bar: Ben & Jerry's, 510 SW Mill St, Portland, OR **97201**

Mississippi Avenue

Restaurant/Bar: Mississippi Pizza, 3552 N Mississippi Ave, Portland, OR **97227**

LGBTQ friendly bookstore:
Reading Frenzy (3628 N Mississippi Ave, Portland, OR **97227**) is an independent press bookshop and event space that's been offering up radness since 1994.
Another Read Through, 3932 N Mississippi Ave, Portland, OR **97227**, 56 Queer-Owned Bookstores to Support, by Oprah Daily, 2021. As of 2021 it's closed.

Restaurant/Bar: Mississippi Studios and Bar, 3939 N Mississippi Ave, Portland, OR **97227**

Store: Rudy's Barbershop, 3956 N Mississippi Ave, Portland, OR **97227**

Q Center, Creative Commons Licenses, via Wikimedia Commons

LGBTQ Center: Q Center, 4115 N Mississippi Ave, Portland, OR **97217**

Morrison Street

Restaurant/Bar:
Holocene, 1001 SE Morrison St, Portland, OR **97214**
Crush Bar, 1400 SE Morrison St, Portland, OR **97214**, has been named among the Amazing Gay Bars Around The World To Visit Before You Die, by BuzzFeed, 2019.
Hot Patata, SW Morrison St & SW 13th Ave, Portland, OR **97205**, included in the Damron Address Book in 1980.

Accommodation: The Nines, a Luxury Collection Hotel, 525 SW Morrison St, Portland, OR **97204**

Club: Olympic Sauna Baths, 359 SW Morrison St, Portland, OR **97204**, included in the Damron Address Book from 1973 to 1977.

Naito Parkway

Restaurant/Bar: Sonny Bowl (SW Morrison St & SW Naito Pkwy, Portland, OR **97204**) has been named among the Best destinations for vegans in the world. As of 2023 it's closed.

Accommodation: Portland Marriott Downtown Waterfront (1401 SW Naito Pkwy, Portland, OR **97201**), TAG Approved LGBTQ friendly accommodation.

Northrup Street

House: Mary Lee Nitschke (1941-2017) was born in Beaver, OK, to Daniel Nitschke and Ruth Davis Nitschke. Raised on a ranch near Perryton, TX, she never lost her affinity for open spaces and life lived close to the land. She was educated at Wichita State University, KS, and Michigan State University where she was awarded a doctorate in psychology in 1978. Dr. Nitschke held positions in the Psychology Department at Concordia College, Mooorhead, MN, and Linfield College, Portland Campus. Reflecting her varied academic interests, she taught a range of courses, including life-span development, health psychology, perspectives on gender and a developmental view of sexuality. After her retirement, she was named Professor Emerita by Linfield College. Her life-long focus on behavioral observation of animals informed much of her work outside of academia. She practiced as an Animal Behavior Society Certified Applied Animal BehavioriSt Further, she directed the Owner Trained Individual Service Dog Program with Animal School Behavior Services (2364 NW Northrup St, Portland, OR **97210**). Dr. Nitschke also consulted nationally on training programs, pet product development, research in animal behavior and litigation involving human-animal interactions. She held professional memberships in several organizations, including the American Veterinary Society of Animal Behavior, American Psychological Society, Interdisciplinary Forum of Applied Animal Behavior, New Guinea Singing Dog Conservation Society and Animals and Society Institute. Dr. Nitschke is survived by her partner, Marian Tews.

Oak Street

Restaurant/Bar:
Valentino's, 555 SW Oak St, Portland, OR **97204**, included in the Damron Address Book in 1977.
Tel & Tel Tavern, 820 SW Oak St, Portland, OR **97205**, Included in the 1964 Directory. Included in the 1964 and 1965 Guild Guide. Later Annex Stereo Room or Annex Derek's, included in the Damron Address Book from 1965 to 1972. Later Derek's Tavern, Included in the 1975 All Lavender International Gay Guide. Later Family Zoo. Included in the Damron Address Book from 1973 to 1980. A visit to the popular gay bar, the Family Zoo is enough to reveal how friendly the animals can be. No one is so got up as they might be in a larger city (Portland has 378,000 people). The instant you walk into this big, gemütlich bar, you feel the difference; it could be a ski lodge—all it lacks are the fire, the buttered rum and the dozing St. Bernard. Edmund White, States of Desire (1980).

Park Avenue

Club: Club Continental, 531 SW Park Ave, Portland, OR **97205**, included in the Damron Address Book from 1978 to 1980.

Restaurant/Bar:
Rafters, SW Park Ave & SW Yamhill St, Portland, OR **97205**, included in the Damron Address Book from 1977 to 1980.
Zorba the Greek, 626 SW Park Ave, Portland, OR **97205**, included in the Damron Address Book from 1972 to 1979.
Embers Lounge, 739 SW Park Ave, Portland, OR **97205**, included in the Damron Address Book from 1975 to 1980.
Hamburger Mary's, 840 SW Park Ave, Portland, OR **97205**, included in the Damron Address Book from 1977 to 1980.

Portland Art Museum

Queer Artists: *The Portland Art Museum in Portland, was founded in 1892, making it the oldest art museum on the West Coast and seventh oldest in the US.*

Address: 1219 SW Park Ave, Portland, OR 97205

Notable queer elements:
John Singer Sargent (1856-1925). Assistant Sketch for the Triumph of Maria Dei Medici (Louvre), (painting, 1877), Franciscan Monk in the Garden of Gethsemane, (painting, 1905-1906).
Marsden Hartley (1877-1943). After the Storm, (painting, 1938).
Thomas Eakins (1844-1916). The Oarsmen, (painting, ca. 1873).

Pine Street

Accommodation: Embassy Suites by Hilton Portland Downtown (319 SW Pine St, Portland, OR **97204**) is located in the heart of Portland's business district and for years, served as the largest and most modern hotel in the Pacific Northwest. Built in a Neo-Classical style by architect Phillip Gevurtz, this grand hotel offers 276 spacious guestrooms and suites with most rooms boasting two outside facing windows for plenty of natural light and gorgeous city views of Downtown Portland. The hotel amenities include an indoor swimming pool, spa, and fitness room. Food and beverage outlet offerings include Mothers Bistro, an iconic Portland restaurant, and Kingsland Kitchen, a British eatery. Formerly known as The Multnomah Hotel, this historic hotel has hosted nine U.S. Presidents from Theodore Roosevelt to Richard Nixon, although President Truman was the only president to stay the night. Embassy Suites by Hilton Portland Downtown, a member of Historic Hotels of America since 2016, dates back to 1912.

Reeder Road

Gay Village: A lot of gay life in the Northwest gets lived out of doors. In the summer Portland gay men ride horses, camp and climb in the Cascades, or sunbathe and frolic in the nude on Sauvie Island (38798 NW Reeder Rd, Portland, OR **97231**), thirteen miles east of Portland, where the Willamette flows into the Columbia. The island is a small farming community and also an animal shelter for wild turkeys, geese, deer and elk. Edmund White, States of Desire (1980).

River Drive

Accommodation: Hyatt House Portland/Downtown (2080 S River Dr, Portland, OR **97201**) is a 3 minute walk from Poets Beach on the banks of the Willamette River and 1 mile from the shops, restaurants and events at Pioneer Courthouse Square. Part of World Rainbow Hotels (WRH), Lesbian and Gay Welcoming Hotels.

River Parkway

Accommodation: Residence Inn Portland Downtown/RiverPlace (2115 SW River Pkwy, Portland, OR **97201**), LGBTQ friendly.

Rosa Parks Way

Restaurant/Bar: Grindhouse Coffee, 1934 N Rosa Parks Way C, Portland, OR **97217**

Russell Street

Restaurant/Bar:
Sloan's Tavern, 36 N Russell St, Portland, OR **97227**
Mint 820 (816 N Russell St, Portland, OR **97227**), lesbian owned.
Russell Street BBQ (325 NE Russell St, Portland, OR **97212**), don't be fooled—this joint has loads of vegetarian options.

Sacajawea Boulevard

Park: Washington Park, near Lewis & Clark Monument, 6200 SW Sacajawea Blvd, Portland, OR **97205**, included in the Damron Address Book from 1972 to 1980.

Salmon Street

Restaurant/Bar: Castaways, 901 SW Salmon St, Portland, OR **97205**, included in the Damron Address Book in 1975.

House: James Beard (1903-1985) was born in Portland, OR, in 1903 to Elizabeth and John Beard. His mother operated the Gladstone Hotel (2223 SW Salmon St, Portland, OR **97205**), and his father worked at the city's customs house. Beard studied locally at Reed College, but in 1922, was expelled from the school for homosexual liaisons with other students and with a professor. (Ironically, in 1974, he received an honorary degree from Reed, after he had become a celebrity.) After the scandal, Beard took voice lessons in London from Enrico Caruso's coach and later returned to Portland, where he pursued a career as an actor. Eventually, Beard relocated to New York City, where he achieved fame as the author of numerous best-selling cookbooks.

Sandy Boulevard

Restaurant/Bar: Escape Bar & Grill (9004 NE Sandy Blvd, Portland, OR **97220**), lesbian owned by DJ Wildfire (Jenn Davis) and her wife Armida Army (Armida Hanlon).

Schuyler Street

Shattuck Road

Oldest Building in America: Tigard Rogers House, 1855, 4504 SW Shattuck Rd, Portland, OR **97221**. The Tigard Rogers House was built by pioneer Andrew Tigard, whose brother Wilson founded the nearby town of Tigard. The property was a modest, frontier-era home. It has a small, gabled roof with an attached shed roof.

Skyline Boulevard

Cemetery: Keith Christopher (1957-1998), a singer/songwriter, actor and AIDS activist, made television history when he appeared as the first openly gay, HIV-positive performer to portray an HIV-positive gay character on NBC's Another World. He was next invited to create the role of Wyatt Sanders, a gay HIV counselor, on the daytime drama The Guiding Light. Christopher dedicated the last years of his life to being a spokesperson for Gay Men's Health Crisis. At GMHC's 1997 AIDS Walk in Central Park, Christopher was a keynote speaker, along with Susan Sarandon, Tim Robbins and Rosie Perez. His song One People was commissioned by the United Nations Environmental Project, and Pieces of Lives was written for and performed by Christopher at the first display of the Names Project Memorial Quilt in New York City. At the time of his death in 1998 he was nearing completion of his first CD, Naked Truth, posthumously released by Significant Other Records. Keith Christopher died of AIDS in New York at the age of 40 on February 23, 1998 and is buried at Mount Calvary Cemetery (333 SW Skyline Blvd, Portland, OR **97221**).

Stark Street

Restaurant/Bar: Food Fight! Grocery, 1217 SE Stark St, Portland, OR **97214**, named among the Best destinations for vegans in the world.

Starky's, Creative Commons Licenses, via Wikimedia Commons

Restaurant/Bar:

Starky's Restaurant and Bar (2913 SE Stark St, Portland, OR **97214**) was a gay bar and restaurant in Portland's Kerns neighborhood. Established in 1984, the venue became a fixture in Portland's gay community before closing in 2015. It hosted LGBT events and served as a gathering space for leather enthusiasts and the Oregon Bears, among other groups. Starky's received a generally positive reception and was most known for its Bloody Marys, brunch, and outdoor seating. Starky's was established in 1984 and housed in a building that was constructed in 1935. Starky's was known for its patio and outdoor seating, in addition to serving American cuisine, including burgers and steak. Joe Waldroff and Greg Simshaw purchased the bar in September 2004. In 2015, Willamette Week described the establishment as a patioed mountain chalet with homestyle food that seems as domestic as Grandpa's house, with busy Thursday karaoke, bottomless mimosas at its essential Sunday brunch, and a charmingly dirty-avuncular bartender who seems to have an answer for everything. Following its closure, the newspaper's Matthew Korfage called Starky's a little mountain chalet and friendly little neighborhood bar catering to longtime regulars in the gay community with raucous karaoke, home-style food and a Sunday brunch that offered up bottomless cheap-bubbly mimosas unless you misbehaved. Beginning in late 2014, Waldroff and Simshaw listed the building and business for sale intermittently, and sold Starky's for $1.2 million in March 2015. The duo planned to retire and expressed a willingness to sell the rights to the name and business. The bar and restaurant closed on September 13, 2015, after operating for 28 years. The building that housed Starky's was demolished during November–December 2015, and was replaced by a three-story apartment building. Starky's served as a gathering space for groups such as Blackout Leather Productions, a nonprofit organization and volunteer group of leather enthusiasts in Oregon and southwest Washington, and the Oregon Bears. Historically, Starky's sold tickets to Portland Gay Men's Chorus performances and hosted (or was a starting location for) gay pride events. The venue also hosted special events such as: a 2009 celebration and fundraiser to send eight musicians from the Rose City Gay Freedom Band to perform at Barack Obama's inauguration, a 2013 PQ Monthly press party, Oregon Bears' 2013 car wash fundraiser for Our House and other nonprofits, the Red Dress Party, and Civic Pride, which was presented by City Club of Portland in June 2014 to commemorate gay pride and LGBT Pride Month. The latter event featured guests from local organizations including: Basic Rights Oregon, Cascade AIDS Project, Equity Foundation, GLSEN Oregon, Oregon Gay and Lesbian Law Association, Oregon Safe Schools and Communities Coalition, PFLAG Portland and the PFLAG Black Chapter, Portland Latino Gay Pride, and Rosetown Ramblers. In 2013, Jaime Dunkle of the Daily Vanguard, Portland State University's student newspaper, included Starky's as one of the Top 5 Gay Clubs/Bars in Portland, writing: For maxing and relaxing: Starky's is the best outdoor gay bar. Word on the street is that they make a killer Bloody Mary and have a yummy brunch menu. They're old school and have been in Portland since 1984. Check it out if you want to get away from the throbbing, meat-market discos. In 2014, GoLocalPDX contributor Byron

Beck included Starky's in his list of the Top 12 Gay Clubs in Portland, writing: Starky's is for those who remember that brunch is best served on Sunday with a Bloody Mary. This true original is more restaurant than bar but that doesn't stop people from coming here for some of the stiffest drinks in town.

Pied Piper (1217 SW Stark St, Portland, OR **97205**), later Riddles and Stark Street Station, is the oldest continuously operating Portland gay bar, operating under various names and owners from the late 1960s. Included in the Damron Address Book in 1971. In the same block is located The Crystal Hotel (1201-1217 SW Stark St, Portland, OR **97205**, formerly Hotel Alma, National Register of Historic Places: 09000706, 2009). The property is operated by McMenamins. Built in 1911 as the Hotel Alma, the building housed a hotel above and auto-focused business on busy Burnside. After WWII hosting the Club Mecca and later the Desert Room, which became a hallmark of vice within a US Senate hearing. By 1978, the building housed a gay bathhouse (Club Portland), and a gay bar, later known as Silverado, until the building was sold in 2007. After an extensive renovation and restoration, McMenamins opened the hotel on May 3, 2011.

Willamette Boulevard

School: The University of Portland (also referred to as UP, 5000 N Willamette Blvd, Portland, OR **97203**) is a private Roman Catholic university located in Portland, OR. It is affiliated with the Congregation of Holy Cross, which also founded UP's sister school the University of Notre Dame. Founded in 1901, UP has a student body of about 4,000 students. UP is ranked 8th in the west for Regional Universities in 2015 by US News & World Report. Notable queer alumni and faculty: Paul Winfield (1941-2004); Mel White (born 1940).

Taylor Street

LGBTQ friendly bookstore:
Scorpio's Adult Bookstore, 209 SW Taylor St, Portland, OR **97204**, included in the Damron Address Book from 1974 to 1980.
Book Bin, 213 SW Taylor St, Portland, OR **97204**, included in the Damron Address Book from 1974 to 1975.

Theatre: Eros Theatre, 314 SW Taylor St, Portland, OR **97204**, included in the Damron Address Book from 1974 to 1979.

LGBTQ friendly bookstore: Looking Glass Bookstore, 318 SW Taylor St, Portland, OR **97204**, active in 1990.

Restaurant/Bar:
Red Carpet at Greyhound Bus Depot, SW Taylor St & SW 6th Ave, Portland, OR **97204**, included in the Damron Address Book from 1966 to 1972.
Happy Hare, 1730 SW Taylor St, Portland, OR **97205**, included in the Damron Address Book from 1965 to 1968.

Wasco Street

Accommodation: Courtyard by Marriott Portland Downtown/Convention Center (435 NE Wasco St, Portland, OR **97232**), TAG Approved LGBTQ friendly accommodation.

House: Harold William Rebarich (1927-2006) was born in Omaha, NE, and raised there. He served in the US Army, received an honorable discharge in 1947, and settled in Southern California where he met John Quitman Lynch. In the 1950s, Lynch and Rebarich moved to Greenwich Village, NY, where Lynch pursued his painting and was even offered tutelage by painter Paul Cadmus. By the early 1960s, they were back in Long Beach, where they remained for the next 25-plus years. In 1963, Rebarich joined the US Postal Service, where he worked for the next 26 years. In the mid-to-late 1980s, Lynch moved to Portland to care for his elderly aunt. After her death, he inherited the home at 3656 NE Wasco St, Portland, OR **97232**, and lived there the rest of his life. Although Lynch and Rebarich visited one another, Rebarich remained at their house in Long Beach, CA. Lynch and Rebarich had a side business selling antiques and collectibles both in Long Beach and in Portland. Rebarich died in November 2006 and Lynch in December 2009.

Washington Street

Restaurant/Bar:
Timber Topper Lounge at Washington Hotel, SW Washington St & SW 12th Ave, Portland, OR **97205**, included in the Damron Address Book in 1970.
Olive Garden Italian, 9830 SE Washington St #205, Portland, OR **97216**
Elephant and Castle, 201 SW Washington St, Portland, OR **97204**, included in the 1975 All Lavender International Gay Guide.
Bohemian, 910 SW Washington St, Portland, OR **97205**, included in the Damron Address Book in 1971.
Flight 181, 1116 SW Washington St, Portland, OR **97205**, included in the Damron Address Book in 1978.
Later New Ritz Disco, included in the Damron Address Book in 1978.
The Buick Café (1239 SW Washington St, Portland, OR **97205**) was a lesbian bar active from the 1940s to the 1950s. It was the hangout for a group of lesbians who congregated at the Music Hall nightclub at Tenth and Stark.

LGBTQ friendly bookstore: A Woman's Place Bookstore, 1300 SW Washington St, Portland, OR **97205**, was a feminist bookstore active in the 1980s.

Water Avenue

Restaurant/Bar: Clarklewis Restaurant, 1001 SE Water Ave, Portland, OR **97214**, Top LGBTQIA+ Owned and Operated Restaurants in America, OpenTable 2021

Woodstock Boulevard

School: Reed College (3203 SE Woodstock Blvd, Portland, OR **97202**) is a private liberal arts college in southeast Portland, OR. Founded in 1908, Reed is a residential college with a campus in Portland's Eastmoreland neighborhood, featuring architecture based on the Tudor-Gothic style, and a forested canyon nature preserve at its center. **Notable queer alumni and faculty:** Guy Sircello (1936-1992), Helen Sandoz (1920–1987), James Beard (1903-1985), Robert Chesley (1943–1990), Tee Corinne (1951-2005), William Dickey (1928–1994).

Yamhill Street

Historic District: Camp Street, SW Yamhill St, Portland, OR **97204**, between 4th & 6th, included in the Damron Address Book from 1972 to 1980.

4th Street

Blue Mouse Theatre

Theatre: Blue Mouse Theatre, 626 SW 4th Street, Portland, OR **97204**, included in the Damron Address Book from 1973 to 1978. This partially excerpted story appeared as the article with the nifty title: THE SAD DEMISE OF THE DESPONDENT RODENT by Loren Shisler in Marquee magazine of the Theatre Historical Soc. in 3rd Qtr. Of 1977, along with six photos. The Blue Mouse wasn't an architectural jewel, though at the time of its opening as the Capitol in July of 1928 it did have a pleasant

Spanish motif with the exterior, interior, and furnishings very well coordinated, and of excellent design. It was of about 850 seats with a small balcony. In 1912, a rather pleasant and pleasing little theatre opened at 11th and Washington Streets in downtown Portland. The name of the theatre was the Globe. It was later taken over and completely remodeled by John Hamrick and opened as the Blue Mouse on November 28th, 1921. In each Northwest city, when the Hamrick chain came in and established themselves, their first house was always called the Blue Mouse. It is interesting to note the origin of the name. One story is that Mr. and Mrs. Hamrick were visiting in London where they attended a musical play titled The Blue Mouse. They were so entranced by the play that they thereafter named their theatres Blue Mouse. There was also a Shubert production of The Blue Mouse. We now have the Blue Mouse launched on its career. The first sound picture in Portland was presented at the Blue Mouse in 1926: John Barrymore in Don Juan. About 1936, the Hamrick-Evergreen Theatres closed the original Blue Mouse and later in October of 1940 Mr. Paul Forsythe would re-open the theatre. He presented family films and kiddie matinees. He was rewarded with success and a host of good patrons, young and old who became loyal Blue Mouse fans. In the meantime, the Capitol Theatre had gone through a period of second run pictures, then vaudeville acts, then an era of strip-tease. It is said that the famous stripper Tempest Storm once for a short time owned and operated the Capitol. The theatre had been closed for some time by 1958 when the original Blue Mouse faced eviction when the property was sold and the building was to be torn down. Mr. Forsythe then removed the Blue Mouse sign from the old house and moved it and his operation over to the Capitol in August of that year. There was, however, one great difference in the operation of the new Blue Mouse as compared to the old situation. Whereas the original Blue Mouse had been located Uptown quite close to a good middle class apartment district, his new Blue Mouse was downtown in a district of old, cheaper hotels and small businesses. Consequently, some policy changes were necessary. The staff became the shepherd and confidant of literally hundreds of lonely souls and habitues of skid row. The theatre became their theatre and they loved the staff that worked there and continued their support of the theatre for many years. In 1977 the Blue Mouse Block was to make way for a huge parking facility. There was a faint outcry to save the Blue Mouse but even if it had been a mighty roar, it was to no more avail than the Save the Fox campaign was in San Francisco in 1963. So now the familiar Blue Mouse sign that had been part of the Portland scene for so long has come down in 1977, the building demolished, and the unusual name no longer is a part of the world of the movie theatre.

1st-68th Avenue

Restaurant/Bar: Harbor Tavern, 736 SW 1st Ave, Portland, OR **97204**, included in the 1964 and 1965 Guild Guide. Included in the 1964 Directory.

Theatre: Sultan Theatre, 1313 SW 1st Ave, Portland, OR **97201**, included in the Damron Address Book in 1974.

Accommodation: Model Inn, 1563 SW 1st Ave, Portland, OR **97201**, included in the Damron Address Book from 1965 to 1969. Included in the 1975 All Lavender International Gay Guide.

Dahl & Penne's, 604 SW 2nd Ave, Portland, OR **97204**, included in the Damron Address Book from 1968 to 1980. Included in the 1975 All Lavender International Gay Guide.

Hobo's | Restaurant & Lounge (120 NW 3rd Ave, Portland, OR **97209**) has been named among the Greatest Gay Bars in the World by Out.com, 2013.

Dema's Tavern, 208 NW 3rd Ave, Portland, OR **97209**, included in the Damron Address Book from 1972 to 1975. Later Darcelle XV Showplace or Tavern, Drag, Cabaret, Dinner, included in the Damron Address Book from 1976 to 1980. It has been named among The 25 Best LGBTQ Bars and Nightclubs in the US, 2019, Matador Network. Named after and owned by Portland's most famous drag queen, Darcelle XV has been busy making drag more mainstream in the city since the 1960s. It's no surprise that the nation's oldest performing drag queen would create such an immersive experience for all of her guests — although the atmosphere has changed over the years. From one-man shows to burlesque and drag shows, this club is one of the best in the country for its ability to entertain any audience — and to draw a crowd of regulars intent on celebrating their lives out in the open. GLD, Gay Lesbian Directory

Dirty Duck, Creative Commons Licenses, via Wikimedia Commons

The Dirty Duck building, or Dirty Duck Tavern building, was located at 421-439 NW 3rd Ave, Portland, OR **97209**, in Portland's Old Town Chinatown neighborhood. Originally called as the Kiernan Building, the one-story structure earned its nickname from Gail's Dirty Duck Tavern, a gay bar that served as a tenant for 25 years. The one-story building was constructed during 1916–1917. It became a contributing structure to the Portland New Chinatown–Japantown Historic District. Bud Clark, who Portland Monthly described as a strong straight ally of the gay community, held campaign events at the bar, and celebrated his victory there after being elected mayor in 1984. In September 1999, the Portland Development Commission (PDC) purchased the property as part of a plan to redevelop the entire block on which the building stood. In 2002, PDC earmarked $2 million for the Blanchet House of Hospitality, a homeless shelter neighboring the Dirty Duck, to construct a new facility at a different location. In return, Blanchet House would deed its property, at the intersection of Northwest Fourth Avenue and Glisan Street, to the commission. However, these plans changed, and before the land swap deal was finalized in 2008, parties agreed that Blanchet House would receive $2 million, acquire the Dirty Duck property, and build a new facility on the same block. Demolition and construction of the new facility was estimated to cost $9–10 million. In November 2008, PDC described the building as functionally and physically obsolete, and in need of a major investment to extend its useful life. In August 2009, members of the city's Historic Landmarks Commission (HLC) criticized plans to demolish the Dirty Duck. The commission held a demolition review in January

2010; their feedback was sent to the Portland Bureau of Development Services, who then submitted a recommendation to Portland City Council, who would ultimately decide the building's fate. In February 2010, Portland City Council approved the building's demolition by a four-to-one vote, despite HLC's recommendation for its preservation. The building housed the gay bar Gail's Dirty Duck Tavern. Mama Bernice, or simply Mama, purchased the bar in 1984. According to her son, who acquired the bar following her death in 1986, she wanted to socialize with the railroaders and seamen, whom she referred to as bluebirds, and who were already patrons of the establishment. She insisted that the bar retain its name and clientele. Mama helped establish the Oregon Bears in 1995, which began with 13 members and has since grown to more than 300, becoming one of the largest bear groups in the US. The bar was the official home of the Oregon Bears until 2007, when they voted to move to Eagle Portland because of its larger size and greater number of services. In 2007, Willamette Week's Byron Beck described Dirty Duck as the quirkiest queer tavern in town and a homebase hole-in-the-wall for a group of gay men with beer guts and bushy brows. Blackout Leather Productions, a nonprofit organization and volunteer group of leather enthusiasts in Oregon and southwest Washington, recognized Dirty Duck Tavern as the Business of the Year in 2004 and 2008, at their annual Rose & Thorn Awards. The bar closed on August 23, 2009, after operating for 25 years.

Wilde Oscar's, 318 SW 3rd Ave, Portland, OR **97204**, included in the Damron Address Book from 1978 to 1980.

Oldest Restaurant in the State and Oldest Bar in the State: Huber's, 411 SW 3rd Ave, Portland, OR **97204**. One of the hallmarks of Huber's in Portland after it was established in 1879 was the free turkey sandwich and coleslaw patrons would get with a drink. The place is still known for its turkey, as well as for drinks.

LGBTQ friendly bookstore:

Pink Cat Adult Books, 523 SW 3rd Ave, Portland, OR **97204**, included in the Damron Address Book from 1974 to 1977.

San Fransisco Book Store, 725 SW 3rd Ave, Portland, OR **97204**, included in the Damron Address Book in 1977.

Accommodation: AC Hotel by Marriott Portland Downtown (888 SW 3rd Ave, Portland, OR **97204**), TAG Approved LGBTQ friendly accommodation.

LGBTQ friendly bookstore:

Dave's Bookstore, 826 SW 3rd Ave, Portland, OR **97204**, included in the Damron Address Book from 1978 to 1979.

Peek-A-Rama Book Store, 834 SW 3rd Ave, Portland, OR **97204**, included in the Damron Address Book from 1976 to 1979.

Sin City Adult Books, 838 SW 3rd Ave, Portland, OR **97204**, included in the Damron Address Book from 1977 to 1980.

Restaurant/Bar:

Dinty Moore's, 924 SW 3rd Ave, Portland, OR **97204**, included in the Damron Address Book from 1970 to 1979. Included in the 1975 All Lavender International Gay Guide.

Mama Bernice's, 1228 SW 3rd Ave, Portland, OR **97204**, included in the Damron Address Book from 1965 to 1966.

LGBTQ friendly bookstore: Hardtime Adult Book Store, 926 SW 3rd Ave, Portland, OR **97204**, included in the Damron Address Book from 1974 to 1980.

Club: Aero Vapor Steam Baths, 1237 or 1239 SW 3rd Ave, Portland, OR **97204**, included in the 1964 and 1965 Guild Guide. Included in the 1964 Directory. Included in the Damron Address Book from 1965 to 1972. Included in the 1975 All Lavender International Gay Guide.

Club Northwest, 217 NW 4th Ave, Portland, OR **97209**, was a lesbian bar. Included in the Damron Address Book from 1969 to 1973. Later Magic Garden, a strip-club, included in the Damron Address Book from 1974 to 1978. As of 2022, it's still open.
Denny's, SW 4th Ave & SW Lincoln St, Portland, OR **97201**, included in the Damron Address Book from 1977 to 1980.
W.C.'s or Water Closet Lounge, 426 SW 4th Ave, Portland, OR **97204**, included in the Damron Address Book from 1976 to 1977.

Club: Vapors, 509 SW 4th Ave, Portland, OR **97204**, included in the Damron Address Book in 1979.

Restaurant/Bar: Buddy's Post, 926 SW 4th Ave, Portland, OR **97204**, included in the Damron Address Book from 1965 to 1969.

Queer Architects: Dublin House Restaurant at the Georgia Pacific Building, SW 5th Ave & SW Salmon St, Portland, OR **97204**, designed by Roland Terry (1969)

Restaurant/Bar:
Yard House, 888 SW 5th Ave #2004, Portland, OR **97204**
Sportsman's Inn, 15 SW 6th Ave, Portland, OR **97204**, included in the Damron Address Book in 1974.

Accommodation: Hilton Portland Downtown (921 SW 6th Ave, Portland, OR **97204**), TAG Approved LGBTQ friendly accommodation.

Restaurant/Bar:
Tiki Tavern, 1728 SE 7th Ave, Portland, OR **97214**, included in the Damron Address Book from 1974 to 1976.
White Owl Social Club, 1305 SE 8th Ave, Portland, OR **97214**
Mamie's Coffee Shop, 302 SW 9th Ave., Portland, OR **97205**, included in the Damron Address Book in 1979.
Fiddler's Three, 728 SW 9th Ave., Portland, OR **97205**, included in the Damron Address Book from 1969 to 1970. Later Roman's Tavern, included in the Damron Address Book from 1971 to 1973. Later Focal Point Tavern, included in the Damron Address Book from 1974 to 1980.
Ben & Jerry's, 301 NW 10th Ave, Portland, OR **97209**

Store: These self-described modern-day, female Robin Hoods raiding men's closets and maniacally dispensing blazers, cardigans, wingtips and bowlers launched their dapper-tomboy brand in early 2013. Models and fans include queer icons like Megan Rapinoe, Kate Moennig, Ellen page and Evan Rachel Wood. Founders Julia Parsley and Emma McIlroy cashed in their 401ks to start the company, a labor of love that eventually came to earn the team $4.5 million in capital to develop more private-label products and build more stores like the one at 404 SW 10th Ave, Portland, OR **97205**.

Restaurant/Bar: Schneidermann's Music Hall, 413 SW 10th Ave, Portland, OR **97205**, opened in 1937 to provide English music hall-style entertainment featuring big name vaudeville acts. Included in the Swasarnt Neft's Gay Guides for 1950. In the late 1940s the hall began booking female impersonators and drew a lesbian and gay male audience. Performers included Lynn Carter and Jerry Kline.

Nortonia Hotel

Heterodoxy Club: *The Nortonia Hotel, which opened in 1908, is now known as the Mark Spencer, a very comfortable hotel in the Theatre District. Even in the early days,* *it was Portland's home-away-from-home for many of the artists who performed in theatric productions. Modern-day theatric artists continue to call the Mark Spencer home while they're in Portland.* TAG Approved LGBTQ friendly accommodation.

Address: The Mark Spencer Hotel, 409 SW 11th Ave, Portland, OR 97205

The Nortonia Hotel, Portland, Vintage Postcard

Place

In Portland Marie Equi met Harriet Speckart, a younger woman, with whom she began a long-term lesbian relationship. Speckart, the niece of Olympia Brewing Company founder, Leopold Schmidt, rebuffed her family's entreaties to abandon her relationship with Equi and struggled to claim her inheritance. They moved together at the Nortonia Hotel. For several years, the Nortonia was called the Bowers. In 1911, H.C. Bowers became the President and Manager. He had managed the Portland Hotel for 17 years. By 1914, Bowers moved on to the Multnomah Hotel and the name was changed back to Nortonia. In 1966, the Hotel was remodeled and the name was changed to Mark Spencer.

Life

Who: Marie Equi (April 7, 1872 – July 13, 1952) and Harriet Frances Speckart (1883-1927)

Marie Equi was a medical doctor in the American West devoted to providing care to working-class and poor patients. She regularly provided birth control information and abortions at a time when both were illegal. She became a political activist and advocated civic and economic reforms, including women's right to vote and an eight-hour workday. In 1892 Equi joined her high school girlfriend, Bessie Holcomb, on an Oregon homestead along the Columbia River. Equi and Holcomb lived a quiet life as close companions in a small house on several rocky acres outside the small city of The Dalles. Their relationship lasted from 1892 until 1901. In 1897 the pair moved to San Francisco, where Equi began studying medicine. She completed two years of coursework, first at the Physicians & Surgeons Medical College and then at the University of California Medical Department. She relocated to Portland, OR – without Bessie Holcomb – and completed her studies at the University of Oregon Medical Department in 1903. She undertook the longest lesbian relationship of her life in 1905 after meeting a younger woman, Harriet Speckart. After ten years of sharing a life together, Equi and Speckart adopted an infant girl, Mary, because Speckart wanted to raise a child. As an adult, Mary recalled that she had called Speckart ma and Equi da since everyone called Equi Doc. In later years the two women separated but remained close until Speckart's death in 1927. When birth control advocate Margaret Sanger lectured in Portland in 1916, Equi became smitten with her. She later wrote letters to Sanger that referred to sexual intimacy between them during Sanger's earlier visit. Archivist Judith Schwartz has described Equi's letters to Sanger as love letters. In 1918, Equi was convicted under the Sedition Act for speaking against US involvement in WWI. She was sentenced to a three-year term at San Quentin State Prison. She was the only known lesbian and radical to be incarcerated at the prison.

Accommodation: Sentinel Hotel (614 SW 11th Ave, Portland, OR 97205). Part of World Rainbow Hotels (WRH), Lesbian and Gay Welcoming Hotels.

Restaurant/Bar:
Chocolate Moose, 1716 SW 11th Ave, Portland, OR 97201, included in the Damron Address Book in 1965. Included in the 1975 All Lavender International Gay Guide.
Red and Black Café, 400 SE 12th Ave, Portland, OR 97214

Club Portland, Creative Commons Licenses, via Wikimedia Commons

Club:
Majestic Hotel & Baths, 303 SW 12th Ave, Portland, OR **97205**, included in the Damron Address Book from 1973 to 1980. Later Club Portland, a gay bathhouse in the historic Hotel Alma building. The building was later renovated into the Crystal Hotel.

Workout Steam Baths & Gym, 531 SW 12th Ave, Portland, OR **97205**, included in the Damron Address Book from 1968 to 1977. Included in the 1975 All Lavender International Gay Guide. Later Olympic Steam Baths, included in the Damron Address Book from 1979 to 1980.

Restaurant/Bar: Brazil Grill, 1201 SW 12th Ave, Portland, OR **97205**, Top LGBTQIA+ Owned and Operated Restaurants in America, OpenTable 2021

Store: Rudy's Barbershop, 212 NW 13th Ave, Portland, OR **97209**

Restaurant/Bar: Either/Or Café (8235 SE 13th Ave #2, Portland, OR **97202**), LGBTQ owned.

Wilhelm Portland Memorial

Address: 6705 SE 14th Ave, Portland, OR 97202

Find a grave

Notable queer burials:

Anne Shannon Monroe (1873–1942) was an American author and lecturer. Anne Shannon Monroe was born in Bloomington, Missouri, the daughter of William Andrew Monroe (1842-1889), M.D., and great-granddaughter of George Shannon of the Lewis and Clark Expedition. From 1907 to 1911 she managed her own advertising office in Portland. In 1913 she bought 300-acre homestead for 16 dollars.

Marie Equi (1872–1952) was an early American medical doctor in the American West devoted to providing care to working-class and poor patients. She regularly provided birth control information and abortions at a time when both were illegal. She became a political activist and advocated civic and economic reforms, including women's right to vote and an eight-hour workday. After being clubbed by a policeman in a 1913 workers' strike, Equi aligned herself with anarchists and the radical labor movement. Equi was a lesbian who maintained a primary relationship with **Harriet Speckart** (1883-1927) for more than a decade. The two women adopted an infant and raised the child in an early example, for the US, of a same-sex alternative family. For her radical politics and same-sex relations, Equi battled discrimination and harassment. In 1918, Equi was convicted under the Sedition Act for speaking against US involvement in WWI. She was sentenced to a three-year term at San Quentin State Prison. She was the only known lesbian and radical to be incarcerated at the prison.

Lion and the Rose Victorian B&B Inn

Accommodation: *Majestic 1906 Queen Anne* LGBTQ owned *home.* GLD, Gay Lesbian Directory

Address: 1810 NE 15th Ave, Portland, OR, 97212
National Register of Historic Places: 93000454, 1993

Lion and the Rose Victorian B&B Inn

Place

The majestic Queen Anne home was built in 1906 for Gustav E. Freiwald, a prosperous German immigrant, owner of the Star Brewery and real estate speculator. The Freiwald house is a unique blend of Craftsman form and Victorian detail. The exterior of the house features an octagonal turret, a wide wrap-around porch with Ionic columns, and a large dormer with arched window and balcony — all Queen Anne conventions. The home's comfortable elegance extends out into the English-style gardens where a brick pathway passes by fountains, statuary, bird baths, rose gardens and a Gazebo. The interior of the house features spacious rooms with large windows, the ornate decorative plaster work of English architecture and elements of medieval architecture (such as oriel windows) — all part of the Craftsman revival under the influence of William Morris and the Arts and Crafts Movement. The interior has been lovingly restored and elegantly decorated with period carpets, wall coverings, draperies and antiques. The house is one of the few remaining grand residences in the area of Portland platted as the Holladay Addition and is now part of the Irvington neighborhood. Dusty and Steve are high tech refugees who moved to Portland in 2002 after living in San Francisco for 25 years. Steve had worked in software marketing and Dusty in Health and Education Administration. Along the way they also ran a 49 seat theater off of Union Square for three years. The Lion and the Rose was in full operation when Steve and Dusty became the second B&B owners. We felt 'called' because we knew the house was meant to be shared says Steve. It is a lot of work, but as Innkeepers we meet new people every day who we would otherwise never encounter says Dusty.

Restaurant/Bar: New Ritz Disco, 605 SE 15th Ave, Portland, OR **97214**, included in the Damron Address Book in 1979.

Accommodation: Hotel Deluxe (729 SW 15th Ave, Portland, OR **97205**), a boutique downtown Portland hotel, is a contemporary tribute to the Golden Era of Hollywood filmmaking, and tastefully balances art deco and art modern styles. Part of World Rainbow Hotels (WRH), Lesbian and Gay Welcoming Hotels.

Other non-queer residents: John Silas Reed (1887-1920), Reed House (NW 21st Ave & NW Davis St, Portland, OR **97210**), from 1900 to 1906.

Restaurant/Bar: Besaw's, 1545 NW 21st Ave, Portland, OR **97209**, Top LGBTQIA+ Owned and Operated Restaurants in America, OpenTable 2021

Accommodation: Portland's White House B&B (1914 NE 22nd Ave, Portland, OR **97212**), gay owned. Historic manor close to shopping, Lloyd Centre, local restaurants.

Restaurant/Bar:
23Hoyt, 529 NW 23rd Ave, Portland, OR **97210**, Top LGBTQIA+ Owned and Operated Restaurants in America, OpenTable 2021
Ben & Jerry's, 39 NW 23rd Pl, Portland, OR **97210**
Hip Chicks do Wine (4510 SE 23rd Ave, Portland, OR **97202**), LGBTQ friendly.

Religious Building: Metropolitan Community Church, NE 24th Ave & NE Broadway, Portland, OR **97232**, included in the Damron Address Book in 1980.

House: David Hopkins (born 1939) and Richard Younge (born 1960) were married on January 28, 2017, at the Arlington Club, a private club in Portland, OR. Gov. Kate Brown of Oregon, a friend of the couple, officiated. Hopkins retired as the president of HereNow Creative Network, a design agency he founded in Portland, now owned by his son. Until 1986 he was the chairman of Beaver State Bank, in Beaverton, OR, of which he was the founder. He is a son of the late Laverne M. Jackson and M. David Hopkins, who lived in Colville, WA. Hopkins's previous marriage ended in divorce. Younge is an independent landscape and architectural designer in Portland. He graduated from Portland State University. He is the son of Tricia A. Younge, who lived in Tampa, FL, and Richard L. Younge, who lived in Portland. The couple met in June 1986 at mutual friend's party in Portland. It was the first time I went to a gay gathering of that ilk, said Hopkins, who was separated from his wife and new to the gay community. As soon as Younge caught sight of what Hopkins was wearing — linen pants, a Chinese steel blue silk shirt with a mandarin collar and sandals — he turned to his partner at the time. Look who just came out, said Younge, referring to Hopkins's dynamic debut. When the two spoke later that evening, they realized they were both avid runners — Younge in marathons and Hopkins in daily conditioning — and decided to meet at noon the next day for a five-mile run. There was no romance, said Hopkins, who knew Younge was off limits because of his partner. They met on the Portland State campus to a run along the Terwilliger greenway, which had a 300-foot climb and views of the city. A month later, their lunchtime run became a three-times-a-week routine. We would meet, run, and I would go back to work," Hopkins said. I learned a lot about the gay world through him. Hopkins soon became known for local initiatives and fund-raisers to increase awareness of gay issues. Younge said: David has this effervescent personality. It seemed like he was everywhere at once. In October 1986, after breaking up with his partner, Younge began dating, but never considered Hopkins a possibility mainly because of the age difference. In January, that perception shifted when they were the only two single men at a dinner party. During dinner we realized we could be a couple, Younge said. After dinner, they had a nightcap at Hopkins's apartment. That's when everything did a 180, Younge added. They began seeing each other frequently, and a couple of weeks later hosted a dinner party. Our friends were going, Oh something is happening here, Hopkins said. By March 1987, they were getting serious. I remember his kids coming over for brunch one day, Younge said, adding that they were a big part of his life. They soon moved in together, and marked each passing decade with a party at the Arlington Club. Anytime Younge brought up marriage, Hopkins shied from it, but undeterred he brought it up once again, jokingly over a drink. Wouldn't it would be great if we got married on our 30th anniversary? Younge said. This time, however, he got the answer he never expected. That sounds good to me, Hopkins said, adding with a laugh, After 30 years, I think it might work. Hopkins and Younge live at 1907 NW 24th Ave, Portland, OR **97210**.

Accommodation: McMenamins Kennedy School Hotel (5736 NE 33rd Ave, Portland, OR **97211**), a converted elementary school, lodge-style stay with multiple restaurants, a soaking pool and its own brewery.

Restaurant/Bar: Ben & Jerry's, 1428 SE 36th Ave, Portland, OR **97214**

Store: Nightingale Acupuncture (5128 NE 42nd Ave, Portland, OR **97218**), sign up for a session with Kristen Dilley, she's one-half of the local herbalist company, Portland Apothecary.

House: Anne Shannon Monroe (1873–1942) was an American author. Born in Bloomington, MO, she was the daughter of William A. Monroe, M.D., and great-granddaughter of George Shannon of the Lewis and Clark Expedition. She wrote popular press articles on a wide variety of subjects, including an early portrayal of a (fictional) female business tycoon, Making of a Business Woman (1912), a notable 1904 study of Mary MacLane's literary inspiration (which Monroe found in Sei Shonagon's work), and the biography of Oregon rancher William Bill Hanley. Many of her books are based on her childhood experiences growing up in the semi-arid, cold ranch-lands of eastern Washington state. She lived at 5906 SE 42nd Ave, Portland, OR **97206**.

School: Warner Pacific College (2219 SE 68th Ave, Portland, OR **97215**) is an urban, Christian liberal arts college located in Southeast Portland, OR. Founded in 1937, the college is accredited by the Northwest Commission on Colleges and Universities. A private college, it is affiliated with the Church of God. Mel White (born 1940), clergyman, author, graduated from Warner Pacific College in 1962. That same year, he married his wife, Lyla Lee Loehr. They had two children, one of whom is the actor/comedian and screenwriter Mike White.

97300

Salem

Salem, OR, has been named among the Gayest Cities in America by The Advocate, 2012
Salem, OR, has been named among the Gayest Cities in America by The Advocate, 2013

Religious Building:
Salem Spirit of Life (420 Pine St NE, Salem, OR **97301**), LGBTQ friendly.
First Congregational Church (700 Marion St NE, Salem, OR **97301**), LGBTQ friendly.

LGBTQ friendly bookstore: Bob's Adult Book Store, 1389 Broadway St NE, Salem, OR **97301**, included in the Damron Address Book from 1978 to 1980.

Historic District: Bus Depot, 500 13th Street SE, Salem, OR **97301**, included in the Damron Address Book from 1975 to 1980.

Restaurant/Bar:
Cellar Bar at Marion Hotel, 201 Liberty St SE, Salem, OR **97301**, included in the Damron Address Book from 1968 to 1973.
Olive Garden Italian, 1302 Lancaster Dr NE, Salem, OR **97301**
Red Lobster, 521 Lancaster Dr NE, Salem, OR **97301**

Tara's Pub, 2290 Front St NE, Salem, OR **97301**, included in the Damron Address Book from 1978 to 1979.
Wooden Shoe, 1391 Broadway St NE, Salem, OR **97301**, included in the Damron Address Book from 1979 to 1980.

Religious Building:
Freedom Friends Church (2425 13th St SE, Salem, OR **97302**), LGBTQ friendly.
Morningside United Methodist Church (3674 12th St SE, Salem, OR **97302**), LGBTQ friendly.

Restaurant/Bar:

Southside Speakeasy, 3529 Fairview Industrial Dr SE, Salem, OR **97302**

Cemetery: Joel Redon (1961-1995) studied writing with Paul Bowles in Morocco and with Elizabeth Pollet at NYU, and wrote columns and reviews for the New York Native in 1986-87. He is the author of Bloodstream (1989), If Not on Earth, Then in Heaven (1991), and Road to Zena (1992). He is buried at Zena Cemetery (Salem, OR **97304**) and his epitaph reads: To have placed the impossible word on the rainbow's arc, then it would have been all said.

Accommodation:
Hopewell B&B (22350 Hopewell Rd NW, Salem, OR **97304**), gay friendly. Lakeside Lodge & Country Cottage on 12 acre farm in the Wine

Country of the Willamette Valley. GLD, Gay Lesbian Directory

Religious Building: Unitarian Universalist Congregation of Salem (3215, 5090 Center St NE, Salem, OR **97317**), LGBTQ friendly.

Accommodation:

Harrison House B&B (2310 NW Harrison Blvd, Corvallis, OR **97330**), LGBTQ friendly.

School: Oregon State University (104 Kerr Administration Building, Corvallis, OR **97331**) has been named among the 100 Best Campuses for LGBT Students by The Advocate College Guide for LGBT Students, 2006. It is a public research university. It was founded in 1856 as Corvallis Academy, the area's first community school for primary and preparatory education. Corvallis area Freemasons played a leading role in developing the early school. Several of the university's largest buildings are named after these early founders. In 1961 it became Oregon State University. The Home Economics Bldg. (3rd floor T-Room) & Student Union (basement T-Room) have been included in the Damron Address Book from 1978 to 1980. Annual LGBT Event Highlights: Welcome Week BBQ (late September), Guess the Hetero Game Show Panel (September), Queer History Month (October), National Coming Out Day (October 11), Coming Out Week (around October 11), Fall Drag Competition (late October), Trans Awareness Week (mid-November), Trans Day of Remembrance

(November 20), World AIDS Day (December 1), Pride Center Birthday (March 14), Day of Silence (April 20), Drag Racs on the Quad (May), Drag Show (May), Queer Pride Week (mid-May), Lavender Graduation (May). **LGBT Resource center/office:** The Pride Center (1555 SW A Ave, 149 MU East, Corvallis, OR **97333**).

Accommodation:
The Harbor Lights Inn (235 SE S 40 Ln, Depoe Bay, OR **97341**), **LGBTQ friendly**.
WorldMark Depoe Bay (939 US-101, Depoe Bay, OR **97341**). Set between the Oregon Coast Highway and the Pacific Ocean shore, this relaxed resort is 2 miles from Fogarty Creek State Recreation Area and 9 miles from Siletz Bay National Wildlife Refuge. Part of World

Rainbow Hotels (WRH), Lesbian and Gay Welcoming Hotels:
Lodge at Detroit Lake (175 Detroit Ave, Detroit, OR **97342**), **gay owned**. Located in the heart of the Willamette National Forest, the lodge offers luxury accommodations featuring flat screen televisions, jetted tubs, kitchenettes and all the charm Detroit Lake has to offer.

Find a grave

Cemetery: Rae Ray Leonard (1849-1921) was an Oregon pioneer who was, in fact, a woman. Born Rae Leonard, she was a cobbler who emigrated to Oregon with her father in 1889, and who, with his apparent approval, began wearing men's clothing and passing as his son Ray. When the elder Leonard died in 1894, Ray took over his local boot and shoemaking business. In 1911, Ray's secret was discovered by a frontier doctor, Mary Canaga Rowlands, when Ray was committed to an asylum under Dr. Rowlands' care. Dr. Rowlands died in 1966, and her autobiography was published in 1995 by her grand-nephew. Ray died in 1921 and his newspaper obituary referred to him as a woman. He is buried at Pioneer Cemetery (Lebanon, OR **97355**).

Park: Yaquina Bay State Recreation Site, Newport, OR **97365**, included in the **Damron Address Book** in 1980.

House: Sue Hardesty (1933–2022) was an American author from Buckeye, Arizona, whose writing focused on plots and characters from the Southwestern US, and social themes of lesbianism and feminism, as well as complex female characters and family relationships. She lived at 156 SW Coast St, Newport, OR **97365**. She was a long-time supporter of the NOW (the Central Oregon Coast Chapter), the Rainbow Round Table of the American Library Association, PFLAG, the Golden Crown Literary Society, and the Lambda Literary Foundation. Sue Aileen Hardesty was born in Buckeye, AZ, and grew up on horseback in the desert area. Her mother was a prospector and a homemaker while her father farmed and ran a ranch. Hardesty grew up with a twin brother and two elder brothers. She graduated from Buckeye Union High School and went on to earn an undergraduate degree in English from Arizona State University followed by a master's degree in Communication. Hardesty taught English and media in high school for twenty-seven years. She met her long-time partner, Dr. Nel Ward, in 1969 at Arizona State University. In 1992, they left the Southwest and moved to the Oregon Coast where they ran a bookstore called 14/Green Gable Books and two B&Bs and also rehabbed houses and re-sold them. For several decades she has been an avid photographer, especially of birds and wildlife, but she's also furnished head shots for various authors, including Lee Lynch. Hardesty was politically and socially active with the Central Coast chapter of PFLAG, with the local NOW, and with the community lesbian group (CLASS) in hosting potlucks and assisting with the monthly newsletter for the group. Hardesty and her wife, Nel Ward, were awarded the Lincoln County CAN award for their contributions to the lesbian community. She retired from all but writing, photography, and managing a guest cottage on the Oregon Coast near the Pacific Ocean. With Nel Ward and Lee Lynch, Hardesty collaborated in the editing and publishing of The Butch Cook Book (2008). Hardesty published her first full-length novel, The Truck Comes on Thursday: Book 1 in the Loni Wagner Series, in 2010 through Teal Ribbon Publications and a second edition through L-Books in 2011. The second book in the Loni Wagner series, Bus Stop at the Last Chance, came out in 2014. In 2019, Hardesty signed with Launch Point Press to reissue the first two books and publish the third and any subsequent books in the series. A novel, Panic, about three teens who get lost in the Arizona desert, was published in 2013 and can be classified as a lesbian YA novel. After releasing Nine Muses: Open the Door to Let Your Muses In in 2020, Hardesty's last venture was the compilation of a book she co-wrote with her wife, Through The Knothole: Musings from Newport (2023) in which she was able to convey her love of Yaquina Bay, the ocean and coastline, and the development of NOAA and the Hatfield Marine Science Center across the bay. Sue said: My joy was the view from the windows of our Newport home with all the boats and ships. I loved the town so much that it became my last project with my spouse, about our impressions, both facts and ideas, while we mused on our lives. She also indulged her love of gadgets with powerful binoculars and camera, toys allowing her to closely observe her surroundings. Over the years, Hardesty served as a reviewer for the American Library Association's Rainbow Round Table, focusing specifically on works by notable lesbian authors.

Accommodation:
A Cottage, 538 SE 2nd Street, Newport, OR **97365**, GLD, Gay Lesbian Directory

The Grand Victorian B&B (105 NW Coast St, Newport, OR **97365**), LGBTQ friendly. GLD, Gay Lesbian Directory
Little Creek Cove (3641 NW Oceanview Dr, Newport, OR **97365**), gay friendly. Little Creek

Cove is the only Newport, OR, hotel that located on the beach; cross the lawn and you have access to three miles of pristine, sandy beach.

Restaurant/Bar:

Over-The-Waves, 2945 NW Jetty Ave, Lincoln City, OR **97367**, included in the Damron Address Book from 1978 to 1980.

Accommodation:
Bella Beach Vacation Rentals (1027 SW 62nd St, Lincoln City, OR **97367**), LGBTQ friendly.
Coast Inn B&B (4507 SW Coast Ave, Lincoln City, OR **97367**), LGBTQ friendly.
Middle Creek Run B&B (25400 Harmony Rd,

Sheridan, OR **97378**) included in Inn Places 1999, Gay & Lesbian Accommodations Worldwide. Gay, Lesbian and gay owned. As of 2021 it's closed.

Cemetery: William Dickey (1928–1994) was a poet and professor of English and creative writing at San Francisco State University. He authored 15 books of poetry over a career that lasted three and a half decades. Dickey was a student of John Berryman at the Iowa Writers' Workshop. Dickey's first collection of poetry, Of the Festivity, was selected by W.H. Auden as the winner of the Yale Series of Younger Poets Competition in 1959. In the foreword to the book, Auden wrote: It is possible to show evidence of great intelligence and sensibility but to be lacking in the first power essential to poetry, the power to speak, Mr. Dickey's lines have both. Dickey lived in San Francisco with his companion Leonard Sanazaro (1949-2004). Dickey died in 1994 at Kaiser Hospital in San Francisco. The cause was complications from HIV-related surgeries. Shortly before his death, Dickey finished a poem, The Death of John Berryman, about the suicide of his former teacher. He is buried at Valley View Cemetery (Silverton, OR **97381**) together with Sanazaro. Leonard Sanazaro was a truly gifted poet whose works appeared widely in literary publications throughout the country. He was born Chicago, IL. He obtained a Bachelor, Lewis University, 1971, and a Master of Arts, University Nevada, 1979. He was a consummate, dedicated English teacher at City College of San Francisco where he taught poetry, the classics, and composition. He was known for his excellence in teaching, high standards, and commitment to helping his students reach their highest potential. He had a brilliant intellect, a great wit and sense of humor, and exceptional courage. He loved the arts and nature. He died in 2004, in San Francisco.

Other non-queer residents: Gordon House, 869 W Main St, Silverton, OR **97381**, designed by Frank Lloyd Wright in 1957.

Accommodation:
Silverton Inn and Suites (301 North Water St, Silverton, OR **97381**), gay owned. The Silverton Inn & Suites is a luxury boutique hotel located less than a mile from The Oregon Garden one of Oregon's most popular destinations, and minutes from The Silver Falls State Park. The Inn's incredible lodging experience includes rooms with their own individual character.

Lee Lynch, author: In 1935 President Franklin D. Roosevelt announced that the Silver Falls area would be turned into a Recreational Demonstration Area. Private land that had been logged was purchased, and workers in the Civilian Conservation Corps were employed to develop park facilities, including the historic South Falls Lodge, completed in the late 1930s. It was used as a restaurant from 1946 until the late 1950s and was listed on the National Register of Historic Places as the Silver Falls State Park Concession Building Area in 1983 (20024 Silver Falls Hwy SE, Sublimity, OR 97385).

97400

Eugene

Eugene, OR, is ranked 21 out of 25 among US Mid-size cities (Population between 100.000 and 250.000) for % of same sex couples (0,998%), and is ranked 13 for # of same sex couples, 663. (US Census 2010)

Madison, WI, has been named among the Gayest Cities in America by The Advocate, 2012

Eugene, OR, has been named among the Gayest Cities in America by The Advocate, 2013

Eugene, OR, has been named among the Queerest City in America by The Advocate, 2016

LGBTQ friendly bookstore:
Mother Kali's Books, 1070 Lawrence St, #A, Eugene, OR **97401**, active in 1990.
Paradox, 825 E 13th Ave, Eugene, OR **97401**, active in 1990.
Climax Book Store, 60 W 13th Ave, Eugene, OR **97401**, included in the Damron Address Book from 1976 to 1980.

Queer Architects: Valley River Inn, 1000 Valley River Way, Eugene, OR **97401**, designed by Roland Terry (1972)

Park: Skinner Butte Park, 248 Cheshire Ave, Eugene, OR **97401**, included in the Damron Address Book from 1975 to 1980.

Restaurant/Bar:
Cassady's at Eugene Hotel, 222 E Broadway, Eugene, OR **97401**, included in the Damron Address Book in 1980.
Hunter Room at Trailways Bus Depot, 959 Pearl St, Eugene, OR **97401**, included in the Damron Address Book from 1968 to 1973. Included in the 1975 All Lavender International Gay Guide.
Luckey's Club (933 Olive St, Eugene, OR **97401**), LGBTQ friendly.
New World Coffee House, 1249 Alder St, Eugene, OR **97401**, between 12th and West 13th, included in the 1965 Guild Guide. Included in the 1975 All Lavender International Gay Guide.

Olive Garden Italian, 1077 Valley River Dr, Eugene, OR **97401**
Pearl Street Station, 412 Pearl St, Eugene, OR **97401**, included in the Damron Address Book in 1979.
Red Lobster, 1085 Valley River Way, Eugene, OR **97401**
Riviera Room, 39 W 10th Ave, Eugene, OR **97401**, included in the Damron Address Book from 1970 to 1980.
Room 13 Lounge at Osburn Hotel, 191 E 8th Ave, Eugene, OR **97401**, included in the 1964 Guild Guide. Included in the 1964 Directory.
The Wayward Lamb (150 W Broadway, Eugene, OR **97401**), was the first gay owned business in Eugene. In Autumn 2018 it became Spectrum Eugene, a dedicated queer establishment.

Accommodation:
The Campbell House Inn and Restaurant (252 Pearl St, Eugene, OR **97401**), LGBTQ friendly.

Excelsior Inn (754 E 13th Ave, Eugene, OR **97401**), LGBTQ friendly.

LGBTQ friendly bookstore: Mother Kali's Books (541 Blair Blvd, Eugene, OR **97402**) was a feminist bookstore active in the 1980s.

Attractions: Oregon Air and Space Museum (90377 Boeing Dr, Eugene, OR **97402**) has been named among the Most beautiful water slides in the world.

Restaurant/Bar:	Hop Valley Brewing Co (990 W 1st Ave, Eugene, OR **97402**), produces Reveal Pale Ale, a portion of whose proceeds support LGBTQ nonprofits.
Izakaya Meiji, 345 Van Buren St, Eugene, OR **97402** Sam Bond's Garage, 407 Blair Blvd, Eugene, OR **97402**	

Accommodation:	River Walk Inn B&B (250 N Adams St, Eugene, OR **97402**), LGBTQ friendly.

School: The University of Oregon (1217 University of Oregon, 1585 E 13th Ave, Eugene, OR **97403**) has been named among the 100 Best Campuses for LGBT Students by The Advocate College Guide for LGBT Students, 2006. Among them Named among the Best of the Best Top 20 Campuses. The Best of the Best Top 20 Campuses rise above expectations as pioneering LGBT leaders in higher education. Non only do the campuses rank among the highest on the Gay Point Average but they also boast the most outstanding accomplishments for LGBT progressiveness across the US. The campuses chosen for the Best of the Best represent a diverse array of demographics such as type of institution, locale, and size. The University of Oregon is a public flagship research university. Founded in 1876, the institution's 295-acre campus is along the Willamette River. The Library 1st floor T-Room has been included in the Damron Address Book from 1976 to 1980. Annual LGBT Event Highlights: Emperors Drag Show (Fall/Spring), Week of Welcome (August), Coming Out Day Celebration (October), Guess the Straight RA (Fall), World AIDS Day (December 1), Queer Film Festival (February), Pride Week (April), Lavender Graduation (April/May), Day of Silence/Night of Noise (Spring), InterSEXtions (Spring), LGBTQA Drag Show (Spring), Queer Prom (Spring). LGBT Resource center/office: Lesbian, Gay, Bisexual, and Transgender Education and Support Services Program (LGBTESSP) (University of Oregon, 164 Oregon Hall, Eugene, OR **97403**). Notable queer alumni and faculty: Arthur Erickson (1924-2009); James Ivory (born 1928); John Walsted (1932–2014); Marie Equi (1872-1952); Olga Broumas (born 1949); Randy Shilts (1951-1994).

Library: Jill Holman is electronic services and science reference librarian at the University of Oregon (1501 Kincaid St, Eugene, OR **97403**).

LGBTQ friendly bookstore: Book and Tea Shop (1646 E 19th Ave, Eugene, OR **97403**) was a feminist bookstore active in the 1980s.

Accommodation:	Phoenix Inn Suites (850 Franklin Blvd, Eugene, OR **97403**), LGBTQ friendly.

LGBTQ friendly bookstore: He & She Adult Bookstore, 288 River Rd, Eugene, OR **97404**, included in the Damron Address Book from 1979 to 1980.

Religious Building: When Eric Marcoux (born 1931) and Eugene Woodworth (1929-2013) met in Chicago in 1953 Marcoux was 23 and Woodworth was 25. They always answered Yes when people asked them if they were brothers. In the last years, when people asked, Marcoux said, No, but thank you for asking, because I am able to tell you that I love this man. Woodworth was a ballet dancer, and Marcoux was just leaving a Trappist monastery. In 2003, for their 50th anniversary, they had a commitment ceremony at the Eugene Zendo Butsugenji (2190 Garfield St, Eugene, OR **97405**). They then officially married in 2013, few days before Woodworth's death.

Accommodation:

The Sea Star Guesthouse (370 1st St SE, Bandon, OR **97411**), LGBTQ friendly.

Store: Visit the McKenzie General Store, 91837 Taylor Rd, McKenzie Bridge, OR **97413**, and you might be forgiven for thinking you'd accidentally stumbled into an alpine village. In reality, the tiny mountain town of McKenzie Bridge is on the edge of the Willamette National Forest and the McKenzie River. Inside you'll find essentials, specialty food items, local brews, meats, cheeses and Oregon-related gifts. There's also a restaurant and beer garden, and an excellent live music program in the summer. Named among the Most charming general stores in every US state, 2018, by Love Food.

Accommodation:
Horse Creek Lodge (56228 Delta Dr, McKenzie Bridge, OR **97413**), gay friendly. Beautiful, comfortable lodging at affordable rates in the heart of the McKenzie River recreational valley. The Chetco River Inn (21202 High Prairie Rd, Brookings, OR **97415**), gay friendly. Modern

inn along a wild & scenic river, near a seacoast town.
South Coast Inn Bed & Breakfast (516 Redwood St, Brookings, OR **97415**) included in Inn Places 1999, Gay & Lesbian Accommodations Worldwide. Gay friendly.

School: Lake on Campus, Southwestern Oregon Community College, 1988 Newmark Ave, Coos Bay, OR **97420**, included in the Damron Address Book from 1978 to 1980.

Restaurant/Bar:
Balboa Club, 112 S Empire Blvd, Coos Bay, OR **97420**, included in the Damron Address Book from 1966 to 1972. Included in the 1975 All Lavender International Gay Guide.
Captain's Cabin at Tioga Hotel, 257 N Broadway, Coos Bay, OR **97420**, included in the Damron Address Book from 1978 to 1980.

Holiday House, Charleston Small Boat Harbor, Coos Bay, OR **97420**, included in the 1975 All Lavender International Gay Guide.
Snappy's, 240 S Broadway, Coos Bay, OR **97420**, included in the Damron Address Book from 1966 to 1972. Included in the 1975 All Lavender International Gay Guide.

Accommodation:
Coos Bay Manor B&B Inn (955 S 5th St, Coos Bay, OR **97420**), gay friendly. High ceilings & large rooms make this home warm and inviting.

Village Green Resort (725 Row River Rd, Cottage Grove, OR **97424**), LGBTQ friendly.

House: Founded in 1975 Oregon Women's Land Trust is a 501(c)(3) membership organization that holds land for conservation and educational purposes in the US state of Oregon. The trust owns 147 acres of land in Douglas County, referred to as OWL Farm (Days Creek Rd, Days Creek, OR **97429**), and the mission states that the Trust is committed to ecologically sound preservation of land, and provides access to land and land wisdom for women. In the mid-1970s there was great interest among women in the lesbian feminist movement in having access to rural land in order to be able to live outside of mainstream patriarchal culture, which was ridden with violence against women, gay people, and the environment. The feminist spirituality movement was also emerging and grounded in reverence for the natural world. For example the magazine WomanSpirit was founded and produced nearby by Jean and Ruth Mountaingrove and had worldwide distribution. Some groups of women traveling or temporarily settled in Oregon, California, and New Mexico were wanting a land-based community where their political and spiritual ideals as lesbians, feminists, and environmentally minded folk could be put into practice. There were a few lands in southern Oregon already owned by feminist lesbians, and some where women lived together collectively but did not own the land. Many women visitors were drawn to the region and wanted to join this exciting and growing community of countrywomen. Initially the farm was to create a place where economically disadvantaged women could stay with other women without the need for permanent residence or invitation. The farm was established as land that was accessible to women and children regardless of their financial status. The land would be held in perpetuity and in its initial form would be open for any women to come live on. Open land trust meetings were held in 1975 and 1976. Women collectively contributed money to buy the land together, giving anywhere between 25 and 5000 dollars. Money and support were raised by women with varying levels of economic means. Women proposed the idea of each woman contributing ten percent of her money so that there could be a collective commitment to recognize class privilege and to make land available for all women, not just those who could afford it. In the spring of 1976, a 147-acre piece of land was found in southern Oregon. Initial conversations about this idea arose from a WomanShare conference about money and power. Over time, the community reorganized financially into a federally recognized 501(c)(3) organization. Over 100 women attended the first meeting that took place at OWL Farm. Soon after this meeting, sixteen women met to form the caretaker collective and moved on to the land in July 1976. As with many back to the land and intentional communities, the community at OWL farm faced challenges related to philosophical and political differences as well as interpersonal issues. These are documented in a number of writings by women who lived in the community. In 1987, a resident caretaker remained and OWL Trust began hosting conferences and other events on the farm. The land continued to provide residential space but was no longer run as a collective. In 1999 the policy that had allowed any woman to live there without any prior vetting or approval was changed to create a more stable and sustainable living environment. According to La Verne Gagehabib and Barbara Summerhawk, Women had profound experiences of creating community together, in various combinations, for periods of months or years. Throughout OWL Farm's first twenty-five years, hundreds of women visited from all over the world. There was the exhilaration, as one ex-resident had shared, of learning how to use a tool one day, and teaching a newly arrived woman how to use it the next. Issues of debate that were taking place in the wider Lesbian Feminist and Separatist Feminist movement were also alive within the OWL Farm community such as childrearing, division of labor, the place of male children in separatist community, private vs common ownership and monogamy vs nonmonogamy. Some children lived on the farm with their mothers. In 2007, OWL Farm found itself on the path of a proposed 3-foot-wide gas export pipeline. The project was stopped through the regulatory process in 2010 and again in 2015, but was proposed again in January 2016 and as of 2018 was still going through the regulatory process. The project is called the Pacific Connector Pipeline, Jordan Cove LNG Terminal and would pipe fracked gas from Canada and the US interior to Coos Bay where it would be compressed into Liquified Natural Gas (LNG) for export by tanker to Russian and China. OWL Trust has taken a leading role in fighting the pipeline, not just across OWL Farm, but across Oregon, due to the direct conflict of this project with the environmental and land preservation mission of the Trust and likely negative impact on women and girls that arise with human trafficking that accompanies large infrastructure projects. Representatives from the Trust have been active members of Landowners United and Citizens Against the Pipeline and was featured by NPR regarding the pipeline. As of 2018, the trust had an active board and had had resident caretakers for most years since it ceased being a residential community. Infrastructure improvements continued with maintenance of buildings, water system improvements and restoration of the farm's original pond. As well as preserving and maintaining OWL Farm, the trust runs educational and wildland access programming in the areas of ecological land management, organic gardening, permaculture and outdoor skills. Regular hikes and gatherings are offered at OWL Farm. The farm is also the last resting place of women members who have requested natural burial or interment of ashes. In the beginning of OWL, (1976) the only buildings were the Main House, a large log cabin, built in 1900; the 52 ft long chicken coop; the log barn, and a small tool shed that sat to the left of the Main House, as you approached the Main House. This small woodshed was the site of the first renovation made on Owl. It would become what was called the Quiet House. Basically, a square box, 12 by 16 ft., in which women built two lofts, added windows, and re-sided the east exterior wall. It was designated as the place for sustained quiet activities, as well as the home space for 4-6 women at a time, in the years '76-79. In later years, this structure would be home to couples and/ or moms with kids, as it was the largest of the small structures on the land. The second building project was the construction of the Little House, located to the east of the Main House, in the meadow above the barn. Built mainly by Spes and Pelican in 1977-78, this is a one-room cabin with a loft. The original intended purpose of this building was to provide a place for the children of OWL Farm and Cabbage Lane (the children went between the lands) to play, sleep, be schooled in. Thus, its original name, the Kids' House. this building was built with discount wood from local mill for $150.00. The third new buildingwas the Tree House, built mainly by Pelican, who wanted to create a space to get away from downtown OWL (where upwards of 30 women could be gathered in and around the main house). This very unique space sits high in the arms of a beautiful immense madrone tree in the forested area north of the Main House. It is perhaps 8ft by 4 ft by 4 ft. An adult woman cannot stand up in it. Most of the major building at OWL was done in the years 1976-1979. In 1989, Boa, Wyrda, Ni Aodagaln,, and lots of drop-in help, added a room onto to the Quiet House. This 8 by 12 ft space provided Felice Ana, Ni Aódagaln's, daughter, with her own bedroom, as well as almost doubling the size of the Quiet House. In 1989, as well, major reroofing of the chicken coop was undertaken and in 1993, the foundation of this 52 ft building was totally redone. In the years 1985-95, the interior of the chicken coop was partially renovated, in order to create two resident living spaces, and two resident work spaces.

| Accommodation: | Summit Prairie Fire Lookout (Tiller, OR **97429**), gay owned. |

LGBTQ Archives: Douglas County Gay Archives, Dillard, OR **97432**, active in 1990.

| Accommodation: Ocean Breeze Motel (85165 US-101, Florence, OR **97439**), LGBTQ friendly. | Camp Yachats Vacation Cottage (95161 S, US-101, Florence, OR **97439**), LGBTQ friendly. |

Umpqua National Forest

Umpqua National Forest, Oregon **97447**, has been named among The Top 10 Destinations in the US for LGBTQ Travelers in the Fall, 2020, Matador Network.

| Accommodation: | Umpqua's Last Resort RV Park & Campground (115 Elk Ridge Ln, Idleyld Park, OR **97447**), gay owned. GLD, Gay Lesbian Directory |

School: Pony Village Shopping Center, 1611 Virginia Ave, North Bend, OR **97459**, included in the Damron Address Book from 1978 to 1980.

| Restaurant/Bar: | Deb's Club, 655 Virginia Ave, North Bend, OR **97459**, included in the Damron Address Book from 1978 to 1979. |

| Accommodation: Daybreak Haven B&B (395 Burchard Dr, Scottsburg, OR **97473**), gay friendly. A small, quiet rural B&B about 20 minutes from the Oregon Coast. The only B&B on the banks of the Umpqua River. Centrally located between numerous Umpqua Valley wineries and the | south central Oregon coast. Providing peace, quiet & comfort. A Peaceful Sanctuary, 203 Deadmond Ferry Rd, Springfield, OR **97477**, GLD, Gay Lesbian Directory |

We sail together: The Radical Faerie movement was founded in California in 1979 by gay activists Harry Hay (1912-2002), Mitch Walker, John Burnside (1916-2008), and Don Kilhefner, who wanted to create an alternative to what they saw as the assimilationist attitude of the mainstream US gay community. Influenced by the legacy of the counterculture of the 1960s, they held the first Spiritual Conference for Radical Fairies in Arizona in September 1979. From there, various regional Faerie Circles were formed, and other large rural gatherings organized. Although Walker and Kilhefner broke from Hay in 1980, the movement continued to grow, having expanded into an international network soon after the second Faerie gathering in 1980. Harry Hay died in 2002, his partner John Burnside died in 2008. In accordance with his wishes, Burnside's ashes were mingled with those of Hay and scattered at the Nomenus Radical Faerie Sanctuary (4525 Lower Wolf Creek Rd, Wolf Creek, OR **97497**). Radical faeries formed Nomenus in 1984 as a consensus-based organization charged to purchase a rural site for gatherings. Initial efforts sought land in California, but after a 1986 gathering near Wolf Creek at Creekland (the historic site of Magdalen Farm, an early rural gay collective which folded in 1978), the land's owner, George Jalbert aka Chenille Dowdy Crow (1945-1987), offered to sell, and the next summer the Nomenus Wolf Creek Sanctuary formed with its inaugural spiritual gathering. During its first decade, Nomenus acted from a San Francisco base to link members in managing the land. The Magdalen Farm collective helped organize the 1976 Faggots and Class Struggle conference, which later led to the birth of the Radical Faeries. Poni Mon Dada aka Roan Simone Poni aka Shrinath (Harry S. Vaughn) (died 1986) was the first Josephine County AIDS death; his ashes are under the comfrey plant in front of Garden House. Assunta Maria Femia (aka Francis Thomas Femia, Sister Species of Crow) also kwno as San Francisco's Wild Nun (1947-2006), was the last resident of Magdalen Farm.

House:

Tee Corrine (1943-2006) and Beverly Anne Brown (1951-2005)'s house, Poppyseed, is near the Old Sunny Valley Town Hall. The sign over her door said Well-behaved women seldom make history. Brown and Corinne lived together at this home at 1199 Sunny Valley Loop, Wolf Creek, OR **97497**, from the early 1990's until 2004.

Ruth Mountaingrove (1923–2016) was an American lesbian-feminist photographer, poet and musician, known for her photography documenting the lesbian land movement in Southern Oregon. She was born Ruth Shook in Philadelphia, PA, to Edith Shelling and Herbert Daniel Shook. She earned a Bachelor of Science in Education degree from Kutztown State Teacher's College in 1945, majoring in science with minors in English and Spanish. In 1946, she published a book of poems, Rhythms of Spring, and married Bern Ikeler. After nineteen years of marriage and five children, they divorced in 1965. Mountaingrove joined the Philadelphia chapter of NOW in 1966, and worked to change abortion laws. She helped found Women in Transition by writing for the newspaper, assisting battered women, and helped facilitate the first lesbian group in the city. She met her future partner Jean in 1970. When she met Jean, realized that she is a lesbian, and started to make a living with writing for a magazine, Country Women, and newspaper, the Women's Press, in Eugene, OR. Because of being lesbians, she and Jean were expelled from their Mountain Grove home. Country Women supported their search for a place to settle around the West Coast. In 1971 they moved to Southern Oregon, taking the name of the intentional community where they lived for two years, Mountain Grove. They moved to Golden, OR, which was a gay commune and founded WomanSpirit), a lesbian feminist quarterly published collectively near Wolf Creek, OR, from 1974–1984. The magazine was established, inspired by the experience of writing for Country Women. It was the first American lesbian/feminist periodical to be dedicated to both feminism and spirituality. Their vision for the magazine was international and radical feminist. We wanted a cultural revolution—a total reordering of institutions and values. It was to be a modest magazine with grand goals. One of the goals is to validate that it's okay to be wherever you are in your own development. Ruth and Jean wanted all women to feel having many other people who shares the same spirit and experiences. The contents of this magazine are pliable as they are what readers supplied and dealt with by anyone who could help at that time, so that the magazine's spirituality is not firm. In the spirit of removing man and men from her descriptions of her work, Mountaingrove and Tee Corinne led ovular photography workshops instead of seminars on photography, where women could learn photography in the context of the women's movement, providing a means for the women to examine the differences between the way men pictured women and the way the women saw themselves. The Blatant Image (a feminist photography magazine) grew out of the ovular workshops. Ruth took the pictures included in the materials Phillis Lyon and Del Martin collected for their magazine called Lesbian Love and Liberation (1973). WomanSpirit was not destined to stay long at Golden, because soon after its founding the Mountaingroves went on to found, or re-found, Rootworks (2000 King Mt Trail, Wolf Creek, OR **97497**), another lesbian community, on a seven-acre tract of land near Sunny Valley, OR. The Mountaingroves purchased the land in 1978 and it's here that Ruth Mountaingrove published the book Turned on Woman's Songbook and a book of poetry, For Those Who Cannot Sleep. Between 1974 and 1986, Mountaingrove spent a 12-year period photographing women in the lesbian community in Oregon and other parts of the US. She photographed meetings of the Oregon Women's Land Trust, documenting their lives at OWL Farm, a southern Oregon lesbian land community providing access to rural land in order to be able to live outside of mainstream patriarchal culture. The Mountaingroves separated in 1985. At Rootworks, there were originally only two houses – the Moonhouse and the Kitchen cabin. In the years that followed the founding, Ruth and Jean added the Sunhouse, a barn (called Natalie Barney), and the All Purpose crafts cabin. In the barn was a study and a feminist library. From 1974 to 1984, Ruth and Jean also published the magazine WomanSpirit from an office in the barn, and The Blatant Image, a feminist magazine about photography, was published there from 1981 to 1983.

Accommodation:
Ocean Haven (94770 US-101, Yachats, OR **97498**), LGBTQ friendly. GLD, Gay Lesbian Directory

The Oregon House (94288 Oregon Coast Hwy, Yachats, OR **97498**) included in Inn Places 1999, Gay & Lesbian Accommodations Worldwide. Gay friendly. GLD, Gay Lesbian Directory

See Vue Motel (95590 US-101, Yachats, OR **97498**), LGBTQ owned. As of 1991, Jacqueline's See Vue Motel was touted as the Oregon Coast's only gay/lesbian oriented motel, owned by two gay guys. As of a decade later, Purple Roofs listed Renée's See Vue Motel as owned by a lesbian activist named Renée LaChance, who labels herself a woman-identified butch Amazon virgin grandma. The place remained lesbian-oriented, but straight-friendly. Most importantly, it had THEME ROOMS. The Study came with a wall of books, the Mountain Shores offers a rustic mountain theme complete with redwood burls, the Far Out West paid homage to the American cowgirl, The Princess and the Pea sounded super creepy and the Far Out East was too problematic for the modern lesbian to truly enjoy. Now, little identical cottages are being built in its place and everybody on the See Vue Inn Facebook is really mad about it and misses the old place. Renée LaChance remains a lesbian environmental activist and works in sustainable construction in Portland, OR. GLD, Gay Lesbian Directory
Shamrock Lodgettes Resort and Spa (105 Hwy 101 N, Yachats, OR **97498**), LGBTQ owned.

97500

Restaurant/Bar:
Medford Hotel & Barbary Coast Bar, 406 W Main St, Medford, OR **97501**, included in the Damron Address Book from 1970 to 1980. As of 2022, it's still open.

Accommodation:
A grand northwest historic lodge, the 71-room Crater Lake Lodge (1211 Ave C, White City, OR **97503**), LGBTQ friendly, originally opened in 1915 and is located on the edge of one of the country's crown jewels – Crater Lake. No place else on earth combines a deep pure lake, so blue in color; sheer surrounding cliffs, almost 2,000 feet high; a picturesque island and a violent volcanic past. The historic lodge is listed in the National Register of Historic Places and was reopened after extensive renovation in 1995 and offers an atmosphere reminiscent of the 1920s, immersing visitors in its rustic

charm. A sense of awe comes over you when entering through the main entrance and viewing the boldly stated fireplace in the Great Hall. Each room provides the expected luxury hotel standards of comfort, privacy, and service. Immerse in the history of Crater Lake Lodge by visiting the Exhibit Room just off the lobby. The Crater Lake Lodge Dining Room overlooks the lake and serves the finest northwest regional cuisine. Crater Lake Lodge is open from late-May thru mid-October. However, Crater Lake National Park offers many year-round things to do. Enjoy adventurous activities such as winter cross-country skiing and snowshoeing, summer camping, boat tours, hiking, and scenic tours around the lake. Crater Lake Lodge, a member of Historic Hotels of America since 2012, dates back to 1915.

Restaurant/Bar:
Red Lobster, 2200 Crater Lake Hwy, Medford, OR **97504**

Olive Garden Italian, 3125 Crater Lake Hwy, Medford, OR **97504**

Attraction: Oregon Shakespeare Festival (15 S Pioneer St, Ashland, OR **97520**), TAG Approved LGBTQ friendly attraction.

Peerless Hotel, Ashland

Accommodation: *Built in 1900 The Peerless Hotel has been lovingly restored and is featured in the Best Selling Book 1,000 Places To See Before You Die.* gay friendly

Address: 243 4th St, Ashland, OR 97520
National Register of Historic Places: 92001328, 1992

Peerless Hotel

Place

The Peerless Rooms Building was built in 1904 by Oscar and Lucinda Ganiard, who built many commercial buildings in Ashland, including the Ganiard Opera House. Long used for lodging in the railroad district (and known as The Ganiard Building), the vernacular brick front commercial style building is typical of the once prevalent rooming houses developed to serve the working-class men and women drawn to Ashland in the early years of the XX century. It was during this time when such single-room occupancy was the norm for residents of a working-class community. Following the 1887 completion of a north-south rail link over the formidable Siskyiou Mountains to the south, the Southern Pacific Company and its employees assumed a major role in the Ashland economy. Since Ashland's primary business district was located along Ashland Creek, over a mile distant from the tracks, a second commercial area developed along Fourth Street in what became known as the railroad district. Given the transitory nature of railroad employment, many of Southern Pacific's employees kept to themselves, avoiding the Ashland community at large. A large number of rooming houses in the Railroad District also provided low-cost housing for a number of young laborers, single women, and traveling salesmen who were drawn to Ashland by the booming economy that the railroad stimulated. It was under the ownership of Sarah Meekly that the building received the name, Peerless Rooms, in 1910. A significant element of the building is the sign painted on the brick proclaiming Peerless Rooms (probably dating from around 1915) with an early Coca-Cola advertisement. The boarding house went through many unproductive uses and sat vacant for many years before Crissy Barnett Donovan purchased the building (In late 1991). Acting as her own general contractor, she launched a massive two-year restoration of the building (including restoration of the Coca-Cola sign, long considered a ghost sign) completing the project in June 1994.

Park: Lithia Park T-Room & Lobby, Winburn Way, Ashland, OR **97520**, included in the Damron Address Book in 1980.

Restaurant/Bar:
Case Coffee Roasters, 44 Lithia Way, Ashland, OR **97520**
Greenleaf Restaurant, 49 N. Main St, Ashland, OR **97520**, GLD, Gay Lesbian Directory
Larks Home Kitchen Cuisine, 212 E Main St, Ashland, OR **97520**

Standing Stone Brewing Company, 101 Oak St, Ashland, OR **97520**
VIllage Commons Tavern, 66 E Main St, Ashland, OR **97520**, included in the Damron Address Book in 1980.

Accommodation:
Arden Forest Inn (261 W. Hersey St, Ashland, OR **97520**), gay owned. A 1890s mansion and carriage house.
Blue Moon B&B (312 Helman St, Ashland, OR **97520**), gay owned. 1896 Farmhouse 4.5 blocks from theatres and one block from historic Railroad District.
An oasis of gentility and charm in the beautiful Rogue River Valley, Ashland Springs Hotel (212 E Main St, Ashland, OR **97520**), TAG Approved LGBTQ friendly accommodation, is the premier choice for lodging in Southern Oregon. A two-year restoration project transformed this historic landmark into a haven of taste and elegance, reminiscent of small European hotels. It was originally known as the Lithia Springs Hotel and opened its doors in 1925, a time when tourism was booming thanks to the popularity of the Chautauqua lecture circuit and the nearby Lithia Springs. The advent of the automobile brought a wave of tourists who came to sample the fabled waters and take in the scenic surroundings. The town fathers envisioned a hotel that would accommodate the area's growing influx of visitors and would rival those back east. Today, the Ashland Springs Hotel continues to offer first-class hospitality to those who are drawn by business, the arts, or the area's natural beauty. Ashland Springs Hotel combines the charm of a B&B, the friendliness of a small inn, the feel of a spa resort, and the safety and convenience of a hotel. This beautifully restored hotel is on the National Register of Historic Places and is located in the heart of downtown Ashland, just steps from the renowned Oregon Shakespeare Festival. Other nearby attractions include the Oregon Cabaret Theater, Lithia Park, wine tastings and gallery tours, skiing, golf, fishing, river-rafting, tax-free shopping, dining, and pampering at the hotel's Waterstone Spa & Salon. Day excursions may include a scenic drive to its sister property, Lake of the Woods Mountain Lodge and Resort - a renovated historic 1920s fishing lodge with marina, general store, 26 cozy cabins, Crater Lake National Park, Oregon Caves, and Chateau and the Oregon Vortex. Ashland Springs Hotel, a member of Historic Hotels of America since 2005, dates back to 1925.
Ashland Creek Inn (70 Water St, Ashland, OR **97520**), LGBTQ owned.
Ashland's Tudor House (271 Beach St, Ashland, OR **97520**), LGBTQ friendly.
Country Willows B&B Inn (1313 Clay St, Ashland, OR **97520**), LGBTQ owned.
Cowslip's Belle B&B (159 N Main St, Ashland, OR **97520**), LGBTQ friendly.

Cemetery: More than 2,000 people attended a funeral Mass on June 17, 2002, for San Francisco police Officer Jon Cook (1964-2002), who was killed when his patrol car crashed into a second police car in the Mission District. Hundreds of officers from throughout Northern California -- from South Lake Tahoe to San Jose to Oakland -- packed St Mary's Cathedral on Geary Boulevard. Other officers stood somberly outside in memory of Cook, 38, the department's first gay officer to be killed in the line of duty. Cook's domestic partner, Jared Strawderman, and relatives followed the flag-draped casket of the officer into the church. Officers, their badges wrapped in black bands of mourning, stood at attention and saluted as police bagpipers played a mournful tune. Strawderman and Cook would have celebrated their third anniversary that same month. Cook when the police car he was driving collided with a second patrol car at 17th and Dolores streets. Four officers, two in each car, had been responding to the Castro to assist in the arrest of a man suspected of gouging out his girlfriend's left eye. Cook was a former biotech researcher who had a master's degree in biotechnology. He served as a lieutenant in Air Force intelligence before he joined the San Francisco Police Department in April 2001. Cook was the 95th San Francisco officer in the department's history to die in the line of duty. He was buried in a private ceremony at Eagle Point National Cemetery (2763 Riley Rd, Eagle Point, OR **97524**).

Park: Valley of the Rogue State Park, rest area & campground, Gold Hill, OR **97525**, included in the Damron Address Book from 1975 to 1976.

Find a grave

Cemetery: Tee Corinne (1943-2006) worked with photography, line drawing, paint, sculpture, ceramics and printing, and she published erotic fiction, poetry, and reviews. She came out in 1975 at which time she was in a relationship with Honey Lee Cottrell. Over the years, Corrine embarked upon relationships with Caroline Overman (early 1980s), Lee Lynch (mid 1980's) and Beverly Anne Brown. Former Josephine County resident Beverly Anne Brown died in 2005 of cancer. Brown was born in Fresno, CA, and grew up in Redding, CA. She attended Reed College in Portland. She wrote In Timber Country: Working People's Stories of Environmental

Conflict and Urban Flight, and was a co-editor of Voices From the Woods: Lives and Experiences of Non-Timber Forest Workers. She was founding director of the Jefferson Center for Education and Research and her final project was a comparative study of contract forest workers in Canada, Mexico and the US. They are buried side by side at Granite Hill Cemetery (2551 Upper River Rd, Grants Pass, OR **97526**).

Accommodation:
Motel Del Rogue (2600 Rogue River Hwy, Grants Pass, OR **97527**), gay friendly. Historic motel sitting on the banks of the Rogue River. In operation since the 1930's. Updated amenities with rustic charm. GLD, Gay Lesbian Directory

TouVelle House B&B (455 N Oregon St, Jacksonville, OR **97530**), LGBTQ owned and gay friendly. Located four short blocks from the Britt Festival, the historic TouVelle House is a classic 1916 Craftsman style home featuring six guest rooms with private baths and air conditioning. The swimming pool and gardens, as well as casually elegant, comfortable public areas throughout the inn invite guests to relax and unwind.

Whispering Pines B&B Retreat (9188 W Evans Creek Rd, Rogue River, OR **97537**) included in Inn Places 1999, Gay & Lesbian Accommodations Worldwide. Gay and Lesbian. As of 2021 it's closed.

97600

LGBTQ Center: Klamath Falls Gay Union, 428 S 9th St, Klamath Falls, OR **97601**, included in the Damron Address Book in 1980.

Restaurant/Bar:

Lighthouse Bar, Klamath Falls, OR **97601**, included in the Damron Address Book in 1980.

Accommodation:
Crystal Wood Lodge (38625 West Side Rd, Klamath Falls, OR **97601**), lesbian owned. Pet friendly accommodations near Crater Lake.
Worldmark Running Y (5432 Running Y Rd, Klamath Falls, OR **97601**) is 7 miles from Train Mountain Railroad Museum. Favell Museum is 30 miles away. Rogue Valley International-Medford Airport is 70 miles away from WorldMark Running Y. Part of World Rainbow Hotels (WRH), Lesbian and Gay Welcoming Hotels.

97700

Restaurant/Bar:
Olive Garden Italian, 63459 US-97, Bend, OR **97701**

Ben & Jerry's, 680 SW Powerhouse Dr, Bend, OR **97702**

Accommodation:
River Wild Retreat (61367 Wild Rapids Dr, Bend, OR **97702**), LGBTQ friendly.
WorldMark Bend - Seventh Mountain Resort (18575 SW Century Dr, Bend, OR **97702**) is within the inside of Deschutes National Forest, the resort with wood-accented lodging is 6.5 miles from downtown Bend and 15.6 miles from skiing at Mt. Bachelor. Part of World Rainbow Hotels (WRH), Lesbian and Gay Welcoming Hotels.
McMenamins Old St Francis School, 700 NW Bond St, Bend, OR **97703**
The Oxford Hotel, 10 NW Minnesota Ave, Bend, OR **97703**, Travellers' Choice Awards, 2022 Best of the Best Hotel in the US, by Tripadvisor.com
Bontemps Motel (74 W Monroe St, Burns, OR **97720**) included in Inn Places 1999, Gay & Lesbian Accommodations Worldwide. Gay friendly.
Cold Springs Resort (25615 SW Cold Springs Resort Lane, Camp Sherman, OR **97730**), LGBTQ friendly.
DiamondStone Guest Lodges (16693 Sprague Loop #8813, La Pine, OR **97739**), LGBTQ friendly.
Birdie 18 Guesthouses at Eagle Crest Resort (1522 Cline Falls Rd #5001, Redmond, OR **97756**), LGBTQ friendly.

WorldMark Eagle Crest (1590 Mountain Quail Dr, Redmond, OR **97756**) is 8 miles from Redmond airport and 18 miles from downtown Bend. Part of World Rainbow Hotels (WRH), Lesbian and Gay Welcoming Hotels.

FivePine Lodge & Conference Center (1021 E Desperado Trail, Sisters, OR **97759**), LGBTQ friendly.

97800

Accommodation:
The Pendleton House Historic Inn B&B (311 N Main St, Pendleton, OR **97801**), LGBTQ owned. An elegant 1917 Italian Renaissance-style mansion.
Geiser Grand Hotel (1996 Main St, Baker City, OR **97814**), LGBTQ friendly.

Barking Mad Farm B&B, 65156 Powers Rd, Enterprise, OR **97828**
Belle Pepper's B&B (101 S Mill St, Joseph, OR **97846**), LGBTQ friendly.
The Bronze Antler B&B (309 S Main St, Joseph, OR **97846**), gay friendly. Award-winning European Arts & Crafts lodging.

House: Shortly after graduating from college, Minor White (1908–1976) purchased a 35 mm Argus camera and traveled to the West Coast. He worked at the Beverly Hotel in Portland, OR, as a night clerk from 1937 to 1938 and began his career in photography. While in Portland, White lived at the YMCA. He was active in the Oregon Camera Club and spent his time photographing, exhibiting, and teaching photography to eager students. In 1938 White was chosen as a creative photographer for the Works Progress Administration. His assignment was to photograph the Portland waterfront and the city's nineteenth-century iron-façade buildings, which were beginning to be demolished. White also arranged two exhibitions for the WPA during that time. One was on early Portland architecture; the other, on the Portland waterfront. In 1940 the WPA sent White to teach photography in its Art Center located in La Grande, OR, near the Idaho border. He lived at 10 Depot St, La Grande, OR **97850**. He later directed the Center and wrote art criticism for local exhibitions while he was there. White returned to Portland in 1941 with the intention of establishing a photography business. In the same year, he participated in the Image of Freedom exhibition at the Museum of Modern Art in New York. Recognizing the high quality of White's work, the museum acquired some of his images for its permanent collection. White's first one-man exhibition of photographs taken in Eastern Oregon was held at the Portland Art Museum in 1942. His photographs were also published in Fair Is Our Land, edited by Samuel Chamberlain during that year. In addition, the Portland Art Museum commissioned White to photograph the Dolph and Lindley houses, two historical residences in the city.

Store: M. Crow & Co., 133 OR-82, Lostine, OR **97857**. This Lostine, OR, destination is a century-old store recently revitalized by artist Tyler Hays. Named among The 5 Best American Mercantiles to Shop for Christmas Gifts, 2017, by Country Living.

Accommodation:

Historic Union Hotel (326 North Main St, Union, OR **97883**), LGBTQ owned.

97900

Cemetery: Joe Little Joe Monahan (1850–1904), born Johanna Monahan, was an American businessman who worked in various prospecting and cattle industries around Silver City, ID, under an assumed masculine name and identity. The revelation of Joe's sex became a sensationalized national news story after his death in 1904. His life was the subject of the 1993 film The Ballad of Little Jo. Monahan had spent his early years in Idaho as a cowboy, and briefly lived in Oregon before returning to Owyhee County, where an 1898 census listed him as a cattle rancher. Monahan was said to have worked in the livery business, then a sawmill, and later saved several thousand dollars in mining, which were stolen in an investment fraud. Monahan voted in an 1880 Republican primary despite women being denied the vote at the time. He is buried at Rockville Cemetery (Jordan Valley, OR **97910**).

Washington

State bordering with: Canada, Idaho, Oregon.

Washington is ranked 8 out of 51 for % of same sex couples (0,725%), and is ranked 10 for # of same sex couples, 19.003. (US Census 2010)

Washington State's LGBTQ and Allied Chamber of Commerce: http://www.thegsba.org/

98000

Accommodation: Emerald Downs Racetrack and Casino (2300 Ron Crockett Dr, Auburn, WA **98001**), Washington State's LGBTQ and Allied Chamber of Commerce member.

Attraction: Rhododendron Species Botanical Garden (2525 S 336th St, Federal Way, WA **98003**), TAG Approved LGBTQ friendly attraction.

Restaurant/Bar: Red Lobster, 2006 S 320th St, Federal Way, WA **98003**

Accommodation: Courtyard by Marriott Seattle Federal Way (31910 Gateway Center Blvd S, Federal Way, WA **98003**), Washington State's LGBTQ and Allied Chamber of Commerce member and TAG Approved LGBTQ friendly accommodation.

Queer Architects: Mr. E. J. Fox residence alterations, 4237 91st Pl NE, Clyde Hill, WA **98004**, designed by Roland Terry (1958)

Alonzo W. and Margaret I. Robertson Residence

Queer Architects: Alonzo W. and Margaret I. Robertson Residence, 9529 Lake Washington Blvd NE, Bellevue, WA **98004**, Designed by Lionel Pries (1955-56). Minor alterations including new kitchen. Survives in private ownership in good condition.

Store: Rudy's Barbershop, 10713 Main St, Bellevue, WA **98004**

Queer Architects: Mr. and Mrs. F. Theodore Thomsen residence, 725 94th Ave SE, Bellevue, WA **98004**, designed by Roland Terry (1959)

Other non-queer residents: Theodore Roethke (1908-1963), 1219 96th Ave SE, Bellevue, WA **98004**, from 1953 to 1954.

Martin Rind house, exterior view of deck, Bellevue, Washington, August 1957, University of Washington Libraries, Special Collections

Queer Architects:

Mr. and Mrs. Russell Stephens residence, 2537 103rd Ave SE, Bellevue, WA **98004**, designed by Roland Terry (1958)

Martin Rind House, 3473 106th Ave SE, Bellevue, WA **98004**, designed by Tucker & Shields (1957).

Restaurant/Bar:

Ben & Jerry's, 166 Bellevue Way NE, Bellevue, WA **98004**

Maggiano's Little Italy, 10455 NE 8th St, Bellevue, WA **98004**

Pagliacci Pizza (8 100th Ave NE, Bellevue, WA **98004**), Washington State's LGBTQ and Allied Chamber of Commerce member.

Taylor Shellfish Oyster Bar (504 Bellevue Way NE, Bellevue, WA **98004**), Washington State's LGBTQ and Allied Chamber of Commerce member.

Hotel 116, a Coast Hotel (625 116th Ave NE, Bellevue, WA **98004**), TAG Approved LGBTQ friendly accommodation.

Seattle Marriott Bellevue (200 110th Ave NE, Bellevue, WA **98004**), Washington State's LGBTQ and Allied Chamber of Commerce member.

W Bellevue (10455 Northeast 5th Place, Bellevue, WA **98004**), Washington State's LGBTQ and Allied Chamber of Commerce member.

The Westin Bellevue (600 Bellevue Way NE, Bellevue, WA **98004**), Washington State's LGBTQ and Allied Chamber of Commerce member.

LGBTQ friendly bookstore: Love Season, 12001 NE 12th St, Bellevue, WA **98005**, included in the 1984 Gayellow Pages.

Queer Architects:

Charles and Mildred Gates Residence, 5315 148th Ave SE, Bellevue, WA **98006**, Designed by Lionel Pries (1950-51). Completely altered by later expansions.

John Clinton Denman, Sr. and Edna Jean Gieselman House, 14845 SE 55th St, Bellevue, WA 98006, designed by Tucker & Shields (1956-1957). Tucker and Shields designed three houses at Hilltop between 1951-1957, this being the last. The house has a post and beam framing system with posts placed 8 feet on center. Interiors were meant to recall Japanese domestic interiors with dark wood structural members juxtaposed with light wall surfaces. Exterior landscaping, seen in the gravel garden paralleling the front walkway, also recalled Japanese domestic precedents. The firm planned the house for John Clinton Denman, Sr. (1913-1994), a pilot for Northwest Airlines, and his wife, Edna Jean Gieselman (1918-1988). When Edna passed away, John remained in the house until at least 1992, and perhaps until his death in 1994. Originally, the Denmans maintained a significant art collection in the house. Featured in Bellevue Modernism Tour Over the Bridge for Gracious Living (2003).

Harry S. and Mary Brown House, 250 145th Ave SE, Bellevue, WA **98007**, designed by Tucker & Shields (1961). Featured in Bellevue Modernism Tour Over the Bridge for Gracious Living (2003).

Restaurant/Bar:
Pagliacci Pizza (15238 Bel-Red Rd, Bellevue, WA **98007**), Washington State's LGBTQ and Allied Chamber of Commerce member.

House: William M. MacLane (1926-2000) was an American artist. In 1982, MacLane sold all his remaining works and moved to Bothell, where he lived another twenty years at 17705 88th Pl NE, Bothell, WA **98011**, quickly fading from public view.

Queer Architects: 19419 Grannis Rd, Bothell, WA **98012**, Designed by Lionel Pries. A parcels of land with houses by both Pries and Robert Fields. They were on the market in 2014 for the sum of $1.18 million.

House: Donn Talenti (1932-2017)'s passion for opera started in New York City where he delighted in sharing performances at the Metropolitan Opera with his family and friends. At 18, Donn met Julian Patrick at The Roxy Theatre. Julian was singing in the chorus and Donn was working as a page. Julian became an accomplished opera singer, performing internationally. They were together for fifty-six years sharing a passionate partnership in life, love and The Arts. Nickolas Donn Talenti was born in New York City. After college, he rose to become a trusted Chief Financial Officer for the Riese Organization of New York of New York City where he remained for thirty-three years, retiring in 1996. Moving to Seattle, Donn became immersed in the Seattle Opera. He was a dedicated member of the Seattle Opera Guild, also serving as President. Donn was a dynamic Seattle Opera Patron and Donor, an Ambassador and Artist Aide. He often hosted visiting opera principle singers from the time they arrived in Seattle until their departure at the conclusion of the opera's performance run. In recent years, as an Ambassador, he shared his knowledge and understanding of the Opera's content with new patrons at McCaw Hall. Although he could have easily retired after arriving in Seattle, Donn chose to create an Encore Career working in the Seattle Opera Ticket office until just days before his death. Besides attending opera, Donn loved theatre performances, gardening, travelling, collecting and movies. Donn always delighted in hosting many family holidays and any opportunity to get his family and friends together. Donn Talenti passed away at his home at 3805 146th St SE, Bothell, WA **98012**, after living in the Seattle and Mill Creek area for 21 years.

Restaurant/Bar:
Top Pot Doughnuts and Coffee (18001 Bothell Everett Hwy, Bothell, WA **98012**), Washington State's LGBTQ and Allied Chamber of Commerce member.

Musuem: The Lavender Palette: Gay Culture and the Art of Washington State at the Cascadia Art Museum (190 Sunset Ave, Edmonds, WA **98020**) was a packed art show and a powerful history lesson. Museum curator David F. Martin put together artwork by dozens of gay men and women who often, just a few short decades ago, had to hide who they were in order to express themselves artistically. The exhibit closed on January 26, 2020. The featured artists included Edmonds native Guy Anderson, illustrator Richard Bennett, Ward Corley, Thomas Handforth, Mac Harshberger, Jule Kullberg, Delbert J. McBride, Orre Nelson Nobles, Malcolm Roberts, potter Lorene Spencer, Sarah Spurgeon, ceramicist Virginia Weisel, Clifford Wright, and also one-time Woodway resident Morris Graves, Leo Kenney, Mark Tobey, Lionel Pries, Leon Derbyshire, and Sherrill Van Cott.

Careladen

House: In the late 1940s Morris Graves (1910-2001) purchased land at 10830 Wachusett Rd, Woodway, WA **98020**, and began construction of a unique cinderblock house he came to call Careladen. One of the first Northwest homes to be made out of cinder block, Graves designed the three-bedroom, 5,181 square-foot home with the help of notable architects Robert Jorgenson, AIA and Robert Shields (one of the grand old men in Northwest architecture). Graves wanted the home, which he dubbed Careläden, to be hidden from the world so he built a high wall around it just to make sure. Unfortunately, he didn't stay long. As the land around the estate was developed and the world encroached on his privacy, he decided to move to Ireland before eventually settling in California. Poet Theodore Roethke and his wife were said to have rented it for a time but the home was eventually sold. Today, the residence remains a unique and stunning escape on 2.5 acres nestled in the woods of Snohomish County. The one-level property boasts 14-foot ceilings and wood-paneled rooms. There have been renovations over the years, which include a new kitchen, family room, sunroom, and an updated master suite. The surrounding wall remains and created a serene courtyard effect from many of the rooms that look out on it. The ground are also loaded with well-landscaped features, including a courtyard with columned portico, pond, pool, and sport court. In the 1950s Graves was not faring very well in his love life. He had been involved with a man named Yonemitsu (Yone) Arashiro, who fell hopelessly in love with him but was taken aback at Graves' contradictory nature. The extant letters between the two men reveal a chronology of hopeful, romantic love, followed by Yone's desperate attempt to resign himself to a hopeless loss of the idea of romantic love. In a letter dated November 13, 1952, he wrote to Graves: You are building your life with one justifiable selfishness. My downfall is that I need someone to love and share the hopes and dreams that belong to nowhere, no other, or even anywhere. A selfish love for two people, for their inner self alone. If I must walk this life alone, I would do so. I cannot comply or try to discharge this inner feeling. So, I am going to resign myself to a solitary life & live another kind of life void of all emotional ties. After Arashiro, Morris Graves met and fell in love with Paul Mills, a Seattle-born museum professional who had attended the University of Washington and was working at the university's Henry Art Gallery as assistant curator in 1952 and '53. Mills, who was 14 years younger than Graves, was living a closeted existence, but that didn't stop Graves from falling for him. Their relationship was brief but intense. Surving letters show Graves for once as the shunned partner. Mills addressed his conflict in an undated letter to Graves: I'm at last beginning to learn something you have learned for yourself and have tried to tell me, the importance of calming down. I have also discovered, by watching myself and seeing what I get confused about and when I get along well, that homosexuality is something that creates too much of a strain on me and makes life difficult for me, hence I had better give that up. The next chapter of my life is going to be devoted to developing a nice, calm middle. I have investigated the extremes of experiences a little too thoroughly. Graves responded: This is what I cannot withhold letting you know: You are in my thoughts almost constantly, but those earlier thoughts which (during the months before winter) were set in motion by you (and willingly together) are now thoughts cheated of their long & urgently needed expressions. You have killed half of my heart, half of my spirit. You have replaced a kind of growing buoyancy with a negative vacancy. You have, at last, by your behaviour, put a kind of solid vacancy into my spirit, into my whole way of being & breathing & searching and that which in my life was, by you, once invited into a renewed living & expanding & creating experience has found finally only the drying effect of your smashing & that is why you, whom I loved, I now feel only hatred for. Mills, resigned to his stand, replied: Morris, the answer seems to be no and quite a final one. And it would only make things more difficult for both of us if we were to see each other again. Mills went on to marry a woman and had children. They remained married until his wife's death in 1999, after which he came out as a homosexual and became an activist in California. His son, Mike Mills, wrote and directed an award-winning fulm titles Beginners in 2010 based on his father's complicated life. Within a few years of the end of his relationship with Mills, Graves met a young man named Richard Svare and had a long-term, productive relationship with him.

Restaurant/Bar: Epulo Bistro (526 Main St, Edmonds, WA 98020), Washington State's LGBTQ and Allied Chamber of Commerce member. Pagliacci Pizza (10200 Edmonds Way, Edmonds, WA 98020), Washington State's LGBTQ and Allied Chamber of Commerce member.

House: In his early twenties, Morris Graves (1910-2001) finished high school in 1932 in Beaumont, TX, while living with his maternal aunt and uncle. He then returned to Seattle, and received his first recognition as an artist when his painting Moor Swan (1933) won an award in the Seattle Art Museum's Northwest Annual Exhibition and was purchased by the museum. He split his time between Seattle and La Conner, WA, where he shared a studio with Guy Anderson. Graves' early work was in oils and focused on birds touched with strangeness, either blind, or wounded, or immobilized in webs of light. Graves began his lifelong study of Zen Buddhism in the early 1930s. In 1932 Graves and Guy Anderson were both living with their parents in Edmonds, just north of Seattle, and the two became lovers. To commemorate a three-way they had with artist Lionel Pries in the 1930s, Morris Graves and Guy Anderson made a two-sided watercolor — Graves' nude study of Anderson on one side, Anderson's study of Graves on the other. In 1934, Graves built a small studio on family property at 186th Pl SW, Edmonds, WA **98026**. When it burned to the ground in 1935, almost all of his work to date was lost with it. In the mid-1930s, Morris Graves met a handsome young man named Sherrill Kinney Van Cott from the small town of Sedro-Woolley, 72 miles north of Seattle. Van Cott had briefly attended the University of Washington after graduating from high school in 1931, but was largely a self-taught artist. He first began exhibiting in the Northwest Annuals at the Seattle Art Museum in 1935 with an oil painting titled Potato Eaters, while Graves also showed two oils. Both artists exhibited in the annuals for the next few years, and in 1939 Van Cott began to exhibit sculpture. The few extant sculptures by Van Cott, using regional materials, appear to have been influenced by the French sculptor Henri Gaudier-Brzeska, who had died at age 24 in WWI. Graves and Van Cott developed a romantic relationship, with Graves exerting a stylistic influence on the slightly younger artist. Van Cott was also a poet, and his writings were compatible with the visual content of his paintings. He focused on insects and other animals, both real and imagined, as well as complex intertwining of the male human form in a fossil-like contained border. Van Cott's last painting, a watercolor titled Weeping Girl, was exhibited at the Northwest Annual from October 7 through November 8, 1942. A month later, he was dead at age 29 from cardiac failure. 20 years earlier, Van Cott had contracted scarlet fever, which caused a severe hearth problem, leaving him practically an invalid for most of his short life. The local art scene had lost a promising talent, and Graves a lover and acolyte. He promoted Van Cott's work long after his death, and preserved many works in his own collection.

Queer Architects:

Inglewood Country Club additions and alterations, 6505 Inglewood Rd NE, Kenmore, WA **98028**, designed by Roland Terry (1962)
Church of the Redeemer parish hall addition, 6211 NE 182nd St, Kenmore, WA **98028**, designed by Roland Terry

Restaurant/Bar:
Pagliacci Pizza (6504 NE Bothell Way, Kenmore, WA **98028**), Washington State's LGBTQ and Allied Chamber of Commerce member.

Ben & Jerry's, 1011 NE High St Suite 103, Issaquah, WA **98029**

Accommodation:

TownePlace Suites Seattle Southcenter (18123 72nd Ave S, Kent, WA **98032**), LGBTQ friendly.

Restaurant/Bar:
Ben & Jerry's, 176 Lake St S, Kirkland, WA **98033**
Pagliacci Pizza (13005 NE 70th Pl, Kirkland, WA

98033), Washington State's LGBTQ and Allied Chamber of Commerce member.

Accommodation:
The Heathman Hotel Kirkland (220 Kirkland Ave, Kirkland, WA **98033**), TAG Approved LGBTQ friendly accommodation.
Decorated in a contemporary coastal style, the 4 star Woodmark Hotel - Still Spa (1200 Carillon

Point, Kirkland, WA **98033**) offer guests a fine-dining restaurant with picturesque views of the Lake Washington and the Seattle skyline. Part of World Rainbow Hotels (WRH), Lesbian and Gay Welcoming Hotels.

Queer Architects: Mr. and Mrs. Steve Wertheimer country residence, 14312 132nd Ave NE, Kirkland, WA **98034**, designed by Roland Terry (1975)

Restaurant/Bar:
Olive Garden Italian, 11325 NE 124th St, Kirkland, WA **98034**
Pagliacci Pizza (11640 98th Ave NE, Kirkland,

WA **98034**), Washington State's LGBTQ and Allied Chamber of Commerce member.

Accommodation:

Courtyard Seattle Kirkland (11215 NE 124th St, Kirkland, WA **98034**), LGBTQ friendly.

Restaurant/Bar:

Red Lobster, 4231 196th St SW, Lynnwood, WA **98036**

Accommodation:
Hampton Inn & Suites (19324 Alderwood Mall Pkwy, Lynnwood, WA **98036**), gay friendly.

Spacious guest rooms, suites and studios. Extended stay suites in North Seattle.

Presentation drawing of the Stixrood House, Mercer Island, WA, c. 1957. Drawing by Tucker and Shields, Architects, courtesy of Sandra Condiotty

Queer Architects:

St. Thomas Episcopal Church parish hall addition, 8398 NE 12th St, Medina, WA **98039**, designed by Roland Terry (1953)

Overlake Golf and Country Club bar-dining room addition, 8000 NE 16th St, Medina, WA **98039**, designed by Roland Terry (1965)
King George Restaurant, 7720 SE 27th St, Mercer Island, WA **98040**, designed by Roland Terry (1969)
Jarvis A. Stixrood House, 8226 SE 41st St, Mercer Island, WA **98040**, designed by Tucker & Shields (1957-1958). The Seattle architectural firm of Tucker and Shields produced this house for Jarvis Alan Stixrood (1920-1981), a mechanical (automotive)

engineer who worked for the Pacific Car and Foundry Company (PACCAR) from the late 1940s until at least the late 1960s. By 1997, this residence had had four owners: Jarvis Stixrood (1958-1962), Ralph Senders (1962-1972), Ronald Coulter (1972-1997) and Jeffry and Sandra Rae Condiotty (1997-present).

Mr. and Mrs. H. A. Kettering residence, 4727 80th Ave SE, Mercer Island, WA **98040**, designed by Roland Terry (1959)

Mrs. E. Heitman Anderson residence, 6627 W Mercer Way, Mercer Island, WA **98040**, designed by Roland Terry (1957)

6914 W Mercer Way, Mercer Island, WA **98040**, designed by Tucker & Shields.

Restaurant/Bar:

Pagliacci Pizza (3077 78th Ave SE, Mercer Island, WA **98040**), Washington State's LGBTQ and Allied Chamber of Commerce member.

Store: Rudy's Barbershop, 16095 Cleveland St, Redmond, WA **98052**

Accommodation:
Seattle Marriott Redmond (7401 164th Ave NE, Redmond, WA **98052**), LGBTQ friendly and

Washington State's LGBTQ and Allied Chamber of Commerce member.

Store: Rudy's Barbershop, West Campus Commons, 15255 NE 40th St, Redmond, WA **98052**

Accommodation:
Hilton Garden Inn Seattle/Renton (1801 E Valley Rd, Renton, WA **98057**), LGBTQ friendly. TownePlace Suites Seattle South/Renton (300 SW 19th St, Renton, WA **98057**), LGBTQ friendly.

Salish Lodge & Spa, 6501 Railroad Ave, Snoqualmie, WA **98065**, Travellers' Choice Awards, 2022 Best of the Best Hotel in the US, by Tripadvisor.com

Skiers Chapel, 1964

Queer Architects:

Skiers Chapel, Snoqualmie Summit, Snoqualmie Pass, WA **98068**, designed by Tucker & Shields (1964). The Chapel is located behind the Forest Ranger Station in the Snoqualmie Pass Summit West complex.

Thunderbird Restaurant, Snoqualmie Pass, WA **98068**, designed by Tucker & Shields (1956). Thunderbird Restaurant later known as Thunderbird Lodge, is a building at Summit West. It is at the top of Thunderbird Hill, off of Wildside. From 1956-1990 it was an active restaurant that served skiers seeking a meal and a mountain view. The building is now abandoned. The exact date that Thunderbird Restaurant shut down is not known, but it is generally believed that around 1990, the restaurant was shut down by the Health Department. The Summit's master development plan released in 1998 called for a full-scale renovation of Thunderbird Restaurant. Reportedly, in the early 2000s, a small movement was started on the Pass to raise money to renovate the lodge, and it has been said that Booth Creek had pledged to put up money to finish the project. This never came about. The project was still on the master development plan when it was approved by the National Forest Service in 2008, and is still on the the most recent version issued in 2010. An inquiry was put on the Summit's Facebook page concerning the future of the lodge in 2012, to which a representative replied no plans to open it any time soon. It is not known at this time what will become of the lodge in the future.

Thunderbird Restaurant, exterior view, Snoqualmie Pass, Washington, December 7, 1956, University of Washington Libraries, Special Collections

Gay Village

Vashon, WA **98070** is ranked 22 out of 25 among US Small cities (Population below 100.000) for % of same sex couples (3,303%), and is ranked 16 for # of same sex couples, 152. (US Census 2010)

Accommodation:
Artist's Studio Loft B&B, 16529 91st Ave SW, Vashon Island, WA **98070**
Bayview Retreat, 9549 SW Bayview Dr, Vashon Island, WA **98070**, GLD, Gay Lesbian Directory
Casa Vista B&B, 6700 SW Luana Beach Rd, Vashon Island, WA **98070**, GLD, Gay Lesbian Directory
Pt. Robinson Keepers' Quarters (3705 SW Point Robinson Rd, Vashon, WA **98070**), gay friendly. Two luxuriously renovated homes perched near a lighthouse on Puget Sound's shore.

Quarters A is a completely furnished 3-bedroom, 2-bath, 2-story home which accommodates up to six adults.
Willows Lodge (14580 NE 145th St, Woodinville, WA **98072**), Washington State's LGBTQ and Allied Chamber of Commerce member.
Pagliacci Pizza (22830 NE 8th St, Sammamish, WA **98074**), Washington State's LGBTQ and Allied Chamber of Commerce member.

Other non-queer residents: Ray Brandes House, 2202 212th Ave SE, Sammamish, WA **98075**, designed by Frank Lloyd Wright in 1952.

98100

Seattle

Seattle, WA, is ranked 2 out of 25 among US Large cities (Population above 250.000) for % of same sex couples (2,306%), and is ranked 4 for # of same sex couples, 6.537. (US Census 2010)

Seattle, WA, is ranked 4 out of 18 among US cities for Percentage of Same-Sex Couple Households, 2017

Seattle, WA, has been named among the Gayest Cities in America by The Advocate, 2010

Seattle, WA, has been named among the Gayest Cities in America by The Advocate, 2011

Seattle, WA, has been named among the Gayest Cities in America by The Advocate, 2012

Seattle, WA, has been named among the Most Lesbianish Cities in America by Jezebel, A supposedly Feminist Website, 2012

Seattle, WA, has been named among the Gayest Cities in America by The Advocate, 2013

Seattle, WA, has been named among the Gayest Cities in America by The Advocate, 2014

Seattle, WA, has been named among the Queerest City in America by The Advocate, 2016

Seattle, WA, has been named among the Queerest City in America by The Advocate, 2017

Seattle, WA, has been named among the Top LGBT-friendly cities by ellgeeBE, 2018

Seattle, WA, has been named among the Top Lesbian Vacation Destinations by Lesbian Business Community, 2019

Airport Way

Restaurant/Bar:
The Palace Theater & Art Bar (5813 Airport Way S, Seattle, WA **98108**), Washington State's LGBTQ and Allied Chamber of Commerce member.

Fran's Chocolates (5900 Airport Way S, Seattle, WA **98108**), Washington State's LGBTQ and Allied Chamber of Commerce member.

Alaska Street

Restaurant/Bar: A la Mode Pies (4225 SW Alaska St, Seattle, WA **98116**), Washington State's LGBTQ and Allied Chamber of Commerce member.

Alaskan Way

Restaurant/Bar:
Poop Deck, South Main St & Alaskan Way S, Seattle, WA **98104**, included in the Damron Address Book in 1970.

Ivar's Acres of Clams, 1001 Alaskan Way, Seattle, WA **98104**, included in The Lady Jai Recommended List, 1954. Washington State's LGBTQ and Allied Chamber of Commerce member.

Pier 57 Miners landing (1301 Alaskan Way, Seattle, WA **98101**), TAG Approved LGBTQ friendly attraction.

Accommodation:
Seattle Marriott Waterfront (2100 Alaskan Way, Seattle, WA **98121**), LGBTQ friendly and Washington State's LGBTQ and Allied Chamber of Commerce member.

The Edgewater Hotel (2411 Alaskan Way, Seattle, WA **98121**), LGBTQ friendly.

Restaurant/Bar: AQUA by El Gaucho (2801 Alaskan Way, Seattle, WA **98121**), Washington State's LGBTQ and Allied Chamber of Commerce member.

Alki Avenue

Beach: Alki Beach, 2665 Alki Ave SW, Seattle, WA **98116**, included in the Damron Address Book from 1977 to 1980.

Andover Park

Restaurant/Bar: Seattle Chocolate (1180 Andover Park W, Seattle, WA **98188**), Washington State's LGBTQ and Allied Chamber of Commerce member.

Aurora Avenue

Restaurant/Bar:
Pagliacci Pizza (719 Aurora Ave, Seattle, WA **98109**), Washington State's LGBTQ and Allied Chamber of Commerce member.
Denny's, 307 Aurora Ave N, Seattle, WA **98109**, included in the Damron Address Book in 1970.

Canlis Restaurant

Queer Architects: Canlis (2576 Aurora Ave N, Seattle, WA **98109**) is a landmark fine-dining destination (since 1950s) offering Pacific NW fare in a mid-XX century-modern home. Recent home to multi-disciplinary pandemic pivots designed to serve the city. Bert Tucker (1910-1983) was an American architect. One of Lionel Pries' students, Robert Shields, became not only a successful architect but also a talented watercolorist, designer, and ceramic artist. In 1946, after serving in the US Navy during WWII, he joined forces with another gay architect, Roland Terry, as well as Bert Tucker. Together, the three men helped to establish a Northwest aesthetic in regional architecture, partially influenced by Pries' knowledge and collecting of Asian art and antiques. Born in Washington, DC, Bert Atherton Tucker was raised in Seattle and graduated from the University of Washington with a Bachelor of Arts degree in English (1931), and Bachelor's degree in Architecture (1940). While still attending school, Tucker worked as a draftsman for architect J.M. Taylor Jr. Upon graduation, he moved to Bremerton and began working for Barry & Kenneth Branch, the largest architectural firm on the Kitsap peninsula. At the age of 35, in 1946, Tucker established a practice with fellow University of Washington graduates Robert Shields and Roland Terry. The talented young firm focused primarily on residential designs for a cross-section of clients from professionals to Seattle's budding creative class. Among the firm's most notable projects during this early period is the W.E. Warren House (1949), the Zoe Dusanne House (1949), the Mayer House (1950), the Burnett Brothers Jewelers Store (1951), and Canlis Restaurant (1951)—all located in Seattle. The Bud Burnett House (1949) in the Broadmoor area, built on stilts into a hillside, was so forward thinking that it continued to be featured as an example of good design in many architectural magazines some 15 years after it was built, and brought the firm many new commissions. After Terry left the partnership to establish his own firm in 1951, Tucker & Shields continued their collaboration until 1962. Still focusing primarily on residential designs, many of their homes were featured in national home building and design magazines such as Sunset and Popular Homes. Many of the firm's projects can be found in Seattle and on the east side communities of Lake Washington. The most notable examples include the Moffett House (1954) in Seattle, the Brown House (1961) in Bellevue, the Denman House (1957) in the Hilltop neighborhood, the Rind House (1961) and the Hayter House in Issaquah (1956). Tucker passed away in Seattle in October of 1983.

Cemetery: Richard W. Ric Weiland (1953–2006) was a computer software pioneer and philanthropiSt He was one of the first five employees of Microsoft Corporation. In 2002, Weiland began seeing Mike Schaefer, an account manager at a software firm and former strategic adviser to the Seattle City Council. Schaefer says he and Ric were drawn together by a shared interest in gay activism. I was first attracted by Ric's commitment to the community, says Schaefer. He was a strong believer in the Seattle Foundation's healthy community model, which included the arts, health, education, and so on. And I was struck by how articulate and focused he was and that he had a really broad portfolio of interests. Mike Schaefer has distributed more than $180 million – nearly 100% of their assets – to 20 charitable organizations since his partner's death in 2006. Weiland is buried at Evergreen-Washelli Memorial Park (11220 Aurora Ave N, Seattle, WA **98133**).

Ballard Avenue

Restaurant/Bar:
Staple & Fancy (4739 Ballard Ave NW, Seattle, WA **98107**), Washington State's LGBTQ and Allied Chamber of Commerce member.
Marine Hardware at Staple & Fancy (4741 Ballard Ave NW, Seattle, WA **98107**), Washington State's LGBTQ and Allied Chamber of Commerce member.
Ballard Pizza Company (5107 Ballard Ave NW, Seattle, WA **98107**), Washington State's LGBTQ and Allied Chamber of Commerce member.
Bramling Cross (5205 Ballard Ave NW, Seattle, WA **98107**), Washington State's LGBTQ and Allied Chamber of Commerce member.

King's Hardware (5225 Ballard Ave NW, Seattle, WA **98107**), Washington State's LGBTQ and Allied Chamber of Commerce member.

Store: Rudy's Barbershop, 5229 Ballard Ave NW, Seattle, WA **98107**

Ballinger Way

Restaurant/Bar: Pagliacci Pizza (20059 Ballinger Way NE, Shoreline, WA **98155**), Washington State's LGBTQ and Allied Chamber of Commerce member.

Barclay Court

Accommodation: Barclay Court Guest Studios (E Barclay Ct, Seattle, WA **98122**), LGBTQ owned.

Bayard Avenue

House: The US Census of 1940 indicated that Roland Terry (1917-2006) lived with his mother on 15th Avenue NW in the Crown Hill neighborhood of Seattle. By 1943, his mother lived at 9800 Bayard Ave NW, Seattle, WA **98117**. When Terry left for his European travels in 1949, he indicated that his home address remained at 9800 Bayard. Terry entered the architecture program at the University of Washington program in architecture in 1935; although he effectively completed the five-year program to earn his B.Arch. by 1940, the degree was not awarded for some years because he was short a few credits. During his years at Washington he benefited from the mentorship of faculty member Lionel Pries. In 1941, Terry won an American Institute of Architects (AIA) Langley Scholarship which allowed him to tour South America and see many examples of the region's early Modern buildings. From 1942 to 1946, Terry served in the military. On Terry's return to Seattle, he joined University of Washington classmates Bert A. Tucker and Robert M. Shields to form Tucker, Shields & Terry. The firm designed custom houses, restaurants and other small buildings, usually in wood and other natural materials, and began to emerge as leaders in Northwest regional Modern architecture. Terry left the partnership in 1949 to study painting in Paris. He studied painting at the Academie Julian, Paris France, during the winter, 1949-1950. The firm continued as Tucker & Shields. In 1950, Tucker, Shields & Terry and Wimberly & Cook were hired to design the Seattle restaurant Canlis. Updates and alterations were later designed by Tucker & Shields, and then by Terry & Moore. The building is considered a Seattle landmark. In 1952, Terry joined Philip A. Moore to form Terry & Moore, a new firm based in Seattle. Terry & Moore executed a large number of houses, often including significant landscape design and interior design, usually in collaboration with emerging designers in those professions.

Bellevue Avenue

Queer Architects: Belroy Apartments, 703 Bellevue Ave E, Seattle, WA **98102**, Designed by Lionel Pries (1931). While in partnership with William J. Bain, Pries worked on the design for the Bel-Roy Apartments, a Capitol Hill landmark completed in 1931.

Restaurant/Bar: Olive Way Tavern, 1706 Bellevue Ave, Seattle, WA **98122**, included in the **Damron Address Book** in 1978.

Belmont Avenue

LGBTQ friendly bookstore: Beyond the Closet Bookstore, 1501 Belmont Ave, Seattle, WA **98122**, active in 1990.

Bergman Road

Accommodation: Waterfall Gardens Private Suites (7269 NE Bergman Rd, Bainbridge Island, WA **98110**), **LGBTQ friendly**.

Blenheim Drive

Queer Architects: John and Fannie Hamrick House, 1932 Blenheim Dr E, Seattle, WA **98112**, Designed by Lionel Pries (1930). John Hamrick was the Pacific Northwest's father of theaters, having started the Rex Theatre, Blue Mouse Theatres, Music Box Theatre, Roxy Theatre and many more. The House was on the market for $3.895 million. Constructed in 1930, the house has been described as classic Santa Barbara Spanish. Possibly meant to evoke Hollywood, the residence eschews windows for interior courtyards, exposed beam ceilings and decorative carvings. Wrough iron balconies and gates, stenciled beams, heraldic shields, and a castone fireplace also evoke the same motifs found in the Music Box Theatre.

Boren Avenue

Restaurant/Bar:
Monastery, 1900 Boren Ave, Seattle, WA **98101**, included in the **Damron Address Book** from 1979 to 1980.
Boren Street, 2015 Boren Ave, Seattle, WA **98101**, included in the **Damron Address Book** from 1978 to 1980.
Thirteen Coins, 125 Boren Ave N, Seattle, WA **98109**, included in the **Damron Address Book** from 1972 to 1976.

Boston Street

Mayer residence exterior showing patio, Seattle, Washington, 1950, University of Washington Libraries, Special Collections

Queer Architects: Millie Mayer House, 1353 E Boston St, Seattle, WA **98112**, designed by Tucker & Shields (1950).

Boston Terrace

Queer Architects: Mr. Robert Block residence remodel and alterations, 1617 E Boston Terrace, Seattle, WA **98112**, designed by Roland Terry (1954)

Bothell Way

Acacia Memorial Park & Funeral Home

Cemetery: *In 1926, the Greater Seattle Masonic Lodge founded Acacia Memorial Park. The acacia tree symbolizes the promise of rebirth in Masonic rites. They sold the cemetery to Fred Burnaby and his family in 1927. The original gardens in the memorial park were designed to form a Celtic cross when looked at from above. Construction on Acacia's original mausoleum began in 1928, and the 1st phase was completed in 1931.*

Address: 14951 Bothell Way NE, Seattle, WA 98155

Notable queer burials:

Alex Calderwood (1966-2013), a founder of the Ace Hotel chain, whose quirky vintage interiors influenced the industry and became the backdrop for countless Instagram pictures. Calderwood, whose dress was rigorously casual and who wore his black hair in a chaotic mop, became the face of a brand that has, as The New York Times put it in 2008, attracted a growing clientele of artistic types short on cash and egalitarians with money to spare. Calderwood was born in Denver and grew up around Seattle, the son of a contractor and a newspaper columnist. He skipped college, became a party promoter and ran a vintage clothing business in Seattle. In the early 1990s, he and a friend risked $12,000 to reinvent the classic barbershop with tile floors, sturdy barbers' chairs and walls covered in old posters and snapshots. As the shop, Rudy's, prospered and expanded to a chain of more than a dozen in the late 1990s, Calderwood and his partners were offered the lease on a 28-room flophouse in a run-down part of Seattle. We put a deal together, jumped into the project with both feet, had absolutely no idea what we were doing and through instinct, came up with something fresh, he told BlackBook magazine in 2009. The then-pioneering blend of reclaimed furniture and touches like street art, turntables in rooms and low prices $65 for a room with a shared bathroom that they used in creating the hotel became Calderwood's signature, and was widely imitated. He and his partners chose the name Ace because the card is the high and the low card in the deck, he said. We employ that high and low principle in our hotel models. In designing a hotel, he said in a 2011 interview with The Times, there's a lot of the pieces of the puzzle. It is not just an interesting design, it is not just the right choice of typeface, it is not finding the executives or team it is all these pieces of the puzzle. By the time of Calderwood's death, Ace had become established in Portland, OR; New York; Palm Springs, CA; and London, with other hotels scheduled to open in Panama and Los Angeles. All arrived complete with buzzword-friendly restaurants and cafes (farm-to-table, nose-to-tail, single-source); in-house music from D.J.'s and bands; and, in some hotels, guitars in the rooms. The people who frequented the Ace Hotel at Broadway and 29th Street in New York, The Times said, thought of it as their club, a place whose aesthetics and business model are redefining the overlapping worlds of drinking, dining, sleeping and shopping. Others, however, derided the hotels as a prepackaged pastiche of counterculture. Yet as the chain grew, Calderwood and his partners separated. One of them, Jack Barron, an architect, said disagreements were not helped by Calderwood's drinking. But Calderwood, in the 2011 interview, said that he had been sober for five months after treatment in a rehabilitation facility. You get to a certain age, and you get to a certain point, where you realize this is just, like, dragging me down, he added. It's not fun anymore. I'm not enjoying it. Calderwood, an aficionado of graphic designers such as Lou Dorfsman and Milton Glaser who was often photographed in jeans, T-shirts and Converse sneakers (he helped design a pair), did not enjoy the label hipster, frequently applied to his hotels, and to him. He seemed to seek to define himself differently. Hotels were art projects, he said, and his business card billed him as a cultural engineer. I'm just a barber and a tattoo pimp, he told Interview magazine early in his career.

Find a grave

We Sail Together: **Jule Kullberg** (1905-1976) and **Orlena F. Harsch** (1904–1995) met at the University of Washington in the 1920s and lived together since then. When Kullberg died in 1976, there was no mention of Harsch in her obituary, even though the women had been a couple for over 40 years. Orlena, in tribute to her life partner, set up the Jule Kullberg Memorial Award with both the Northwest Watercolor Society and WPW. Before Orlena's death in 1995, most of Kullberg's paintings were dispersed to friends and students without record.

Monte Edgar Brown (1914-1999) was the chairman and publisher of the Seattle Daily Journal of Commerce. He was the longtime partner of Ward Corley. Monte Brown died at his Seattle home. The newspaper was later run by Monte Brown's nephew, Denis Brown, and Denis' son, Phil Brown.

Boylston Avenue

LGBTQ Center:
Gay Community Center, 110 Boylston Ave E, Seattle, WA **98102**, included in the Damron Address Book in 1978.
In 1999 the Gay City offices were at 128 Boylston Ave E, Seattle, WA **98102**. It's now Fred Wildlife Refuge. Gay City is Seattle's LGBTQ Center.

House: Jule Kullberg (1905-1976) dedicated her life to teaching at the expense of pursuing a national career in fine arts. Although she painted and exhibited locally, her influence as a teacher was also substantial. Some of her students went on to become major figures in the region, including Fay Chong, Morris Graves, Leo Kenney, Neil Meitzler, and Malcolm Roberts. Kellberg never his her relationship with her life partner, Orlena F. Harsch (1904-1995), so she naturally would have been a trusted figure among her gay students. Jule Helen Kullberg was born an only child in Sain Paul, MN, and moved as a baby with her parents to Seattle the year of her birth. Her mother, Pauline Broadum, was a German immigrant, and her father, John Emil Kullberg, was a Swedish immigrant who worked as a salesman and real estate investor. Mr Kullberg was interested in parapsychology and, as a member of the Seattle Psychic Research Society, lectured on his own psychic experiences as well as the practice of automatic writing. Jule studied at the University of Washington, graduating with a BA in dramatic art in 1927. During her time as a student, she designed stage sets and props for various UW productions. She later entered the University of Oregon on a Carnegie Scholarship, and consequently studied with Dong Kingman at Mills College in Oakland, CA, and with George Grosz in New York. While attending the University of Washington, Kullberg met a fellow student, Orlena Harsch, who was pursuing a career as a teacher. Harsch came from both an artistic and academic family. Her father, Howard Harsch, was an extremely talented photographer who had studios in Seattle and Yakima. Her brother, Alfred E. Harsch, became a prominent Seattle attorney and professor at the University of Washinton, serving in their School of Law for 35 years. After graduating from the UW, Kullberg taught public speaking, science and world history at Prosser High School in Washington before accepting a teaching position in the Bothell school district in 1928. Orlena also joined the Bothell faculty by 1932. It was around this time that the two women started living together as a couple. When Jule accepted a position to teach drama and English at Seattle's Broadway High School in 1935, Orlena moved in with Jule in her parents' home until they rented an apartment at 505 Boylston Ave E, Seattle, WA **98102**, on Capitol Hill that same year. Jule had always liked to sketch and paint in watercolor, through her education had been primarily in the dramatic arts. One of her friends, artist Edmond James Fitzgerald, admired her painting and encouraged her to return to the university to advance her art education. With a new focus on the visual arts, she became a very active member of Women Painters of Washington (WPW), one of the region's most prominent arts organizations. Orlena secured a teaching job at Highline High School, in nearby Burien, where she also became itivolved in the school's theater productions. Around this time the couple purchased a cabin on Whidbey Island for weekend getaways and as a summer residence. In the late 1930s, they began following, their lifelong passion for travel by visiting Jule's aunt Emma Olson, who lived outside Gothenburg, Sweden. As the new decade began, they had purchased a home on Seattle's Queen Anne Hill and then sold the cabin and built a larger country home at Coupeville, also on Whidbey Island. The women did much of the construction work themselves, and Jule decorated the interior and exterior of the home as well as customizing the furniture with designs based on Pennsylvania Dutch and Swedish iconography, celebrating her own paternal heritage. The Coupeville area attracted a number of lesbian couples who also found the beauty of the island a safe refuge from the city. Orlena began working at Seattle's Queen Anne High School in 1943, initially teaching French and then becoming the school's head counselor. She was active in the Administrative Women in Education organization, assisting international students after the war. Jule became a prominent member of the Northwest Watercolor Society and began showing her work in their annual exhibitions at the Seattle Art Museum in 1943. She would be involved with that organization for the next thirty years, exhibiting twenty-one watercolors during the period of her membership. Jule's teaching position changed in 1946 when Broadway High School student were redirected to other districts as the school merged with the neighboring Edison Technical School. The following year the couple spent a month during the summer on a driving trip to allow Jule to sketch up and down the West Coast. Since Jule never learned to drive, Orlena indulged her partner's artistic pursuits by driving her wherever she thought she would find inspiration. Their love of the ocean caused them purchase yet another home, this time at Arch Cape on the Oregon Coast, where Jule could paint and entertain friends and family. The new Broadway-Edison became a school for adults as well as accornmodating WWII veterans to assist in their training and reintegration into the job market through the GI Bill. Jule continued her position at the technical school and became head of their flourishing art department by 1953, hiring prominent local artist friends such as Jacob Elshin, Fay Chong, and Yvonne Twining Humber to teach night classes. This school became the starting point for numerous future successful Northwest artists, including Doris Totten Chase, who had taken painting classes there at the beginning of her career. In 1948 the Northwest Watercolor Society held its first national exhibition at the Riverside Museum in New York. Five of Jule's watercolors were among the 101 paintings exhibited by forty-three artist members of the organization. This was a significant honor for the contributing artists and a validation of their talents and advocacy of the difficult medium. Jule and Orlena were both savy in financial matters, and besides their teaching jobs, they had extra income from investments in apartment buildings in Seattle. This allowed them to build a new studio home in 1948 on Seattle's posh Queen Anne Hill with a spectacular view of the city and Puget Sound. They would often open their home to artists and arts organizations, especially WPW, which held its annual Christmas parties there for several years. Jule honed her art skills and learned printmaking as well. In 1950 she taught screen printing for members of WPW and became their president in 1954. Her artistic ambitions were generally aimed at teaching and promoting younger artists, although she exhibited her own work in group presentations locally as well as in New York, Hawaii, and California. Jule and Orlena never hid the fact that they were a couple. Their families and artist friends accepted their relationship as a matter of fact and gave them their support and love. In 1963 both women took sabbaticals from their educational careers and indulged in a nine-month trip around the world. Their financial acumen had allowed them to travel extensively, with regular trips to Hawaii, Palm Springs, and other locations that welcomed gay visitors. Jule retired from teaching in 1965 to concentrate on travel and painting. Orlena soon followed suit. From February to April, 1971, actor Richard Chamberlain rented Jule and Orlena's home through discreet connections in local gay circles. The actor, who was closeted at the time, could live freely with his then boyfriend in a nonthreatening atmosphere. When Chamberlain occupied the upstairs quarters of their home, the women went to Honolulu, Alaska, and the Oregon Coast to give him some privacy. Jule and Orlena continued to support their former students, younger artists, and professional women as time and finances allowed.

Queer Architects: Designed by noted architect Robert Shields, A.I.A., 1005 Boylston Ave E, Seattle, WA **98102**, is a stylish contemporary retreat located in the historic

Harvard/Belmont district, offering the ultimate in elegance & privacy.

Broad Street

Restaurant/Bar: Space Needle (400 Broad St, Seattle, WA **98109**), TAG Approved LGBTQ friendly attraction, has been named among the Bars & Restaurants Where You Can Be Your Full Queer Self in Seattle by Travel Out Seattle, 2018.

Broadway

Gay City, Creative Commons Licenses, via Wikimedia Commons

Club: Crystal Steam Baths, 722 Broadway, Seattle, WA **98122**, included in the 1964 and 1965 Guild Guide. Included in the 1964 Directory. Included in the Damron Address Book in 1979. Included in the 1975 All Lavender International Gay Guide.

Sam Hill House, Creative Commons Licenses, via Wikimedia Commons

House: Sam Hill House (E Highland Dr & Broadway E, Seattle, WA **98102**) is a historic, privately owned home located in the Capitol Hill neighborhood. The property forms part of the city-designated Harvard-Belmont Landmark District. The concrete building was constructed between 1909 and 1910 by railroad magnate Sam Hill in preparation for a planned visit to Seattle by a member of the Belgian royal family. Following Hill's 1931 death, the home remained vacant until its purchase in 1937 by Theodore and Guendolen Plestcheeff. Guendolen Plestcheeff, a notable local preservationist, remained resident at the property until her death in 1994. After spending time in Ireland, Morris Graves (1910-2001) returned to Seattle in 1964, living for several months in the so-called Pletscheff Mansion. In 2016 the home went on sale for $15 million.

AIDS Memorial: Capitol Hill Station Plaza (140 Broadway E, Seattle, WA **98102**), Seattle AIDS Legacy Memorial, since 1 December 2019, without names. The Seattle AIDS Legacy Memorial (SALM) will ensure that an historic epoch, the early days of the AIDS crisis in Seattle and neighboring communities, is accurately and comprehensively told by those who were on the front lines of the initial battle against AIDS and the fear and discrimination created by the epidemic. SALM's Community Advisory Group is guided by three goals/mandates: Create a place of reflection and remembrance; Tell the history of Seattle/King County's AIDS crisis of the 1980s-90s and to capture the lessons of the crisis and diverse community responses to it; and Provide a call to action to end AIDS and to protect against discrimination and stigma. Former Seattle City Councilmember Tom Rasmussen, along with Leonard Garfield, executive director of the Museum of History & Industry, and Michele Hasson, community volunteer, convened a group of stakeholders in summer 2015 to assess interest in creating a memorial to recognize those lost during the AIDS crisis of the 1980s-90s as well as our communities' responses to it. Seattle City Council provided funding to MOHAI to identify sites for the memorial, engage with community leaders, identify design parameters and goals, and seat a Community Advisory Group, with three subcommittees: Community In-reach, Content & Experience, and Fund Development. The group concluded the best of these to be a site consisting of the northern edge of Cal Anderson Park, the adjacent public plaza at the Capitol Hill Link light rail Transit-oriented Development (CHTOD), and the connecting festival street block of East Denny Way.

Restaurant/Bar: Two-O-Six Tavern, 206 Broadway E, Seattle, WA **98102**, included in the Damron Address Book in 1978.

Store: Fantasyland, 219 Broadway E, Seattle, WA **98102**, included in the Damron Address Book in 1980.

Restaurant/Bar: Le Faux Playhouse (5415, 300 Broadway E, Seattle, WA **98102**) at Julia's on Broadway puts on Seattle's longest running celebrity impersonation show. The nationally acclaimed drag show is often hosted by some of biggest names in drag, including Seattle's supremely talented Jinkx Monsoon, winner of Rupaul's Drag Race Season 5.

LGBTQ friendly bookstore: A Different Drummer, 420 Broadway E, Seattle, WA **98102**, included in the Damron Address Book in 1980.

Restaurant/Bar:
Pagliacci Pizza (426 Broadway E, Seattle, WA **98102**), Washington State's LGBTQ and Allied Chamber of Commerce member.

Queer Architects: Jade Pagoda Restaurant remodel, 606 Broadway E, Seattle, WA **98102**, designed by Roland Terry (1962)

Restaurant/Bar:
Lionhead (618 Broadway Ave. East, Seattle, WA **98102**) gay owned by James Beard Award-winning chef Jerry Traunfeld and his husband, Stephen Hudson. Top LGBTQIA+ Owned and Operated Restaurants in America, OpenTable 2021
Poppy (622 Broadway E, Seattle, WA **98102**), Washington State's LGBTQ and Allied Chamber of Commerce member, gay owned by local celebrity chef Jerry Traunfeld, who used to be executive chef of The Herbfarm (as well as a former Top Chef: Masters contestant).
Jimmy's on Broadway (1100 Broadway, Seattle, WA **98122**), Washington State's LGBTQ and Allied Chamber of Commerce member.

Accommodation:
B&B on Broadway (722 Broadway E, Seattle, WA **98102**) included in Inn Places 1999, Gay & Lesbian Accommodations Worldwide. Gay friendly. GLD, Gay Lesbian Directory
The Bacon Mansion B&B (959 Broadway East, Seattle, WA **98102**), Washington State's LGBTQ and Allied Chamber of Commerce member. Washington on Capitol Hill close to downtown. Included in Inn Places 1999, Gay & Lesbian Accommodations Worldwide. Gay friendly. GLD, Gay Lesbian Directory
Silver Cloud Hotel (1100 Broadway, Seattle, WA **98122**), Washington State's LGBTQ and Allied Chamber of Commerce member and TAG Approved LGBTQ friendly accommodation, is located in the Capitol Hill neighborhood of Seattle. We have 179 rooms and suites with complimentary Internet access. Part of World Rainbow Hotels (WRH), Lesbian and Gay Welcoming Hotels.

Restaurant/Bar: DJ Wildfire and her wife Armida run the Inferno (formerly Hot Flash) all-women's dances that take place throughout the month in either Seattle or Portland. With the tagline Open Minds = Happy Times, this power couple is in it to win it. Uniting the community at Neighbours Nightclub (1509 Broadway, Seattle, WA **98122**) on the first and third Saturdays of the month is only the beginning for the Inferno Gals. Neighbours Nightclub is Seattle's longest-running and largest LGBT nightclub. Since 1982, it has been welcoming visitors—regardless of sexual orientation or gender identity—to dance the night away and enjoy performances from some of the world's biggest entertainers.

House: Ralph Edward Spencer (1914-1973) was an American artist. In the 1940s he lived at 2327 Broadway E, Seattle, WA **98102**. Lorene and Ralph Spencer owned and operated the Spencer Potter Studio in South Seattle in the Mid-XX century producing a variety of stoneware bowls, vases, plates, mugs, etc. Lorene also produced painted ceramic tiles that often used impressions from a modified printing block. The Pottery was known for its high quality local sourced clays and the glazes mixed from Washington State minerals gathered by Ralph Spencer. Although Lorene and Ralph Spencer were both gay, they maintained their marriage until Ralph's death in 1973. Afterward, Lorene and her life partner, Ruth Henry, had a close friendship with Bud McBride and Richard Scheneider, who sold Lorene's work along with their own Crow Valley pottery, as well as work by other talented artists, until their retirement in 1995. Born in Spirit Lake, ID, to George Forrest Spencer and Emma Anna Bailey. Lorene Rhua Flower met Ralph E. Spencer while he was serving in the Coast Guard at Astoria, OR, and they soon married. Ralph lived in Spirit Lake, Idaho, until 1935, when he moved to Seattle to attend the University of Washington. He studied chemical engineering at the UW until he enlisted in the Coast Guard in 1942, serving as a motor machinist's mate in Depoe Bay, OR. In her later years, Lorene explained that both she and Ralph were aware of their homosexual orientations but, like many gay people of their generation, they had innocently thought that if they married and had children, these feelings would resolve and change to heterosexual orientation, which, naturally, did not happen. However, they decided not to act on their same-sex attractions and remained a couple. After their marriage, Ralph and Lorene worked in a family business running a fishing resort on the Umpqua River in Oregon, where they built boats and manufactured docks. After a few years, in 1948, they sold their share of the business and moved to Newberg, OR, where they made their first ceramic works. After some initial success, they started marketing their work through the Meier & Frank department store in Portland. Newberg's largely conservative political leanings became too stressful and so the family headed for Seattle in 1951, there establishing the Spencer Pottery business. By 1955, Spencer Pottery was located in the Seattle suburb of Tukwila. The Spencers were active members of the Clay Club, founded in 1948 in Seattle. Other Clay Club members included Virginia Weisel and architect Robert Shields.

Brooklyn Avenue

Other non-queer residents: Robinson Jeffers (1887-1962), 4215 Brooklyn Ave NE, Seattle, WA **98105**, from 1910 to 1911.

California Avenue

Restaurant/Bar:
Ma'ono, 4437 California Ave SW, Seattle, WA **98116**.
Pagliacci Pizza (4449 California Ave SW, Seattle, WA **98116**), Washington State's LGBTQ and Allied Chamber of Commerce member.

Campus Parkway

Restaurant/Bar: Pagliacci Pizza (Lander Hall, 1245 NE Campus Pkwy, Seattle, WA **98195**), Washington State's LGBTQ and Allied Chamber of Commerce member.

School: The University of Washington (320 Schmitz Hall, 1410 NE Campus Parkway, Seattle, WA **98195**) has been named among the 100 Best Campuses for LGBT Students by The Advocate College Guide for LGBT Students, 2006. It is a public flagship research university based in Seattle. Founded in 1861, Washington is one of the oldest universities on the West Coast. Smith Hall T-rooms and G.P.A. Union Bldg. have been included in the Damron Address Book from 1972 to 1980. The Husky Den and ballroom additions in the Husky Union Building (4001 E Stevens Way NE, Seattle, WA **98195**) were designed by Tucker & Shields. Annual LGBT Event Highlights: Welcome Week (last week of September), Coming Out Day (October 11), World AIDS Day (December 1), Drag Show (February), Ally Week (February), Q Center Birthday (February), Mother's Day Celebration (May), Pride Week (May), Lavender Graduation (June). LGBT Resource center/office: Q Center (450 Schmitz Hall, P.O. Box 355838, Seattle, WA **98195**). Notable queer alumni and faculty: Alice B. Toklas (1877–1967), Bert Tucker (1910-1983), Bobbi Campbell (1952-1984), Jack Nichols (1938–2005), Jon-Henri Damski (1937–1997), Josephine Herbst (1892–1969), Jule Kullberg (1905-1976), Lionel Pries (1897–1968), Nicholas Heer (born 1928), Orlena F. Harsch (1904–1995), Pehr Hallsten (1897-1965), Reah Whitehead (1883–1972).

Queer Artists: Whale's Jaw, Dogtown Common, (painting, 1934), by Marsden Hartley (1877-1943), Henry Art Gallery, University of Washington, 15th Ave NE & NE 41st St University of Washington campus, Seattle, WA **98195**.

Cherry Street

Restaurant/Bar: The Fox & Hounds, 122 Cherry St, Seattle, WA **98104**, included in The Lady Jai Recommended List, 1954.

Commodore Way

Queer Architects: Mr. and Mrs. Austin Case residence, 3718 W Commodore Way, Seattle, WA **98199**, designed by Roland Terry (1957)

Delmar Drive

William MacLane house, exterior view, Seattle, Washington, July 23, 1953, University of Washington Libraries, Special Collections

Queer Architects: William MacLane House, 2402 Delmar Dr E, Seattle, WA **98102**, designed by Tucker & Shields (1953). Photographer Carl Natelli worked in conjunction with William M. MacLane (1926-2000), who acted as a distributor for the work of a number of artists and photographers from the region and beyond. MacLane had been a combat artist during WWII, and he continued to make art his profession when he returned to Washington after the war. He worked in pencil-and-ink drawings that portrayed sailors, soldiers, and surfers in addition to Northwest subjects like rugged lumberjacks and beachgoers. Most of MacLane's works reflect the vocabulary of the midcentury physique genre: muscular models, sexually charged scenes, but no overt sex displayed. His artwork is clearly designed to appeal to a gay audience since his scenes always show a heavy sensuality and (when there are two or more figures) there is a subtle but obvious sexual tension to the scenes. MacLane was prosperous enough in 1953 to build a starkly modern house overlooking Portage Bay that was featured in the Seattle Times in 1955. The artist worked in a variety of mediums including pen and ink, watercolor, and oils. In 1982, MacLane sold all his remaining works and moved to Bothell, where he lived another twenty years, quickly fading from public view.

Denny Blaine Place

Queer Architects: Mr. and Mrs. Louis Dulien residence, 4000 E Denny Blaine Pl, Seattle, WA **98112**, designed by Roland Terry (1954)

Denny Way

Queer Architects: Frol and Peaseley office alterations at the John Hancock Building, 204 Denny Way, Seattle, WA **98109**, designed by Roland Terry (1969)

Restaurant/Bar: The Hub (421 Denny Way, Seattle, WA **98109**) was the first lesbian bar to open in Seattle, active from 1950 to 1966. Owned by Marjory Taylor and Anne Thompson.

Dexter Avenue

Accommodation:
Holiday Inn Seattle Center (211 Dexter Ave N, Seattle, WA **98109**), **LGBTQ friendly**.
Oakwood Seattle South Lake Union (717 Dexter Ave N, Seattle, WA **98109**) is located in Seattle in the Washington State Region, 900 yards from Space Needle, while the original Starbucks store is 1.1 miles from the property. Part of **World Rainbow Hotels (WRH), Lesbian and Gay Welcoming Hotels**.

Restaurant/Bar: Chez Paul, 1107 Dexter Ave N, Seattle, WA **98109**, included in the **Damron Address Book** from 1977 to 1980.

Queer Architects: Clark's Restaurant Enterprises office, 1319 Dexter Ave N, Seattle, WA **98109**, designed by Roland Terry (1976)

Dravus Street

Restaurant/Bar: Pagliacci Pizza (1614 W Dravus St, Seattle, WA **98119**), Washington State's LGBTQ and Allied Chamber of Commerce member.

Eastlake Avenue

Restaurant/Bar: Eastlake East, 101 Eastlake Ave E, Seattle, WA **98109**, included in the **Damron Address Book** in 1980.

Edgecliff Drive

Other non-queer residents: William Tracy House, 18971 Edgecliff Dr SW, Normandy Park, WA **98166**, designed by Frank Lloyd Wright in 1954.

Elliott Avenue

Queer Architects: Office, 2819 Elliott Ave, Seattle, WA **98121**, designed by Roland Terry (1968)

Evergreen Point Road

Beach: BA (Bare Ass) beach near Evergreen Point Floating Bridge, Evergreen Point Rd & SR-520, Medina, WA **98039**, included in the **Damron Address Book** from 1976 to 1980.

Fairview Avenue

Accommodation: Residence Inn Seattle Downtown/Lake Union (800 Fairview Ave N, Seattle, WA **98109**), **LGBTQ friendly**.

Fauntleroy Way

Store: Rudy's Barbershop, 4480 Fauntleroy Way SW, Seattle, WA **98126**

Federal Avenue

Park: Broadway Playfield, 500 Federal Ave E, Seattle, WA **98102**, included in the Damron Address Book from 1977 to 1980.

Freemont Avenue

Restaurant/Bar:
Dancing Machine, 3400 Fremont Ave N, Seattle, WA **98103**, included in the Damron Address Book from 1976 to 1978.
Too Hi Tavern, 3405 Fremont Ave N, Seattle, WA **98103**, included in the Damron Address Book in 1977.

Green Lake Drive

Restaurant/Bar: Ben & Jerry's, 7900 E Green Lake Dr N Suite 104, Seattle, WA **98103**

Greenwood Avenue

House: Roland Terry (1917-2006) was a Pacific Northwest architect from the 1950s to the 1990s. He was a prime contributor to the regional approach to Modern architecture created in the Northwest in the post-WWII era. One of Lionel Pries' students, Robert Shields, became not only a successful architect but also a talented watercolorist, designer, and ceramic artist. In 1946, after serving in the US Navy during WWII, he joined forces with Roland Terry, another gay architect, as well as Bert Tucker. Together, the three men helped to establish a Northwest aesthetic in regional architecture, partially influenced by Pries' knowledge and collecting of Asian art and antiques. Terry was born in Seattle, the son of Clyde Casper Terry (1884-1919) and Florence E. Beach (1880-1958). Clyde's father was a preacher in Port Townsend, WA, in 1880, while Florence's worked as a farmer in Ottawa, KS, in 1900. He lived for most of his life in the Puget Sound. At one year of age, Roland lived with his parents at 5610 Greenwood Ave N, Seattle, WA **98103**, in Seattle's Phinney Ridge neighborhood near Woodland Park. This residential area was new at the time, with many small bungalows lining this section of Greenwood Avenue. Right after their marriage, Clyde worked as a teacher at the Young Men's Christian Association (YMCA). According to Clyde Terry's WWI registration documentation, he was self-employed as a contracting engineer in Seattle, WA. Clyde died very young, at age 35 in 1919, creating unsettled financial conditions for his wife and son. He and his mother, Florence, moved periodically. At the age of three, just after his father's death, he lived with his widowed mother and grandmother in Compton, CA. Between 1920 and 1932, mother and son shuttled between two addresses in Seattle, possibly two properties that the family owned. Florence and Roland resided at 306 N 56th St, Seattle, WA **98103**, but, by 1925, they returned to dwell at 5610 Greenwood Avenue, where they also stayed in 1927 and 1928. In 1930-1931, their address was back at 306 North 56th Street, and the following year, at 5610 Greenwood Avenue. The 1930 US Census indicated that Roland, his mother, and his widowed paternal grandmother, Emma C. Terry lived at 5612 Greenwood Avenue. The census reported that they lived at 306 North 56th Street, but this address was adjacent to 5612 Greenwood.

Hospital: In 1975 the Lesbian Clinic was active at the Fremont Women's Clinic (6817 Greenwood Ave N, Seattle, WA **98103**).

Hamlin Street

Queer Architects: Seattle Yacht Club interior additions and alterations, 1807 E Hamlin St, Seattle, WA **98112**, designed by Roland Terry (1961)

Harrison Street

Park: Seattle Center, near International Foutain, 305 Harrison St, Seattle, WA **98109**, included in the Damron Address Book from 1976 to 1980.

Queer Architects: Le Tastevin restaurant, 19 W Harrison St, Seattle, WA **98119**, designed by Roland Terry (1982)

Henderson Street

Restaurant/Bar: Bird On A Wire Espresso (3507 SW Henderson St, Seattle, WA **98126**), lesbian owned since 2002.

Highland Drive

Queer Architects:
Residence at 4105 E Highland Dr, Seattle, WA **98112**, designed by Roland Terry (1960)
Mr. and Mrs. E. Dickenson Peaseley residence addition, 321 W Highland Dr, Seattle, WA **98119**, designed by Roland Terry (1970)

Hillside Drive

Jay Jacobs residence, exterior view, Seattle, Washington, June 8-11, 1953, University of Washington Libraries, Special Collections

Queer Architects: Jay Jacobs Residence, 849 Hillside Dr E, Seattle, WA 98112, designed by Tucker & Fields (1953)

Howell Street

Restaurant/Bar:
Thirsty Tavern, 1114 Howell St, Seattle, WA **98101**, included in the Damron Address Book in 1980. Later Re-bar, named among the Greatest Gay Bars in the World by Out.com, 2007. Named among the Greatest Gay Bars in the World by Out.com, 2013.
Dylan's Tavern, 1224 Howell St, Seattle, WA **98101**, included in the Damron Address Book in 1977. Later Marshall's Office, included in the Damron Address Book from 1978 to 1980.

International Boulevard

Cemetery: Cal Anderson (1948–1995) was an American politician. A Democrat, he served in both chambers of the Washington State Legislature, representing the 43rd Legislative District in Pos. 1 in the State House of Representatives, as well as in the State Senate. Anderson was Washington's first openly gay legislator. Anderson served in Vietnam before his political career where he won two Bronze Star Medals and four Army Commendation Medals. On November 9, 1987, Anderson was appointed to a state house vacancy by King County Council, becoming Washington state's first openly gay legislator. He represented the 43rd legislative district, focused on downtown Seattle. In November 1994, he was elected to the Washington State Senate, taking office in January 1995. He served only briefly in the Senate, dying on August 4, 1995 of AIDS. He is buried at Washington Memorial Park (16445 International Blvd, SeaTac, WA **98188**). Future Seattle mayor Ed Murray served as his campaign manager during the 1988 legislative race. On April 10, 2003, Seattle's Broadway Park was renamed Cal Anderson Park in his honor.

Accommodation: The Coast Gateway Hotel (18415 International Blvd, Seattle, WA **98188**), TAG Approved LGBTQ friendly accommodation.

Holiday Inn Express Hotel & Suites SEA-TAC (19621 International Blvd, SeaTac, WA **98188**), LGBTQ friendly.

Jackson Street

Restaurant/Bar: Annex or The Silver Slipper, 210 S Jackson St, Seattle, WA **98104**, was a lesbian bar active from 1969 to the late 1970s. Included in the Damron Address Book from 1970 to 1977. Included in the 1975 All Lavender International Gay Guide.

Accommodation: Embassy Suites by Hilton Seattle Downtown Pioneer Square (255 S King St, Seattle, WA **98104**), Washington State's LGBTQ and Allied Chamber of Commerce member.

Queer Architects: Seattle First National Bank Branch, 502 S Jackson St, Seattle, WA **98104**, Designed by Lionel Pries. After losing his job at the University of Washington, Pries designed exterior and interior decorative elements for the International Distric branch of Seattle. First National Bank while working for the firm Durham, Anderson and Freed.

John Street

Webb Moffet house, exterior view of patio and garden, Seattle, Washington, May 1954, University of Washington Libraries, Special Collections

Queer Architects: Webb Moffett House, 3767 E John St, Seattle, WA 98112, designed by Tucker & Fields (1954).

Theodore Roethke (1908-1963), 3802 E John St, Seattle, WA **98112**, from 1957 to 1963.

Mrs. Paul Siegel residence, 3814 E John St, Seattle, WA **98112**, designed by Roland Terry

Kenilworth Place

Dr. and Mrs. Russell Anderson residence, 5126 Kenilworth Pl NE, Seattle, WA **98105**, designed by Roland Terry (1955)

Lake City Way

Mojito (7545 Lake City Way NE, Seattle, WA **98115**), Washington State's LGBTQ and Allied Chamber of Commerce member.

Lake Washington Boulevard

Kurt Cobain House, 171 Lake Washington Blvd E, Seattle, WA **98112**

Lakeside Avenue

Leschi Park, 201 Lakeside Ave S, Seattle, WA **98122**, included in the Damron Address Book from 1977 to 1980.

Laurelhurst Drive

Lionel H. Pries Residence

Queer Architects: Lionel H. Pries Residence, 3132 W Laurelhurst Dr NE, Seattle, WA **98105**, Designed by Lionel Pries (1947-48). Partial third floor added about 1969-70; full third floor added ca. 1980. Survives in private ownership in good condition, but exterior appearance was changed by added floor.

Leary Way

Restaurant/Bar: Frēlard Pizza Company (4010 Leary Way NW, Seattle, WA **98107**), Washington State's LGBTQ and Allied Chamber of Commerce member.

Lenora Street

Queer Architects: Warwick Seattle Hotel, 401 Lenora St, Seattle, WA **98121**, designed by Roland Terry (1978), **LGBTQ friendly**.

Lorentz Place

LGBTQ Center: In 1975 the Lesbian Mothers National Defense Fund was active at 2446 Lorentz Pl N, Seattle, WA **98109**.

Lynn Street

House: Paul Mills (1924-2004) was a museum professional who had attended the University of Washington and was working at the university's Henry Art Gallery as assistant curator in 1952 and '53. Morris Graves met and fell in love with him. Mills, who was 14 years younger than Graves, was living a closeted existence, but that didn't stop Graves from falling for him. Their relationship was brief but intense. Surving letters show Graves for once as the shunned partner. Mills went on to marry a friend from high school, Jan Dowd, in 1955 and had children. They remained married until his wife's death in 1999, after which he came out as a homosexual and became an activist in California. His son, Mike Mills, wrote and directed an award-winning fulm titles Beginners in 2010 based on his father's complicated life. Paul Chadbourne Mills was born in Seattle, WA, the son of Reed Chadbourne Mills (1895–1982) and Lillian Hoey (1896–1977). In the 1940s the family lived at 2605 E Lynn St, Seattle, WA **98112**. After high school, he enlisted in the Army and was sent to Alaska as part of the communication corps. From 1945 to 1948 he attended Reed College in Oregon and for the next three years worked as a reporter with the Bellevue American in Washington state. In 1953 he earned a bachelor's degree in art history from the University of Washington. Mills' lifelong career in the arts began with a part-time job at the university's Henry Gallery, where he served as assistant curator for a year beginning in 1952. He went on to the fledgling Oakland Museum, starting as art curator before being named director, a post he held until 1970. Mills was active in the Bay Area Figurative Movement and the Pop Art Movement. He gave Richard Diebenkorn his first show, said his daughter, and wrote notably about painter David Park, who was the focus in his 1961 (master's) thesis in art history from UC Berkeley. That work -- known as the only firsthand book on the artist -- was published in 1988 as The New Figurative Art of David Park. During the 1960s, he and his wife were also active in Oakland's civil rights movement, and Mills helped his wife open a collection of stores and restaurants in Oakland, the Bret Harte Boardwalk, in 1963. They also worked for passage of bonds for a new building for the Oakland Museum of California, Katie Mills said. The couple moved to Santa Barbara in 1970 when Mills took over as director of the Santa Barbara Museum of Art. For three decades Mills was a powerful force in the public arts scene, ranging from spearheading a project to line the breakwater and Stearns Wharf with flags to raising money for the rainbow sculpture, Chromatic Gate, near Fess Parker's Doubletree Resort. Mills was a champion of many local causes, serving on the boards of the Santa Barbara Flag Project, Santa Barbara Maritime Museum, Santa Barbara Trust for Historic Preservation, Contemporary Arts Forum, Prime Timers and Gay Santa Barbara. His daughter Katie Mills, of Los Angeles, said he is probably the busiest person ever to die. He was drawn to flag design and he designed the Santa Barbara County flag, which hangs in the county Courthouse arch. In a 2001 News-Press interview, Mills said, Flags are a combination of modern design and history. Heraldry I find interesting. In 1977, Mills started the Santa Barbara Flag Project, 36 colorful flags that line the breakwater, each representing a community organization. The project also encompasses the Cedric Boeske Memorial, a dozen historic flags of California on Stearns Wharf. When his wife died in 1999, Mills came out as a gay man. He served as vice president of Gay Santa Barbara and organized Pride art shows. His daughter said he also joined Trinity Church and actively explored his beliefs and religion. He also joined Santa Barbara Prime Timers, of which he served as president. Mills remained vibrant, loving and clear-minded up until the very end of his busy life, said his daughter. Many never guessed the extent of his illness because he remained so active and committed to his causes. In addition to his daughter Katie, Mills is survived by a daughter, Megan Kitchen of Santa Barbara, a son, Mike Mills of Los Angeles.

Paul Mills died of lung cancer. He was 79. The Paul Mills Archives of California Art are held at the Oakland Museum.

Queer Architects: Sylvester residence garden development plan, 4215 E Lynn St, Seattle, WA **98112**, designed by Roland Terry (1981)

Madison Street

Accommodation:
Renaissance Hotel (515 Madison St, Seattle, WA **98104**), Washington State's LGBTQ and Allied Chamber of Commerce member.
Hotel Sorrento (900 Madison St, Seattle, WA **98104**), Washington State's LGBTQ and Allied Chamber of Commerce member. Since 1909, the Sorrento Hotel on Seattle's First Hill has been a special place where memories are made, and traditions are born.

Pony, Creative Commons Licenses, via Wikimedia Commons

Restaurant/Bar:
Pony (1221 E Madison St, Seattle, WA **98122**) has been named among the Greatest Gay Bars in the World by Out.com, 2013. It has been named among the Amazing Gay Bars Around The World To Visit Before You Die, by BuzzFeed, 2019. It has been named among The 25 Best LGBTQ Bars and Nightclubs in the US, 2019, Matador Network. Serving as a tribute to the West Village and Castro bars of the 1970s, Pony in Seattle is housed in a 1930s-era gas station — now transformed into a beloved hangout space for hipsters and members of the LGBTQ community alike. Meeting somewhere in the middle, the bar and club blares punk rock, disco, new wave, and indie rock music for the Seattle queer hipsters to shimmy and shake to all night long. If you're looking for a party in Seattle, put on your dancing shoes and head to the Pony.
Madison Pub, 1315 E Madison St, Seattle, WA **98122**
Queen Bee Café (2200 E Madison St B, Seattle, WA **98112**), Washington State's LGBTQ and Allied Chamber of Commerce member.
The Bottleneck Lounge (2328 E Madison St, Seattle, WA **98112**), Washington State's LGBTQ and Allied Chamber of Commerce member.
Two Doors Down (2332 E Madison St, Seattle, WA **98112**), gay owned.
Cafe Flora (2901 E Madison St, Seattle, WA **98112**), Washington State's LGBTQ and Allied Chamber of Commerce member.
Pagliacci Pizza (3015 E Madison St, Seattle, WA **98112**), Washington State's LGBTQ and Allied Chamber of Commerce member.

Mr. and Mrs. Richard Weisfield House, exterior view of deck, Seattle, Washington, September 6-8, 1961, University of Washington Libraries, Special Collections

Queer Architects: Richard Weisfield House, 2563 Magnolia Blvd W, Seattle, WA **98199**, designed by Tucker & Shields (1961).

Magnolia Way

House: Julian Patrick (1927–2009) was an American operatic baritone and voice teacher. His life partner of 56 years was Donn Talenti. They lived at 1511 Magnolia Way W, Seattle, WA **98199**. Julian Earnest Patrick was born in Meridian, MS, and grew up in Birmingham, AL, where he was a member of the Apollo Boys Choir. After graduating from the Cincinnati Conservatory of Music, he began his professional career as a musical theatre performer in the 1950s; appearing in the original Broadway productions of The Golden Apple (1954), Bells Are Ringing (1956), Juno (1959), Once Upon a Mattress (1959), and Fiorello! (1959). He also studied singing privately in New York City with Cornelius L. Reid. After the 1950s Patrick worked mainly as a performer in operas, making appearances at the Dallas Opera, the De Nederlandse Opera, the Grand Théâtre de Genève, the Houston Grand Opera, the Lyric Opera of Chicago, the Metropolitan Opera, the Opéra national du Rhin, the San Francisco Opera, the Vienna Volksoper, and the Welsh National Opera among other major opera houses. In 1968 he starred as Private Don Hanwell in the world premiere of Hugo Weisgall's Nine Rivers from Jordan at the New York City Opera. He was particularly active with the Seattle Opera where he notably created the role of George Milton in the world premiere of Carlisle Floyd's Of Mice and Men in 1970. He also taught on the music faculty of the University of Washington for many years and sang Alberich in the Seattle Opera performances of Wagner's Ring of the Nibelung, being declared by the Seattle Opera General Director Speight Jenkins as the world's greatest living Alberich.

Main Street

Shelly's Leg Sign, Creative Commons Licenses, via Wikimedia Commons

Restaurant/Bar: In acting class I made a friend and we went to Shelly's Leg, the most fabulous disco ever, which I'm afraid has closed now. Shelly was a radical lesbian whose real leg was shattered in an accident; with the insurance money she opened her place. That was in 1972 and it was Seattle's first disco: beautiful paintings, deco decor, lines outside every night. Edmund White, States of Desire (1980). Shelly's Leg, 77 South Main St, Seattle, WA 98104, under Alaska Way Viaduct and Main Street, near the waterfront, was the first openly gay operated bar in Seattle. Included in the Damron Address Book from 1975 to 1978. Also Cascades, included in the Damron Address Book from 1977 to 1980. Later Poopdeck Tavern, included in the 1975 All Lavender International Gay Guide. It operated from 1973 until sometime circa 1978. Shelly Bauman was born in Chicago on July 23, 1947. She studied dance there until she was 16, at which time she became a runaway due to family tension. She performed striptease in Chicago, Hawaii, and Florida, moving to Rainier Valley, Seattle in 1968 to continue her profession there. She quit dancing after the Bastille Day accident. As a consequence of the accident she founded Shelly's Leg. She died in her home in Bremerton, Washington on November 18, 2010. On 14th of July, 1970 at the Seattle Bastille Day parade in Pioneer Square, Seattle, Bauman was in attendance enjoying the parade. At 10pm a parade consisting of a Dixieland band, two cars, and an old fire engine exited the Sinking Ship to begin a performance. The water cannon on the fire engine was set up to fire confetti. The cannon was fired, and somehow it did not shoot confetti, but rather a ball of wet paper which hit Bauman. Bauman's lower abdomen was severely injured, and doctors were forced to amputate her left leg. When Bauman recovered, she pursued a lawsuit against the cannon operator, the parade organizers, and the city of Seattle. Her case settled with her receiving US$330,000. She used this money to found a nightclub which she named Shelly's Leg. Bauman purchased a hotel in Pioneer Square, Seattle and in 1973 converted it into a gay bar and nightclub. Bauman would attend parties there in her wheelchair. The dancing at Shelly's Leg came to an abrupt end at around 1am on December 4, 1975. A fuel truck carrying an attached tank trailer struck a guardrail and jackknifed on the slick asphalt of the lower deck of the nearby Highway 99 viaduct near South Washington and South Main streets. The trailer detached from the truck, hit a roadway column, overturned and split open, spilling a river of flaming fuel onto the cars of a Burlington Northern Railway train, some parked vehicles and the building housing Shelly's Leg. The wall of fire was so hot, it shattered the disco's windows. Everyone made it out safely through a rear door. Bauman and her co-proprietors were able to renovate the club using insurance money. Nevertheless, the club's popularity was permanently damaged by the incident. Ultimately, the club's final demise was caused by a financial dispute among the three owners that led to the club being padlocked by the Internal Revenue Service, and Shelly's Leg thus abruptly closed. The sign from the nightclub is now an exhibit at Museum of History & Industry (MOHAI).

Malden Avenue

LGBTQ center: Seattle Counseling Service for Homosexuals, 318 or 320 Malden Ave E, Seattle, WA **98112**, included in the 1971 Homosexual National Classified Directory. At the same address was the Dorian Society of Seattle, included in the 1971 Homosexual National Classified Directory. Included in the Damron Address Book from 1972 to 1973.

Marion Street

Maison Blanc

Restaurant/Bar: Maison Blanc, 306 Marion St, Seattle, WA **98104**, included in The Lady Jai Recommended List, 1954. The Maison Blanc occupied an 1880 mansion. Charles Joseph Ernest Blanc opened Maison Blanc in 1916, during Prohibition. Blanc was the founder of the Chef's de Cuisine organization. His restaurant décor featured antiques and various forms of art, including marble statues, bronzes, ceramics, and oil paintings. Described as a timely addition to Maison Blanc, The Rathskellar below stairs at #306, claimed to be one of the most authentic German beer cellars in the country. Included in The Lady Jai Recommended List, 1954.

Market Street

Restaurant/Bar: In 2012, Cupcake Royale **lesbian owned** by Jody Hall who created a formal Political Action Committee (PAC) to distribute $7,000 to the fight for marriage equality in Washington state via a rainbow cupcake. Owner of six stores in the area, Hall has been asking her customers to Legalize Frostitution for years, and they are listening. Get your frosting on at Cupcake Royale in Ballard (2052 NW Market St, Seattle, WA **98107**), Madrona (1101 34th Ave, Seattle, WA **98122**), West Seattle, Capitol Hill (1301 4th Ave, Seattle, WA **98101**), Queen Anne, or the company's pre-order only Bellevue store.

McGilvra Boulevard

Smith residence interior, Seattle, Washington, 1952, University of Washington Libraries, Special Collections

Queer Architects:

Mrs. Letha Woodley residence alterations, 334 McGilvra Blvd E, Seattle, WA **98112**, designed by Roland Terry (1954)

Paul Smith House, remodel, 350 McGilvra Blvd E, Seattle, WA **98112**, designed by Tucker & Shields (1952).

Mr. and Mrs. John Amberg residence, 450 McGilvra Blvd E, Seattle, WA **98112**, designed by Roland Terry (1958)

Mr. and Mrs. Tibor Freesz residence, 456 McGilvra Blvd E, Seattle, WA **98112**, designed by Roland Terry (1956)

Frank Preston House, 745 McGilvra Blvd E, Seattle, WA **98112**, designed by Tucker & Fields (1959). Featured in Guide to Architecture in Washington State: An Environmental Perspective (1980).

The Hauberg town house, 1101 McGilvra Blvd E, Seattle, WA **98112**, designed by Roland Terry (1953)

Preston residence exterior showing patio, Seattle, Washington, 1953, University of Washington Libraries, Special Collections

Melrose Avenue

House: In the late 1930s, Malcom Roberts was in a romantic but open relationship with painter Morris Graves (1910-2001). In 1939 they moved into a home at 136 Melrose Ave E, Seattle, WA **98102**, on Capitol Hill, with composer John Cage and his beard wife, Xenia. Roberts' high-strung personality was at odds with that of the mischievous Graves, so their living arrangement soon came to an end. Morris Graves, Guy Anderson, and Richard Bennett remained friends throughout the 1940s, and Graves would often visit the couple at their cabin at Robe Ranch, where they all shared ideas and produced work in the Northwest wilderness. Mark Tobey would also visit occasionally, but his disdain for outdoor activities led Margaret Callahan to remark: Nature in the raw for Mark Tobey means dinner in the open at a city park such as Golden Gardens or Volunteer Park.

Restaurant/Bar:
Terra Plata (1501 Melrose Ave, Seattle, WA **98122**), Washington State's LGBTQ and Allied Chamber of Commerce member.
Mamnoon (1521 Melrose Ave, Seattle, WA **98122**), Washington State's LGBTQ and Allied Chamber of Commerce member.

Mercer Street

Queer Architects:
Dick Peaseley's office remodel, Mercer St & 2nd Ave N, Seattle, WA **98109**, designed by Roland Terry (1983)
Mercer Street Restaurant, 3rd Ave N & Mercer St, Seattle, WA **98109**, designed by Roland Terry (1961)

Restaurant/Bar: The John McNamara Lobby Bar (155 Mercer St, Seattle, WA **98109**), LGBTQ friendly.

Attractions: Pacific Northwest Ballet (301 Mercer St, Seattle, WA **98109**), TAG Approved LGBTQ friendly attraction.

House: Morris Graves (1910–2001) was an American painter. In the 1940s he lived at 909 E Mercer St, Seattle, WA **98102**. He was one of the earliest Modern artists from the Pacific Northwest to achieve national and international acclaim. His style, referred to by some reviewers as Mysticism, used the muted tones of the Northwest environment, Asian aesthetics and philosophy, and a personal iconography of birds, flowers, chalices, and other images to explore the nature of consciousness. An article in a 1953 issue of Life magazine cemented Graves' reputation as a major figure of the 'Northwest School' of artists. He lived and worked mostly in Western Washington, but spent considerable time traveling and living in Europe and Asia, and spent the last several years of his life in Loleta, California. The Lavender Palette: Gay Culture and the Art of Washington State at the Cascadia Museum in Edmonds was a packed art show and a powerful history lesson. Museum curator David F. Martin put together artwork by dozens of gay men and women who often, just a few short decades ago, had to hide who they were in order to express themselves artistically. The Morris Graves painting Preening Sparrow was featured in the famous Life magazine story about Northwest School artists Anderson, Graves, Tobey and their straight friend Kenneth Callahan.

Queer Architects: Universal Services, Inc. office remodel, 109 W Mercer St, Seattle, WA **98119**, designed by Roland Terry (1961)

Northgate Way

Accommodation: Hotel Nexus (2140 N Northgate Way, Seattle, WA **98133**), gay friendly and Washington State's LGBTQ and Allied Chamber of Commerce member. This hotel in North Seattle is undoubtedly one of the area's favorites, offering the finest amenities at truly affordable rates.

Queer Architects: Northgate Apartments alterations, NE Northgate Way & 3rd Ave NE, Seattle, WA **98125**, designed by Roland Terry (1960)

Store: Facèré Jewelry Art Gallery (550 NE Northgate Way, Seattle, WA **98125**) represents the work of artists from the US and abroad, showcasing an extensive collection of contemporary jewelry art made with precious and non-precious metals, as well as nontraditional materials. Established in the early 1980s in Downtown Seattle by local entrepreneur, author, and art enthusiast Karen Lorene, Facèré Gallery has now expanded to two locations inside the Seattle and Bellevue studios of Green Lake Jewelry Works, a custom jeweler that has been open for over 20 years. Green Lake Jewelry Works is recognized locally and nationally for their exceptionally handcrafted custom engagement rings and unique custom jewelry pieces. In their studios, master jewelers create and craft a variety of jewelry pieces marrying new technology (CAD, CAM, CNC) and classic jewelry-making techniques like hand-carved wax, lost wax casting, setting, filigree and metal fabrication.

Occidental Avenue

Restaurant/Bar:
Hank's, 100 Occidental Ave S, Seattle, WA **98104**, included in the Damron Address Book in 1973.
107 Club or Club-One-O-Seven or One-O-Seven Club, 107 Occidental Ave S, Seattle, WA **98104**, included in the Damron Address Book from 1971 to 1979.
Trojan Shield, 117 Occidental Ave S, Seattle, WA **98104**, included in the Damron Address Book from 1974 to 1976.

Club: Atlas Club Baths, 118 ½ Occidental Ave S, Seattle, WA **98104**, included in the 1966 Lavender Baedeker. Included in the Damron Address Book from 1965 to 1970. Included in the 1975 All Lavender International Gay Guide.

Restaurant/Bar: Taylor Shellfish Oyster Bar (410 Occidental Ave S, Seattle, WA **98104**), Washington State's LGBTQ and Allied Chamber of Commerce member.

Olive Way

Queer Architects: El Gaucho restaurant entrance alterations, 7th Ave & Olive Way, Seattle, WA **98101**, designed by Roland Terry (1955)

Restaurant/Bar: Clark's Around the Clock, 100 Olive Way, Seattle, WA **98101**, included in the Damron Address Book from 1969 to 1973. Included in the 1975 All Lavender International Gay Guide.

Accommodation: The Mayflower Park Hotel (405 Olive Way, Seattle, WA **98101**) was constructed in 1927, opening under the name of the Bergonian, and is the oldest continuously operating hotel in downtown Seattle. The building's facade—complete with ornate terra cotta detailing—evokes a sense of history the minute the building meets your gaze. Walk inside and the high ceilings, stained-glass windows and a magnificent five-tier crystal chandelier reinforce the atmosphere of Old World charm. Smaller details like the 1770 Grandfather Clock and the 1810 English Mohagany Breakfront add hints of a classical European-style hotel, while each of the 160 guest rooms and suites offer all the modern amenities a savvy traveler has come to expect, from complimentary wireless high-speed Internet access to Aveda toiletries. The Mayflower Park Hotel is centrally located within Seattle, opening directly into Westlake Center and the Monorail Station located on the top floor, which puts the Seattle Center, Space Needle and Experience Music Project within reach. Also located next door Seattle's Light Rail, which offers our hotel guests transportation within the Seattle area and to and from SeaTac Airport. The Pike Place Market, Waterfront and Seattle Art Museum are just a short walk away. Mayflower Park Hotel was awarded Best Historic Hotel (76-200 Guestrooms) for the 2017 Historic Hotels Awards of Excellence. Mayflower Park Hotel, a member of Historic Hotels of America since 1999, dates back to 1927.

Restaurant/Bar: Crescent Tavern, 1413 E Olive Way, Seattle, WA **98122**, was a lesbian bar from the late 1960s to the late 1970s. Included in the Damron Address Book from 1977 to 1980. On October 19, 1974, the Lesbian Mothers National Defense Fund held its first benefit fundraiser at the Crescent Tavern. The group, which had been meeting for some months, scheduled the fundraiser two days after founding member Geraldine Cole's 21st birthday, because We thought it would be fun to be legal (Cole). This was one of the first organizations in the US to offer legal advice, support, and other resources to lesbians involved in child custody battles. The Arterial Tavern begins appearing in city guides at this address in 1939 and it is listed as the Crescent Tavern in the 1948. It is said to have been an old carriage house, although the current building wasn't constructed until 1924. It now caters to older gay men, with a broad mix for karaoke.

LGBTQ friendly bookstore: Book Project, 1502 E Olive Way, Seattle, WA **98122**, included in the Damron Address Book in 1980.

House: Leo Kenney (1925–2001) was an American abstract painter, described by critics as a leading figure in the second generation of the Northwest School of artists. William Leo Kenney was born in Spokane, WA, the son of Raymond Augustus Kenney (1888–1942) and Dorris Della Woodfin Putman (1900–1955), and moved to Seattle with his family at age six. In the 1940s the family lived at 1562 Olive Way, Seattle, WA **98101**. He was interested in art from a young age, copying pictures from newspapers and art magazines. He had an early love of surrealism, and did very well in art classes. Although an intensely energetic kid, he had health problems related to his small stature. At one point in his teenage years he suffered a case of mumps so serious that he had to spend several weeks in bed, his weight dropping to 70 pounds. He attended Broadway High School, on Seattle's Capitol Hill. An art teacher, Jule Kullberg, sent him to see the works of Mark Tobey and Morris Graves at the Seattle Art Museum. I was never so knocked out as when I first saw Graves' Morning Star and In the Night, Kenney recalled in a 1999 interview. It was an epiphany to come upon his work - the originality of it. Kenney was dumbfounded when, following the attack on Pearl Harbor and the beginning of American involvement in WWII, his Japanese friends from Broadway High were removed from school for shipment to internment camps. It was the awakening of my social consciousness, he later recalled. In 1942 Kenney's older brother Jack was drafted into the US Army; shortly after that, his father died. An average student at best, he dropped out of high school on his 18th birthday. He was promptly called up by the draft, but, being underweight, was rejected. He went to work at the Douglas Aircraft assembly plant in Long Beach, CA. Kenney returned to Seattle in 1944. After his mother remarried and moved to Long Beach, he moved in with the family of a friend, Jack Griffin. He routinely painted through the night in the basement room he shared with Griffin, who was so impressed with Kenney's work that he took some of his paintings to the Frederick & Nelson's department store in downtown Seattle, which had a small art gallery. Kenney's first exhibition, along with sculptor James W. Washington, Jr., took place there in 1944. The gallery manager then brought Kenney's work to the attention of Dr. Richard Fuller, the director of the Seattle Art Museum, which bought its first Kenney painting, The Inception of Magic, in 1945. The artist was just 20 years old. At a young age Kenney had read Salvador Dalí's autobiography and the works of poet André Breton, and had become fascinated with surrealism. The influence is plain in his dark, figurative works of the 1940s and '50s. Taking Breton's proclamation that only the marvelous is beautiful to heart, he painted automatically, without conscious planning. Except for a few portraits done for friends, he never tried to reproduce reality in his paintings, always searching instead for deeper meaning. He never saw the world as others see it, said a longtime friend and patron, Merch Pease. His work is highly personal. It's pure invention.

Restaurant/Bar: CC Attle's (1701 E Olive Way, Seattle, WA **98102**) has been named among the Greatest Gay Bars in the World by Out.com, 2013.

Olympic Place

Park: Kinnear Park, 899 W Olympic Pl, Seattle, WA **98119**, included in the Damron Address Book from 1977 to 1980.

Pacific Highway

Queer Architects: Hilton Hotel alterations at Sea-Tac, 17620 Pacific Hwy S, Seattle, WA **98188**, designed by Roland Terry (1979)

Parkside Drive

Queer Architects: John and Dorothy Hall Residence, 1510 Parkside Dr E, Seattle, WA **98112**, Designed by Lionel Pries (1952-53). Omitted from Lionel H. Pries, Architect, Artist, Educator, as it was discovered only in 2007, the house was demolished in 2009.

Phinney Avenue

Restaurant/Bar:
A la Mode Pies (5821 Phinney Ave N, Seattle, WA **98103**), Washington State's LGBTQ and Allied Chamber of Commerce member, has been named among the Bars & Restaurants Where You Can Be Your Full Queer Self in Seattle by Travel Out Seattle, 2018.
Windy City Pie, 5918 Phinney Ave N, Seattle, WA **98103**

Store: Rudy's Barbershop, 6415 Phinney Ave N, Seattle, WA **98103**

Pike Street

Restaurant/Bar: Victoria Tavern, 91 Pike St, Seattle, WA **98101**, included in the Damron Address Book from 1972 to 1979.

LGBTQ friendly bookstore: Left Bank Books, 92 Pike St, Seattle, WA **98101**, active in 1990. 56 Queer-Owned Bookstores to Support, by Oprah Daily, 2021.

Restaurant/Bar:
Hideout Tavern at Pike Public Market, 93 Pike St, Seattle, WA **98101**, included in the Damron Address Book in 1972. It's now Daily Dozen Doughnut, Washington State's LGBTQ and Allied Chamber of Commerce member.
Hard Rock Cafe (116 Pike St, Seattle, WA **98101**), Washington State's LGBTQ and Allied Chamber of

Club: Metropolitan Health Club, 120 Pike St, Seattle, WA **98101**, included in the Damron Address Book from 1977 to 1979.

LGBTQ friendly bookstore: Carcinogen Books, 611 Pike St, Seattle, WA **98101**, included in the Damron Address Book from 1977 to 1980.
Commerce member.

Restaurant/Bar:
The Daily Grill (629 Pike St, Seattle, WA **98101**), Washington State's LGBTQ and Allied Chamber of Commerce member.

The Pike Street Tavern or Mike's Pike St. Tavern, 824 Pike St, Seattle, WA **98101**, included in the 1963 and 1966 Lavender Baedeker. Included in the 1964 and 1965 Guild Guide. Included in the Damron Address Book from 1965 to 1977. Included in the 1975 All Lavender International Gay Guide.

Club Z, Creative Commons Licenses, via Wikimedia Commons

Club: Club Z or Zodiac Club Baths, 1117 Pike St, Seattle, WA **98101**, was a gay bathhouse. Included in the Damron Address Book from 1979 to 1980.

Restaurant/Bar:
Starbucks Reserve Roastery (1124 Pike St, Seattle, WA **98101**), Washington State's LGBTQ and Allied Chamber of Commerce member.
Tavolàta (501 E Pike St, Seattle, WA **98122**), Washington State's LGBTQ and Allied Chamber of Commerce member.

LGBTQ Center: Gay City: Seattle's LGBTQ Center, 517 E Pike St, Seattle, WA **98122**

Restaurant/Bar:
Kaladi Brothers Coffee (517 E Pike St Ste C, Seattle, WA **98122**), Washington State's LGBTQ and Allied Chamber of Commerc998.e member.

Store:
Opened in 1993, Babeland (707 E Pike St, Seattle, WA **98122**) is lesbian owned by Claire Cavanah and Rachel Venning. They now have shop in New York and Los Angeles and host a website that sells their products and provides sex education. We are lesbians, and that has put a distinctly queer stamp on the business, the owners said in 2010. We know how important a great dildo can be, how hot the right harness can make you feel, how hard it can be to open up to a salesperson who may not know anything about lesbian sexuality. Babeland has been named among the Top 10 Lesbian-Owned Companies by Curve Magazine, 2010.

Doghouse Leathers (715 E Pike St, Seattle, WA **98122**), Washington State's LGBTQ and Allied Chamber of Commerce member. The goal at Doghouse Leathers is to provide quality leathers at fair prices by servicing the needs and desires of the Seattle Men's Leather, Kink, Bear and Puppy Communities.

Out of the Closet, 1016 E Pike St, Seattle, WA **98122**

Restaurant/Bar:

Brass Door, 722 E Pike St, Seattle, WA **98122**, included in the Damron Address Book from 1979 to 1980.

Larry's Greenland or Mr. Larry's, 801 Pike St, Seattle, WA **98101**, included in the Damron Address Book from 1976 to 1980.

Capitol Cider (818 E Pike St, Seattle, WA **98122**), Washington State's LGBTQ and Allied Chamber of Commerce member. Featuring hard cider, gluten-free food, live music, & arts events.

The Pike Street Tavern, 824 E Pike St, Seattle, WA **98122**, included in the 1964 Directory.

Lamplighter, Pike St, Seattle, WA **98101**, between 8th & 9th, included in the Damron Address Book in 1965.

The Easy Bar (916 E Pike St, Seattle, WA **98122**) was a lesbian bar active from 1993 to 1998.

Comet Tavern (922 E Pike St, Seattle, WA **98122**), Washington State's LGBTQ and Allied Chamber of Commerce member.

Poquitos (1000 E Pike St, Seattle, WA **98122**), Washington State's LGBTQ and Allied Chamber of Commerce member.

Big Mario's Pizza (1009 E Pike St, Seattle, WA **98122**), Washington State's LGBTQ and Allied Chamber of Commerce member.

The Wildrose, Creative Commons Licenses, via Wikimedia Commons

Restaurant/Bar:

The Wildrose bar (1021 E Pike St, Seattle, WA **98122**), lesbian owned by Shelley Brothers and Martha Manning, part of the Lesbian Bar Project, 2020. It is the only lesbian bar in the city, one of the oldest lesbian bars on the West Coast, opened in 1984, and one of the few lesbian bars left in the US. Lesbian Bars originated to create safe spaces for queer women, and then their allies, to socialize free from societal stigmas, and legal prohibition. Advancements in the LGBTQIA community have afforded many in it greater acceptance, but to say that there is no work to be done, is wrong. We are experiencing such dramatic polarization, in our country, and regarding our civil liberties, spaces for our community must be preserved. They are living testimonies of our struggle. Often Lesbian Bars have the impossible position of pleasing all age groups, as there are rarely multiple spaces in cities. But this provides a unique cross section of ages that is ideal in sharing stories, and history, as well as engaging in activism now. — Martha Manning, Co-

Owner of Wildrose. In general, we need to protect businesses and organizations led by, and for, women. It's imperative. Lesbian Bars in particular have closed by the droves across the country to the point where a small handful are now left. If we have no spaces to gather, we have no spaces in which to create, nurture and inspire our community. If we let this happen, we will regret it. There is no replacement for the human connections we make together as a community. — DJ LA Kendall, Patron of Wildrose. The Wildrose has been named among the Bars & Restaurants Where You Can Be Your Full Queer Self in Seattle by Travel Out Seattle, 2018.

Kozy Korner Kafe, 1101 E Pike St, Seattle, WA **98122**, included in the Damron Address Book from 1977 to 1979.

Eleven Eleven Club or Tavern, 1111 E Pike St, Seattle, WA **98122**, included in the Damron Address Book from 1973 to 1977. It's now Cupcake Royale & Vérité Coffee, Washington State's LGBTQ and Allied Chamber of Commerce member.

LGBTQ Publisher: Jon, 1302 E Pike St, Seattle, WA **98122**, included in the 1963 and 1964 Directory. Sometime around 1945 Jon Arnt (1906-1982) began his own photo studio, and for two decades he recorded the usual array of marriage, anniversary, and other formal portrait. He also became the official photographer for Seattle University, where he took pictures sports teams, prom couples, faculty members, and various campus scenes. What the priests at the Jesuit university did not know (at least so one assumes) was that the Kansas native was also recording the glories of local manhood. Arnt would visit nearby gymnasiums and invite a few of the better-looking men to come to his studio at #1302, and pose for his camera. Many times the photographer would convince the men to disrobe completely and would take nude pictures of them. This was not so odd in the early days, since it was assumed that before the images were published the photographer would black out the private parts by inking in a posing strap. If Arnt had tried to market the pictures of the models when they were au naturel, he could have been arrested and sent to prison. Still, some of these nudes did survive unretouched, and now they are extremely rare. Arnt was famous for his bronze-toned photos, and there is a great warmth and richness in these images. Most of the men whom he photographed were presumably heterosexual, but they were captured with an eye toward the sensuality that was conveyed by their bodies. It was Arnt's appreciation for beauty that lends a special luminous quality to his masterful images. Arnt was apparently well connected in the burgeoning Seattle homosexual community, as recorded other gay subjects. He took a few photos of the female impersonators at the Garden of Allah, as well as at least one moody portrait of ballet impresario and Seattle native Robert Joffrey. Arnt was truly not just a regional master but an equal to others all over the world. He would occasionally send photos to a few crypto-gay publications that maintained the illusion that they promoted exercise and a healthy life. They fooled very few. Arnt continued his photography business until the mid-1960s, but he seems to have gradually decreased his involvement in physique studies. This is almost certainly related to the fact that the laws against obscenity were beginning to break down around 1966-67, and it soon became possible to exhibit not just nude photos but pictures of actual sex acts. At this point the great majority of physique photographers called it quits. They had never wanted to produce pornography; art was their goal (with a little erotic spice stirred in). The Seattle photographer had to find another was to make a living, so surprisingly he fround employment as the city's night coroner. It must have been a grisly business, but it left Arnt free to pursue his picture taking during the day. Around 1972 he retired to a little residence on Camano Island, and it was there he died at the age of 75.

Accommodation: Palihotel Seattle (107 Pine St, Seattle, WA **98101**) is a boutique hotel with The Hart & The Hunter Restaurant, bar, and coffee outpost set in the city's downtown core, steps away from world Famous Pike Place Market. Part of World Rainbow Hotels (WRH), Lesbian and Gay Welcoming Hotels.

LGBTQ friendly bookstore: In 1975 the Lesbian Separatist Study Group was active at the Madwoman Feminist Bookcenter (317 Pine St, Seattle, WA **98101**).

Queer Architects: Best's Apparel store entrance remodel, Pine St & 5th Ave, Seattle, WA **98101**, designed by Roland Terry (1964)

Queer Architects: Store Building for Mr. and Mrs. Robert J. Cole, 616 Pine St, Seattle, WA **98101**, designed by Roland Terry (1952)

Accommodation: Grand Hyatt Seattle (721 Pine St, Seattle, WA **98101**), Washington State's LGBTQ and Allied Chamber of Commerce member and TAG Approved LGBTQ friendly accommodation. 457 stylish guestrooms & suites features opulent bathrooms, high-speed internet available,32`flat panel TV, breathtaking views of the city & lakes. Rooms have private entry foyer and separate bath tub. Part of World Rainbow Hotels (WRH), Lesbian and Gay Welcoming Hotels.

Restaurant/Bar: The Carlile Room (820 Pine St, Seattle, WA **98101**), Washington State's LGBTQ and Allied Chamber of Commerce member. Serving classic seventies-era lounge cocktails, a thoroughly modern and progressive menu with plant house features, favorite local meats and a hearty late night menu.

LGBTQ friendly bookstore: Centurion Book Store, 903 Pine St, Seattle, WA **98101**, included in the Damron Address Book in 1969. Included in the 1975 All Lavender International Gay Guide.

Club: The Pines, 912 Pine St, Seattle, WA **98101**, included in the Damron Address Book from 1978 to 1980.

Restaurant/Bar: Spag's Tavern, 926 Pine St, Seattle, WA **98101**, corner of Terry, included in the Damron Address Book from 1965 to 1980. Included in the 1975 All Lavender International Gay Guide.

El Capitan & SCS, Creative Commons Licenses, via Wikimedia Commons

LGBTQ Center: Seattle Counseling Service (SCS, 1216 Pine St, Seattle, WA **98101**) was originally Seattle Counseling Service for Sexual Minorities.

Restaurant/Bar: Cherry Street Coffee House (320 E Pine St, Seattle, WA **98122**), Washington State's LGBTQ and Allied Chamber of Commerce member.

Manray, Creative Commons Licenses, via Wikimedia Commons

Restaurant/Bar: Manray Video Bar, 514 E Pine St, Seattle, WA **98122**

Fogón Cocina Mexicana, Creative Commons Licenses, via Wikimedia Commons

LGBTQ friendly bookstore: Lambda Nearly New Store, 600 E Pine St, Seattle, WA **98122**, included in the Damron Address Book in 1980. Later Brob House Books, active in 1990. Later R Place, a gay bar. It's now Fogón Cocina Mexicana, Washington State's LGBTQ and Allied Chamber of Commerce member.

Rudy's Barbershop, Creative Commons Licenses, via Wikimedia Commons

Store: Rudy's Barbershop, 614 E Pine St, Seattle, WA **98122**

Restaurant/Bar:
Linda's Tavern (707 E Pine St, Seattle, WA **98122**), Washington State's LGBTQ and Allied Chamber of Commerce member.
Mothers Tavern, 725 E Pine St, Seattle, WA **98122**, included in the Damron Address Book in 1980.
Support two lesbian owned businesses at once when you dine at The Tin Table (915 E Pine St, Seattle, WA **98122**) and dance the night away at Century Ballroom (915 E Pine St, Seattle, WA **98122**) on Capitol Hill. Owner of both establishments, Hallie Kuperman, has an eye for classic dance and a taste for excellent food and wine. Not only does she own the Century Ballroom, she has also been the lead instructor since its inception in 1997. Want to learn how to Lindy Hop, Swing, Salsa, Waltz, West Coast Swing, or Country Western Two-Step? Century Ballroom has classes for all levels and interests. As for the Tin Table, the exposed brick and modern vibe induces a calming sensation for its patrons. Reservations are required and the price is mid-range and worth every penny. Delight in a new vino or savor the made-from-scratch entrée fresh from the oven. Whatever you do, save some room for dancing.

Store: Sugar Pill (900 E Pine St, Seattle, WA **98122**) is Capitol Hill's neighborhood herbal apothecary, featuring medicinal and culinary herbs, cocktail bitters and bartending essentials, gourmet salts, pantry staples and hard to find chocolates, as well as a divine selection of natural products for your body and home. Experienced herbalists are on staff and consultations are always free of charge. Community Herbalist & Homeopathic Consultant Karyn Schwartz is the Capitol Hill apothecary's heart and soul. Her business is run by more than dollars and cents – there's a whole lotta love involved, too.

Prefontaine Place

Restaurant/Bar: Silver Slipper Tavern, 109 ½ Prefontaine Pl S, Seattle, WA **98104**, included in the Damron Address Book from 1979 to 1980.

Prospect Street

Queer Architects: Residence and office alterations, 803 E Prospect St, Seattle, WA **98102**, designed by Roland Terry (1956)

LGBTQ Archives: Lesbian and Gay Alliance of the Pacific Northwest, 1425 E Prospect St, Seattle, WA **98112**, active in 1990.

Exterior view of the Burnett House, Seattle, 1952; University of Washington Libraries, Special Collections

Queer Architects: Bud and Adele Burnett House, 3717 E Prospect St, Seattle, WA **98112**, designed by Tucker & Fields (1949)

Queen Anne Avenue

Restaurant/Bar: Pagliacci Pizza (550 Queen Anne Ave N, Seattle, WA **98109**), Washington State's LGBTQ and Allied Chamber of Commerce member.

Accommodation: Nestled in Uptown Queen Anne, the MarQueen Hotel (600 Queen Anne Ave N, Seattle, WA **98109**) is in the center of the vibrant and popular Seattle. Part of World Rainbow Hotels (WRH), Lesbian and Gay Welcoming Hotels.

Restaurant/Bar:
5 Spot (1502 Queen Anne Avenue North, Seattle, WA **98109**), Washington State's LGBTQ and Allied Chamber of Commerce member.
Queen Anne Coffee co. (1811 Queen Anne Ave N, Seattle, WA **98109**), Washington State's LGBTQ and Allied Chamber of Commerce member, gay owned, has been named among the Bars & Restaurants Where You Can Be Your Full Queer Self in Seattle by Travel Out Seattle, 2018.
How To Cook A Wolf (2208 Queen Anne Ave N, Seattle, WA **98109**), LGBTQ owned and Washington State's LGBTQ and Allied Chamber of Commerce member.

Rainier Avenue

Queer Architects: Clark's Pancake Chalet, Rainier Ave S & S Charlestown St, Seattle, WA **98118**, designed by Roland Terry (1962)

Restaurant/Bar: Pagliacci Pizza (4901 Rainier Ave S, Seattle, WA **98118**), Washington State's LGBTQ and Allied Chamber of Commerce member.

Store: Rudy's Barbershop, 4903 Rainier Ave S, Seattle, WA **98118**

Republican Street

Restaurant/Bar: Taylor Shellfish Oyster Bar (124 Republican St, Seattle, WA **98109**), Washington State's LGBTQ and Allied Chamber of Commerce member.

Roy Street

Cornish College of the Arts

School: *Cornish College of the Arts was founded in 1914 as the Cornish School of Music, by Nellie Cornish, a teacher of piano. Cornish would go on to serve as the school's director for its first 25 years, until 1939. The Cornish School of Music began its operations in rented space in the Boothe (or Booth) Building on Broadway and Pine Street.*

Address: 710 E Roy St, Seattle, WA 98102

Notable queer alumni and faculty:

Clifford Wright (1919-1999) was an American artist. In an article for The Gay & Lesbian Review (2005), Edward Field noted that the openly gay Ralph Pomeroy was accepted by Yaddo 1955, where he scandalized the sedate arts colony by having an open affair with painter Clifford Wright. Described in one exhibition as the painter of the grotesque, Clifford Wright studied in Seattle at the Cornish School and with Mark Tobey from 1937 to 1943. He exhibited at the Seattle Art Museum and the Museum of Modern Art. Wright lived in New York where he married Elsa Gress, a leading feminist writer of Denmark, and went there to live with her and their children on the Island of Mon south of Copenhagen. He did designs for the Royal Danish Opera and has also illustrated books.

Karen Irvin (1909-1999) joined the Cornish school in 1945 after being a student there since the 1920s, with additional studies in New York. By the late 1930s, Irvin was a noted local performer and dance instructor, along with her lesbian accompanist Catherine Rogers, who remained a fixture at Cornish for several decades. Around 1952, when Irvin became head of the dance department, she met Pamelia (Mea) Hartman, and they soon became lovers. In 1956 the two women, along with close friend and artist Malcom Roberts, founded the Cornish Ballet. Irvin, Hartman, and Roberts guided the ballet into becoming the leading regional company of the time. Besides Irvin's choreography, the trio designed and built the stage sets, made the costumes, and even sold tickets. Irvin remained head of the department for 27 years, during which time the ballet company continued to prosper. Born in Hastings, PA, Karen Irvin moved with her family to Seattle, Washington at age 8. It was there that she began to study ballet with Caird Leslie, Lee Foley, and ultimately with Nellie Cornish of the Cornish School (now Cornish College of the Arts). She studied briefly in New York, then returned to the Northwest where she opened a ballet studio in West Seattle. Irvin joined the Cornish faculty in 1945, and in 1952 she became head of the Institution's dance department. Four years later, she co-founded Cornish

Ballet -- an early contributor to the regional ballet movement -- with her longtime companion, Mea Hartman. Irvin headed the dance department at Cornish for 27 years, and was responsible for designing the College's dance degree program. She trained dancers for companies such as the Joffrey Ballet, Twyla Tharp Dance, the Pennsylvania Ballet, and National Ballet of Canada, and worked to raise Seattle's stature in the dance world.

Megan Terry (1932–2023) was an Obie Award winner, a founding member of the Open Theater group and a prolific feminist playwright who wrote and directed a rock musical on the New York stage that predated Hair. In high school, she worked with the Seattle Repertory Playhouse, learning early that politics and theater could be powerful but prickly bedfellows. The playhouse closed in 1951 under pressure from the House Un-American Activities Committee. Marguerite won a scholarship to the Banff School of Fine Arts in Canada, where she earned a certificate in acting, directing and design. Returning to her home state, she completed her bachelor's degree in education at the University of Washington. She then took a teaching job at the Cornish School of Allied Arts, today Cornish College of the Arts, in Seattle.

Merce Cunningham (1919–2009) was an American dancer and choreographer who was at the forefront of the American modern dance for more than 50 years. He was born in Centralia, WA in 1919, the second of three sons. Both his brothers followed their father, Clifford D. Cunningham, into the legal profession. Cunningham first experienced dance while living in Centralia. He took tap class from a local teacher, Mrs. Maude Barrett. He attended the Cornish College of the Arts from 1937 to 1939 to study acting, but found drama's reliance on text and miming too limiting and concrete. Cunningham preferred the ambiguous nature of dance, which gave him an outlet for exploration of movement. During this time, Martha Graham saw Cunningham dance and invited him to join her company. In 1939, Cunningham moved to New York.

Nellie Cornish (1876-1956) was a pianist, teacher, writer, and founder of the Cornish School (now Cornish College of the Arts). She was influenced by the pedagogical ideas of Maria Montessori as well as Calvin Brainerd Cady's ideas about teaching broader values through music education. Martha Graham described her as a small, round, plump little lady with the dynamism of a rocket. Cornish returned to Seattle, where she founded the Cornish School in 1914. Within three years it had enrolled over 600 students, and was the country's largest music school west of Chicago. The curriculum soon expanded to include subjects as diverse as eurhythmics, French language, painting, dance (folk and ballet), and theater. She went on to serve as the school's director for the next 25 years. Although she often moved among the rich and famous, Cornish did not have any particularly large sum of her own money, and was at times totally broke. Neither Cornish not the school itself owned the custom-built 1921 building now known as Kerry Hall: the school was a tenant renting the building, which in turn was rather heavily mortgaged by the group of supporters who owned it. In 1923, the entire financial arrangement nearly came crashing down, and only some last minute donations prevented the school from having to move to Los Angeles. The next year, the realty company that owned the building converted itself into a foundation to support the school, and took on its debts. However, there was no endowment, and finances remained precarious even through what Cornish called the school's golden years in the mid-1920s. This remained the case even after the mortgage was paid off and the building donated to the school in 1929, and financial difficulties inevitably grew during the Great Depression. The Board neither raised an endowment nor otherwise put the school on a financial footing that would allow it to do more than tread water. Ultimately, this led Cornish to resign her position as head of the school in 1939. After leaving her school, Cornish spent three years of rest and gardening in California; spent half a year in an unsuccessful New York-based venture to improve children's radio programming; and then spent four years as head of the Pittsfield Community Music School (Pittsfield, MA). She spent her last years mainly in California, and sometimes in Seattle. Cornish never married. According to Nancy Wilson Ross, Twice she was deeply in love and lost the men to other women. She adopted the orphaned Elena Miramova as her daughter.

Robert Joffrey, dancer and choreographer, studied at Cornish at some point, and is listed as a member of the alumni association. Joffrey began his dance training at nine years old in Seattle as a remedy for asthma under instructor Mary Anne Wells.

Sand Point Way

House: Ramona Solberg (1921-2005) created eccentric yet familiar jewelry using found objects; she was an influential teacher at the University of Washington School of Art and often referred to as the grandmother of Northwest found-art jewelry. She was an art instructor in and around Seattle for three decades as well as a prolific jewelry artist. Solberg eschewed precious materials and made necklaces and pins out of found objects from cultures around the world — bottle tops, dice, sardine cans, dominos, beads, bone. The apartment at 6345 Sand Point Way NE, Seattle, WA **98115**, where she lived alone was jammed with boxes and drawers of such items, many of which she collected during her extensive travels. The resulting pieces were large and substantial, meant to be worn rather than displayed in cases. Sarah Spurgeon passed away in October 1985, surrounded by loved ones and in the arms of her intimate friend, Ramona Solberg. Solberg was prolific, said Karen Lorene, who represented Solberg for 20 years at the Facere Jewelry Art Gallery. If you see a Ramona piece you almost always know it's a Ramona piece. She always said, I'm the Henry Ford of jewelry. She wanted everyone to be able to afford her work. While her necklaces could fetch prices north of $6,000, she continued to make a pin called a fibula that never sold for more than $125. Ramona Lorraine Solberg was born in Watertown, SD, but her family relocated to Seattle, WA, before Solberg's second birthday. She enlisted in the Women's Army Corps in 1943 during WWII and served until 1950. Using her G.I. Bill benefits, she went to Mexico where she studied jewelry and textile design at the University of Michoacan in Morelia and textiles at the Belias Artes in San Miguel de Allende. She then studied in Oslo, Norway at Statens Kunst og Handverk Skole and worked with jewelry and enameling. Upon returning to the US, she completed both a Bachelor's of Arts and a Master's of Fine Arts degree at the University of Washington and also studied with Ruth Pennington. From 1951 to 1956 Solberg taught at James Monroe Jr. High School, and then worked until 1967 as an associate professor at Central Washington University in Ellensburg, WA. From that time until her 1983 retirement, Solberg was an art professor at the University of Washington. Solberg is often associated with Pacific Northwest artists and jewelers she taught like Laurie Hall, Ron Ho, Kiff Slemmons, and Nancy Worden. Though Solberg made some jewelry in her studies, she did not create her first piece of jewelry using beads and found objects until 1956, while at Central Washington State College.

Her jewelry was large, rather than typical delicate, precious jewelry. She created her jewelry to be worn and to be worn by large women. In the 1960s, she began traveling. Her first round-the-world trip included visits to Japan, Taiwan, Hong Kong and Nepal, picking up beads at every stop. When she returned, she published a book Inventive Jewelry Making in 1972. Solberg and a Seattle group called Friends of the Crafts began making annual travels through Europe, the Middle East, Southeast Asia, Africa and even one trip to Antarctica to both study crafts in other areas and obtain artifacts that could be used in their own works. Solberg was honored as a Fellow of the Council by the American Craft Council for leadership and ability as an artist and/or teacher. Craft historian Vicki Halper curated a 2001-2002 major traveling exhibition, and wrote a comprehensive, illustrated accompanying publication, after conducting an extensive (35 page transcribed) oral history.

Restaurant/Bar: Pagliacci Pizza (6224 Sand Point Way NE, Seattle, WA **98115**), Washington State's LGBTQ and Allied Chamber of Commerce member.

Seaview Avenue

Restaurant/Bar: Ray's Catering, 6049 Seaview Avenue Northwest, Seattle, WA **98107**, GLD, Gay Lesbian Directory

Queer Architects: The Windjammer Restaurant at Shilshole Bay, 7001 Seaview Ave NW, Seattle, WA **98117**, designed by Roland Terry (1962)

Seneca Street

Restaurant/Bar: Sportland, 95 Seneca St, Seattle, WA **98101**, included in the 1975 All Lavender International Gay Guide.

Shenandoah Drive

Queer Architects: Mr. and Mrs. David E. Wyman residence remodeling, Broadmoor, 1239 Shenandoah Dr E, Seattle, WA **98112**, designed by Roland Terry (1960)

Shorewood Drive

Shorewood Dr SW, Burien

Queer Architects: 12139 Shorewood Dr SW, Burien, WA **98146**, designed by Tucker & Shileds.

Spring Street

Accommodation: Executive Hotel Pacific (400 Spring St, Seattle, WA **98104**). Part of World Rainbow Hotels (WRH), Lesbian and Gay Welcoming Hotels.

House: In 1955, Roland Terry (1917-2006) resided at 1105 Spring St, Seattle, WA **98104**. Following on in 1960, Terry opened his own practice as Roland Terry & Associates and continued to design notable houses and other structures, as well as restaurants and other interiors in Seattle, San Francisco and Honolulu. Terry took his longtime associate, Robert H. Egan into partnership in 1974 forming Terry & Egan, a partnership that endured until 1987. Terry was elected a Fellow in the American Institute of Architects in 1980; he received the AIA Seattle Chapter Medal in 1991, the highest award given by the chapter.

Queer Architects: Ann Parry residence remodel, 1223 Spring St, Seattle, WA **98104**, designed by Roland Terry (1975)

Stevens Way

Restaurant/Bar: Pagliacci Pizza (Husky Union Building, 4001 Northeast, E Stevens Way NE, Seattle, WA **98105**), Washington State's LGBTQ and Allied Chamber of Commerce member.

Stewart Street

Restaurant/Bar: Scout PNW @ Thompson Hotel (110 Stewart Street Thompson, Seattle, WA **98101**) has been named among the Bars & Restaurants Where You Can Be Your Full Queer Self in Seattle by Travel Out Seattle, 2018.

Accommodation: Thompson Hotel (110 Stewart St, Seattle, WA **98101**), Washington State's LGBTQ and Allied Chamber of Commerce member, is a contemporary urban landmark at the center of a spectacular cascadian landscape, and located in the center of Seattle near the Puget Sound waterfront. Part of World Rainbow Hotels (WRH), Lesbian and Gay Welcoming Hotels.

Queer Architects: New Washington Hotel alterations, 2nd Ave & Stewart St, Seattle, WA **98101**, designed by Roland Terry (1956)

Restaurant/Bar: Miller's Guild (612 Stewart St, Seattle, WA **98101**), Washington State's LGBTQ and Allied Chamber of Commerce member.

Accommodation: Hotel Max (620 Stewart St, Seattle, WA **98101**). Part of World Rainbow Hotels (WRH), Lesbian and Gay Welcoming Hotels.

House: Gypsy Rose Lee (1914-1970) lived at 1007 Stewart St, Seattle, WA **98101**, in 1914 (demolished).

Stone Way

Restaurant/Bar:
Sea Wolf Bakers (3621 Stone Way N Suite D, Seattle, WA **98103**), Washington State's LGBTQ and Allied Chamber of Commerce member.
Super Bueno (3627 Stone Way N, Seattle, WA **98103**), Washington State's LGBTQ and Allied Chamber of Commerce member.
Pagliacci Pizza (4003 Stone Way N, Seattle, WA **98103**), Washington State's LGBTQ and Allied Chamber of Commerce member.

Sylvester Road

Accommodation: Soundview Cottage B&B, 17600 Sylvester Rd SW, Seattle, WA **98166**, GLD, Gay Lesbian Directory

Terry Avenue

Restaurant/Bar: Cuoco (310 Terry Ave N, Seattle, WA **98109**), Washington State's LGBTQ and Allied Chamber of Commerce member. At Trattoria Cuoco, the focus is on the pasta station located front and center. This casual spot is as perfect for a cocktail and a bite as it is for a full-out Italian meal.

Charles & Emma Frye Art Museum

Queer Artists: *The Frye Art Museum is an art museum located in the First Hill neighborhood of Seattle. The museum emphasizes painting and sculpture from the XIX century to the present. Its holdings originate in the private collection of Charles (1858–1940) and Emma (d. 1934) Frye. Charles, owner of a local meatpacking plant, set aside money in his will for a museum to house the Fryes' collection of over 230 paintings. The Frye Art Museum opened to the public in 1952, and was Seattle's first free art museum. The museum building was originally designed by Paul Thiry, although it has since been considerably altered.*

Address: 704 Terry Ave, Seattle, WA 98104

Notable queer elements:

John Singer Sargent (1856-1925). A'Aranjuez, (painting, ca. 1912), Mrs. Frederick Roller, (painting, 1895).
Marsden Hartley (1877-1943). Nova Scotia Woman Churning, (painting, 1938-1939).
Thomas Eakins (1844-1916). Maybelle, (painting, 1898).

Accommodation: Pan Pacific Seattle (2125 Terry Ave, Seattle, WA **98121**), TAG Approved LGBTQ friendly accommodation.

Thomas Street

Restaurant/Bar: Aluel Cellars (801a E Thomas St, Seattle, WA **98102**), Washington State's LGBTQ and Allied Chamber of Commerce member.

Store: Local, independent animal clinic Urban Animal (909 E Thomas St, Seattle, WA **98102**) is a go-to spot when you need to take care of your loved one in his/her time of need. Veterinarian Cherri Trusheim envisioned Urban Animal as a safehaven for pets during their recovery. The principles of affordable care provided by individuals who are highly trained and experienced have helped set Urban Animal apart from other veterinary clinics.

Tolo Road

Accommodation: Ashton Woods (5515 NE Tolo Rd, Bainbridge Island, WA **98110**), LGBTQ owned.

Twin Maple Lane

House: Richard Svare (1930-2004) was an accomplished vocalist, teacher and actor, known for Pretty Smart (1987), Bare et liv - historien om Fridtjof Nansen (1968) and Olympus Force: The Key (1988). Within a few years of the end of his relationship with Paul Mills, Morris Graves met Richard Svare and had a long-term, productive relationship with him. Richard John Svare grew up in Tacoma and got some preparation for his international lifestyle early-on. His father, pastor Trygve Svare of Trinity Lutheran in Tacoma, served as cultural attaché to Norway and Svare attended the University of Norway at Oslo for post-graduate work in theater, specializing in the plays of Ibsen. Before that, he studied at University of Washington and Pacific Lutheran University, where he graduated in 1950. Svare studied voice at PLU and privately in Oslo, where he trained with Ellen Schytte-Jacobsen, known for teaching the great Norwegian soprano Kirsten Flagstad. He worked in Oslo as a translator and currier for the 1952 Winter Olympics ski-jumping teams. Languages came easily to Svare. Besides English, he spoke Norwegian, Swedish, Danish, French, German and Greek. It helps to be musical, he explained. Growing up, Svare sang with the church choir at Trinity Lutheran. He was a soloist at the PLU choir and in 1952 joined the Compline Choir at Seattle's St. Mark's Cathedral, where he sang for two years. He also taught drama and English at Cleveland High School during that time. It was Richard's cousin, Dale Keller, who introduced Svare to Morris Graves during the completion of Careläden, one of Graves' houses, in 1951. Richard, a voice major at University of Washington, fell deeply and swiftly under the charismatic spell of Morris Graves. Though twenty years younger, he became intricately involved with the day-to-day minutia in the life of an internationally celebrated artist, acting as companion, organizer, secretary, and confidant. Through Graves, Svare got to know artist Mark Tobey. Tobey and Graves had a famously competitive relationship, but Svare said he never witnessed any strife. Graves would occasionally invite Tobey to dinner, then drive down to Seattle to get him (Tobey didn't drive). In 1954, Svare left the Northwest art scene behind to move to Ireland with Graves. Increasingly frustrated by the post-World War II development around his Edmonds property, Graves wanted to escape to a quieter place. His Machine Age Noise paintings of the early '50s express his rage at the encroaching bulldozers and chainsaws. Svare and Graves moved to County Cork, where they bought and restored Woodtown Manor (near Dublin), a 35-acre country estate with an imposing stone house built in 1750. They lived a very exciting life: traveling, meeting people, said their friend, Jan Thompson. They had a special bond. Movie director John Huston also had a house in Ireland, and Svare and Graves spent much time with the Huston family during those years. They often visited Paris, including a 1961 trip for Tobey's show at the Musée des Arts Décoratifs at the Louvre. In 1963 Morris had become disenchanted. He needed change, more solitude. He returned to the US in search of what became known as The Lake, his last habitation in Northern California. accompany Morris but moved to Stockholm where he founded and directed the Scandinavian Theater Company, a professional English language repertory theatre based in Stockholm. Among the actors who performed with the touring company were Peggy Ashcroft, John Gielgud, E.G. Marshall, Sada Thompson and Esther Rolle. Svare didn't like to talk about what prompted his move, but said he felt he needed to be doing his own work again. He and Graves remained close friends. In 1969, Svare acted in the Russian film One Life and later moved to the Greek island of Corfu, where he helped organize an annual arts festival. He appeared in a number of European feature films and Euro Television productions, including Drifting Cities. He migrated to Athens, Greece and spent two decades as an actor, interrupted briefly as Administrative Director for the Merce Cunningham Dance Company in New York City in 1976-78. He was somewhat of a local celebrity in Athens, having appeared in numerous Greek and European film and television productions, as well as various commercials. He was living in a modest apartment not too far from the Pláka, along with his two Lhasa Apso dogs, both of which had easily extracted Richard's absolute devotion; he adored them. In fact, when he planned to return to the United States, he couldn't bear the idea the dogs would have to fly in cargo. He had heard somewhere that the captain of an air flight could decide if a small pet could ride topside, beneath the legs of a doting owner. He spent weeks chasing this possibility, which, of course, did not pan out at all. When he moved back to Seattle, he moved in to his old family home at 5741 Twin Maple Ln NE, Seattle, WA **98105**, in the Ravenna area, in the basement where he had spent a part of his boyhood. His older sister, Betty, was living upstairs. He wrote Morris Graves: His Houses, His Gardens, for which one of the more difficult tasks before him was to severely edit out the significant extent of his deep, personal relationship with Graves. He had no intention of thickening the book with personal anecdotes or explicating those historical events that amplified Graves as an eccentric recluse. While the book doesn't approach the paintings of Morris Graves, it does go into detail about those things that were absolutely necessary for Morris to make the paintings. Richard set about not only describing the physical habitations of Morris Graves, two of which he shared with Morris, but also the nearly insurmountable difficulties in realizing all four—The Rock, Careläden, Woodtown Manor, and The

Lake. Also he detailed the reasons Morris became disenchanted with one place then left it for another. Even though they parted their physical union in the 1960's, they communicated frequently by phone until Morris Graves died in 2001. Clearly a well of mutual respect and trust had deepened between them. Svare also wrote works concerning ancient gardens. Titles of his manuscripts include: The Gardens of Greece: Known and Unknown, The Forgotten Gardens of Byzantium, Voyages: The Sea- A Literary Photographic Collection of the Sea, Hoi Polloi, and a number of other short stories and poems. Svare also authored an introduction to Galen Garwood's multi-media production of Adagio, presented at the Washington State Historical Society's The Memory and Mourning of Artists in 1997. Svare died of lung cancer at his Seattle home, after a lifetime of involvement in the arts. With his trained voice, crop of snowy hair and courteous manner, Svare was known for his kindness, wit and intelligent conversation, as well as his generous support of other artists. Svare spent the last decade of his life in Seattle, but for most of his adult years, he lived in Europe, often in the company of accomplished people, including movie director John Huston, and actors Alan Bates, John Gielgud, Peggy Ashcroft and Laurence Olivier. He loved to recall the time, in 1957, when he and Graves were bidden to Paris for Thanksgiving with the Duke and Duchess of Windsor. They arrived at the opulent house by cab an hour late. Svare remembered the scene vividly: The Duke came running down this great staircase with all the pugs running after him, saying I'm so sorry — we have the most impossible place to find! Svare said. It was the height of noblesse oblige. He was incredibly polite. The meal, of course, was incredible, too, served on table linens as sheer as handkerchiefs. The turkey arrived at the table already carved and perfectly reassembled. Ten people attended the dinner, mostly Americans, and Svare sat near the Duchess, to her left. She kept a little gold notebook and gold pencil at her place and each time something went wrong or she didn't like something, she'd make a little note, he said. She picked her teeth with a gold toothpick.

Union Street

Restaurant/Bar: Goldfinch Tavern (99 Union St, Seattle, WA **98101**), Washington State's LGBTQ and Allied Chamber of Commerce member.

Accommodation: Four Seasons Hotel (99 Union St, Seattle, WA **98101**), LGBTQ friendly, Washington State's LGBTQ and Allied Chamber of Commerce member.

Historic District: Union St & 2nd Ave, Seattle, WA **98101**, included in the Damron Address Book from 1977 to 1980

Queer Architects:
Dublin House Restaurant, 321 Union St, Seattle, WA **98101**, designed by Roland Terry (1959)
Sanky's Gift Shop at the Washington Building, 4th Ave & Union St, Seattle, WA **98101**, designed by Roland Terry (1959)

Waldorf Apartments, ca. 1906

House: Jon Arnt (1906-1982) was a well respected physique photographer working in Seattle during the late 1940s - 1950s. Arnt's work was regularly published in magazines. Jon Clayton Arnt was born in Beloit, Mitchell, KS, to Casper Dayton Arnt (1882-1971) and Fannie Bone (1873-1968). He lived in Racine, WI, in 1935 and Spokane City, WA, in 1940. In the early 1940s he moved to Seattle, where he found work taking photos at Boeing Aircraft. He lived at Waldorf Hotel (7th Ave & Pike St, Seattle, WA **98101**). In the 1940 he worked for Grady Studios, 420 Union St, Seattle, WA **98101**. The Waldorf Hotel was constructed in 1906. In the 1960s, it was converted to low rent apartments known as the Waldorf Towers. The building was demolished in 2000 to make way for the Washington State Convention Center.

Queer Architects: Kalua Room Restaurant at the Windsor Hotel, 6th Ave & Union St, Seattle, WA **98101**, designed by Roland Terry (1958)

Restaurant/Bar:
Loulay Kitchen & Bar (600 Union St, Seattle, WA **98101**), Washington State's LGBTQ and Allied Chamber of Commerce member.
Cortina and Cortina Café (621 Union St, Seattle, WA **98101**), Washington State's LGBTQ and Allied Chamber of Commerce member.
Street Treats (2407 E Union St Ste C, Seattle, WA **98122**), Washington State's LGBTQ and Allied Chamber of Commerce member. Mobile dessert/ice cream catering food truck.

University Street

Fairmont Olympic Hotel

Accommodation: *The Fairmont Olympic Hotel is the premier accommodations in Seattle. Fairmont Olympic Hotel, a member of* Historic Hotels of America *since 2018, dates back to 1924. The Marine Room at the Olympic Hotel was dubbed the Snake Pit by its gay clientele. Included in the* Swasarnt Neft's Gay Guides for 1949 and 1950*. Included in* The Lady Jai Recommended List, 1954*. Included in the* 1964

Directory. *Included in the* 1975 All Lavender International Gay Guide. *Remodeled in the 1960s, gone were the maritime murals by Eric Trumbull and the ship décor. The Marine Room closed in 1974 to reopen as a discotheque, the Downstairs, which was itself later renamed the Yellow Submarine Room. The Terrace Room at the Olympic Hotel has been included in the* Damron Address Book *from 1972 to 1976.*

Address: 411 University St, Seattle, WA 98101

Place

The recently renovated Fairmont Olympic Hotel, LGBTQ friendly, has redefined downtown sophistication in Seattle, Washington. Open since the 1920s, this hotel has almost a century of service under its belt and has a reputation to match. Celebrating its inauguration with a grand ball, the Fairmont Olympic has continued the tradition of treating every moment like that first night - with impeccable service, attention to detail, and pride. Blending mid-century modernity with classic elegance in each of its updated 450 guestrooms, the Fairmont Olympic has everything a traveler seeking a premier experience in Seattle could want and need. Featuring amenities such as an in-room refreshment center, blackout curtains, premium television channels, bathrobes and designer toiletries, the Fairmont Olympic Hotel provides world class luxuries to world class guests. Also boasting two award-winning restaurants, Shucker's and The Georgian, dining at the Fairmont Olympic is an exceptional experience for all. The Terrace features live music and Fourth Ave features a cup of coffee to rival all others. As the city around it has grown, it has become obvious that the Fairmont Olympic Hotel is the heart of the metropolis that is Seattle. Guests can spend their day leisurely saltwater fly fishing, kayaking along Lake Washington, paddling in salty Puget Sound, golfing at the Golf Club at Newcastle, taking in a show at the Pacific Northwest Ballet or the Paramount Theatre, and end the evening with any number of exciting festivals and shows depending on the time of year.

Queer Architects: Salsbury Store storefront remodel, 412 University St, Seattle, WA **98101**, designed by Roland Terry (1955)

University Way

LGBTQ Center: In 1975 the Lesbian Resource Center was active at the University YWCA (4224 University Way NE, Seattle, WA **98105**).

Store: Rudy's Barbershop, 4738 University Way, Seattle, WA **98105**

LGBTQ friendly bookstore: It's About Time (5241 University Way NE, Seattle, WA **98105**) was a feminist bookstore active in the 1980s.

Upland Terrace

Lysle A. Woods house, interior view of living room, Seattle, Washington, 1956, University of Washington Libraries, Special Collections

Queer Architects: Lysle A. Woods House, 6604 Upland Terrace S, Seattle, WA **98118**, designed by Tucker & Shields (1956)

Valley Street

Queer Architects: Louise Routh residence modernization, 7 Valley St, Seattle, WA **98109**, designed by Roland Terry (1956)

Viewmont Way

Queer Architects: 2530 W Viewmont Way W, Seattle, WA **98199**, Designed by Lionel Pries (1930s). A French Norman house in Magnolia that Pries designed while with Bain & Pries. It was on the market in 2014 for $1.285 million. The renovated 1930 brick home features hardwood floors, open beam ceilings, a circular staircase and two fireplaces. A gorgeous spire accompanied by the well-manicured grounds and a Puget Sound backdrop make for one hell of a Pacific Northwest postcard.

Vinton Court

Queer Architects: Mrs. Fay Wilson residence, 10003 Vinton Ct NW, Seattle, WA **98177**, designed by Roland Terry

Wall Street

Queer Architects: Skyway Luggage additions and alterations, 10 Wall St, Seattle, WA

98121, designed by Roland Terry (1956)

Store: Rudy's Barbershop, 89 Wall St, Seattle, WA **98121**

Ward Street

Queer Architects: Alterations, Gene and Betty Taylor House, 173 Ward St, Seattle, WA **98109**, Designed by Bruce Goff (1975-76).

Washington Street

Restaurant/Bar:
Stage Door, 158 S Washington St, Seattle, WA **98104**, included in the Damron Address Book from 1966 to 1970. Included in the 1975 All Lavender International Gay Guide.
Columbus Tavern, 167 S Washington St, Seattle, WA **98104**, included in the Damron Address Book from 1975 to 1980.
Silver Star, 173 S Washington St, Seattle, WA **98104**, included in the Damron Address Book from 1968 to 1977. Included in the 1975 All Lavender International Gay Guide.
El Toro Lounge & Jim's Chop House, 201 S Washington St, Seattle, WA **98104**, included in the Damron Address Book from 1978 to 1979.

Webster Point

Max and Helen Gurlich Residence

Queer Architects: Max and Helen Gurlich Residence, 3006 Webster Point Rd NE, Seattle, WA **98105**, Designed by Lionel Pries (1964-65). The estate located at the water's edge on Webster Point is known as being the last large project that Lionel Pries ever built. Along with his wife Helen, businessman and art patron Max Gurlich lived here until his death in 2009. Survives in fine condition; sold to new owners in late 2010, the grand Northwest-style house was again on the market in 2014 for $5.9 million. The home boasts terrazzo floors, vaulted ceilings, Shoji-style window screens and of course blisteringly-good views from just about every room.

Western Avenue

Attractions: Seattle Architecture Foundation (1010 Western Ave, Seattle, WA 98104), TAG Approved LGBTQ friendly attraction.

Restaurant/Bar:
Place Pigalle at Pike Place Public Market, 1531 Western Ave, Seattle, WA 98101, included in the Damron Address Book from 1972 to 1976.
Honest Biscuits (1901 Western Ave Suite E, Seattle, WA 98101), Washington State's LGBTQ and Allied Chamber of Commerce member. Southern food with all local ingredients & a fabulous water view. NGLCC Certified LGBT Business Enterprise.
indi Chocolate (1901 Western Ave D, Seattle, WA 98101), Washington State's LGBTQ and Allied Chamber of Commerce member.
Aerlume (2003 Western Ave Suite C, Seattle, WA 98121), Washington State's LGBTQ and Allied Chamber of Commerce member.
Etta's (2020 Western Ave, Seattle, WA 98121), Washington State's LGBTQ and Allied Chamber of Commerce member. An inspired seasonal, market fresh seafood menu driven by their proximity to Pike Place Market. An instant classic for lunch, dinner and market brunch.
2024 Tavern or Twenty-Twenty-Four Tavern, 2024 Westlake Ave, Seattle, WA 98121, included in the Damron Address Book from 1976 to 1980.

LGBTQ publisher: Seal Press, 3131 Western Ave, #410, Seattle, WA 98121, active in 1990.

Westlake Avenue

Restaurant/Bar: Mama Dot's, 233 Westlake Ave N, Seattle, WA 98109, was a lesbian bar active in the 1970s. Included in the Damron Address Book in 1980.

Store: Ladies' Rest Room, William O. McKay Company (609 Westlake Ave N, Seattle, WA 98109) was a spot for the lady motorist to rest and refresh herself while awaiting the repairs on their car. The William O. McKay Company operated a Ford and Lincoln dealership and repair facility.

Restaurant/Bar: Joker, 8th Ave & Westlake Ave, Seattle, WA 98121, included in the Damron Address Book from 1976 to 1977.

Accommodation: Courtyard by Marriott Seattle Downtown/Lake Union (925 Westlake Ave N, Seattle, WA 98109), Washington State's LGBTQ and Allied Chamber of Commerce member.

Queer Architects: Kim's Broiler, 1844 Westlake Ave N, Seattle, WA 98109, designed by Roland Terry (1972)

Restaurant/Bar: Shake Shack, 2115 Westlake Ave, Seattle, WA 98121

Whitman Court

Restaurant/Bar: Pagliacci Pizza (Willow Hall, 4294 Whitman Ct NE, Seattle, WA **98195**), Washington State's LGBTQ and Allied Chamber of Commerce member.

Willow Street

House: Jean Swallow (1953-1995) was a lesbian writer and editor. Her work included newspaper editing for the Charlotte Observer, poetry, novels, essays, and grant-writing. Her anthology Out From Under was published in 1983 and was the first book by and about lesbians in recovery from substance abuse. In 1986 her novel Leave a Light on for Me was published; it was reissued in 1991. She continued to write shorter pieces, poems and stories, which she collected in How (Some of) It Works. The success of Out from Under led to a follow-up volume published as The Next Step in 1993. Both volumes were welcome additions to the literature of lesbians in recovery. Swallow died of an apparent suicide on January 16, 1995 in Seattle. She lived at 5134 S Willow St, Seattle, WA **98118**. At the time of her death Swallow had been clean and sober for 14 years. In 1995 Swallow had just finished a draft of a book of interviews with photographs by Geoff Manasse; the draft was published under the title Making Love Visible: In Celebration of Gay and Lesbian Families. The book A Woman Determined was published in 1998.

Yesler Way

Restaurant/Bar: In the 1940s, Leo Kenney (1925–2001), American abstract painter, described by critics as a leading figure in the second generation of the Northwest School of artists, worked at the Pioneer Café (119 Yesler Way, Seattle, WA **98104**) in the Korn Building. Later Cavalier Inn, included in the Damron Address Book from 1971 to 1972. Later Doll House, included in the Damron Address Book from 1973 to 1975. The Korn Building was designed by Elmer Fisher in 1889 for Moses Korn to replace an earlier building that had been destroyed during the great Fire of 1889. In fact, this is one of the first commissions that Fisher received after the Fire. The Korn Building resembles a less solid version of the New England Hotel, also designed by Fisher in 1889-1890, in the gridlike divisions of the elevation, the repeated use of arches, the treatment of the corner elevation and the raised parapet which used to rise above it. The New England Hotel also stands on a corner- the northwest corner of Main and First Avenue South. Moses Korn, who ran Korn Druggists, was an important entrepreneur before and after the Fire of 1889. The Pioneer Building is located very close to the Korn Building and was also designed by Fisher. Elmer Fisher's life remains something of a mystery, since the recent discovery that it is unlikely that he was really from Scotland, as he stated and none of the accomplishments he claimed, outside of his work in British Columbia, can be corroborated; however, after the Fire of 1889, he was the most prolific architect in Seattle. He is credited with almost half of the major buildings in downtown Seattle between 1889 and 1891.

Historic District: 2nd Ave & Yesler Way, Seattle, WA **98104**, included in the Damron Address Book from 1972 to 1975.

Restaurant/Bar:
The Mocambo Room, 203 Yesler Way, Seattle, WA **98104**, included in the 1963 and 1966 Lavender Baedeker. Included in the 1964 and 1965 Guild Guide. Included in the 1964 Directory. Included in the Damron Address Book from 1965 to 1979. Included in the 1975 All Lavender International Gay Guide.
Broadcast Coffee Roasters (1918 E Yesler Way, Seattle, WA **98122**), Washington State's LGBTQ and Allied Chamber of Commerce member. 2018 GSBA Board Chair's Award. NGLCC Certified LGBT Business Enterprise.

Restaurant/Bar:
614 or Six Fourteen Club, 614 1st Ave, Seattle, WA **98104**, near Pioneer Square, included in the 1966 Lavender Baedeker. Included in the Damron Address Book from 1965 to 1973. Included in the 1975 All Lavender International Gay Guide.
Pennyland, 1003 1st Ave, Seattle, WA **98101**, included in the 1975 All Lavender International Gay Guide.

Accommodation: Alexis Hotel (1007 1st Ave, Seattle, WA **98104**), LGBTQ friendly.

Holyoke Building

School: *The Holyoke Building (or Holyoke Block) is a historic building located in downtown Seattle, WA. It is a substantial five story brick structure with stone trimmings. Construction began at the corner of First Avenue and Spring Streets just before the Great Seattle fire of 1889. Completed in early 1890, it was the first permanent building completed and ready for occupancy in downtown Seattle following the fire. Today the Holyoke Building is one of the very few such buildings still standing in Seattle outside of the Pioneer Square district and is a historic remnant of the northward expansion of Seattle's business district between the time of the great fire and the Yukon Gold Rush in 1897.*

Address: 1018 1st Ave, Seattle, WA 98104
National Register of Historic Places: 76001888, 1976

Holyoke Building, Creative Commons Licenses, via Wikimedia Commons

Place

The Holyoke Building housed many social and artistic clubs and organizations throughout its history. As early as 1895 it housed the Conservatory of Arts on the top floor. Later in the 1920s the Seattle Musical Club brought many local artists and musicians together in the building and other private and social clubs shared the building with toiletry manufactures and offices. The Holyoke Building is a subdued example of the Victorian Commercial style with elements of Romanesque style and remains almost completely intact from when it was built even down to the storefronts, which had been altered over time but have now been restored. Following this restoration in 1975 by the building's owner Harbor Properties and it became a City of Seattle Landmark in 1978.

Life

Who: Nellie Centennial Cornish (July 4, 1876 - April 24, 1956)
Born in Nebraska, Nellie Cornish grew up first in Arlington, OR, and then in Blaine, WA, as the daughter of the town's first mayor, lawyer Nathan Armfield Cornish. In her early teens, she lived about half a year in Portland, OR, where she studied piano under Ebenezer Cook, a teacher of strong local reputation. Shortly after, her father's fortunes and her mother's health began to fail. Her parents moved to Spokane, WA, where her mother died two years later; Nellie stayed in Blaine much of that time, teaching fourth grade although still in her teens. Her father remarried to a woman she did not like, leading to a break with him. In her early twenties, she gave music lessons and did other tutoring in northwestern Oregon. She moved to Seattle in 1900, and took a studio in 1902 in the Holyoke Building (the center of Seattle music instruction at the time), which gave her a chance to meet nearly all of the city's leading music teachers. In 1904, she traveled to Boston for the summer to learn the Evelyn Fletcher-Copp's Montessori-influenced method of teaching piano to young children. From this, she evolved her own technique of teaching. By 1911, when she left for Los Angeles, CA, to study for six weeks with Calvin Brainerd Cady, she was a very well established Seattle music teacher, with a suite of five studio rooms and two assistants. (She would later hire Cady as a faculty member at the Cornish School.) She returned to Seattle and modified her approach to teaching to incorporate Cady's ideas about using music education to impart a broader spiritual approach to life in general. However, the combination of disappointment in romance and a reconciliation with her father led her to turn over her studio to one of her assistants, Martha Sackett, and join her father in Alturas, California, where he had somewhat recovered his fortune. A plan for father and daughter to travel together to Europe was scotched by the outbreak of WWI; plans to study in New York City also fell through, as did an effort to establish herself in Salt Lake City.

LGBTQ friendly bookstore:
Magazine City Adult Books, 1210 1st Ave, Seattle, WA **98101**, included in the Damron Address Book from 1977 to 1980.
Henry's Adult Book Store, 1212 1st Ave, Seattle, WA **98101**, included in the Damron Address Book in 1980.

Arlington Hotel, 1904, Creative Commons Licenses, via Wikimedia Commons

The Garden of Allah was a mid-XX century gay cabaret that opened in 1946 in the basement of the Victorian-era Arlington Hotel (1215 1st Ave, Seattle, WA **98101**) in Seattle's Pioneer Square. Included in the Swasarnt Neft's Gay Guides for 1950. Included in The Lady Jai Recommended List, 1954. It was Seattle's most popular gay cabaret in the late 1940s and 1950s and one of the first gay-owned gay bars in the US. Prior to becoming a cabaret, the space had been a speakeasy, during Prohibition, and then a tavern. The Garden catered to all factions of the LGBT community, though heterosexual patrons, tourists and military personnel on leave also visited. Acts were primarily female impersonation, though some male impersonators also performed; the former sometimes included striptease. One act was the professional female-impersonation Jewel Box Revue, though that act was largely geared to and supported by hetero people. Patrons report that the cabaret became like a family or support group, and Don Paulson, author of An Evening at the Garden of Allah: A Gay Cabaret in Seattle, noted that he believes the sense of community and group consciousness produced by the Garden was what made the gay rights movement of later decades possible. Jack Starr aka Jackie Starr (born 1915), called the most beautiful man in America by gossip columnist Walter Winchel, and the male Gypsy Rose Lee, was one of the most successful female impersonators at the Garden of Allah. Starr was a classically trained singer, a ballet dancer, an actor, and an excellent striptease artist. By 1929, he was performing in drag in Chicago and during the 1930s, he performed in New York. He joined the Jewel Box Revue in the late 1930s and moved to the west coast by 1940. He headlined at the Garden of Allah for the next ten years. Around 1950, Starr married a man named Bill Scott. The two remained together until Scott's death sometime in the late 1960s. Starr died in the late 1980s. The Garden of Allah was opened in 1946 by Fred Coleman and Frank Reid. It was Seattle's first gay-owned and operated gay bar. It was located in the basement of the Arlington Hotel, on 1st Avenue between University Street and Seneca Street. It was a known for vaudeville acts and female impersonation. The Garden of Allah was described as a safe place for both gay men and lesbians to gather. The Garden closed in 1956, when a combination of a rate raise from the musicians' union and a raise in city taxes on locales that provided both entertainment and alcohol put it out of business.

Queer Artists: SAM traces its origins to the Seattle Fine Arts Society (organized 1905) and the Washington Arts Association (organized 1906), which merged in 1917, keeping the Fine Arts Society name. In 1931 the group renamed itself as the Art Institute of Seattle. The Art Institute housed its collection in Henry House, the former home, on Capitol Hill, of the collector and founder of the Henry Art Gallery, Horace C. Henry (1844–1928).

Address: 1300 1st Ave, Seattle, WA 98101

Notable queer elements:

John Singer Sargent (1856-1925). Coming Down from Mont Blanc, (painting, 1902), Leon Delafosse, (painting, ca. 1895-1898), View in the Dolomites, (painting, 1914), Yachts at Anchor, Palma de Majorca, (painting, 1912).
Marsden Hartley (1877-1943). Berlin Abstraction, (painting, 1914-1915), Gloucester Fantasy, (painting, 1936), Little Canyon, Talpa, (painting, ca. 1918), Roses, (painting).

LGBTQ friendly bookstore: Sultan's Lavender Cinema & Bookstore, 1313 1st Ave, Seattle, WA **98101**, included in the **Damron Address Book** from 1974 to 1980.

Postcard view of the Arcade Building, Seattle, c. 1910

Office: Working from a studio at the Arcade Building (1318 1st Ave, #3027, Seattle, WA **98101**), Jon Arnt (1906-1982) produced wonderful prints of handsome men, both competitive bodybuilders and those with more lyrical builds. Although his work appeared in a number of popular physique magazines in the 1950s, he was never as prolific (or as commercially successful) as his contemporaries Lon of New York (Lon Hanagan), Bruce of Los Angeles (Bruce Bellas) or the great Douglas of Detroit (Douglas Juleff). The 1st Ave. Movie Arcades has been included in the **Damron Address Book** from 1972 to 1980. Built in 1901-1903, the mammoth Arcade Building, with its extensions, occupied all of the 2nd Avenue westside street frontage between Union Street and Seneca Street. It stood on the northwest corner of 2nd Avenue and

Seneca Street and southwest corner of 2nd Avenue and University Street. The Arcade Building was razed. The Seattle Art Museum occupied a portion of the site after 1991.

Restaurant/Bar: Lou's Arcade, 1406 1st Ave, Seattle, WA **98101**, included in the 1975 All Lavender International Gay Guide.

LGBTQ friendly bookstore: John's Adult Books, 1410 1st Ave, Seattle, WA **98101**, included in the Damron Address Book from 1978 to 1980.

Restaurant/Bar: High's, 1411 1st Ave, Seattle, WA **98101**, included in the 1975 All Lavender International Gay Guide.

LGBTQ friendly bookstore:
Champ Arcade, 1413 1st Ave, Seattle, WA **98104**, included in the Damron Address Book from 1978 to 1980.
Adult Book Store, 1415 1st Ave, Seattle, WA **98101**, included in the Damron Address Book from 1972 to 1980. It's now The Pike Brewing Company, Washington State's LGBTQ and Allied Chamber of Commerce member.

Restaurant/Bar: Amusement Center, 1416 1st Ave, Seattle, WA **98101**, included in the 1975 All Lavender International Gay Guide.

LGBTQ friendly bookstore: Seattle Magazine City, 1604 1st Ave, Seattle, WA **98101**, included in the Damron Address Book in 1980.

Restaurant/Bar:
Johnny's Handlebar, 2018 1st Ave, Seattle, WA **98121**, included in the Damron Address Book from 1975 to 1980.
Tug's Belltown Tavern, 2207 1st Ave, Seattle, WA **98121**, included in the Damron Address Book in 1980.
Haddads, 2400 1st Ave, Seattle, WA **98121**, included in the Damron Address Book in 1976.

Club: Dave's Steam Baths, 2402 1st Ave, Seattle, WA **98121**, at Battery, included in the 1964 Directory. Included in the 1965 Guild Guide. Included in the 1975 All Lavender International Gay Guide.

Ace Hotel

Accommodation: *Ace Hotel Seattle is a former Salvation Army halfway house located in the Belltown neighborhood.* gay owned *and* LGBTQ friendly.

Address: 2423 1st Ave, Seattle, WA 98121

Place

The first Ace Hotel was opened in 1999. Friends Alex Calderwood (1966-2013), Wade Weigel, and Doug Herrick purchased and transformed a Seattle halfway house into an affordable hotel that would appeal to the creative class. Calderwood and Weigel had previously founded Rudy's, a reinvigorated traditional barbershop concept they started in Seattle, which eventually expanded to more than a dozen West Coast locations. They also founded Neverstop, a marketing and advertising company. In 2006, Jack Barron and Michael Bisordi (Tungsten Partners) joined the team as owners. That year the group opened a second hotel in Portland, followed by properties in Palm Springs and New York in 2009. In 2011, Ace Hotel collaborated with the cosmetics brand uslu airlines to create a nail polish sold in the hotels' mini-bars. In 2013, an Ace Hotel opened in the Shoreditch neighborhood of London. The company opened a property in Panama City, Panama, as the American Trade Hotel. Calderwood had defined a goal of opening a new Ace Hotel every one to two years. He died at age 47 in November 2013, shortly after the opening of the London Shoreditch hotel. Soon after, the downtown Los Angeles location opened in a former theatre, followed by a hotel in Pittsburgh in late 2015 and in New Orleans in spring 2016. A location in Kyoto, Japan designed by Kengo Kuma is expected to open in late 2019.

Restaurant/Bar: El Gaucho (2505 1st Ave, Seattle, WA **98121**), Washington State's LGBTQ and Allied Chamber of Commerce member.

Accommodation: The Inn at El Gaucho (2505 1st Ave, Seattle, WA **98121**), Washington State's LGBTQ and Allied Chamber of Commerce member.

Restaurant/Bar: Popeye, 315 1st Ave N, Seattle, WA **98109**, included in the Damron Address Book in 1977.

Store: Rudy's Barbershop, 109 1st Ave S, Seattle, WA **98104**

Restaurant/Bar: Dead Line (114 1st Ave S, Seattle, WA **98104**), Washington State's LGBTQ and Allied Chamber of Commerce member.

Club: South End Baths, 115 ½ 1st Ave S, Seattle, WA **98104**, included in the 1964 and 1965 Guild Guide. Included in the Damron Address Book from 1974 to 1980. Included in the 1975 All Lavender International Gay Guide.

Store: TomboyX (1910 1st Ave S, Seattle, WA **98134**) just keeps getting cooler. Many ladies (especially the gay ones) prefer a men's-style cut to their underwear, but would prefer they were cut to fit different types of bodies. Like women's bodies. That's why Fran and Naomi invented TomboyX. Naomi Gonzalez and Fran Dunaway have teamed up to create the perfect fusion of women's wear and tomboy style. With an impressive line that features jeans, casual wear, jewelry, and even underwear, TomboyX has the style the celesbians can't wait to put in their closet. Notable ambassadors for the brand include actress Traci Dinwiddie, singer Catie Curtis, and rocker Hannah Thomas.

Club: Dave's Baths, 2402 1st Ave N, Seattle, WA **98109**, included in the Damron Address Book from 1965 to 1980.

Historic District: 2nd Ave & Yesler Way, Seattle, WA **98104**, included in the Damron Address Book from 1972 to 1975.

Restaurant/Bar: Chicken Coop, 411 2nd Ave, Seattle, WA **98104**, included in the Damron Address Book in 1974.

Smith Tower

Attractions: Smith Tower, 506 2nd Ave, Seattle, WA **98104**, at Yesler Way, Historic site with views and a vintage bar. Smith Tower is a skyscraper in the Pioneer Square neighborhood of Seattle. Completed in 1914, the 38-story, 484 ft tower is the oldest skyscraper in the city and was among the tallest skyscrapers outside New York City at the time of its completion. The Submarine Room, in the Basement of Smith Tower, has been included in the Damron Address Book from 1966 to 1973. Included in the 1975 All Lavender International Gay Guide. Also The Dorian Group, included in the 1984 Gayellow Pages.

Theatre: Florence Theatre, 512 2nd Ave, Seattle, WA **98104**, included in the Swasarnt Neft's Gay Guides for 1950. The Florence Theatre was built in 1920. It seated 450 and was still listed in the 1950's. It later became a burlesque theatre known as the New Paris Theatre, then a legitimate theatre known as the Pioneer Square Annex Theatre. The building is still standing but vacant in 2022.

Restaurant/Bar:
Grubstake Café, 608 ½ 2nd Ave, Seattle, WA **98104**, included in the Damron Address Book in 1971.
The 611 or Six Eleven Tavern or Six Eleven Club, 611 2nd Ave, Seattle, WA **98104**, included in the 1963 and 1966 Lavender Baedeker. Included in the 1964 and 1965 Guild Guide. Included in the Damron Address Book from 1966 to 1980. Included in the 1975 All Lavender International Gay Guide.

Accommodation: Courtyard by Marriott Seattle Downtown/Pioneer Square (612 2nd Ave, Seattle, WA **98104**), Washington State's LGBTQ and Allied Chamber of Commerce member.

Queer Architects: Trident Club in the Norton Building, 801 2nd Ave, Seattle, WA **98104**, designed by Roland Terry (1959)

Historic District: Union St & 2nd Ave, Seattle, WA **98101**, included in the Damron Address Book from 1977 to 1980

Restaurant/Bar: The Captains Room, 1117 2nd Ave, Seattle, WA **98121**, included in **The Lady Jai Recommended List, 1954**.

Burnett Brothers jewelry store interior, Seattle, Washington, between 1950 and 1963, University of Washington Libraries, Special Collections

Queer Architects: Burnett Brothers Jewelers Store, 1316 2nd Ave, Seattle, WA **98101**, designed by Tucker & Shields (1950)

Club: Atlas Baths, 1318 2nd Ave, Seattle, WA **98101**, included in the **Damron Address Book** from 1971 to 1979.

Historic District: Penny's Corner, 2nd Ave, Seattle, WA **98101**, between Pike & Union, included in the **Damron Address Book** from 1972 to 1974.

Accommodation: Kimpton Palladian Hotel, 2000 2nd Ave, Seattle, WA **98121**. An eclectic, edgy ambiance where old-world vintage meets contemporary innovation to capture the hip heritage of Belltown. As The Trevor Project's Premier National Hotel Partner, Kimpton Hotels are involved on local and national levels hosting fundraisers across America. In 2022, when you made a reservation, they donated $10 per night to The Trevor Project, plus you got 15% off our Best Flexible Rate.

Restaurant/Bar: Tavolàta (2323 2nd Ave, Seattle, WA **98121**), Washington State's LGBTQ and Allied Chamber of Commerce member.

Connect Lounge (2330 2nd Ave, Seattle, WA **98121**) has been named among the Bars & Restaurants Where You Can Be Your Full Queer Self in Seattle by Travel Out Seattle, 2018.

Jim's Side Pocket or The Light Spot, 2nd Ave S & S Washington St, Seattle, WA **98104**, included in the 1975 All Lavender International Gay Guide. Wayner's Tavern, included in the Damron Address Book from 1977 to 1978.

The Golden Horseshoe, 207 2nd Ave S, Seattle, WA **98104**, included in the 1963 and 1966 Lavender Baedeker. Included in the 1964 and 1965 Guild Guide. Included in the 1964 Directory. Included in the Damron Address Book from 1965 to 1976. Included in the 1975 All Lavender International Gay Guide.

Good Bar (240 2nd Ave S, Seattle, WA **98104**), Washington State's LGBTQ and Allied Chamber of Commerce member, has been named among the Bars & Restaurants Where You Can Be Your Full Queer Self in Seattle by Travel Out Seattle, 2018. Good Bar is located in the historic and ever-changing neighborhood of Pioneer Square. Good Bar offers classic cocktails, an extensive beer list, a thoughtful wine program and friendly, detailed service. Our food is straightforward and delicious, always made from quality ingredients. NGLCC certified LGBT business.

Flanigan's Pub, 400 2nd Ave Ext S, Seattle, WA **98104**, included in the Damron Address Book in 1980.

The Double Header Lounge, also Casino and Mrs Peabody's, 407 2nd Ave Ext S, Seattle, WA **98104**, included in The Lady Jai Recommended List, 1954. Included in the Damron Address Book from 1965 to 1980. Included in the 1966 Lavender Baedeker. Included in the 1975 All Lavender International Gay Guide. The Double Header was one of the oldest continuously operating gay and lesbian bars in the country, opened in 1934. The LGBT establishment closed in December 2015. The bar was located in the Pioneer Square neighborhood.

Busy Bee Cocktail Lounge, 417 2nd Ave S, Seattle, WA **98104**, included in the Damron Address Book from 1966 to 1969. Included in the 1975 All Lavender International Gay Guide.

The 611 Tavern, 611 2nd Ave S, Seattle, WA **98104**, included in the 1964 Directory.

Coffee Coral, 3rd Ave & Yesler Way, Seattle, WA **98104**, included in the 1975 All Lavender International Gay Guide.

Caper at the Morrison Hotel, 509 3rd Ave, Seattle, WA **98104**, included in the Damron Address Book from 1966 to 1971. Included in the 1975 All Lavender International Gay Guide.

The County-City Building and City Hall Park, October 26, 1917 Courtesy Seattle Municipal Archives

Office: Reah Whitehead (1883–1972) was one of the first female lawyers in Washington state and the first female Justice of the Peace in King County and Washington state. She had her office at 412 County City Building (516 3rd Ave, Seattle, WA **98104**). Whitehead was born in Kansas City, MO, the daughter of Stanley E. Whitehead and Esther Gideon. She attended the University of Washington School of Law. She graduated and passed the Washington State Bar examination in 1905. Reah Whitehead began her legal career as a stenographer. In 1899, at 16 years old, she worked in a law office in Skagway, AK: she was the youngest court reporter in Alaska. After graduation and passing the bar examination, she worked for Judge Thomas Burke. She then moved to the position of chief clerk in the King County Prosecutor's Office with Chief Prosecutor MacKintosh. In 1909 she was named Deputy Prosecuting Attorney by Chief Prosecutor George Vanderveer, the first woman prosecutor in the King County and the State of Washington. In 1914 she was elected Justice of the Peace, the first female Justice of the Peace in King County and Washington state. Her mother, Esther T. Bosley, ran her campaign. She served in the role King County's only female Justice of the Peace until 1941 for seven terms. She prepared the Drafts of Bills for and assisted in procuring passage of laws for Women's State Reformatory and Filiation Proceedings. Her mother, Esther Bosley, was the driving force for the funding of the Women's Industrial Home and Clinic in Medical Lake, Washington; her daughter drafted the bill for the measure aimed to grant funding from state social welfare agencies, which passed. She was on the Board of Travelers Aid. She was honorary member of the American Woman's Association. In 1926 she was selected to represent Washington State at the American Women's Association convention in New York City. In 1936 she strongly opposed the reinstatement of public whipping as a means to punishing criminals, according to her a society's failure. Reah Whitehead moved to Seattle, Washington, in 1890 with her family. In 1931, at 48 years old, Reah Whitehead married Frank Sidney Harrison, a retired grocery man. They later divorced and Harrison died in 1955. After her marriage she lived in an old rectory, restored as manor. She spent the summers in a cabin on Lake Sammamish, commuting daily to Seattle. Whitehead retired in 1941 and was replaced by Evangeline Starr. She died on October 13, 1972, at 89 years old.

Restaurant/Bar: The Madison Tavern, 922 3rd Ave, Seattle, WA **98104**, near 1st Bank Building, included in the 1963 and 1966 Lavender Baedeker. Included in the 1964 and 1965 Guild Guide. Included in the 1964 Directory. Included in the Damron Address Book from 1965 to 1968. Included in the 1975 All Lavender International Gay Guide. Later Nine-Twenty-Two Club, included in the Damron Address Book from 1969 to 1976. Included in the 1975 All Lavender International Gay Guide. Later Riverboat Tavern, included in the Damron Address Book in 1979.

Queer Architects: Allen, DeGarmo, and Leedy office plan at Northern Life Tower, 1212 3rd Ave, Seattle, WA **98101**, designed by Roland Terry

Theatre: Winter Garden Theatre, 1515 3rd Ave, Seattle, WA **98101**, included in the Swasarnt Neft's Gay Guides for 1950. Opened as the Winter Garden Theatre on December 3, 1920. This theatre was also known as the Garden Theatre and last operated as the Garden Art Theatre screening adult movies. It was closed in the 1980s and has been in retail use, which ceased in June 2016.

Restaurant/Bar: Zach's Key, 2620 3rd Ave, Seattle, WA **98121**, included in the Damron Address Book in 1974.

Queer Architects:

Richard and June Lentz house, 14301 3rd Ave NW, Seattle, WA **98177**, designed by Roland Terry (1988)

Terry & Egan & Associates office remodeling, 427 3rd Ave W, Seattle, WA **98119**, designed by Roland Terry (1974)

Bank of California Center, 900 4th Ave, Seattle, WA **98164**, designed by Roland Terry (1972)

Accommodation: YMCA, 909 4th Ave, Seattle, WA **98101**, included in the 1975 All Lavender International Gay Guide.

Library: Seattle Public Library-Central Library (1000 4th Ave, Seattle, WA **98104**) has been named among the Most beautiful libraries in the world, 2019. Bonita C. Corliss (born 1954) has worked at the Seattle Public Library in a variety of professional positions. She was 1995-1996 recipient of an American Library Association/United States Information Agency fellowship and thus worked at the American Library in Paris. In 1992 she presented a paper topic on lesbian literature at the American Library Association annual conference in New Odeans. And from 1993-1995 Bonita was a member of the book awards committee of the Gay. Lesbian and Bisexual Task Force.

Accommodation:

Kimpton Hotel Monaco (1101 4th Ave, Seattle, WA **98101**), LGBTQ friendly. This top-rated boutique hotel near the famed Pike Place Market downtown adds a spark to any Seattle visit. As The Trevor Project's Premier National Hotel Partner, Kimpton Hotels are involved on local and national levels hosting fundraisers across America. In 2022, when you made a reservation, they donated $10 per night to The Trevor Project, plus you got 15% off our Best Flexible Rate.

W Seattle (1112 4th Ave, Seattle, WA **98101**), Washington State's LGBTQ and Allied Chamber of Commerce member.

Restaurant/Bar: The Capital Grille, 1301 4th Ave, Seattle, WA **98101**

Queer Architects: Japan Air Lines ticket office, 1302 4th Ave, Seattle, WA **98101**, designed by Roland Terry (1959)

Restaurant/Bar: Yard House, 1501 4th Ave #118, Seattle, WA **98101**

Colonial Theatre

Theatre: Colonial Theatre, 1515 4th Ave, Seattle, WA **98101**, included in the Swasarnt Neft's Gay Guides for 1950. Included in the Damron Address Book in 1973. Included in the 1975 All Lavender International Gay Guide. The Colonial Theatre opened in 1913 in what is now the heart of downtown Seattle. It had a Kimball organ. The Tiger Lily was shown on opening night. Seattle theater king John Danz bought the Colonial Theatre in 1917 or 1918. A new Wurlitzer organ was added around that time. This theatre thrived until the early-1960s.

Restaurant/Bar: Lola (2000 4th Ave, Seattle, WA **98121**), Washington State's LGBTQ and Allied Chamber of Commerce member. Lola features the classic produce of the Pacific Northwest mingled with cooking styles of Greece; the menu offers modern Mediterranean and North African riffs on local ingredients.

Accommodation: Hotel Andra (2000 4th Ave, Seattle, WA **98121**), Washington State's LGBTQ and Allied Chamber of Commerce member and TAG Approved LGBTQ friendly accommodation.

Restaurant/Bar: Dahlia Lounge (2001 4th Ave, Seattle, WA **98121**), Washington State's LGBTQ and Allied Chamber of Commerce member. The smell of the wood burning grill, a swirl of world-class wine, a bite from the fresh northwest sea bar, Dahlia Lounge is the quintessential Seattle restaurant experience.

Queer Architects: Sixth and Lenora building, 2033 4th Ave, Seattle, WA **98121**, designed by Roland Terry (1974)

House: Gypsy Rose Lee (1914-1970) lived at 323 4th Ave N, Seattle, WA **98109**, in 1915 (demolished).

> *Michael Jensen, author: Everyone knows the Space Needle is a great place to go for views of downtown Seattle, but from the observation deck at Columbia Center (701 5th Ave, Seattle, WA 98104) you get amazing views of the entire Puget Sound region. You can see the Olympics to the west, the Cascades to the east, Mount Rainier to the south, as well as Puget Sound, Lake Washington and almost all of Seattle. It's breathtaking!.*

Accommodation: Kimpton Hotel Vintage Park (1100 5th Ave, Seattle, WA **98101**), LGBTQ friendly. Stately yet easygoing hotel in the heart of the downtown that pays homage to Washington wine country. As The Trevor Project's Premier National Hotel Partner, Kimpton Hotels are involved on local and national levels hosting fundraisers across America. In 2022, when you made a reservation, they donated $10 per night to The Trevor Project, plus you got 15% off our Best Flexible Rate.

Queer Architects:

Plaza 5 Restaurant, 1200 5th Ave, Seattle, WA **98101**, designed by Roland Terry (1963)

Crissey Store remodel, 1329 5th Ave, Seattle, WA **98101**, designed by Roland Terry (1955)

Tall's 5th Avenue, 1409 5th Ave, Seattle, WA **98101**, designed by Tucker & Shields (1948).

Restaurant/Bar: Frolik Kitchen+Cocktails (1415 5th Ave, Seattle, WA **98101**), Washington State's LGBTQ and Allied Chamber of Commerce member, has been named among the Bars & Restaurants Where You Can Be Your Full Queer Self in Seattle by Travel Out Seattle, 2018.

Accommodation:
Motif (1415 5th Ave, Seattle, WA **98101**), Washington State's LGBTQ and Allied Chamber of Commerce member. Ideally situated in Downtown Seattle with 319 newly redesigned guest rooms and suites featuring Wi-Fi, In-Room Alexa, mini-fridge and in-room safe. Signature rooftop restaurant and lounge onsite. Part of World Rainbow Hotels (WRH), Lesbian and Gay Welcoming Hotels.
The Westin Seattle (1900 5th Ave, Seattle, WA **98101**), TAG Approved LGBTQ friendly accommodation.

Restaurant/Bar:
Mr Mike's, 5th Ave & Pike St, Seattle, WA **98101**, included in the 1975 All Lavender International Gay Guide.
Palace Kitchen (2030 5th Ave, Seattle, WA **98121**), Washington State's LGBTQ and Allied Chamber of Commerce member. Cozy into a dimly lit booth, or watch the kitchen crank from the lively bar. A long-time favorite for locals and industry folk for treats from the applewood grill until 1am.

Queer Architects: Crissey Flowers and Gifts, 2100 5th Ave, Seattle, WA **98121**, designed by Roland Terry (1974)

Accommodation:
The four-star Hyatt House Seattle/Downtown (201 5th Ave N, Seattle, WA **98109**) is located just across the street from Seattle's famous Space Needle, offering contemporary guestrooms with kitchen amenities. Part of World Rainbow Hotels (WRH), Lesbian and Gay Welcoming Hotels.
Crowne Plaza Seattle Downtown (1113 6th Ave, Seattle, WA **98101**), Washington State's LGBTQ and Allied Chamber of Commerce member and TAG Approved LGBTQ friendly accommodation.

Queer Architects: Washington Athletic Club, 1325 6th Ave, Seattle, WA **98101**, designed by Roland Terry

Accommodation:
The Inn at the Washington Athletic Club (1325 6th Ave, Seattle, WA **98101**), Washington State's LGBTQ and Allied Chamber of Commerce member.
Sheraton Grand Seattle (1400 6th Ave, Seattle, WA **98101**), Washington State's LGBTQ and Allied Chamber of Commerce member and TAG Approved LGBTQ friendly accommodation.

Restaurant/Bar:
Gabe's, 1421 6th Ave, Seattle, WA **98121**, included in the 1975 All Lavender International Gay Guide.
As a 100% gay owned business and the 6th largest LGBTQ owned business in the region, Marination (2000 6th Ave, Seattle, WA **98121**), Washington State's LGBTQ and Allied Chamber of Commerce member, is brimming with Pride and aloha. Established in 2009, Marination serves Hawaiian-Korean curb cuisine. Kamala and Roz say they believe in delivering daily Aloha to Seattle and their thousands of customers seem to agree. Marination is a staple in Seattle's foodie industry. Dubbed America's Sauciest Food Truck, Marination extends well beyond the mobile feel to also include brick and mortar locations in some of the city's best avenues. Marination Ma Kai on Alki (1660 Harbor Ave SW, Seattle, WA **98126**) offers a spectacular view of the Seattle skyline and the freshest fish tacos in the area. Marination Station on near Broadway (1412 Harvard Ave, Seattle, WA **98122**) is the quick pick-me-up you need to succeed through the rest of the day. And then there's Marination Mobile, more commonly known as BIG BLUE. A NGLCC certified LGBT business.

Accommodation: Offering convenience and comfort in the heart of Seattle, the Hyatt Place Seattle Downtown, (110 6th Ave N, Seattle, WA **98109**) delights guests with warm hospitality and courteous, personalized service offerings. Part of World Rainbow Hotels (WRH), Lesbian and Gay Welcoming Hotels.

Restaurant/Bar: Seoul Tofu House, 516 6th Ave S, Seattle, WA **98104**

Accommodation: Civic Hotel (325 7th Ave, Seattle, WA **98109**), Washington State's LGBTQ and Allied Chamber of Commerce member.

Theatre: Place Upstairs Tavern Theatre, 1404 7th Ave, Seattle, WA **98101**, included in the Damron Address Book in 1977.

Restaurant/Bar: Roost, 1416 7th Ave, Seattle, WA **98101**, included in the Damron Address Book in 1974.

Queer Architects: Roosevelt Hotel alterations, 1531 7th Ave, Seattle, WA **98101**, designed by Roland Terry (1962). Part of World Rainbow Hotels (WRH), Lesbian and Gay Welcoming Hotels.

Restaurant/Bar: Canlis, 2576 7th Ave N, Seattle, WA **98109**

Accommodation: Hyatt At Olive 8 (1635 8th Ave, Seattle, WA **98101**), Washington State's LGBTQ and Allied Chamber of Commerce member and TAG Approved LGBTQ friendly accommodation. From the moment you walk through the doors you'll see why our downtown Seattle hotel is one of the most celebrated LEED certified buildings in the city. Part of World Rainbow Hotels (WRH), Lesbian and Gay Welcoming Hotels.

Restaurant/Bar: Annex, 1914 8th Ave, Seattle, WA **98101**, included in the Damron Address Book from 1976 to 1977. Later Park Bench, included in the Damron Address Book from 1979 to 1980.

Religious Building: Raymond Hunthausen (1921–2018) was an American prelate of the Catholic Church. He served as Bishop of Helena from 1962 to 1975 and as Archbishop of Seattle from 1975 to 1991. He was appointed Archbishop of Seattle, Washington by Pope Paul VI and retired effective August 21, 1991 (his 70th birthday), after years of controversies that included an investigation coordinated by Joseph Cardinal Ratzinger, who later became Pope Benedict XVI. The oldest of seven children, Raymond Hunthausen was born in Anaconda, Montana, to Anthony Gerhardt Hunthausen and Edna Marie Tuchscherer. He studied chemistry at Carroll College and graduated cum laude in 1943. He then entered the seminary and was ordained in 1946. He would later pursue a Master's degree at the University of Notre Dame. From 1946 to 1957 Fr. Hunthausen was as an assistant professor of chemistry at Carroll College. He also served as football and basketball coach during the last four years of that period. In 1957 he was appointed the president of Carroll College. We was thirty-five years old: the youngest president in Carroll's history then and now. In 1962 Saint John XXIII appointed him to succeed Bishop Joseph Gilmore as the sixth bishop of Helena. Within months of his ordination as bishop, he was summoned to Rome for the convening of the Second Vatican Council. He was a council father at all four sessions of the Council and remains the only living American bishop to have attended all four sessions. He was the newest and youngest American bishop at the start of the Council. One area of controversy involved ministry to LGBT Catholics in the Seattle Archdiocese. Archbishop Hunthausen and many of the priests in the Seattle Archdiocese had long supported LGBT Catholics. The Archbishop openly supported civil rights for gays and lesbians in 1978 when there was an initiative in Seattle designed to take away those rights. In addition, many priests in the Archdiocese presided at a weekly Mass held by Dignity in various Catholic parishes...eventually landing in 1980 at St. Joseph's on Capitol Hill. Archbishop Hunthausen himself had presided at the Dignity Mass at St. Joseph's. This practice was not unique in Seattle as many Dignity chapters across the country held Masses in Catholic parishes in the 1970s and early 1980s. Given this reality, when the Archdiocese of Seattle was asked to allow attendees at the 1983 biennial convention of Dignity/USA to use St. James Cathedral (804 9th Ave, Seattle, WA **98104**) for a Mass during their convention, the Archbishop promptly and enthusiastically approved the request. While it is true that this could have been viewed as just another a Dignity Mass on Catholic Church property, two things set it apart. First, it was the only time Dignity/USA (the umbrella group for all Dignity chapters) had been officially invited to a Mass on Church property; and, second, the welcome extended by the Seattle Archdiocese was all encompassing. The Archbishop himself had originally planned to celebrate the Mass but was called to Rome and unable to do so. Instead, he sent a videotaped message of welcome to the convention attendees which was played at the convention's Opening Ceremony at the Sheraton Hotel. In addition, an official welcome from the Archdiocese appeared in both the printed convention brochure and booklet. In the end, over 1000 people attended the Mass at St. James, and it was by far the highlight of the convention. It also, alas, turned out to be the pinnacle of acceptance of LGBT Catholics by the hierarchy of the Church. The Archbishop's courageous and loving act was later investigated by the Congregation for the Doctrine of the Faith and, as a result, Dignity chapters across the country were either evicted from Church Property or had their ministry to LGBT Catholics co-opted and replaced by Archdiocesan sponsored LGBT ministries. The Archdiocesan ministry in Seattle lasted at St. Joseph's from 1988-2001 until Dignity/Seattle decided that actions taken by the new Archbishop (Brunette), such as opposition to gay civil rights legislation, were incompatible with Dignity's values. Dignity voted to relocate off Church property rather than continue to collaborate with an Archdiocese which had become increasingly unwelcoming to the LGBT Catholic community, their families and friends. Archbishop Hunthausen was a champion and stalwart pastoral minister for the LGBT community, and suffered professionally and personally as a result. He did everything in his power, within the confines and restrictions of the intolerant Vatican policies, to care for his entire flock, consistent with his view of the gospel. Archbishop Hunthausen retired in 1991 and resided near Helena, Montana, with his brother, Father Jack Hunthausen. He continued to hear confessions once a week in East Helena. As of October 2011, Hunthausen was the last living American bishop to have attended all four sessions of the Second Vatican Council. On July 22, 2018, he died in his home in Helena at the age of 96. He is the second archbishop interred in the crypt at St. James Cathedral.

Restaurant/Bar: Tip Inn, 1926 9th Ave, Seattle, WA **98101**, included in the Damron Address Book in 1975.

Other non-queer residents: Jimi Hendrix (1934-1970), 124 10th Ave, Seattle, WA **98122**, in 1946.

Restaurant/Bar: Lost Lake Café & Lounge (1505 10th Ave, Seattle, WA **98122**), Washington State's LGBTQ and Allied Chamber of Commerce member.

House: Nicholas Heer (born 1928) is an American Arabist and Islamist educator. He is a member of American Oriental Society, Middle East Studies Association, American Association Teachers of Arabic (treasurer 1964-1976, president 1981, director 1982-1984). Seattle's first gay-rights organization was the Dorian Society, founded in 1966 by University of Washington professor Nicholas Heer and other local activists. Nicholas Lawson Heer was born in Durham, NC, the son of Clarence Heer and Jean Douglas MacAlpine. He has a Bachelor degree from Yale University, 1949, and a Doctor of Philosophy degree from Princeton University, 1955. Heer was translation analyst for the Arabian American Oil Corporation, Saudi Arabia, 1955-1957; assistant professor at Stanford University, 1959-1962; visiting lecturer at Yale University, 1962-1963; assistant professor at Harvard University, 1963-1965; associate professor, University of Washington, Seattle, 1965-1976; professor of Near Eastern languages and civilization, University of Washington, Seattle, 1976-1990; professor emeritus, University of Washington, Seattle, since 1990; department chairman of Near Eastern languages and civilization, University of Washington, Seattle, 1982-1987; Middle East curator at Hoover Institution, Stanford, CA, 1958-1962. Nicholas Lawson Heer has been listed as a noteworthy language educator by Marquis Who's Who. Due in part to the proximity of the University of Washington, Seattle University and Cornish College, students of nursing, law and music have lived at the Fairfax Apartments, 1508 10th Ave E, Seattle, WA **98102**, as have university teachers of Spanish and History, a Japanese translator and language instructor. Longtime resident Nicholas Heer came to Seattle from the east coast to teach at the University of Washington. He was one of the founders and first president of the Dorian Society in 1967, the city's first social organization for advocacy and outreach for Seattle's gay community. He briefly left retirement to teach Arabic to students after 9/11.

Restaurant/Bar: Oddfellows Café + Bar (1525 10th Ave, Seattle, WA **98122**), Washington State's LGBTQ and Allied Chamber of Commerce member.

Pagliacci Pizza (2400 10th Ave E, Seattle, WA **98102**), Washington State's LGBTQ and Allied Chamber of Commerce member.

Gay Village

Capitol Hill, 11th Ave, Seattle, WA **98122**

Rainbow Crosswalks: In 2015, Seattle unveiled 11 rainbow crosswalks in the LGBTQ-friendly Capitol Hill neighbourhood (Pine & Broadway, 10th Ave & Pike, 11th Ave & Pine, 10th Ave & Pine, Pike & Broadway, ...). The city pledged to maintain them for years to come. They, like all the rainbow crosswalks, are a favorite place to stop for photos, for both tourists and locals alike.

Restaurant/Bar:
Kurt Farm Shop (1424 11th Ave, Seattle, WA **98122**), LGBTQ owned.
Grim's Provisions & Spirits (1512 11th Ave, Seattle, WA **98122**), Washington State's LGBTQ and Allied Chamber of Commerce member.
Queer/Bar (1518 11th Ave, Seattle, WA **98122**), Washington State's LGBTQ and Allied Chamber of Commerce member. Formerly Purr.

Accommodation: Landes House (712 11th Ave E, Seattle, WA **98102**) included in Inn Places 1999, Gay & Lesbian Accommodations Worldwide. Gay and Lesbian. As of 2021 it's closed.

Queer Architects: Mr. and Mrs. A. W. Paterson residence, 2616 11th Ave E, Seattle, WA **98102**, designed by Roland Terry (1958)

Attraction: Seattle Men's Chorus and Seattle Women's Chorus (319 12th Ave, Seattle, WA **98122**), TAG Approved LGBTQ friendly attraction.

Restaurant/Bar:
Ba Bar Restaurant, 550 12th Ave, Seattle, WA **98122**
Rhein Haus (912 12th Ave, Seattle, WA **98122**), Washington State's LGBTQ and Allied Chamber of Commerce member.
Barrio Mexican Kitchen & Bar (1420 12th Ave, Seattle, WA **98122**), Washington State's LGBTQ and Allied Chamber of Commerce member.

Theatre: Three Dollar Bill Cinema (1620 12th Ave, Seattle, WA **98122**) hosts Translations: The Seattle Transgender Film Festival, as well as some really fun summer movies in the park events in the Capitol Hill neighborhood.

The Cuff Complex, Creative Commons Licenses, via Wikimedia Commons

Restaurant/Bar: The Cuff Complex (1533 13th Ave, Seattle, WA **98122**) has been named among the Bars & Restaurants Where You Can Be Your Full Queer Self in Seattle by Travel Out Seattle, 2018. Named among the Greatest Gay Bars in the World by Out.com, 2013. Serving the Seattle gay community for over 25 years, The Cuff Complex is the home bar for many of Seattle's leather, bear, bike, and fetish groups.

LGBTQ Center: Gay Community Center, 105 14th Ave, Seattle, WA **98122**, included in the **Damron Address Book** from 1979 to 1980.

Restaurant/Bar: Rione XIII (401 15th Ave E, Seattle, WA **98112**), Washington State's LGBTQ and Allied Chamber of Commerce member.

Store: Rudy's Barbershop is a chain of barbershops founded in Seattle and located primarily on the United States West Coast. The first Rudy's was opened by Alex Calderwood, David Petersen and Wade Weigel in 1993. Rudy's Barbershops are known for their casual, retro-hip aesthetic. Alex Calderwood, a club promoter, was inspired to found the first Rudy's during occasional visits to Sig's, a neighborhood barbershop. Seeking to combine the traditional barbershop experience with trendier hairstyles that would appeal to a younger clientele, Calderwood, along with partners Weigel and Petersen, opened the first location in Seattle's Capitol Hill neighborhood in 1993 (428 15th Ave E, Seattle, WA **98112**). The name Rudy was inspired by the character of the same name from the television program Fat Albert and the Cosby Kids.

LGBTQ friendly bookstore: Red and Black Books, 430 15th Ave E, Seattle, WA **98112**, active in 1990.

Restaurant/Bar:
Mother Morgan's Gumbo Factory, 431 15th Ave E, Seattle, WA **98112**, included in the **Damron Address Book** from 1973 to 1975.
Nuflours Bakery (518 15th Ave E, Seattle, WA **98112**), Washington State's LGBTQ and Allied Chamber of Commerce member.

Park: Volunteer Park, 1247 15th Ave E, Seattle, WA **98112**, near Seattle Asian Art Museum, included in the Damron Address Book from 1972 to 1980.

Lake View Cemetery

Cemetery: *Lake View Cemetery is a private cemetery located in the Capitol Hill neighborhood, just north of Volunteer Park. Known as Seattle's Pioneer Cemetery, it is run by an independent, non-profit association. It was founded in 1872 as the Seattle Masonic Cemetery and later renamed for its view of Lake Washington to the east.*

Address: 1554 15th Ave E, Seattle, WA 98112

Notable queer burials:

Denise Levertov (1923–1997) was an American poet. She was a recipient of the Lannan Literary Award for Poetry. Levertov's 'What Were They Like?' is currently included in the Pearson Edexcel GCSE (9–1) English Literature Poetry Anthology. In 1994 she was diagnosed with lymphoma, and also suffered pneumonia and acute laryngitis. Despite this she continued to lecture and participate at national conferences, many on spirituality and poetry. In February 1997 she experienced the death of Mitch Goodman. In December 1997, Denise Levertov died at the age of 74 from complications due to lymphoma. Her papers are held at Stanford University. The first full biography appeared in October 2012 by Dana Greene Denise Levertov: A Poet's Life (Chicago: University of Illinois, 2012). Donna Krolik Hollenberg's more substantial biography, A Poet's Revolution: The Life of Denise Levertov, was published by the University of California Press in April 2013.

Elizabeth Ordway (1828–1897), an early advocate for woman suffrage in Washington territory, was one of the first group of young women recruited to become teachers and wives in pioneer Seattle in the 1860s. Despite the expectation that these Mercer Girls would marry, Ordway remained single and became a successful teacher, school administrator, and suffrage activist. The suffrage activism of Ordway and some of the other Mercer Girls reflected their educational levels, professional status, and the values associated with personal autonomy that promoted their decisions to migrate across the continent to build new lives. Ordway received a good education for a woman of her time, matriculating at the Ipswich Academy, MA, with Mary Abigail Dodge (an American writer and essyist better known as Gail Hamilton). She taught in Lowell, MA, before migrating to Washington when she was in her mid-30s. In March of 1864 she left Lowell with 10 other ladies, known as Seattle's Mercer Girls, and went to Washington Territory where she continued to teach. She taught first in schools in Beginning in Coupeville, WA, on Whidbey Island and in the lumber communities of Port Gamble and Port Madison on the Kitsap Peninsula. She developed a reputation as the best teacher in the territory and traveled around the area to turn around problem schools. She also launched and taught in Seattle's first dedicated school building. In 1867 she was teaching at Port Madison and then in August of 1870 she became the first pulbic school teacher in Seattle. In 1871 Ordway appeared on stage with Susan B. Anthony in Seattle during Anthony's tour of the Northwest promoting the cause of women voting. Ordway became active in the Female Suffrage Association formed after Anthony spoke and served as a delegate to the territorial suffrage convention. Anthony formed the Washington Territory Woman Suffrage Association, a crucial vehicle for suffrage lobbying in the ensuing decades. Thereafter, Ordway returned to teaching in Kitsap County and, in 1881, became the first woman to be elected as a school superintendent in territorial Washington. She served Kitsap County in that position for eight years, solidifying her position as a builder of public schools in Washington territory. In 1891 she moved to Seattle and assisted the prepartation of the Washingtons educational exhibit for the Chicago World's Fair of 1893. A woman friend described Ordway as admired for her charm and wit, a clever and interesting conversationalist who loved a good argument, and Washington's first career woman. Ordway died in Seattle the at age 69, and is remembered by a description she applied to herself: The Mercer Girl who reserved her affections for her students. In 1953 the Retired Teachers Association placed a monument headstone on her grave in the Captain Sylvanus Libby family plot.

We Sail Together: **Virginia Weisel** (1923-2017) was an accomplished ceramic artist and sculptor in the Pacific Northwest for many decades. The Kiln, a ceramic establishment in Bellevue, was owned and operated by a lesbian couple, Virginia Weisel and her life partner, Aurilla Doerner. The women had been together for nearly ten years before establishing their own business where Virginia, a seasoned ceramic artist, was in charge of production and Rilla provided the financial stability for their success. They offered classes through the studio and participated in all the region's finest crafts exhinitions. Virginia was known for her classically inspired modern stoneware and especially for her unique and innovative glazes. Weisel's ashes were scattered at her parents' grave, the same location as **Aurilla Doerner**, her life partner who died in 1996.

Gaslight Inn, Creative Commons Licenses, via Wikimedia Commons

Accommodation: Gaslight Inn (1727 15th Ave., Seattle, WA **98122**) is a beautifully appointed arts and crafts inn in the heart of the gay neighbourhood known as Capitol Hill. Named Featured Inns of 1999 by Inn Places, Gay & Lesbian Accommodations Worldwide. Gay and Lesbian. GLD, Gay Lesbian Directory

Other non-queer residents: Theodore Roethke (1908-1963), Malloy Apartments (4337 15th Ave NE, Seattle, WA **98105**), from 1947 to 1950.

Park: Cowen Park, 5849 15th Ave NE, Seattle, WA **98105**, included in the Damron Address Book from 1977 to 1980.

Restaurant/Bar:
Pagliacci Pizza (8024 15th Ave NE, Seattle, WA **98115**), Washington State's LGBTQ and Allied Chamber of Commerce member.
Thunderbird Tavern, 7515 15th Ave NW, Seattle, WA **98117**, included in the 1964 and 1965 Guild Guide.
Chocolopolis (WorkLofts, 1631 15th Ave W #111, Seattle, WA **98119**), Washington State's LGBTQ and Allied Chamber of Commerce member.

LGBTQ Center: Gay Community Center, 1726 16th Ave, Seattle, WA **98122**, included in the Damron Address Book in 1977.

Religious Building: Metropolitan Community Church, 128 16th Ave E, Seattle, WA **98112**, included in the Damron Address Book from 1974 to 1980.

Accommodation:
Salisbury House B&B Inn (750 16th Ave E, Seattle, WA **98112**), LGBTQ friendly.
Roberta's B&B (1147 16th Ave E, Seattle, WA **98112**) included in Inn Places 1999, Gay & Lesbian Accommodations Worldwide. Gay friendly. As of 2021 it's closed.

Religious Building: The Rev. Mineo Katagiri (1919-2005) was a United Church of Christ clergy who advocated for social justice and racial equality and was an early supporter of LGBTQ rights. Katagiri was born in Haleiwa, HI. His father and mother were Buddhist and worked as barbers on the north shore of Oahu. His father supplemented the family income through selling home-brewed liquor and hand-carved sashimi. During his youth Mineo witnessed and experienced the horrible conditions and injustices of the plantation system—sugar cane and pineapple fields—where many Asian immigrants worked long days for meager wages. Years later he would write: My hatred of the plantation system has become an emotional one. My life has therefore been one of quest for means and methods of breaking such a system. Mineo enrolled in the University of Hawaii in 1937, intending to become a lawyer so as to work for social change. An athlete who played baseball and basketball, he became active in the university YMCA to participate in its sports programs. His leadership abilities became evident as he was elected to the student council of the university and the vice-president, and later president, of the YMCA. His life changed dramatically in August 1939 when he traveled to the World Conference of Christian Youth in Amsterdam as part of the YMCA's delegation. Europe was aflame with the rise of Nazi Germany and its persecution of Jews. Following the conference, Mineo and some friends toured Europe. While in Germany he became gravely ill with an infection and high fever. Fearing that he might die in Nazi Germany, he prayed to God that if he recovered, he would give his life to Christian service. He did recover quickly and upon his return to the university changed his focus to ministry. He graduated in 1941 and enrolled in Union Theological Seminary in New York City. Union was a high-profile seminary at that time, with a renowned faculty and a focus on social justice. Mineo thrived there and through the counsel of some friends he associated with the Congregational Church (which became the United Church of Christ in 1957). After the Japanese attacked Pearl Harbor in December 1941, there was pressure in the Japanese-American community for young men to enlist in the US military. As Mineo was preparing to graduate from seminary in 1944, he received a draft notice. By that time he was strong in his pacifist beliefs and claimed conscientious objector status. This was not a popular stance within his family and community. Mineo served briefly as a pastor in rural Kentucky and then outside Chicago. However, he encountered much resistance because of the strong anti-Japanese sentiment in the U.S. at the time. So in January 1945, he returned to Hawai'i and married his childhood sweetheart, Nobu Sasai. Three daughters were born into the family in the years following as he pastored congregations on Oahu, Maui, and Kauai. He also taught at Doshisha University in Kyoto, Japan. In 1959, the Katagiri family moved to Seattle, where Mineo became the campus minister at University Congregational United Church of Christ (4515 16th Ave NE, Seattle, WA **98105**). There his charismatic, active, open-minded style flourished in interactions with university students. As the turbulent 1960s unfolded, U.S. church leaders began searching and experimenting on how to do authentic ministry in cities. In 1965, United Church of Christ officials in Seattle decided to create an Ecumenical Metropolitan Ministry to engage urban problems and needs. Because of his success in campus ministry, Katagiri was invited to head this new ministry initiative. Katagiri understood that in this role he should be learning about and listening to the multitude of voices and communities in the city and working in partnerships to improve peoples' lives. One of the Seattle communities he encountered early in this ministry were the gay men who gathered in the bars and restaurants around Pioneer Square. In March 1966, a small group of gay and lesbian activists met in Katagiri's office and formed the Dorian Society, Seattle's first gay rights group. Katagiri continued to meet with the group and provide meeting space for them. In November 1966, when the Seattle City Council was considering whether to limit or curtail gay clubs, Katagiri was chosen to be a spokesperson for the gay community before the Council. The Council decided to allow gay clubs to remain. Modeled on the innovative dialogues between homosexuals and clergy that the Council on Religion and the Homosexual began in San Francisco in 1964, Katagiri hosted similar daylong gatherings with gay and church leaders for listening and learning. Katagiri also worked with the gay community to provide opportunities for journalists and church leaders to take tour of gay clubs and establishments to get firsthand, personal knowledge of LGBTQ persons. Katagiri was driven by his passionate belief in the integrity and dignity of every human being. Therefore, he worked for economic and racial justice as well as LGBTQ equality. He served as president of the Seattle-King County Economic Opportunity Board and was on the boards of the Central Area Civil Rights Committee and the Seattle Urban League. He founded and led the Asian Coalition for Equality. Katagiri's vigorous and faithful ministry and leadership took him to a national church position in 1970 as the Director of Mission Priorities for the United Church of Christ in New York City. In 1975, he was called to be the Conference Minister for the Northern California UCC. He supported the collective ordination of Stacy Cusulos, Jody Parsons and Loey Powell on April 2, 1978 and led a prayer in that ordination service, Stacy served as the Associate Conference Minister for Youth and Young Adults. When another pastor tried to have her removed from that position because she was known to be lesbian, Katagiri's strong defense of Cusulos and her fitness for ministry were instrumental in keeping her in that position. Katagiri retired in 1984 and lived in San Francisco. He died at the age of 86. An overwhelming majority of the members of the University Congregational United Church of Christ voted in 1994 to let the Rev. Peter Ilgenfritz and his partner, David Shull, become the congregation's associate ministers. The pair, who met while at Yale Divinity School in 1986, are believed to be the first gay couple in the country to share a ministry at a nongay church.

Restaurant/Bar: The Lumber Yard Bar (9619 16th Ave SW, Seattle, WA **98106**), Washington State's LGBTQ and Allied Chamber of Commerce member.

Accommodation:
Seahurst Garden Studio (13713 16th Ave SW, Seattle, WA **98166**), LGBTQ owned.
Foxglove Guesthouse (117 18th Ave E, Seattle, WA **98112**), gay owned. On a quiet tree lined street this classic Seattle house has been completely restored and outfitted with the modern traveller in mind.

House: William M. MacLane (1926-2000) was an American artist. William Millea MacLane was born in Baltimore, MD, and in the 1940s he lived at 5026 18th Ave NE, Seattle, WA **98105**.

Restaurant/Bar: Fuel Coffee (610 19th Ave E, Seattle, WA **98112**), Washington State's LGBTQ and Allied Chamber of Commerce member.

Queer Architects: Florence Beach Terry residence, 9807 19th Ave NW, Seattle, WA **98117**, designed by Roland Terry (1937).

Accommodation: Sleeping Bulldog B&B (816 19th Ave S, Seattle, WA **98144**), gay owned. A modern B&B that is conveniently located to downtown, Seattle's waterfront and both Sports Arenas. GLD, Gay Lesbian Directory

House: Carl Natelli (1913-2008) was born in Seattle to Anthony and Barbara Mayo Natelli. The family lived at 1523 19th Ave S, Seattle, WA **98144**. He was the seventh of twelve siblings (four boys and eight girls); he attended Mt. Virgin Elementary, and graduated from Franklin High School in 1932. He was drawn to the performing arts in high school, and participated in skits, plays and comedy routines. After graduating, he pursued his passion for music by singing in the St. James Cathedral choir under the direction of Dr. Palmer, whom he greatly admired. During WWII he played the organ at the cathedral, and eventually became well respected in the pipe organ community. During the 1970's he helped design, build and pay for the Balcom and Vaughan organ at St. Edwards church where he played for ten years. For many years he has served as a respected advisor and inspiration to the music department at St. James. Besides music, Carl's other passions included Asian Art and photography. He photographed and processed his own prints professionally until the early 1980's. Carl was an avid reader who enjoyed history, politics, art and religion, and participated in the Great Books discussion program during the 1980's. He was gifted with an almost photographic memory as well as perfect pitch, and could well be described as a dapper artistic gentleman who could passionately contribute to any conversation. In 1977 he retired from the Railroad as a traffic analyst, a job he approached with consummate professionalism.

Queer Architects:

Mr. and Mrs. Ark Chin residence, 1920 20th Ave S, Seattle, WA **98144**, designed by Roland Terry (1953)

Delta Delta Delta (Tri-Delta) sorority house additions and alterations, 4527 21st Ave NE, Seattle, WA **98105**, designed by Roland Terry (1956)

House: Morris Graves (1910-2001) was born in Fox Valley, OR, where his family had moved about a year before his birth, from Seattle, WA, in order to claim land under the Homestead Act. He was named in honor of Morris Cole, a favored minister of his Methodist parents. He had five older brothers, and eventually, two younger siblings. Constant winds and cold winters made it much more difficult than expected to establish a working farm, and the struggle led to bankruptcy of the senior Graves' once-thriving paint and wallpaper store in Seattle. In 1911, a few months after Morris' birth, the family returned to the Seattle area, settling north of the city in semi-rural Edmonds, WA. He was a self-taught artist with natural understandings of color and line. Graves dropped out of high school after his sophomore year, and between 1928 and 31, along with his brother Russell, visited all the major Asian ports of call as a steamship hand for the American Mail Line. On arriving in Japan, he wrote: There, I at once had the feeling that this was the right way to do everything. It was the acceptance of nature not the resistance to it. I had no sense that I was to be a painter, but I breathed a different air. In the 1940s the Graves' family lived at 5217 21st Ave NE, Seattle, WA **98105**.

Accommodation: Chambered Nautilus B&B Inn (5005 22nd Ave NE, Seattle, WA **98105**), LGBTQ friendly.

Restaurant/Bar: Fuel Coffee (2300 24th Ave E, Seattle, WA **98112**), Washington State's LGBTQ and Allied Chamber of Commerce member.

Purr, Creative Commons Licenses, via Wikimedia Commons

Restaurant/Bar:
Purr Cocktail Lounge (2307 24th Ave E, Seattle, WA **98112**) has been named among the Greatest Gay Bars in the World by Out.com, 2013.

That's Amore Italian Café (1425 31st Ave S, Seattle, WA **98144**), Washington State's LGBTQ and Allied Chamber of Commerce member, Top LGBTQIA+ Owned and Operated Restaurants in America, OpenTable 2021

Red Cow (1423 34th Ave, Seattle, WA **98122**), Washington State's LGBTQ and Allied Chamber of Commerce member.

Queer Architects: Mr. and Mrs. Marvin Mohl residence, 35th Ave E & E John St, Seattle, WA **98112**, designed by Roland Terry (1956)

House: Malcolm Roberts (1913-1990) was an American artist. In the 1940s he was living at 319 36th Ave, Seattle, WA **98122**. He studied at the Chicago Art Institute, the University of Washington and in Europe. He was credited as Seattle's first Surrealist and exhibited frequently at the Northwest Annuals at the Seattle Art Museum. He produced paintings in oil and gouache for the WPA as well as lithographs. Roberts utilized elements of the northwest landscape in his surreal compositions, especially coast and shoreline related material such as shells, driftwood and beach detritus. Some of his art reflects his homosexual orientation and he was connected romantically with other male artist's including Morris Graves and Guy Anderson. His later work of the 1950s and 1960s turned away from Surrealism. Malcolm Roberts began art instruction in 1928 at the classes of the Seattle Fine Arts Society under Mark Tobey. In the late 1930s, Roberts was in a romantic but open relationship with painter Morris Graves. In 1939 they moved into a home on Melrose Avenue East, on Seattle's Capitol Hill, with composer John Cage and his beard wife, Xenia. Roberts' high-strung personality was at odds with that of the mischievous Graves, so their living arrangement soon came to an end. In 1940, Roberts collaborated with Jane Givan and Robert Iglehart to produce stage and costume designs for Bonnie Bird's newly formed American Dance Theatre at Cornish. The dances utilized diverse music selections, including Bach's Third English Suite, John Cage's America Was Promises (set to Archibald MacLeish's poem), and Any Man's Safa by George McKay. The soloist included Bonnie Bird, then head of Cornish's dance department, as well as Syvilla Fort and Dorothy Herrman. When Roberts' father died, he left Malcolm with a trust fund that would enable him to live comfortably and indulge his artistic pursuits. The following year, he married a lesbian friend named Ann Erickson (1913-1991) in Pasadena, where she had moved the previous year from Seattle. Ann was part of the cultural circle Roberts traveled in, and the two had been very close friends for several years. Altought they gave birth to a child, the marriage soon ended. Malcolm Roberts developed a fine reputation in Southern California, even designing a large home for mobster Mickey Cohen. According to Roberts' friend Ivar Haglund, Cohen ordered Roberts to furnish the home entirely with antiques, but they had to be new antiques. He complied and, drawing on his Surrealist past, created a bust of Queen Victoria with a state-of-the-art FM radio hidden inside. In the early 1970s he formed a design business with Seattle decorators Barbara Thomas and Jean Anderson. He lived the remainder of his life in a small, elegant apartment and never returned to painting again.

Brown residence exterior from rear, Seattle, Washington, 1952, University of Washington Libraries, Special Collections

Queer Architects: Monte Edgar Brown (1914-1999) was the chairman and publisher of the Seattle Daily Journal of Commerce. He was the son of Monte Frank Brown (1880–1941) and Nettie Cecilia Curran (1884–1968). He graduated from University of Washington, class of 1937. After serving as a major in the Marine Corps during WWII, Brown returned to Seattle to help run the Journal of Commerce which was published by his father, Monte F. Brown, until his death in 1941. Monte Edgar Brown became sole publisher in 1964. After WWII, Ward Corley came to Seattle for an unknown reason, and slowly became part of Seattle's gay artistic circles. He was briefly involved with architect Robert Shields and later had a longterm relationship with Monte Edgar Brown. It is not known if the two men met in the marines or if Brown was the reason Corley moved to Seattle. Monte Brown came from a prominent and successful family that owned and operated the Daily Journal of Commerce, where Ward found employment until 1959. In 1959 he was diagnosed with a terminal liver disease. He went immediately in California for treatment from a liver specialist. In a letter to Morris Graves dated April 21, 1959, Corley wrote: My week-end in San Francisco was made extremely pleasant because of Monte (prior to becoming set up here in Palo Alto). He had me in the finest suite, as those things go, in the St. Francis, even asking them to give me quarters that were not modern, but with antique furniture or at least French in feeling... The result was a king of high-powered almost savage elegance that was so pleasant under the circumstances. Unlike Corley, his boyfriend Monte Brown had a very supportive family in Seattle who were aware of their relationship. Ward returned to Seattle to live with Monte in a home built directly behind Monte's parents' home at 1111 38th Ave (demolished), that included a studio where he could paint. They continued to support Ward through his illness and even cared for him in their own home when he was particularly weak. The Monte E. Brown House at 338 39th Ave E, Seattle, WA **98112**, was designed by Tucker & Shields in 1951.

Queer Architects: Richard, Jr., and Ruth Lea Residence, 230 40th Ave E, Seattle, WA **98112**, Designed by Lionel Pries (1956-57). An extraordinary home designed around a collection of Japanese art, it was demolished in 2006.

Julian and Marajane Barksdale House

Queer Architects: *The Julian & Marajane Barksdale house is located in the Cedar Park neighborhood in northeast Seattle, east of the center of Lake City. The Barksdale house represents the post-WWII modern design work of Seattle architect and educator Lionel H. Pries, who is considered one of the fathers of modern architecture in the Pacific Northwest.*

Address: 13226 42nd Ave NE, Seattle, WA 98125
National Register of Historic Places: 13000995, 2013.

Julian and Marajane Barksdale House, Creative Commons Licenses, via Wikimedia Commons

Place

The house has an area of 2690 s.f. (2160 s.f. main floor; 530 s.f. basement) enclosed by an irregular perimeter. A curved gravel driveway leads from 42nd Avenue to the northwest-facing front entrance. The northeast wall of the house has the form of a zig-zag oriented to views of Lake Washington. From the front entrance, the interior spaces are designed in a spatial sequence that leads to the views of the lake. The primary exterior materials are cedar siding stained dark brown and concrete block. The primary interior rooms are finished in mahogany veneer plywood. The house was designed by architect and educator Lionel H. Pries. The first phase was constructed in 1949-50 (although it includes a cottage daring from 1926). An addition, also by Lionel Pries, was constructed in 1954-55. The house remained in the ownership of the Barksdale family until 2006, when it was purchased by the present owners. As a result, it is an almost completely unaltered example of the mid-century modern architecture of Lionel Pries. Stylistically, it is an exceptional example of the emerging regional modernism of the Pacific Northwest of the late 1940s.

Life

Who: Lionel H. (Spike) Pries (June 1, 1897 – April 7, 1968)
Lionel Pries was a leading architect, artist, and educator in the Pacific NorthweSt Pries was born in San Francisco and raised in Oakland. He graduated with a B.A. in Architecture from the University of California, Berkeley, in 1920, where he studied under John Galen Howard. He then studied under Paul Cret at the University of Pennsylvania, earning his M.A. in 1921. After travel in Europe, he returned to San Francisco where he practiced architecture for the next four years, although he spent a year in Santa Barbara (designing buildings for the Bothin Helping Fund) after the 1925 earthquake. In 1928, Pries moved to Seattle to join Penn classmate William J. Bain in the firm Bain & Pries. Initially successful, the firm could not survive the Depression and dissolved in late 1931. Thereafter Pries focused on his career as an educator, although he occasionally took on architectural projects under his own name. Pries joined the faculty of the Department of Architecture at the University of Washington in fall 1928 and soon became the center of the school. From 1928 to 1958, he was the inspirational teacher of a generation of architecture students at Washington, among them Minoru Yamasaki, A. Quincy Jones, Ken Anderson, Paul H. Kirk, Roland Terry, Fred Bassetti, Victor Steinbrueck, Perry Johanson, Wendell Lovett, and many others. From 1931 to 1932, Pries served as Director of the Art Institute of Seattle (predecessor to the Seattle Art Museum). For a time he was part of the circle of Northwest artists that included Kenneth Callahan, Morris Graves, and Guy Anderson. Pries exhibited as an artist (oils, watercolors, drypoint prints) in the late 1920s and from the mid-1930s to the mid-1940s. Beginning in the late 1920s and continuing to 1942, Pries travelled to Mexico every summer and regularly interacted with leaders in Mexican art including William Spratling, Frederick W. Davis, Rene d'Harnoncourt, Juan O'Gorman, and others. Pries's architectural works from the late 1930s to the 1960s showed a mix of Modernism and regionalism, reflecting the profound influence of what he encountered in Mexico. Pries was gay, but deeply closeted in the University of Washington community. He anticipated teaching at least until he reached retirement age, but was forced to resign his university position in 1958 after he was picked up in a vice sting in Los Angeles. The reason for Pries's abrupt departure from the university was concealed at the time. Pries worked as a drafter until he was able to retire in 1964, then lived quietly until his death in 1968.

Queer Architects: Mr. Richard Lea apartment residence at Washington Park Tower, 1620 43rd Ave E # 1C, Seattle, WA **98112**, designed by Roland Terry (1967)

Beach: Madison Park Beach, 1900 43rd Ave E, Seattle, WA **98112**, included in the Damron Address Book from 1972 to 1980.

Queer Architects: Lakecrest/Shoremont Apartments, 2012 43rd Ave E, Seattle, WA

98112, Designed by Lionel Pries (1926-31). This apartment complex was built in four sections. The first (northern) section was designed in 1926-28 by William J. Bain, Sr., and was originally known as the Shoremont Apartments. A compatible addition was constructed in 1930-31 by Bain and his partner, Lionel Pries; they received a state AIA Honor Award for the design. The southern section, two buildings originally known as the Lakecrest Apartment Court, was designed in 1928-29 as one of the earliest works of Paul Thiry and James M. Taylor. The final building, at the northeast corner, was designed in 1952-53 by Frederick Anhalt, and is perhaps the only apartment building that he actually designed. The complex is still owned by the Heathman family, who purchased it in 1944.

Restaurant/Bar: Endolyne Joe's (9261 45th Ave SW, Seattle, WA **98136**), Washington State's LGBTQ and Allied Chamber of Commerce member.

Accommodation: Chittenden House B&B (5649 47th Ave SW, Seattle, WA **98136**), LGBTQ friendly.

47th Ave SW, Seattle

Queer Architects:

9830 47th Ave SW, Seattle, WA **98136**, designed by Tucker & Shileds.
Julia Flett (Mrs. Arthur) Morris Residence, 3704 48th Ave NE, Seattle, WA **98105**, Designed by Lionel Pries (1947-48). Minor alterations including added garage and new kitchen. Survives in private ownership in fine condition.

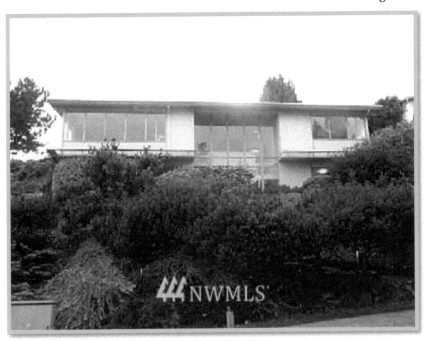

3855 51st Ave NE, Seattle

Queer Architects:
3855 51st Ave NE, Seattle, WA **98105**, designed by Tucker & Shields.
Dr. and Mrs. George Kennaugh residence remodel, 5736 64th Ave NE, Seattle, WA **98105**, designed by Roland Terry (1959)

Oldest Building in America: Maynard's House, 1860, 3045 64th Ave SW, Seattle, WA **98116**. This building was built for pioneer David Doc Maynard, an Indian agent whose job was to manage Indian affairs. The nondescript, shingle home is a private residence. There's no plaque indicating its status as the oldest building in the city, and the property has no special historic designation.

34th-205th Street

The Dancing Machine, Creative Commons Licenses, via Wikimedia Commons

The Dancing Machine (Fremont Ave N & N 34th St, Seattle, WA **98103**) was a gay bar active in 1975.
Cafe Turko, 750 N 34th St, Seattle, WA **98103**

Rudy's Barbershop, 475 N 36th St, Seattle, WA **98103**

Fuel Coffee (1705 N 45th St, Seattle, WA **98103**), Washington State's LGBTQ and Allied Chamber of Commerce member.

Changes Bar & Grill, Creative Commons Licenses, via Wikimedia Commons

Restaurant/Bar: Guild II 45th Theater on 45th Street, Wallingford, Seattle, WA, closed in July 2017 closing. To its right, Changes Bar & Grill (2103 N 45th St, Seattle, WA **98103**) is a gay bar since 1989.

Blue Moon Tavern

Restaurant/Bar: *Former haunt of Theodore Roethke & other counterculture literati, now a music venue & student hive. The Blue Moon is a tavern located on the west edge of the University District. It opened in April 1934, four months after the repeal of Prohibition, and has been visited by many counterculture icons over the years. Included in the* Damron Address Book *from 1972 to 1977.*

Address: 712 NE 45th St, Seattle, WA 98105

Original sign of the Blue Moon Tavern, Creative Commons Licenses, via Wikimedia Commons

Place

The Blue Moon is the first and oldest tavern in the U-District. It was an instant hit with students, together with the still-thriving Duchess Tavern in Ravenna (which was established in the same year as the Blue Moon). Under state law, students had to trek one mile from campus to purchase drinks. The Blue Moon was one of the rare bars outside of the Central District to serve African American servicemen during WWII. The tavern also provided a haven for UW professors who were caught up in the McCarthyist purge, such as Joe Butterworth, who used the bar as his writing desk. Its heyday continued into the 1950s and 1960s. Regulars included authors Tom Robbins and Darrell Bob Houston, poets Theodore Roethke, Richard Hugo, Carolyn Kizer, Stanley Kunitz, and David Wagoner, and painters Richard Gilkey and Leo Kenney. Other visitors included Dylan Thomas, Ken Kesey, Allen Ginsberg and Mik Moore. A popular story claims that sometime in the late 1960s, Tom Robbins tried to call the artist Pablo Picasso in Barcelona from a pay phone at the Blue Moon Tavern. Supposedly, Robbins got through to Picasso, but the artist refused to accept the overseas collect calling charges. The Blue Moon declined in the 1970s. Efforts to redevelop the property in 1989 were derailed by community activists led by Walt Crowley; however, an attempt in 1990 to gain landmark status failed. Developers spared the tavern after landmark status was denied. The Blue Moon remains one of the few surviving blue-collar landmarks in Seattle. In 1995, the alley to the west of the Blue Moon was named Roethke Mews in honor of the bar's famous patron Theodore Roethke.

Life

Who: William Leo Kenney (March 5, 1925 – February 26, 2001)
In the late 1940s Leo Kenney lived in a small apartment near the University of Washington with the brilliant, combative, hard-drinking painter Richard Gilkey. The two became fixtures at the Blue Moon Tavern, the locus of Seattle's nascent Beat culture. In 1948 two of Kenney's paintings were accepted by

the Seattle Art Museum for its Annual Exhibition of the Artists of the Pacific Northwest (the Northwest Annuals); one of them, Third Offering, won a prize and cash award. The following year SAM presented a solo exhibition of Kenney's work. At age 24 he most likely was (and still is) the youngest artist to have a solo show at the museum. As the Pacific Northwest's most popular young painter he soon found himself overwhelmed with commissioned work, and fled to California, where he would stay for the next several years. After briefly returning to Douglas Aircraft, he stumbled onto a job, in 1952, as a display artist at Gump's, a major seller of Asian art in San Francisco. He spent the next six years there, becoming the company's director of display, then moved to a different art dealership, W. & J. Sloane. He painted only sporadically during this time, but learned a great deal about Asian art. His fascination with an Eastern symbol, the mandala, led to a shift in his work away from the figure and into a pure abstraction of glowing colors and simple, geometric forms, detailed with obsessive intricacy. In 1960 he quit his job in order to refocus on painting. Kenney's 1962 experiments with mescaline had a pronounced effect on his art. The writer Deloris Tarzan Ament would later say: Figures and representational images disappeared. In their place appeared a long series of paintings that were variations on an inner circle radiating misty echoes like the reverberations of a gong. They are elemental forms, drenched with archetypal resonance; symbols of source as well as pure studies of light and form. As the 1960s progressed the world seemed to be catching up to Kenney's proto-psychedelic visions. He moved back to Seattle in 1964, and subsequent gallery shows were met with strong sales and critical acclaim. In 1967 the American Academy of Arts and Letters recognized him with a display of his work at the Academy and an award of $2,500. His paintings were included in the West Coast Now traveling exhibition. Mark Tobey and Morris Graves' agent in New York, Marian Willard, arranged a New York exhibition for Kenney at the Willard Gallery in 1968. The show was such a success that Willard immediately wanted to schedule an encore. The Seattle Art Museum, initially somewhat skeptical of Kenney's newer work, slated a solo exhibition for 1973, in tandem with an exhibition at Seattle's Foster/White Gallery. Despite his success, Kenney was growing tired of the symmetric shapes of his most popular work, and began loosening up his composition and breaking his shapes into pieces. As he explored these new directions he became increasingly uncomfortable with the pressure to churn out new paintings. His meticulous attention to detail had always necessitated a slow working pace, and now, in his late forties, burdened by ill health and a drinking problem, he simply couldn't produce enough work to keep up with demand. By the late 1970s his celebrity began to recede. He painted sporadically and sold work out of his studio to help pay his expenses, but was never able to complete enough paintings for another gallery exhibition. Kenney remained a master colorist and technician among Northwest painters. However, injuries and alcohol greatly reduced his artistic output. His old friend and patron Merch Pease helped him reorder his health and his finances somewhat, and in 1996 the Port Angeles Fine Art Center mounted Leo Kenney: Geometrics, a showing of his work since the 1973 Seattle Art Museum show. In 2000 the Museum of Northwest Art in La Conner, Washington presented Celebrating the Mysteries, a comprehensive overview of Kenney's 50-year career curated by Barbara Straker James. Though ailing, Kenney happily gabbed with guests and old friends for several hours at the exhibition's opening celebration. Suffering from cancer and emphysema, Kenney died on February 26, 2001, in Seattle. In 2014, several of his works were included in Modernism in the Pacific Northwest: the Mythic and the Mystical, a major exhibition at the Seattle Art Museum.

House: Pehr Hallsten (1897-1965) was born in Hammerdal, Sweden. He emigrated to the US in 1920, and moved to Seattle in the 1930s. Fluent in seven or eight languages, he made a living teaching languages, working as a laborer, and for the WPA. In 1953 he graduated from the University of Washington; his M.A. thesis was a translation of Strindberg's Stora Landsvagen into English. He began to have success in the late '50s as a painter. Pehr was the companion of artist Mark Tobey, living together in Seattle, Washington and Basel, Switzerland. At age 56, Pehr decided to paint after watching artist friend, Helmi Juvonen. Helmi told Wes Wehr, (artist and friend) she had given Pehr some Windsor and Newton watercolors and paper, and that Pehr said painting looked easy when he watched her work. Helmi's studio and Pehr's reading room were in the same building, the Kennedy (907 NE 45th St, Seattle, WA 98105), next to the University Way post office. Pehr would spend time at the Kennedy, due to his partner, Mark Tobey, required solace whenever he was working.

Store: Rudy's Barbershop, 3620 NE 45th St, Seattle, WA 98105

Queer Architects: Alpha Tau Omega Fraternity House, 1800 NE 47th St, Seattle, WA **98105**, Designed by Lionel Pries. This is a Bain & Pries building that one can easily see from the street.

Park: Woodland Park, 1000 N 50th St, Seattle, WA **98103**, included in the Swasarnt Neft's Gay Guides for 1950. Lower side, included in the Damron Address Book from 1977 to 1980.

Restaurant/Bar: mkt. (2108 N 55th St, Seattle, WA **98103**), Washington State's LGBTQ and Allied Chamber of Commerce member.

Queer Architects: Ernst and Marie Levy House, 2129 NE 55th St, Seattle, WA **98105**, designed by Tucker & Shields (1948-1949). The German refugee Ernst Levy (1881-1968) taught in the Law School at the University of Washington between 1936-1952. He began his teaching career in 1919 at the University of Frankfurt, before moving to Freiburg in 1922, where he attained the rank of full professor. In 05/1928, he became a tenured professor at the University of Heidelberg, and taught here until Nazi persecution forced all Jewish professors out of the school in 1936. He and his wife, Zerline Marie Wolff (1884-1974), came to the US and settled for 16 years in Seattle. They later moved back to Basel, Switzerland, and Davis, CA, in later years. This relatively small, 1,530-square-foot house was completed in 1949. This modest, one-floor residence had a basement, and was designed by Robert M. Shields (1917-2012) of the firm of Tucker, Shields and Terry.

Queer Architects: Mr. and Mrs. Philip Padelford residence recreation room addition, 610 NW 56th St, Seattle, WA **98107**, designed by Roland Terry (1955)

Store: Contractor Nicole Dumas, owner of Dumas Build (523 NE 81st St, Seattle, WA **98115**), was lead carpenter for Seattle Homes & Lifestyles' Kitchen of the Year. Rated favorably on Angie's List, Yelp, the Better Business Bureau, and by various customers on their official website (dumasbuildllc.com), Dumas Build offers high quality renovations for your outdated kitchens, baths, basements, decks, and more.

Restaurant/Bar: Pagliacci Pizza (851 NW 85th St, Seattle, WA **98117**), Washington State's LGBTQ and Allied Chamber of Commerce member.

Store: Lorene Spencer (1923-2016) was an American potter. The Lavender Palette: Gay Culture and the Art of Washington State at the Cascadia Museum in Edmonds was a packed art show and a powerful history lesson. Museum curator David F. Martin put together artwork by dozens of gay men and women who often, just a few short decades ago, had to hide who they were in order to express themselves artistically. The exhibit closed on January 26, 2020. The featured artists included Edmonds native Guy Anderson, illustrator Richard Bennett, Ward Corley, Thomas Handforth, Mac Harshberger, Jule Kullberg, Delbert J. McBride, Orre Nelson Nobles, Malcolm Roberts, potter Lorene Spencer, Sarah Spurgeon, ceramicist Virginia Weisel, Clifford Wright, and also one-time Woodway resident Morris Graves, Leo Kenney, Mark Tobey, Lionel Pries, Leon Derbyshire, and Sherrill Van Cott. Born in Spirit Lake, ID, to George Forrest Spencer and Emma Anna Bailey. Lorene Rhua

Flower met Ralph E. Spencer while he was serving in the Coast Guard at Astoria, Oregon, and they soon married. In her later years, Lorene explained that both she and Ralph were aware of their homosexual orientations but, like many gay people of their generation, they had innocently thought that if they married and had children, these feelings would resolve and change to heterosexual orientation, which, naturally, did not happen. However, they decided not to act on their same-sex attractions and remained a couple. After their marriage, Ralph and Lorene worked in a family business running a fishing resort on the Umpqua River in Oregon, where they built boats and manufactured docks. After a few years, in 1948, they sold their share of the business and moved to Newberg, Oregon, where they made their first ceramic works. After some initial success, they started marketing their work through the Meier & Frank department store in Portland. Newberg's largely conservative political leanings became too stressful and so the family headed for Seattle in 1951, there establishing the Spencer Pottery business. The Spencers were active members of the Clay Club, founded in 1948 in Seattle. Other Clay Club members included Virginia Weisel and architect Robert Shields. Upon relocating to the Washington State area, they opened Spencer Pottery, a pottery supply shop and studio in the family's new home, which many of us will recognize as the tall, angular building at the bottom of Brummer's Hill (5023 S 144th St, Seattle, WA 98168), more recently Bonsai Northwest and now Forever Roofing. Lorene and Ralph Spencer produced a variety of stoneware bowls, vases, plates, mugs, etc. Lorene also produced painted ceramic tiles that often used impressions from a modified printing block. The Pottery was known for its high quality local sourced clays and the glazes mixed from Washington State minerals gathered by Ralph Spencer. Pottery was a family enterprise, with Ralph collecting the high-quality, locally sourced clay and minerals used in the glazes, as well as constructing equipment for the studio. Their highly prized work was shown in galleries and exhibitions throughout the Pacific Northwest and across the country. In addition to pottery, Lorene also created paintings and sculptures, some of which are in the permanent collection of the Museum of History and Industry (MOHAI) in Seattle. Spencer Pottery sold high-quality clay and glazes to other artists and Seattle public schools. During their heyday, Spencer Pottery would receive visits from their friends from the Seattle arts scene, including painters William Cumming (a 1934 Foster High graduate), Kenneth Callahan, sculptor George Tsutakawa, and pottery master Shoji Hamada. A newspaper article about the couple noted, The more highly automated our world becomes, the more necessary are artists like the Spencers, who demonstrate that man still can think, and create for himself. And a woman for herself. Although Lorene and Ralph Spencer were both gay, they maintained their marriage until Ralph's death in 1973. Afterward, Lorene and her life partner, Ruth Henry, had a close friendship with Bud McBride and Richard Scheneider, who sold Lorene's work along with their own Crow Valley pottery, as well as work by other talented artists, until their retirement in 1995. In later years, Lorene Spencer first lived in Olympia, and then, in 2008, moved to Apache Junction, Arizona, where Ruth and her remained until their respective deaths.

Restaurant/Bar: Pagliacci Pizza (315 N 145th St, Seattle, WA 98133), Washington State's LGBTQ and Allied Chamber of Commerce member.

Accommodation: Seattle Airport Marriott (3201 S 176th St, Seattle, WA 98188), LGBTQ friendly.

Find a grave

We Sail Together: Carl Natelli (1913-2008) was a photographer whose work was published in both gay and bodybuilding magazines. Some of his best work was done with the bodybuilder Edmund Pinnell around 1958. He is buried together with Hyung K. Kim (1927-2002) at Holyrood Catholic Cemetery (205 NE 205th St, Shoreline, WA **98155**).

Queer Architects:

King George Restaurant, N 185th St & Aurora Ave N, Shoreline, WA **98133**, designed by Roland Terry (1970)

Bagley Wright House, 134 Huckleberry Ln, Shoreline, WA **98177**, Designed by Arthur Erickson (1977).

Mr. and Mrs. Roy Boese residence alterations, 11115 7th Ave NW, Seattle, WA **98177**, designed by Roland Terry (1960)

Miss Myrtle Warneke residence remodel, 18055 8th Ave NW, Shoreline, WA **98177**, designed by Roland Terry (1958)

Tukwila Motor Hotel, 205 Strander Blvd, Tukwila, WA **98188**, designed by Roland Terry (1967)

Restaurant/Bar:
Bahama Breeze, 15700 Southcenter Pkwy, Tukwila, WA **98188**
Ben & Jerry's, 2800 Southcenter Mall K2688

Kiosk 9250, Tukwila, WA **98188**
Olive Garden Italian, 310 Strander Blvd, Tukwila, WA **98188**

98200

AIDS Memorial: Plaza west of old Mission Bld., Pacific & Wetmore Ave. (3000 Rockefeller Ave, Everett, WA **98201**), Snohomish County AIDS Memorial, since 1 December 2005. In May of 2000, an idea was born, that all those who have suffered from the AIDS epidemic should somehow be memorialized. A group at the local Underground Bar began a fund raising campaign with shows and auctions. It seemed at the time that the cemetery would be a logical setting, so three plots located on a triangular space near the entrance to the park were to be purchased from Evergreen Cemetery in Everett. For whatever reason, after having raised nearly $10,000, the original project lost steam. Recently, the remaining members of the AIDS Memorial Committee decided to get the project back on track. Discovering that Evergreen Cemetery had changed management and that the new management did not seem clear on what or where the memorial should be, perhaps not even sure they wanted an AIDS Memorial on their grounds. A new location for the AIDS Memorial was proposed - the old Snohomish County Campus. A proposal was sent to the County Executive and after some time, the AIDS Memorial Committee met with Snohomish County Facilities Manager and agreed to a proposed site choice on the campus, the plaza west of the old Mission Building at Pacific and Wetmore Avenue. On March 17, 2005, the AIDS Memorial Committee visited the studio and gardens of George Little and David Lewis on Bainbridge Island well known for their innovative and beautifully crafted outdoor garden art. On World AIDS Day, December 1, 2005, the AIDS Memorial of Snohomish County was dedicated with a ceremony held at the site. Representatives from the county and state governments joined a crowd of local citizens at the Mission Building Plaza to confirm the pledge to remember those who have suffered from the AIDS epidemic.

LGBTQ friendly bookstore: Everette Books & Magazines, 1808 Hewitt Ave, Everett, WA **98201**, included in the Damron Address Book from 1978 to 1980.

Historic District: Greyhound Bus Depot, 3201 Smith Ave, Everett, WA **98201**, included in the Damron Address Book from 1977 to 1980.

Restaurant/bar:
The London Cafe and Bar, 2008 Hewitt Ave, Everett, WA **98201**, included in the Damron Address Book from 1974 to 1980. Included in the 1975 All Lavender International Gay Guide.

The Monte Cristo Hotel-Bar, 1507 Wall St, Everett, WA **98201**, included in the 1975 All Lavender International Gay Guide.
Olde Imperial, 1607 Hewitt Ave, Everett, WA **98201**, included in the 1984 Gayellow Pages.

Accommodation:
Best Western Navigator Inn & Suites (10210 Evergreen Way, Everett, WA **98204**), gay friendly. Whether you need a room for one

night or an extended stay, this hotel offers great rates, hotel services, and full kitchen amenities to accommodate your needs.

House: Morris Graves (1910-2001)'s first one-man exhibition was in 1936 at the Seattle Art Museum (SAM); that same year he began working under Bruce Inverarity at the Seattle unit of the WPA's Federal Art Project. His participation was sporadic, but it was there that he met Mark Tobey and became impressed with Tobey's calligraphic line. In January 1937 Graves traveled to New York City to study with the controversial Father Divine's International Peace Mission movement in Harlem; on his return, in May, he bought 20 acres (81,000 m2) on Fidalgo Island, near Rodger Bluff, WA **98221**. In 1938 he quit the FAP and went to the Virgin Islands and Puerto Rico to paint. In 1940, Graves began building a house, which he named The Rock, on an isolated promontory on his Fidalgo Island property. He lived at The Rock with a succession of cats and dogs, all called Edith, in honor of poet Edith Sitwell. Graves was known for his personal charm and bursts of puckish humor, but also spent long periods in semi-isolation, absorbed in nature and his art. At the Rock, with WWII erupting, he retreated for a particularly long time and created a very large number of paintings. Many of them, such as Dove of the Inner Eye (1941) and Bird in the Night (1943), featured what would become Graves' iconic motif of birds trapped in layers of webbing or barbs, representing the artist's fears for the survival of man and nature in the face of modern industry and warfare. His near-isolation was interrupted in the Spring of 1942 when the Museum of Modern Art in New York opened its Americans 1942: 18 Artists from 9 States exhibition. Critics raved over Graves' contributions, all of which were quickly snapped up by museums and collectors. At the same time the U.S. Army came looking for him, as he had failed to achieve the conscientious objector status he had applied for. There was also suspicion of him due to his association with the International Peace Mission and the fact that among his few regular visitors at the Rock had been the brilliant Japanese-American designer George Nakashima and his Japanese-born wife Miriam, prior to their being sent to the Minidoka relocation center. While his work was receiving further exhibition in New York and Washington, DC, and phenomenal sales, the artist himself spent much of that same time in the stockade at Camp Roberts, CA, where he went into a deep depression. He was finally released from military service in March 1943. With help from longtime supporters Elizabeth Willis, Nancy Ross, and Marian Willard, owner of the Willard Gallery in New York, Graves' work continued to enjoy popularity throughout the war years and beyond, with numerous exhibitions. The cabin he built burned to the ground a few months after his death in 2001, taking the life of its caretaker with it. And nowadays, not only can't you get a piece of The Rock you can't get to the rock: the land is still privately owned. To get a glimpse of the face of Rodger Bluff and the surrounding area from the closest place politely possible: hike the Tursi Trail connector. Park in the pullout at the junction of Campbell Lake Road and Donnell Road and take a short walk east along Campbell Lake Road for a great view of the valley, the bluff and the lake; hike Trail 247 in the ACLF for a view from higher elevation or hike or drive to the top of Mt Erie, 1,000 feet above The Rock to see the surroundings islands, lakes and mountains.

Accommodation:
Majestic Inn and Spa, 419 Commercial Ave, Anacortes, WA **98221**, Travellers' Choice Awards, 2022 Best of the Best Hotel in the US, by Tripadvisor.com

Maggie's Cabin (19016 640th Ln NE, Baring, WA **98224**), LGBTQ friendly.
Sky Cabins (63814 NE 190th St, Baring, WA **98224**), LGBTQ friendly.

Oldest Restaurant in the State: Horseshoe Café, 1886, Comford food, 113 E Holly St, Bellingham, WA **98225**. What people say: The Horseshoe, with its all-day breakfast, averages a middling 3.5 stars out of 5 from customer reviews on Yelp. Those who love it rave about its fried chicken, while others hail the establishment's comfortable old-style decor. Well, it is more than 130 years old.

Store: Make.Shift (306 Flora St, Bellingham, WA **98225**) is an alternative art and music venue downtown. They're open from Tuesday to Saturday from noon to 5pm, in addition to special events.

LGBTQ friendly bookstore:

Village Books and Paper Dreams, 1200 11th St, Bellingham, WA **98225**, 56 Queer-Owned Bookstores to Support, by Oprah Daily, 2021.
Great Northern Bookstore, 1306 Railroad Ave, Bellingham, WA **98225**, included in the Damron Address Book from 1978 to 1980. Included in the 1984 Gayellow Pages.

Park: Cornwell Park, 3424 Meridian St, Bellingham, WA **98225**, included in the Damron Address Book from 1978 to 1980.

Theatre: Green Apple Cinema, 1211 N State St, Bellingham, WA **98225**, included in the 1984 Gayellow Pages.

Restaurant/Bar:
Aslan Brewing Company, 1330 N Forest St, Bellingham, WA **98225**
The Black Drop, 300 W Champion St, Bellingham, WA **98225**
Boundary Bay Brewery & Bistro, 1107 Railroad Ave, Bellingham, WA **98225**
Chuckanut Brewery & Kitchen, 601 W Holly St, Bellingham, WA **98225**
Fairhaven Stones Throw Brewery, 1009 Larrabee Ave, Bellingham, WA **98225**
Fiamma Burger, 1309 Railroad Ave, Bellingham, WA **98225**
Honey Moon Alley Bar & Ciderhouse, 1053 N State St Alley, Bellingham, WA **98225**
The Hut, 1317 ½ N State St, Bellingham, WA **98225**, included in the Damron Address Book from 1978 to 1980. Later Toyon, included in the 1984 Gayellow Pages.
Iron Bull, 1316 Bay St, Bellingham, WA **98225**, included in the Damron Address Book from 1972 to 1975.

Kulshan Brewing Co, 2238 James St, Bellingham, WA **98225**
Leaf and Ladle, 1113 N State St, Bellingham, WA **98225**
The Local Public House, 1427 Railroad Ave, Bellingham, WA **98225**
Makizushi, 1530 Cornwall Ave, Bellingham, WA **98225**
Mallard Ice Cream, 1323 Railroad Ave, Bellingham, WA **98225**
Redlight, 1017 N State St, Bellingham, WA **98225**
Rumors Cabaret (1119 Railroad Ave, Bellingham, WA **98225**), gay friendly.
Shirlee Bird Café, Sycamore Square, 1200 Harris Ave #100, Bellingham, WA **98225**
Structures Brewing, 1420 N State St, Bellingham, WA **98225**
Up & Up Tavern, 1234 N State St, Bellingham, WA **98225**, included in the Damron Address Book from 1975 to 1977.
Wander Brewing, 1807 Dean Ave, Bellingham, WA **98225**

Accommodation:
The Chrysalis Inn & Spa Bellingham, Curio Collection by Hilton (804 10th St, Bellingham,

WA **98225**), Washington State's LGBTQ and Allied Chamber of Commerce member.

Restaurant/Bar:

Olive Garden Italian, 4276 Guide Meridian, Bellingham, WA **98226**

Accommodation:

Squalicum Lake Cottage (Squalicum Lake Rd, Bellingham, WA **98226**), LGBTQ friendly.

Park: Whatcom Falls Park, 1401 Electric Ave, Bellingham, WA **98229**, included in the Damron Address Book from 1978 to 1980.

Restaurant/Bar:
Anchor, 154 1st St, Bellingham, WA **98229**, included in the Damron Address Book in 1978.

K2, 1538 Kentucky St, Bellingham, WA **98229**

LGBTQ friendly bookstore:

Blaine Amusements, 481 ½ Peace Portal Dr, Blaine, WA **98230**, and 715 Peace Portal Dr, Blaine, WA **98230**, included in the Damron Address Book from 1978 to 1980.
Blaine Books, 715 Peace Portal Way, Blaine, WA **98230**, included in the 1984 Gayellow Pages.

Accommodation:
Smuggler's Inn B&B (2480 Canada View Dr, Blaine, WA **98230**), LGBTQ friendly.
Worldmark Birch Bay (4810 Beachcomber Dr, Blaine, WA **98230**). Situated in the charming coastal community of Blaine, just south of the Canadian border in Northern Washington. Furnished balcony with BBQ facilities is featured in each apartment. Part of World Rainbow Hotels (WRH), Lesbian and Gay Welcoming Hotels.

Other non-queer residents: Edward Roscoe Murrow (1908-1965), 387 Chuckanut Dr, Bow, WA **98232**, from 1913 to 1918.

Restaurant/Bar:
Tweet's Café (5800 Cains Ct, Bow, WA **98232**), LGBTQ owned.

Olive Garden Italian, 1809 Marketplace Dr, Burlington, WA **98233**

Accommodation:
The Quintessa on Whidbey Island (3493 French Rd, Clinton, WA **98236**) has been named among the 10 Best Romantic Lesbian Resorts in the United States by Dopes on the Road, 2018. It is a nine-bedroom vacation home near Seattle WA popular for weddings and large groups. The Quintessa is located within minutes to many attractions including a nine-hole golf course straight out of the Scottish Highlands, a variety of beaches, and an abundance of local artists' studios. Take a drive to nearby Langley The Village by the Sea, featuring a vintage movie house, live music and theater, eclectic boutiques, art galleries, antique shops, bookstores, and fabulous food options.

Queer Architects: Stephen and Harriette Lea Residence, 29807 WA-525, Coupeville, WA **98239**, Designed by Lionel Pries (1949-51 and 1963). Survives in private ownership with some changes.

Accommodation:
Inn on Orcas Island (114 Channel Rd, Deer Harbor, Orcas Island, WA **98243**), gay owned. Charming, serene, waterfront luxury in the Puget Sound.
The Place at Cayou Cove (161 Olympic Lodge Ln, Deer Harbor, WA **98243**), gay friendly. 2006 Andrew Harper Travel B&B of the Year. Featured Sunset Magazine, Orcas Island's most luxurious waterfront B&B cottages are located on five acres of beautiful gardens with over 500 ft of private beach.
Mt Baker B&B (9434 Cornell Creek Rd, Deming, WA **98244**), LGBTQ friendly. GLD, Gay Lesbian Directory

Crow Valley School Museum, Eastsound

Museum: Crow Valley School, originally called Pleasant Valley, was built in 1888, one year before the Territory of Washington was admitted to the Union as the State of Washington.

Address: 1701-1703 Crow Valley Rd, Eastsound, WA 98245

Place

Crow Valley School was built on an acre of land donated by settler Peter Frechette. Students from grades one through eight were taught in the school house, which had a capacity of 57 (though most years saw about 27 students in attendance.) In 1893 there were 63 days of school compared with a State minimum of 180 today. The length of school terms was dependent on funds and the availability of teachers, who were paid about $50 per month. Some teachers would move from one school district to another, and sometimes their pupils would follow. Irene Bellvue recalls following her teacher to three different schools, one on another island. Crow Valley School was closed in 1918, after which students attended the consolidated Eastsound School. The building continued to be used as a community meeting place, including use as a church and a Sunday School. In 1929 the school house was purchased by The Willing Workers women's club, many of whom were former students, and became The Crow Valley Club. This club made a few changes to the school house, including an opening to the main room which served as their kitchenette. Using a kerosene stove they held community dinners and entertained in this space. In 1987 the school house was placed on the National Register of Historic Places. Shortly later it was painstakingly restored over hundreds of hours by Richard Schneider and Bud McBride, the founders of Crow Valley Pottery. Crow Valley School is one of the finest examples of an intact one room school house in our state and in 1989 was recognized for its renovation during the Washington Centennial Celebration by the Governor's wife Jean Gardner and Secretary of State Ralph Munro, both co-chairs of the Centennial Committee. Richard Schneider and Bud McBride received the State Historic Preservation Officer's 1997 Annual Award For Outstanding Achievement in Stewardship for the Crow Valley School.

Life

Who: Richard Eugene Schneider (April 5, 1928 - February 15, 2015)
Richard Schneider and his lifelong partner, Albert (Bud) McBride, Delbert J. McBride and Oliver Tiedemann started Klee Wyk Studio. Born to Dorothy and Clarence Schneider in Seattle, WA, Richard grew up on Orcas Island with his two sisters, Joyce and Viola. Klee Wyk made a big splash locally through its use of Northwest Coast Indian imagery in design work. Klee Wyk's design legacy is still evident in the recently restored West Seattle High School mural in Seattle. Several Seattle apartment buildings still have Klee Wyk tile murals with Indian themes installed on the outside. Local collectors have coffee tables, fountains, fireplaces and back splashes designed specifically for their homes. Bread-and-butter items like wind chimes and pendants were also designed and sold to tourists and visitors to the gallery. The construction of I-5 eventually ended the cooperative. Subsequently, in 1959, Richard and Bud McBride opened what was then called the Crow Valley Shop, 2274 Orcas Rd, Eastsound, WA **98245**. With their experience, the shop became known for their wind bells, pendants, pottery and vases largely decorated by Richard. Richard and Bud McBride ran Crow Valley Pottery on Orcas Island until their retirement in 1995. Richard and Bud restored the original Crow Valley schoolhouse and donated it to the Historical Museum in Eastsound. As an avid historian, Richard studied and knew more about Orcas Island history and his lineage than one would expect. Richard and Bud moved the Dixon House across Crow Valley to restore and show.

Accommodation:

Kangaroo House B&B (1459 N Beach Rd, Eastsound, WA **98245**), LGBTQ friendly.

San Juan Island

San Juan Island (WA **98250**) has been named among the Most beautiful islands in the world, 2019

Accommodation:
Bird Rock Hotel (35 First St N, Friday Harbor, WA **98250**), LGBTQ friendly.
Olympic Lights B&B (146 Starlight Way, Friday Harbor, WA **98250**), LGBTQ friendly.
Elements San Juan Islands Hotel and Spa (410 Spring St, Friday Harbor, WA **98250**), LGBTQ friendly.
Harrison House Suites B&B (235 C St, Friday Harbor, WA **98250**), LGBTQ friendly.
Hillside House B&B (365 Carter Ave, Friday Harbor, WA **98250**), LGBTQ friendly.

Juniper Lane Guest House, 1312 Beaverton Valley Road, Friday Harbor, WA **98250**, GLD.
Gay Lesbian Directory
Trumpeter Inn B&B (318 Trumpeter Way, Friday Harbor, WA **98250**), LGBTQ friendly.
Tucker House Inn B&B (275 C St, Friday Harbor, WA **98250**), LGBTQ friendly.
Wildwood Manor (5335 Roche Harbor Rd, Friday Harbor, WA **98250**), LGBTQ owned.
Triangle Recreation Camp, 47715 Mountain Loop Hwy, Granite Falls, WA **98252**, has been named among the 8 LGBTQ Outdoor Resorts That Put the Camp in Camping, 2021, Matador Network.

House: Guy Anderson (1906-1998) grew up in a semi-rural setting north of Seattle, in the town of Edmonds, WA. Some of his early paintings portrayed his family home. A piano was an important presence in his house. His father, Irving Lodell Anderson, was a carpenter-builder and also a musician. His mother was Edna Marie Bolduc. From an early age Guy was intrigued by other cultures; he was particularly fascinated by the woodcarvings of Northern Coastal native tribes, and by the collection of Japanese prints owned by his piano teacher. As soon as he was old enough to do so on his own, he began commuting to the Seattle Public Library by bus to study art books. After graduating from Edmonds High School, Anderson briefly studied with Alaskan scenic painter Eustace Ziegler, who encouraged Anderson's career-long preference for oil paints, and taught him how to draw nude figures, which would become important features of his work. In 1929, Anderson applied for and won a Tiffany Foundation scholarship and spent the summer studying at the Tiffany estate on Long Island, New York. As there were no art museums in Seattle at that time, he delighted in weekend visits to the Museum of Modern Art in Manhattan, examining the works of Rembrandt, Goya, Whistler, and many others. On his return to Washington in the fall of 1929, Anderson set up a studio in an outbuilding on his parents' property, and had paintings included in a group show at the Fifth Avenue Gallery in downtown Seattle. The show piqued the interest of 19-year-old painter Morris Graves, who lived near Anderson, and the two became lifelong friends. In 1934 they traveled together to California in a beat-up panel truck, attempting to sell their paintings along the way. They also spent time painting near Monte Cristo in the North Cascade mountains. With the opening of the Seattle Art Museum in 1933, Anderson befriended its founder, Dr. Richard Eugene Fuller, and worked there for several years, off-and-on, as an installer and children's art teacher. His lifelong interest in Asian art and culture was deepened by both close exposure to the museum's major collection of Asian art and artefacts, and by socializing and sometimes painting with members of Seattle's vibrant Asian arts community. In the Northwest Annual Exhibition of 1935 he won the Katherine Baker Purchase Award, and the museum mounted a solo exhibition of his work the following year. In 1937, Anderson helped refurbish a burned-out house Morris Graves had discovered near the small town of La Conner, WA, in the Skagit Valley, about sixty miles north of

Seattle. The two decorated the earthen-floored studio with furniture made of driftwood and raw cedar logs. Like many artists during the Great Depression, Anderson worked for the Works Progress Administration's Federal Art Project. Hired by the program's Washington director, R. Bruce Inverarity, he taught at the Spokane Art Center in 1939-40, alongside painters Carl Morris and Clyfford Still, sculptor Hilda Deutsch, and muralist Ruth Egri. The center was widely praised as being among the most popular and productive of the more than 100 community art centers opened nationwide by the FAP. Throughout the 1940s and 50s Anderson was very much involved in Seattle's bustling art community. Morris Graves and Mark Tobey had become artists of international reputation; Tobey's studio and the home of painters Margaret and Kenneth Callahan become centers of lively socializing and philosophical debate. Otto Seligman and Zoe Dusanne were championing abstract art at their respective galleries, while SAM, the Henry Art Gallery, and the Frye Art Museum cautiously supported it. Anderson taught at the Helen Bush School in Seattle and Ruth Pennington's Fidalgo Art School in La Conner, while working at SAM, building stone mosaic patios for well-to-do patrons, and producing driftwood art for the commercial market. He lived in Seattle's University District, but spent much of his time painting at Graves' studio in La Conner or at the Callahans' summer place in Granite Falls, Washington. After a very successful show at SAM in 1945, he purchased his own cabin in Granite Falls. In September 1953 he became nationally known when Life magazine ran a major feature presenting Anderson, Mark Tobey, Morris Graves, and Kenneth Callahan as the big four of Northwest mystic art. In 1959 Anderson left Seattle for good. He rented a house on the edge of La Conner, where he found inspiration from the vast skies and natural settings of the surrounding area. He gathered rocks and driftwood, which he composed around his rustic home in various assemblages. For a time, he rented a studio on the main street of La Conner. Later, he bought property at 415 Caledonia St, La Conner, WA **98257**, building a house and studio there. He began painting large works on roofing paper purchased from a local lumber company. Working with large sheets of paper on the floor in the studio above his living room, Anderson used thinned oil paint and large brushes. The scale of the format enabled his brushstrokes to become expansive and expressive, while its texture gave unexpected complexities which he valued. Over the years his art ranged from densely worked and tightly composed figurative images of Northwest landscapes to large, sweeping brushstrokes with flowing, symbolic and iconographic forms. Anderson always preferred a limited palette of mostly muted earthy tones, sometimes accented with brilliant red. The male nude—often placed horizontally—figures prominently in many of his paintings. His works are often inspired by, and titled after, Greek mythology and Native American iconography. In 1966 Anderson traveled to Europe for the first time with friends and fellow artists Clayton and Barbara James. In 1975 he was awarded a Guggenheim Fellowship, which, among other things, allowed him to visit major museums in Boston, New York, and Washington, D.C., and travel extensively in Mexico. In 1982 he visited Osaka, Japan for an exhibition featuring his work. He received a Lifetime Achievement Award at the Seattle Center in 1995, and many who knew him personally considered him a living treasure. Anderson was a complex, affable, and generous man with a wide-ranging mind and a devious sense of humor. His paintings can be read in many ways, but he cherished the premise of the human figure—a prominent feature in many of his works—as being symbolic of the journey of life. Guy Anderson never quite achieved the international stature of his friends Mark Tobey and Morris Graves. This was partly due to bad luck - such as a newspaper strike leaving his first solo exhibition in New York (at the Smolin Gallery in 1962) unreviewed - but he turned down other important exhibition opportunities, including one at the Phillips Collection in Washington, DC, simply because he felt he didn't have enough material of sufficient quality ready. He remained a pre-eminent artist with strong sales and major commissioned projects in the Pacific Northwest. His expressions of northwest atmospheres with their mythological allusions are distinctive, even as they evoke the coastal Skagit River country where he lived. In the 1980s, with his health declining, Anderson arranged to be cared for as an elder, and he became increasingly dependent on a younger companion, Deryl Walls. Walls eventually became executor of his estate, and made the controversial decision to end Anderson's long association with Francine Seders, who had been his agent since 1966. Anderson continued living in the house he had built on Caledonia Street, where he received visitors and continued painting into his late eighties. Walls eventually moved Anderson into his own home on Maple Street in La Conner, where Anderson was cared for while surrounded by his paintings. Walls hosted birthday parties for Anderson which were well attended by collectors, fellow artists, and admirers. He remained lucid and enjoyed visitors at La Conner until shortly before he died aged 91 years.

Accommodation:
The Heron Inn (117 Maple Ave, La Conner, WA 98257), LGBTQ owned.

The Wild Iris Inn, 121 Maple Avenue, La Conner, WA 98257, GLD, Gay Lesbian Directory
Country Cottage of Langley B&B (215 Sixth St, Langley, WA 98260), LGBTQ friendly.

Michael Jensen, author: Lopez Island (WA 98261), part of the San Juan Islands. An amazing place to go for a bike ride through bucolic farms, pristine beaches, and gorgeous views. Only hours from Seattle, yet utterly unspoiled.

Queer Architects:
Richard and Ruth Lea Residence, 2200 Davis Bay Rd, Lopez Island, WA 98261, Designed by Lionel Pries (1946-47). Survives in ownership of the Lea family.
Office and studio on Lopez Island, 2076 Vista Rd, Lopez Island, WA 98261, designed by Roland Terry (1963)

Accommodation:
Inn at Swifts Bay (856 Port Stanley Rd, Lopez Island, WA 98261) has been named Featured Inns of 1999 by Inn Places, Gay & Lesbian Accommodations Worldwide. Gay friendly and gay owned. As of 2021 it's closed.
Mt. Baker Lodging (7509 Mt Baker Hwy, Maple Falls, WA 98266), TAG Approved LGBTQ friendly accommodation.

Mt Baker Lodging Cabins and Condos (7463 Mt Baker Hwy, Maple Falls, WA 98266), LGBTQ friendly.
Holiday Inn Express & Suites Marysville (8606 36th Ave NE, Marysville, WA 98270), TAG Approved LGBTQ friendly accommodation.

Restaurant/Bar:

Olive Garden Italian, 10326 Quil Ceda Blvd, Tulalip, WA 98271

Accommodation:

Tulalip Resort Casino (10200 Quil Ceda Blvd, Tulalip, WA **98271**), TAG Approved LGBTQ friendly accommodation.

LGBTQ friendly bookstore: Main St. Books, 110 E Main St #100, Monroe, WA **98272**, 56 Queer-Owned Bookstores to Support, by Oprah Daily, 2021.

House: Between 1980-2006, Abdelwahid Elhassan, was Roland Terry (1917-2006)'s companion. In his later years, Terry lived quietly at his property near Mount Vernon, Washington. In 1993, Roland Terry's office and home was located at 1512 Beaver Marsh Rd, Mount Vernon, WA **98273**.

LGBTQ friendly bookstore: Great Northern Bookstore, 515 N 1st St, Mount Vernon, WA **98273**, and 420 Myrtle St, Mount Vernon, WA **98273**, included in the Damron Address Book from 1978 to 1980.

Accommodation: White Swan Guest House (15872 Moore Rd, Mt Vernon, WA **98273**) included in Inn Places 1999, Gay & Lesbian Accommodations Worldwide, Gay friendly. As of 2021 it's closed.

Park: Hillcrest Park, 1717 S 13th St, Mount Vernon, WA **98274**, included in the Damron Address Book from 1978 to 1980.

Accommodation: TownePlace Suites Seattle North/Mukilteo (8521 Mukilteo Speedway, Mukilteo, WA **98275**), LGBTQ friendly. Whidwood On Whidbey Island, Coupeville, Whidbey Island (Coupeville, WA **98277**), gay owned. The New York Times calls centrally located Coupeville the logical home base for exploring the islands. Use Whidwood as your base for exploring nearby shops, galleries, parks, gardens & beaches.
Spring Bay Inn (464 Spring Bay Trail, Olga, WA **98279**), LGBTQ friendly.
Blue Moon Beach House (3267 Shoreline Dr, Camano, WA **98282**), LGBTQ friendly.

Attraction: North Cascades Institute (810 Moore St, Sedro-Woolley, WA **98284**), TAG Approved LGBTQ friendly attraction.

Cemetery: Sherrill Van Cott (1913-1942) was born in Fargo, ND. Sherrill Van Cott was a busy, cheerful high school student in rural, semi-isolated Sedro-Woolley, Washington, involved in the arts in school and cartoonist for the school year book. He graduated in 1931, just as the Great Depression settled in as long-term hardship for the country. Shortly after graduation, unable to find work, Van Cott began serious self-study in the arts, with occasional professional help in sculpture and painting. Childhood rheumatic fever returned as heart disease in his early twenties, an additional impediment to his growing skills and critical success as a modernist painter and sculptor in northwest Washington. He persisted in spite of his growing illness and was becoming collected by prestigious Northwest arts collectors and organizations when he died at age 29. In the mid-1930s, Morris Graves met a handsome young man named Sherril Kinney Van Cott from the small town of Sedro-Woolley, 72 miles north of Seattle. Van Cott had briefly attended the University of Washington after graduating from high school in 1931, but was largely a self-taught artist. He first began exhibiting in the Northwest Annuals at the Seattle Art Museum in 1935 with an oil painting titled Potato Eaters, while Graves also showed two oils.

Both artists exhibited in the annuals for the next few years, and in 1939 Van Cott began to exhibit sculpture. The few extant sculptures by Van Cott, using regional materials, appear to have been influenced by the French sculptor Henri Gaudier-Brzeska, who had died at age 24 in WWI. Graves and Van Cott developed a romantic relationship, with Graves exerting a stylistic influence on the slightly younger artist. Van Cott was also a poet, and his writings were compatible with the visual content of his paintings. He focused on insects and other animals, both real and imagined, as well as complex intertwining of the male human form in a fossil-like contained border. Van Cott's last painting, a watercolor titled Weeping Girl, was exhibited at the Northwest Annual from October 7 through November 8, 1942. A month later, he was dead at age 29 from cardiac failure. 20 years earlier, Van Cott had contracted scarlet fever, which caused a severe hearth problem, leaving him practically an invalid for most of his short life. He is buried at Union Cemetery (Sedro-Woolley, WA **98284**). The local art scene had lost a promising talent, and Graves a lover and acolyte. He promoted Van Cott's work long after his death, and preserved many works in his own collection. In February 1945, Fortune magazine paid a small tribute to Van Cott and Graves, exposing the work to some of the younger generation of gay artists, like Leo Kenney and Ward Corley.

Queer Architects: Sue Hauberg residence and equestrian center at Victoria Heights, 315th St NW, Lake Ketchum, WA **98292**, designed by Roland Terry (1984)

98300

Accommodation: August Inn (14117 Lyle Point Rd, Anderson Island, WA **98303**), **LGBTQ friendly**.

Alexander's Country Inn B&B (37515 706 E, Ashford, WA **98304**), **gay friendly**.

Theatre: Bremerton Cinema, 317 N Callon, Bremerton, WA **98310**, included in the **1984 Gayellow Pages**.

House: Jack Lenor Larsen (1927–2020) was an American textile designer, author, collector and promoter of traditional and contemporary craftsmanship. He developed under the Northwest artists influence as a young gay man in Seattle. His retrospective at the Musée of Arts Décoratifs, Palais du Louvre, in 1979-80 made him and Mark Tobey two of only four Americans to be so honored. Through his career he was noted for bringing fabric patterns and textiles to go with modernist architecture and furnishings. Some of his works are part of permanent collections at prominent museums including Museum of Modern Art, Victoria and Albert Museum, Art Institute of Chicago, Musée des Arts Décoratifs at the Louvre, and the Minneapolis Institute of Art which has his most significant archive. Jack Lenor Larsen was born in Seattle, WA, to Mabel Bye and Elmer Larsen. His father was a building contractor. His parents were Canadians of Danish-Norwegian ancestry who moved to Bremerton, WA, from Alberta in Canada. In the 1940s the family lived at 925 Times Ave, Bremerton, WA **98312**. He was educated in Bremerton before enrolling at the School of Architecture at the University of Washington, where he struggled with drawing, and became interested in interior design, weaving, and furniture design. The following year he moved to Los Angeles to focus on fabrics; he worked as a weaver's apprentice and also taught actress Joan Crawford to weave. In 1949 he studied ancient Peruvian textiles in Seattle and opened a studio in the city. In 1951, he earned his Master of Fine Arts degree from the Cranbrook Academy of Art, Michigan, and moved to New York, where he opened a studio.

Restaurant/Bar:
Goe Duck Tavern, just S. of Dosewallips St. Park, 306996 US-101, Brinnon, WA **98320**,

included in the Damron Address Book from 1973 to 1976.
Ben & Jerry's, 4635 Point Fosdick Dr NW Building 11, Suite 400, Gig Harbor, WA **98335**

Queer Architects: Dr. and Mrs. J. E. Haddon residence patio alterations, 1735 Ohio Ave, Bremerton, WA **98337**, designed by Roland Terry (1955)

Park: Evergreen Park, 1500 Park Ave, Bremerton, WA **98337**, included in the Damron Address Book from 1974 to 1976.

Restaurant/Bar:
Anchor Wash, 1st St, Bremerton, WA **98337**, included in the Damron Address Book from 1978 to 1980.
Beach Tavern, 1st St, Bremerton, WA **98337**, included in the Damron Address Book from 1973 to 1976.

Skipper's Tavern, 116 1st St, Bremerton, WA **98337**, on pier by ferry terminal, included in the Damron Address Book from 1972 to 1977. Included in the 1975 All Lavender International Gay Guide.

Accommodation:
Olympic Vacation and Camping Rentals, 57 Arden St, Port Hadlock, WA **98339**. The vacation rental units are located in the same house, which is situated just 4 blocks from the water in a quiet neighborhood in Port Hadlock, WA, adjacent to Port Townsend. A 1 BR/1BA Studio is on the ground floor and a 2BR/1BA occupies the entire second floor. These units have both been fully renovated and are available separately or as an entire unit. Olympic Camping Rentals provides you with oversized tents, comfortable chairs, great bedding and real kitchen gear.

Cemetery: Oliver Tiedeman (1919-1986) was an artist and worked professionally together with Delbert McBride from their studio in Nisqually named Klee Wyck. He specialized in Northwest Indian art and their murals can be seen in many places. One is the bas-relief work on the outside of the Bremerton Naval Hospital in Bremerton, WA. Del McBride changed the world of local craft by incorporating elements of his Native American heritage into a range of contemporary designs for artistic and utilitarian purposes. In 1950 he formed Klee Wyk Studio with his cousin Oliver Tiedemann, a talented designer and painter. They were soon joined by Del's brother, Albert (Bud) McBride, and Bud's life partner, Richard Schneider. The studio was located in the Nisqually flats, north of Olympia. For over ten years, Klee Wyk Studio produced architectural and decorative tile murals, fabrics, hand-printed cards, and utilitarian objects that were among the finest regional midcentury designs utilizing Northwest Coast Native American motifs. The name Klee Wyk was a homage based on Canadian artist Emily Carr's memoir Klee Wyck of 1941. Tiedeman is buried at Lakebay Cemetery (222 Cornwall Rd SW, Washington **98349**).

World Heritage List: Olympic National Park (3002 Mt Angeles Rd, Port Angeles, WA **98362**)

Accommodation:

Maple Rose Inn (112 Reservoir Rd, Port

Angeles, WA **98363**) included in Inn Places 1999, Gay & Lesbian Accommodations Worldwide. Gay friendly, gay owned and gay

operated. It's now Inn at Rooster Hill.

Store: Port Gamble General Store & Café, 32400 N Rainier Ave, Port Gamble, WA **98364**. This three-story general store dates back to 1916. It sells souvenirs and an assortment of goods, and it also houses a full-service restaurant and a small museum. Named among the 25 Charming General Stores Across the Country, by Bob Vila, Tried, True, Trustworthy Home Advice.

Accommodation:

Resort At Port Ludlow, 1 Heron Rd, Port Ludlow, WA **98365**

Other non queer residents:

Walker Ames House, 2-98 N Rainier Ave, Poulsbo, WA **98370**
Site Of Historic Blockhouse Fortification, Poulsbo, WA **98370**

Port Townsend

Cemetery: James Broughton (1913–1999) was an American poet and poetic filmmaker. He was part of the San Francisco Renaissance, a precursor to the Beat poets. He was an early bard of the Radical Faeries as well as a member of The Sisters of Perpetual Indulgence, serving the community as Sister Sermonetta. He died in 1999 with champagne on his lips, in the house in Port Townsend, where he and his partner Joel Singer lived for 10 years. Before he died, he said, My creeping decrepitude has crept me all the way to the crypt. His gravestone at Laurel Grove Cemetery (Port Townsend, WA **98368**) reads, Adventure – not predicament.

Accommodation:
Chevy Chase Beach Cabins (3710 S. Discovery Rd, Port Townsend, WA **98368**), gay owned. Seven miles outside of Port Townsend, on 1/4 mile of private beach, the newly-renovated cabins are part of a resort complex operating for over one hundred years.
The English Inn (718 F St, Port Townsend, WA **98368**), gay friendly. Stunning Italianate-style Victorian home c.1885, is now a traditional English style B&B.
Ravenscroft Inn (533 Quincy St, Port Townsend, WA **98368**) has been named Featured Inns of 1999 by Inn Places, Gay & Lesbian Accommodations Worldwide. Gay friendly.

The James House (1238 Washington St, Port Townsend, WA **98368**), gay friendly. Sitting high on the bluff with the best water and mountain views, the inn is within walking distance of fine restaurants and the shopping district.
Green Cat Guest House B&B (25445 Tytler Rd NE, Poulsbo, WA **98370**), gay friendly. Surrounded by the majestic waterways and mountain ranges of Puget Sound - Wedding venue, established B&B- hot tub, sauna, wi-fi, cable tv.
Poulsbo Inn & Suites (18680 WA-305, Poulsbo, WA **98370**), LGBTQ friendly. GLD, Gay Lesbian Directory

School: Jamie Pedersen (born 1968) is an American lawyer and politician from the state of Washington who has served as a member of the Washington State Legislature since January 2007. He currently represents the 43rd District in the Washington State Senate. Pedersen grew up in Puyallup, and attended Puyallup High School (105 7th St SW, Puyallup, WA **98371**). Pedersen is openly gay and is one of seven LGBT members of the Washington State Legislature. Pedersen is married to Eric Cochran Pedersen, a high-school assistant principal whom he met in 2004 while attending Seattle's Central Lutheran Church. Pedersen and his husband have four sons: Trygve Cochran Pedersen and a set of triplets - Leif, Anders, and Erik - born in early 2009. The children were all given traditional Norwegian names by Pedersen who is ethnically Norwegian.

Willcox House

Queer Architects: Willcox House, 2390 Tekiu Point Rd NW, Seabeck, WA **98380**, Designed by Lionel Pries (1937). During the 1940s and '50s, Clark Gable was one of many celebrities -- including Errol Flynn, Spencer Tracy, Ernest Hemingway and John Wayne -- who were guests at the home of Col. Julian Willcox. The original owners of the Willcox House were Col. Willcox, his wife Constance and her sister Agnes Britt. The colonel and his wife had one son, Julian Jr. The Britt sisters were the daughters of a wealthy San Francisco judge who made his fortune by handling the Camp Pendleton land acquisition. Col.Willcox, an officer in the Marine brigade stationed in Bremerton, began his connection with Hollywood as a consultant for the movie Tell it to the Marines starring Clark Gable. The colonel soon became part of an elite Hollywood circle and invited many of his new friends to his Kitsap County oasis. Later the house was used as a boys' school and a conference center. In 1988 it was converted into an inn, now closed.

Accommodation:
Holiday Inn Express & Suites Sequim (1441 E Washington St, Sequim, WA **98382**), **TAG Approved LGBTQ friendly accommodation**. The Sunset Marine Resort (40 Buzzard Ridge Road, Sequim, WA **98382**), **LGBTQ owned**, has been named among the 10 Best Romantic Lesbian Resorts in the United States by Dopes on the Road, 2018. It is made of private vacation cabins on the Olympic Peninsula with panoramic waterfront views of the Puget Sound. The waterfront lodging is less than 2 hours from Seattle and Victoria BC. Whether your idea of lodging is a simple jump off point for the Olympic National Park, a quiet beachfront cabin to relax and rejuvenate, a gathering place for connecting families and friends or a place to sit and watch the sunset,

The Sunset Marine Resort is a great option.

Olive Garden Italian, 3204 NW Randall Way, Silverdale, WA **98383**

Red Lobster, 3208 NW Randall Way, Silverdale, WA **98383**
Stables, Silverdale, WA **98383**, included in the Damron Address Book from 1974 to 1977.

98400

Tacoma

Tacoma, WA, has been named among the Gayest Cities in America by The Advocate, 2013

Tacoma, WA, has been named among the Gayest Cities in America by The Advocate, 2014

Tacoma, WA, has been named among the Queerest City in America by The Advocate, 2015

Suquamish Clearwater Casino Resort (15347 Suquamish Way NE, Suquamish, WA **98392**),

Washington State's LGBTQ and Allied Chamber of Commerce member.

Queer Architects:
First Presbyterian Church, 20 Tacoma Ave S, Tacoma, WA **98402**, Designed by Ralph Adams Cram (1923)

Washington State History Museum, 1911 Pacific Ave, Tacoma, WA **98402**, Designed by Charles Moore, his last work.

The Museum of Glass, 1801 Dock St, Tacoma, WA **98402**, Designed by Arthur Erickson with Nick Milkovich (1996).

Restaurant remodeling for Mr. John Swan, 740 St Helens Ave, Tacoma, WA **98402**, designed by Roland Terry

Queer Artists: The Fence, (painting, ca. 1914), by John Singer Sargent (1856-1925), Tacoma Art Museum, 1701 Pacific Ave, Tacoma, WA **98402**.

LGBTQ friendly bookstore:
Jerry's Adult Bookstore, 1305 Commerce St, Tacoma, WA **98402**, included in the Damron Address Book in 1980.

King's Books, 218 St Helens Ave, Tacoma, WA **98402**, 56 Queer-Owned Bookstores to Support, by Oprah Daily, 2021.

Tacoma Magazine Center, 1346 Pacific Ave, Tacoma, WA **98402**, included in the Damron Address Book from 1978 to 1980.

Historic District: Fun Circus, S 13th St & Pacific Ave, Tacoma, WA **98402**, included in the Damron Address Book from 1976 to 1980.

Barbary Coast, 1554 Jefferson Ave, Tacoma, WA **98402**, included in the Damron Address Book from 1973 to 1980.

Flamingo Lounge, 1516 Broadway, Tacoma, WA **98402**, included in the Damron Address Book from 1976 to 1980.

The Mix, 635 St Helens Ave, Tacoma, WA **98402**, GLD, Gay Lesbian Directory
Murphy's Café, 938 Pacific Ave, Tacoma, WA **98402**, included in the Damron Address Book from 1966 to 1972. Included in the 1975 All Lavender International Gay Guide.
Pacific Grill (1502 Pacific Ave, Tacoma, WA **98402**), gay owned.
Sand Box, 1309 Commerce St, Tacoma, WA **98402**, included in the Damron Address Book from 1971 to 1974. Later Fickle Fox, included in the Damron Address Book in 1975. D.J.'s, included in the Damron Address Book from 1976 to 1980. Also Mister's, included in the Damron Address Book in 1978.
Tin Pan Alley, 815 ½ Pacific Ave, Tacoma, WA **98402**, included in the Damron Address Book in 1980.
Vern's, S 9th St & Pacific Ave, Tacoma, WA **98402**, included in the Damron Address Book in 1976.
Winthrop Hotel Bar, S 9th St & Broadway, Tacoma, WA **98402**, included in the 1964 Directory. Included in the Damron Address Book in 1972. Included in the 1975 All Lavender International Gay Guide.

Accommodation:
Hotel Murano (1320 Broadway, Tacoma, WA **98402**). Part of World Rainbow Hotels (WRH), Lesbian and Gay Welcoming Hotels.

LGBTQ friendly bookstore: Imprints Bookstore & Gallery, 917 N 2nd St, Tacoma, WA **98403**, active in 1990.

Accommodation:
Chinaberry Hill Victorian Inn & Cottage (302 N Tacoma Ave, Tacoma, WA **98403**), LGBTQ friendly.

Geiger Victorian B&B (912 N I St, Tacoma, WA **98403**), LGBTQ friendly.

Park: Wright Park, 501 S I St, Tacoma, WA **98405**, Duck Pond and Beach, included in the Damron Address Book from 1976 to 1980.

Store: Rudy's Barbershop, 2722 N Proctor St, Tacoma, WA **98406**

Oldest Building in the State: Fort Nisqually Granary, 5519 Five Mile Dr, Tacoma, WA **98407**. The historically significant granary is one of the few surviving Hudson's Bay Company structures in the United States and is also a rare remaining example of post-on-sill timber construction in the country. Records show that the granary's construction took place between July 1850 and January 1851.

House: Grenville Michael Scott (1922-2013) was born in Portland, OR, in 1922, but did most of his best work in California. His parents separated and divorced shortly after he was born, and he and his mother lived in Tacoma, at 4109 N Stevens St, Tacoma, WA **98407**, for the next twenty years. After attending Stadium High School, Scott went to the University of Washington and pledged at the Sigma Chi fraternity in 1941, but after Pearl Harbor he left school in 1942 to join the army. Apparently, his duties in the service did not prevent him from returning to the UW, and he is shown in uniform in the 1944 Tyee as a member of the Purple Shield Society. He finally graduated in 1947, and sometime around 1950 moved to San Francisco, where he found work in advertising for the National Distillers Corporation. It was in the Bay Area where he began to discover and expand his photographic talents, as well as his sexuality. San Francisco was mobbed with servicemen who were returning from the Pacific theater, and a surprising number of them ended up in Scott's bed, as well as being recorded on black-and-white film and, occasionally, in color trasparencies. Grenville Scott eventually moved to Los Angeles, where he bought a gracious home in the Toluca Lake neighborhood of the San Fernando Valley. There he installed a pool and had tall cinder-block walls built around his little domain, where he often held wild parties for his friends and paramours. From the late 1950s to the early 1980s, Mike Scott (as he usually called himself) began taking photos with an astonishing frenzy. He took thousands of black-and-white images and even more color slides and transparencies. This was a risky business at the time because these photos were almost exclusively of male nudes, and not coyly posed or attired in posing pouches. Since he did not intend to sell his images, he could make them as bold and sexy as he wished. Mike Scott continued taking photos well into the 1980s, but by then he had slowed down and his preferred format changed to Polaroid instant photos. Then in 2013, while 92-year old Washington native was crossing the road near his home, he was struck by a SUV and died after a few weeks in the hospital. Fortunately, his photographs survived more or less intact.

Restaurant/Bar:	
The Mix, 635 St Helens Ave, Tacoma, WA **98407** Olive Garden Italian, 1921 S 72nd St, Tacoma, WA **98408**	Red Lobster, 1929 S 72nd St, Tacoma, WA **98408**

Tacoma Cemetery

Cemetery: *The Old Tacoma Cemetery, located on 42 acres in the heart of Tacoma, opened in 1875. The cemetery contains many of the founding fathers of the great City of Destiny. On any particular day you will find walkers enjoying the natural beauty of this Victorian cemetery with the many majestic trees located throughout the grounds.*

Address: 4801 S Tacoma Way, Tacoma, WA 98409

Life

Jack Tuell (1923-2014) was born in Tacoma, WA, the youngest of six sons of Harry Tuell and Ann Bertelsen Tuell. His father Harry was a mortician, and the family lived for a time in the Tuell Funeral Home. In the 1940s the family lived at 820 N Lawrence St, Tacoma, WA **98406**. He served in the Army Air Forces during WWII. His last posting was at Lowry Field in Denver, CO. At a young adult fellowship meeting at Trinity Methodist Church in Denver, he met Marjorie Beadles, a native of Tacoma like himself. They were married in June, 1946. In 1948 he graduated from the University of Washington with a law degree. He practiced law for two years in Edmonds, Washington. During this time he felt a call to ministry and headed off to Boston University School of Theology where he was awarded the Jacob Sleeper Fellowship and graduated summa cum laude. He was ordained as an elder in the Pacific Northwest Conference of The Methodist Church in 1958. Tuell served as pastor of several local churches and as a district superintendent in Washington. He also served the national church as a delegate to the General Conferences of 1964-1972 and was an alternate member of the Judicial Council from 1964-68. This was a critical period of time with the preparations and immediate aftermath of the 1968 Methodist and Evangelical United Brethren merger that formed The United Methodist Church. In 1972 he was elected bishop by the Western Jurisdictional Conference of The United Methodist Church. Tuell served as the bishop of the

Portland Episcopal Area for eight years and then moved to the Los Angeles Episcopal Area for the next twelve years where he was the top official for 195,000 members in more than 400 churches. As the bishop in Los Angeles, Tuell inherited lawsuits demanding $366 million after the bankruptcy of the Pacific Homes retirement facilities in three states and was instrumental in negotiating a settlement of the complex litigation. He also advocated immigrant rights, signed a protest letter calling US arms policy idolatrous and marshaled clergymen against a national lottery game show. But his stance on gay issues continued to reflect the official policy as stated in the Book of Discipline: The practice of homosexuality is incompatible with Christian teaching, although gay people, like all others, have sacred worth. He shuffled a gay clergyman to a non-pastoral job. He recalled later that in a conversation with another church leader he coined the phrase fidelity in marriage and celibacy in singleness which was adopted as official church policy to help filter out gay and lesbian candidates for ministry. Tuell was well-known as an expert on United Methodist polity and law. Beginning with the 1972 edition, he took on the role--from Bishop Nolan Harmon--of author of The Organization of The United Methodist Church. This book served as the standard polity textbook in seminaries for United Methodist pastors. The book was revised after each General Conference to include changes that assembly made to the Book of Discipline, the denomination's law book. Tuell's last edition was published after the 2008 General Conference. Tuell served as president of two United Methodist general agencies, the Commission on Christian Unity and Interreligious Concerns and the Board of Pension and Health Benefits. He delivered the episcopal address at the 1988 General Conference and served as president of the Council of Bishops from 1989 to 1990. In 1992, Tuell retired from the episcopacy and moved with Marjorie back to the Seattle Area. In retirement he continued his work as legal advisor in the church. He regularly provided counsel to other bishops on matters of church law. He argued cases before the Judicial Council. He taught classes on United Methodist polity. He was asked by other bishops to preside, i.e. serve as judge, at church trials. As Tuell later wrote, it was the seventh trial at which he presided that had a profound impact on his thinking on the church's stance on homosexuality. This was the 1999 trial of the Rev. Gregory Dell, a Chicago clergy accused of disobeying church law by performing a commitment service for two gay parishioners. Dell was convicted and suspended from the ministry for a year. For months Tuell reflected on the conviction. Dell, a minister he described as dedicated, energetic, compassionate, caring and able, had been ousted. Anguished friends had been telling him their gay and lesbian children didn't feel at home in the churches where they were raised. Ecclesiastically speaking, the decision was correct, he later wrote. As I understand the Spirit of God, it was wrong. Is it reasonable to believe that God would create some with an orientation toward the same gender, put them within the same strong drive of sexuality and love which is present in heterosexual persons, and then decree that such a drive is to be absolutely repressed and denied? This not only defies reason, but it is cruel, unfeeling and arbitrary ... Tuell publicly expressed his change of heart during a guest sermon at his Des Moines, WA, church in February 2000. I stated flatly that I was wrong and called on the church to prayerfully seek a new inclusiveness, he later wrote. I was 76 years old. His change of heart was widely publicized. Tuell actively advocated for the denomination to eliminate its ban on clergy officiating at same-sex unions and the prohibition against self-avowed practicing gay clergy. In 2004, Tuell appeared as a witness for the defense in the church trial of the Rev. Karen Dammann, a minister accused of violating church doctrine by living openly as a lesbian. She was acquitted. That year he also published From Law to Grace: An Autobiography. He even appeared in frail health at the 2012 General Conference in Tampa, Florida to protest church policy. Although he was not able to witness this change in policy, he was courteous but relentless in his efforts to build bridges that might allow this change to happen. Tuell received honorary degrees from Pacific School of Religion, Alaska Methodist University, and University of Puget Sound. A fund in honor of the Tuells was created at the School of Theology at Claremont to be used for future scholarships. The Pacific Northwest Conference established the Bishop Jack and Marjorie Tuell Center for Leadership Excellence, which aims to nurture clergy and lay members to lead congregations toward vitality.

Perry Watkins (1948-1996) was an African-American gay man, one of the first servicemembers to challenge the ban against homosexuals in the US military, and the only person ordered reinstated to active military duty by a court after being dismissed for homosexuality. Watkins died in 1996, at his home in Tacoma, of complications relating to AIDS.

School: The University of Puget Sound (1500 N Warner St, CMB 1062, Tacoma, WA **98416**) has been named among the 100 Best Campuses for LGBT Students by The Advocate College Guide for LGBT Students, 2006. Among them Named among the Best of the Best Top 20 Campuses. The Best of the Best Top 20 Campuses rise above expectations as pioneering LGBT leaders in higher education. Non only do the campuses rank among the highest on the Gay Point Average but they also boast the most outstanding accomplishments for LGBT progressiveness across the US. The campuses chosen for the Best of the Best represent a diverse array of demographics such as type of institution, locale, and size. The University of Puget Sound is a private liberal arts college. It was founded by the Methodist Episcopal Church in 1888 in downtown Tacoma. The idea for a college in Tacoma originated with Charles Henry Fowler, who had previously been the president of Northwestern University. Fowler was in Tacoma for a Methodist conference when he spoke of his vision of a Christian institution of learning in the area. Two cities vied for the location of the school: Port Townsend and Tacoma. The committee eventually decided on Tacoma. Annual LGBT Event Highlights: Queer History Month (October), National Coming Out Day (October 11), Queer 101 Forum (October 11), Coming Out Dance (October 11), Drag 101 (October), Intersex Awareness Day (October), Masquerade Ball (October 28), Transgender Day of Remembrance (November), World AIDS Day (December 1), Conspiracy of Hope Marriage Booth (February), Day of Silence (April), Annual Drag Show (April), Take Back the Night (April). LGBT Resource center/office: Student Diversity Center (3211 North 15th St, Tacoma, WA **98416**).

Cemetery: Bobbi Campbell (1952-1984) was an openly gay public health nurse, the first person in The US to come out publicly as having AIDS. A self described AIDS Poster Boy, he advocated for people living with AIDS to empower themselves and was instrumental in the founding and organizing of the People With AIDS Movement. Bobbi was born in Columbus, GA and raised in Tacoma. He came out to his parents when he was 18 and they were supportive of him. He graduated with a degree in nursing from The University of Washington, Seattle. While living in San Francisco, he was a registered nurse in graduate school studying to become an adult health nurse practitioner at The University of California, San Francisco. Beginning in February 1981 with a case of shingles, he experienced a number of strange illnesses including anemia. After a hiking trip with his boyfriend in Pinnacles National Monument in September, he noticed purple lesions about the size of a quarter on the heel of each of his feet. Initially believing that the lesions were blood blisters, he became more concerned when the purple spots did not heal after three weeks. Upon visiting his primary care physician, she referred him to a specialist with the Kaposi's Sarcoma Task Force. During this time in San Francisco within the gay community, there were a large number of diagnosed cases of Kaposi's Sarcoma, a very rare cancer which most often afflicted elderly Jewish men. He was diagnosed with gay cancer in the Fall of 1981, the 16th case in San Francisco at the time. On December 10, 1981 in his first article for The Sentinel, Bobbi became the first person in The US to publicly disclose that he was suffering from Kaposi's Sarcoma and that he had gay cancer when he proclaimed himself to be the KS Poster Boy. As a member of the drag troupe The Sisters of Perpetual Indulgence as Sr Florence Nightmare, R.N., he coauthored Play Fair, a safer-sex manual. In 1982 along with several other persons diagnosed with the new disease, Bobbi helped found People With AIDS San Francisco, the first support organization in the country at the time founded by people living with AIDS. In August 1983, he appeared on the cover of Newsweek with his partner, Bobby Hilliard, in a story entitled Gay America. On August 15 1984 surrounded by his parents and partner, Bobbi Campbell died of complications from AIDS at San Francisco General Hospital. At a time when life expectancy for AIDS patients was dramatically shorter than it is today, he had lived for over three and a half years with the disease. He is buried at New Tacoma Cemeteries & Funeral Home (9212 Chambers Creek Rd W, University Place, WA **98467**).

Queer Architects:

Mr. and Mrs. Corydon Wagner III residence, 29 Country Club Dr SW, Lakewood, WA **98498**, designed by Roland Terry (1962)
Mr. and Mrs. J.P. Weyerhaeuser III residence additions and alterations, 11409 Gravelly Lake Dr SW, Lakewood, WA **98499**, designed by Roland Terry (1985)

Other non-queer residents: Chauncey Griggs House, 6816 79th St W, Tacoma, WA **98499**, designed by Frank Lloyd Wright in 1946.

98500

Accommodation:
The Governor, a Coast Hotel (621 Capitol Way S, Olympia, WA **98501**), TAG Approved LGBTQ friendly accommodation.

Swantown Inn B&B (1431 11th Ave SE, Olympia, WA **98501**), LGBTQ friendly.

House:

Barbara Ann Gibson (1931-2017) was a civil rights and peace activist, a widely-admired teacher of literature and feminism, a poet, a playwright, a mental health counselor, and a spiritual director. She was a fierce advocate for justice and was creative in many media. She lived at 2438 Crestline Dr NW, Olympia, WA **98502**. The name of the small town where Barbara grew up Normal, Illinois always amused her, as she herself was far from conventional. She attended Oberlin College and received a BA from the University of Iowa in 1953 and an MA from Wayne State University in 1957. She taught creative writing at the University of Wisconsin-Milwaukee from 1961 to 1970, a vibrant time in the world and in her life. In Milwaukee she was active in CORE and the NAACP, had her family home firebombed by racists and received hate mail, spoke at many antiwar rallies, was a frequent contributor to the local underground newspaper, and was an advocate for gay rights in the early days of gay liberation. She continued her teaching career at Thomas Jefferson College in Michigan, focusing on feminist studies as well as writing. Barbara moved from the Midwest to the Pacific Northwest in the late 1970s. She received a Master of Education from the University of Washington and became a mental health counselor at The Evergreen State College. As her life progressed, Barbara became less involved in radical politics and immersed herself in spiritual teachings, receiving a Doctor of Ministry from Matthew Fox's University of Creation Spirituality and a Spiritual Director Certification from St. Placid Priory Spirituality Center. She wrote several mystical plays about the deity Sophia. She served on the board of Interfaith Works in Olympia, and was a founder of their Moments of Blessing. She loved her church, Community for Interfaith Celebration, and was intimately involved with it until she became too diminished by age to attend. Barbara was wildly creative, freewheeling, kind, generous, warm, insightful, fair, funny, playful, curious, outspoken. She had a vivid personality and was a powerful presence. She brought people together and formed communities. She doted on cats and dogs and loved the animals of the woodland. She swam in lakes and rivers and seas. She loved the grandeur and grace of trees and their colors at different times of the year. She never failed to make people laugh, no matter how dire the situation. Barbara leaves behind numerous writings, including the play The Abolitionist's Wife, performed at Olympia Family Theater. Her books of poetry include This Woman; Psalms for Troubled Times; Olympia; On the Bridge: New Olympia Poems; and Waiting to Fly, her reflections on the end of life. She also leaves many paintings, fabric art pieces, songs, and a legacy of justice advocacy and love of beauty. Her written work incorporates simple but profound language, liberating theology, ancient traditions re-thought and re-worked, and messages to inspire and comfort. Barbara Ann Gibson died at the home that she shared with her beloved wife Carol D. McKinley (born 1942).

Delbert J. McBride (1920-1998) was an artist, historian, curator, museum promoter, cultural ambassador, researcher, writer, and educator, of Spokane and Olympia, WA. Early in his life, Richard Schneider and his lifelong partner, Albert (Bud) McBride, Delbert McBride and Oliver Tiedemann started the Nisqually Valley Klee Wyk Studio (422 Nisqually Cut Off Rd SE, Olympia, WA **98513**), which specialized in Native American art design. From 1961-1966 Del McBride served as curator of art at Eastern Washington State Historical Society's Cheney Cowles Memorial Museum in Spokane. Delbert McBride is one of the artists featured in The Lavender Palette: Excerpts, which is a selection of works from our original exhibition The Lavender Palette: Gay Culture and the Art of Washington State. Museum curator David F. Martin put together artwork by dozens of gay men and women who often, just a few short decades ago, had to hide who they were in order to express themselves artistically. The featured artists included Edmonds native Guy Anderson, illustrator Richard Bennett, Ward Corley, Thomas Handforth, Mac Harshberger, Jule Kullberg, Delbert J. McBride, Orre Nelson Nobles, Malcolm Roberts, potter Lorene Spencer, Sarah

Spurgeon, ceramicist Virginia Weisel, Clifford Wright, and also one-time Woodway resident Morris Graves, Leo Kenney, Mark Tobey, Lionel Pries, Leon Derbyshire, and Sherrill Van Cott. Born in Olympia, Washington, Delbert J. McBride is known as an important Northwest historian. He was Curator of Art at The Cheney Cowles Museum in Spokane (now Northwest Museum of Arts and Culture) and curator at the Washington State Capital Museum in Olympia for many years. Lesser known is the fact that McBride also produced original works of art in several mediums. As a painter, McBride exhibited in local museums and institutions such as the Seattle Art Museum, Tacoma Art Museum, and the University of Puget Sound. In the design field, McBride founded Klee Wyk Studios along with cousin Oliver Tiedeman and brother Bud McBride. They were later joined by Bud's life partner Richard Schneider. The studio was located in the Nisqually Flats, north of Olympia, beginning in the early 1950s. The name Klee Wyk was a homage based on Canadian artist Emily Carr's memoir Klee Wyck of 1941. For ten years, Klee Wyk Studios produced architectural and decorative tile murals as well as utilitarian objects that were among the finest mid-century designs. The artists' use of Northwest Native American motifs reflects the McBrides' Quinault and Cowlitz heritage. McBride and Klee Wyk Studios were the subjects of several retrospectives at the Washington State History Museum in Tacoma. Their reputations were established and preserved largely through the efforts of Northwest art historian Maria Pascualy. Personal and professional papers of Delbert McBride amassed from childhood until just before his death in 1998 -- Includes papers and stories passed down from family members, work-related documentation, correspondence, organizational minutes and newsletters, personal notations on a variety of topics, drawings and sketches, research material, and newspaper clippings. The first portion of the collection is arranged to reflect McBride's life, starting with his family and family associated groups such as the Cowlitz and Quinault, moving to his education, essays and other writings, and job applications. The second portion follows his career: The Klee Wyk Studio, Cheney Cowles Museum, State Capitol Museum, and activities as curator emeritus. The papers from his years at the State Capitol Museum include research material and notes gathered for exhibits. Includes personal correspondence with friends (1935-1998), providing insight into McBride's personal life as a gay man, artist, and activist. Includes papers reflecting organizational membership, arranged alphabetically by name of organization, of which McBride may or may not have been a member; flyers, posters, magazines, newsletters, and other materials on a variety of topics reflecting his various interests, particularly art, artists, Native Americans, and the Nisqually Valley. Due to the repressive social attitudes toward homosexuality in the 1950s, McBride sought out discreet national publications and organizations aimed at gay men and their suppressed libidos. He collected erotic photographs from various studios, including Bob Mizer's Athletic Model Guild (AMG), whose nearly naked models were promoted under the guise of aesthetic source material or as role models for the attainment of a physical ideal. According to Del's brother Bud, McBride made an erotic film accompanied with graphic illustrations that were submitted to AMG, but neither the film or any record of publications containing his illustrations had been located. Del also belonged to the Frontier Athletic Club based out of San Diego and Tijuana, Mexico, and received their awkward, handmade, mimeographed newsletter that promoted the sale of erotic photographs of sexy men. He would later subscribe to the post-Stonewall International Phallic Society newsletter, based out of Las Vegas, another venue for male erotica. Around 1959, Del McBride met the esteemed scholar and archeologist Clark W. Brott, who became his close friend, confidant, model, professional peer, and sexual partner. Brott was curator and director for the Washington State Historical Society (WSHS) in Tacoma from 1960 to 1962, but also became involved in the Klee Wyk Studio as a photographer. Although married with children, he was primarily attracted to men, which was a source of personal conflict for many years. Judging by their lifelong correspondence in McBride's archive at WSHS, he was also McBride's most significant love. Although McBride would confide in Brott when interested in other men, whether for relationships or sexual conquests, his emotional attachment seemed most centered on his relationship with Brott, even after their physical relationship had ended. In 1966 Del McBride returned to Thurston County to become curator of the Washington State Capitol Museum in Olympia. After he retired in 1982 continued to act as consultant on issues ranging from Native American native art and culture to historic preservation for numerous agencies and organizations. Cowlitz/Quinault artist Del McBride's work was preserved by his family, whereas the nieces and nephews of other gay artists did not often keep sketches of their uncles' lovers. Del McBride changed the world of local craft by incorporating elements of his Native American heritage into a range of contemporary designs for artistic and utilitarian purposes. Albert Edward (Bud) McBride, Jr. (1927-2012) was born in Olympia, WA, the son of Albert Edward McBride and Pauline Leona McAllister. He was a descendant of the pioneer McAllister, Mounts, McLeod families and Chief Sca-da-wah of the Cowlitz Tribe. He graduated from Lincoln High School, Tacoma, in 1945. He served in the Army 1945-1947 in Japan. For over ten years, Klee Wyk Studio produced architectural and decorative tile murals, fabrics, hand-printed cards, and utilitarian objects that were among the finest regional midcentury designs utilizing Northwest Coast Native American motifs. The name Klee Wyk was a homage based on Canadian artist Emily Carr's memoir Klee Wyck of 1941. Then Bud McBride opened Crow Valley Pottery on Orcas Island with partner Richard Schneider where business flourished for 35 years until retirement. Bud and Richard undertook the restoration of the 1888 Crow Valley School, completing the restoration for the centennial celebration. The school has recently been dedicated to the Orcas Island Historical Society. Bud McBride, Jr. passed away peacefully on January 10, 2012, in his home at the McBride Nisqually family farm. He was survived by his life partner, Richard E. Schneider.

Restaurant/Bar:

Red Lobster, 4505 Martin Way E, Olympia, WA 98516

Cemetery: Robert Arthur (1925-2008) was an American actor. Since the late 1970s he has headed the California-based Project Rainbow organization to help aid Gay senior citizens. He never married, but dated actresses Jane Russell, Rhonda Fleming, Jan Sterling, Jane Greer, Ava Gardner and Zsa Zsa Gabor. Robert Arthur was born in Aberdeen, WA, the son of Edward Paul Arthaud (1899–1987) and Gertrude Bertha Sather Arthaud (1902–1995). He graduated from Aberdeen High School in 1943. He attended the University of Washington and was in the US Navy training program. He won a high school radio announcing contest and later became a professional announcer and disc jockey before embarking on his film career. Baby-faced support actor, he portrayed earnest collegiate and rookie types in military films, melodrama and film noir of the 1950s. After his first notable movie performance in the 1948 picture Green Grass of Wyoming, he had notable roles in the films Yellow Sky (1948), Twelve O'Clock High (1949), September Affair (1950), Air Cadet (1951), Ace in the Hole (1951), The Ring (1952), Take the High Ground! (1953), Top of the World (1955) and Hellcats of the Navy (1957). His television program credits include The Lone Ranger, Four Star Playhouse and Gomer Pyle, USMC. He quit acting in the 1960s and eventually became an insurance salesman. He was a drama coach and also ran a small theatre group in Los Angeles at one time. He is buried at Fern Hill Cemetery (2212 Roosevelt St, Aberdeen, WA **98520**).

Club: Crystal Steam Baths, 107 F St, Aberdeen, WA **98520**, included in the 1984 Gayellow Pages.

Accommodation: Canterbury Inn (643 Ocean Shores Blvd., Ocean Shores, WA **98569**), gay friendly. Voted one of the best vacation getaways in Washington, Ocean Shores offers six miles of sandy beach, 23 miles of interconnecting fresh water canals and a quaint beach town to shop and explore.

Michael Jensen, author: Seabrook (WA 98571). This beach town on the Washington coast is a stellar example of New Urbanism, which means the town is designed to be pedestrian friendly (bikes are available for anyone to grab one and start riding), shared outdoor spaces including fire pits, large grass lawns, and a cohesive look and feel to the town that makes it feel like a place from a different era.

Queer Architects: Alderbrook Inn alterations, 10 E Alderbrook Dr, Union, WA **98592**, designed by Roland Terry (1976)

Accommodation: Westport Bayside B&B (1112 S Montesano St, Westport, WA **98595**), LGBTQ friendly. A perfect place to come home to after a day of salmon fishing, clamming, sightseeing, horseback riding or bicycling. GLD, Gay Lesbian Directory

98600

Accommodation: Carson Ridge Luxury Cabins, 1261 Wind River Rd, Carson, WA **98610**
The Villa at Little Cape Horn, 48 Little Cape Horn Rd, Cathlamet, WA **98612**, GLD, Gay Lesbian Directory

Lone Fir Resort (16806 Lewis River Rd, Cougar, WA **98616**), LGBTQ owned.
Mt Adams Lodge at the Flying L Ranch (25 Flying L Ln, Glenwood, WA **98619**), LGBTQ friendly.

Maryhill Museum of Art, Goldendale

Museum: *With Queen Marie of Romania and American businessman Samuel Hill, Loie Fuller helped found the Maryhill Museum of Art in rural Washington State, which has permanent exhibits about her career.*

Address: 35 Maryhill Museum Dr, Goldendale, WA 98620

Life

Who: Loie Fuller (also Loïe Fuller; January 15, 1862 – January 1, 1928)

Loie Fuller was an American actress and dancer who was a pioneer of both modern dance and theatrical lighting techniques. Born Marie Louise Fuller in the Chicago suburb of Fullersburg, now Hinsdale, IL, Fuller began her theatrical career as a professional child actress and later choreographed and performed dances in burlesque (as a skirt dancer), vaudeville, and circus shows. An early free dance practitioner, Fuller developed her own natural movement and improvisation techniques. In multiple shows she experimented with a long skirt, choreographing its movements and playing with the ways it could reflect light. By 1891, Fuller combined her choreography with silk costumes illuminated by multi-coloured lighting of her own design, and created the Serpentine Dance. After much difficulty finding someone willing to produce her work when she was primarily known as an actress, she was finally hired to perform her piece between acts of a comedy entitled Uncle Celestine, and received rave reviews. Almost immediately, she was replaced by imitators (originally Minnie Renwood Bemis). In the hope of receiving serious artistic recognition that she was not getting in America, Fuller left for Europe in June 1892. She became one of the first of many American modern dancers who traveled to Europe to seek recognition. Her warm reception in Paris persuaded Fuller to remain in France, where she became one of the leading revolutionaries in the arts. A regular performer at the Folies Bergère with works such as Fire Dance, Fuller became the embodiment of the Art Nouveau movement and was often identified with Symbolism, as her work was seen as the perfect reciprocity between idea and symbol. Fuller began adapting and expanding her costume and lighting, so that they became the principle element in her performance—perhaps even more important than the actual choreography, especially as the length of the skirt was increased and became the central focus, while the body became mostly hidden within the depths of the fabric. An 1896 film of the Serpentine Dance by the pioneering film-makers Auguste and Louis Lumière gives a hint of what her performance was like. (The unknown dancer in the film is often mistakenly identified as Fuller herself; however, there is no actual film footage of Fuller dancing.) Fuller's pioneering work attracted the attention, respect, and friendship of many French artists and scientists. Fuller was also a member of the Société astronomique de France (French Astronomical Society). Fuller held many patents related to stage lighting including chemical compounds for creating color gel and the use of chemical salts for luminescent lighting and garments (stage costumes US Patent 518347). She attempted to create a patent of her Serpentine Dance as she hoped to stop imitators from taking her choreography and even claiming to be her. Fuller submitted a written description of her dance to the US Copyright Office; however, a US Circuit Court judge ended up denying Fuller's request for an injunction, as the Serpentine Dance told no story and was therefore not eligible for copyright protection. At that time dance was only protected if it qualified as dramatic and Fuller's dance was too abstract for this qualification. The precedent set by Fuller's case remained in place from 1892 until 1976, when Federal Copyright Law explicitly extended protection to choreographic works. Fuller supported other pioneering performers, such as fellow US-born dancer Isadora Duncan. Fuller helped Duncan ignite her European career in 1902 by sponsoring independent concerts in Vienna and BudapeSt Loie Fuller's original stage name was Louie. In modern French L'ouïe is the word for a sense of hearing. When Fuller reached Paris she gained a nickname which was a pun on Louie/L'ouïe. She was renamed Loïe - this nickname is a corruption of the early or Medieval French L'oïe, a precursor to L'ouïe, which means receptiveness or understanding. She was also referred to by the nickname Lo Lo Fuller. Fuller formed a close friendship with Queen Marie of Romania; their extensive correspondence has been published. Fuller, through a connection at the US embassy in Paris played a role in arranging a US loan for Romania during WWI. Later, during the period when the future Carol II of Romania was alienated from the Romanian royal family and living in Paris with his mistress Magda Lupescu, she befriended them; they were unaware of her connection to Carol's mother Marie. Fuller initially advocated to Marie on behalf of the couple, but later schemed unsuccessfully with Marie to separate Carol from Lupescu. Fuller occasionally returned to America to stage performances by her students, the Fullerets or Muses, but spent the end of her life in Paris. She died of pneumonia at the age of 65 on January 1, 1928 in Paris, two weeks shy of her 66th birthday. She was cremated and her ashes are interred in the columbarium at Père Lachaise Cemetery in Paris. Her sister, Mollie Fuller, had a long career as an actress and vaudeville performer.

Restaurant/Bar:

Maryhill Winery, 9774 WA-14, Goldendale, WA **98620**

Red Lobster, 203 Three Rivers Dr, Kelso, WA **98626**

Accommodation:

Anthony's Home Court Cabin Rentals, 1310 Pacific Ave, Long Beach, WA **98631**. Walk to the ocean, on the Long Beach Peninsula just 2 hours from Portland, OR.

WorldMark Long Beach (420 Sid Snyder Dr SW, Long Beach, WA **98631**). This sleek apartment hotel is a minute's walk from the beach, the peninsula's main street, and 6 miles from Cape Disappointment Light House beside the Columbia River. Part of World Rainbow Hotels (WRH), Lesbian and Gay Welcoming Hotels.

Moby Dick Hotel, Restaurant and Oyster Farm (25814 Sandridge Rd, Nahcotta, WA **98637**), LGBTQ friendly.

Heron Hollow at Ocean Park (25815 Park Ave, Ocean Park, WA **98640**), gay owned. This beach house has wonderful views of the ocean and surrounding wetlands and woods.

Shakti Cove Cottages (25301 Park Ave, Ocean Park, WA **98640**), secluded in a grove of trees, on 3 beautiful acres. A stream that flows through the property and a private walking path to the beach. Shakti Cove has 12 cottages all with kitchenettes. Its truly a magical place that soothes the soul. Included in Inn Places 1999, Gay & Lesbian Accommodations Worldwide. Gay and Lesbian. GLD, Gay Lesbian Directory

Worldmark Surfside Inn (31512 J Pl, Ocean Park, WA **98640**) is 5 minutes' walk from the beach. The property is located in Ocean Bay Park, less than 5 minutes' walk from 28 miles of Washington coastline. Part of World Rainbow Hotels (WRH), Lesbian and Gay Welcoming Hotels.

Carson Ridge Luxury Cabins, 1261 Wind River Road, Carson, WA **98641**, GLD, Gay Lesbian Directory

Bloomer Estates Vacation Rentals, PO Box 345, Seaview, WA **98644**, GLD, Gay Lesbian Directory

Sou'wester Lodge and Trailer Park, 38th St. (Beach Access Road) & J Place, Seaview, Long Beach, WA **98644**, GLD, Gay Lesbian Directory

The Inn at Crippen Creek Farm (15 Oatfield Rd, Skamokawa, WA **98647**), LGBTQ friendly.

The Inn at Lucky Mud (44 Old Chestnut Dr, Skamokawa, WA **98647**), LGBTQ friendly.

Vancouver

Vancouver, WA, has been named among the Gayest Cities in America by The Advocate, 2011

Find a grave

Mary Carolyn Davies (1888–1974) was an American poet and prose writer. The editors of Poetry, Harriet Monroe and Alice Corbin Henderson included Davies in their 1917 selection for The New Poetry: An Anthology. According to Adrienne Munich and Melissa Bradshaw, authors of Amy Lowell, American Modern, what connects these poets is their appartenance to the queer sisterhood. Davies was born in Sprague, WA, a tiny town about forty miles southwest of Spokane. Davies moved to Portland at age twelve. She graduated from Washington High School in Portland in 1910 and spent a year teaching school on the Crooked River and in Rockaway. In 1911 she entered the University of California at Berkeley, where she was the first woman to win the Bohemian Club prize for poetry and the Emily Chamberlin Cook Prize for Poetry as a freshman; but dropped out after a year. She moved to New York City, where she supported herself by hack literary work, while also writing poetry in her spare time. Davies's first book, a collection of war poems called The Drums in our Street, was published in 1918 and was dedicated to my three brothers. She moved back to Oregon and married Leland Davis (a marriage which ended in divorce). During the 1920's she published in magazines that included Collier's, Cosmopolitan, Good Housekeeping, McClure's, and Poetry, and in prominent anthologies like the Bookman Anthology of Verse and Modern American Poetry. She was elected president of the Women's Press Club of Oregon in 1920, and president of the Northwest Poetry Society in 1924. She published little after that time, however, and largely disappeared from public life after she moved back to New York City during the 1930s. In 1940 the Oregonian reported that she was destitute; the paper's poetry editor, Ethel Romig Fuller, visited her in New York, and found her living in a deplorable state. She died in 1974 and is buried in a twin tomb with Margaret D. Nash in Vancouver, WA.

Ulysses Simpson Grant (1822-1885), Grant House (1106 E Evergreen Blvd, Vancouver, WA **98661**), from 1852 to 1853.
George Catlett Marshall (1880-1959), 1310 E Evergreen Blvd, Vancouver, WA **98661**, from 1936 to 1938.

Attractions: Fort Vancouver National Historic Site (612 E Reserve St, Vancouver, WA **98661**) includes four sites central to life in the Pacific Northwest. These sites include army barracks, a fur trading post, an air travel museum, and the home of the doctor who helped form the state of Oregon. Among the 50 most popular historic sites in America, 2022.

Restaurant/Bar: Olive Garden Italian, 8101 NE Parkway Dr, Vancouver, WA **98662**	Red Lobster, 8219 NE Vancouver Mall Dr, Vancouver, WA **98662**
Accommodation: Husum Riverside B&B (866 WA-141, White Salmon, WA **98672**), LGBTQ friendly. 7 miles	from the Hood River, to the White Salmon River and Mt Adams.
Restaurant/Bar:	Olive Garden Italian, Columbia Crossing Shopping Center, 16405 SE Mill Plain Blvd, Vancouver, WA **98684**

98800

Accommodation: Coast Wenatchee Center Hotel (201 N Wenatchee Ave, Wenatchee, WA **98801**), TAG Approved LGBTQ friendly accommodation. Mary Kay's Romantic Whaley Mansion Inn (415 S 3rd St, Chelan, WA **98816**) included in Inn Places 1999, Gay & Lesbian Accommodations Worldwide. Gay friendly. Located 5 minutes walk from Lake Chelan, the WorldMark Chelan - Lake House (402 W Manson Hwy, Chelan, WA **98816**) offers an outdoor pool, sun loungers and hot tub. Part of	World Rainbow Hotels (WRH), Lesbian and Gay Welcoming Hotels. Icicle Village Resort (505 US-2, Leavenworth, WA **98826**), Washington State's LGBTQ and Allied Chamber of Commerce member. Hotel, condos, dining at JJ Hills Fresh Grill, Junction Activity Center & Alpine Spa along with mini golf, sports court, swimming pools and much more. Pine River Ranch All Suite B&B (19668 WA-207, Leavenworth, WA **98826**), LGBTQ friendly. GLD, Gay Lesbian Directory

98900

Cemetery: Rand Snyder (1960-1996) lived with HIV and AIDS for years and years. Well before his symptoms began to show, he became a leader in AIDS activism in NYC. He fought this illness in the streets and with every bone in his body. With his lover, David, and many other friends by his side, Rand died at Bellvue Hospital in July 1996. He is buried at Terrace Heights Memorial Park (3001 Terrace Heights Dr, Yakima, WA **98901**).

Restaurant/Bar: Chinook Hotel Bar, 402 E Yakima Ave, Yakima, WA **98901**, included in the Damron Address Book from 1978 to 1980. Olive Garden Italian, 222 E Yakima Ave, Yakima, WA **98901**	Queen of Hearts Tavern, 18 N 1st St, Yakima, WA **98901**, included in the 1964 and 1965 Guild Guide. Included in the 1975 All Lavender International Gay Guide. Red Lobster, 905 N 1st St, Yakima, WA **98901**

Central Washington University

School: *Central Washington University has been named among the* **100 Best Campuses for LGBT Students** *by The Advocate College Guide for LGBT Students, 2006. It is a public university.*

Address: 400 E University Way, Ellensburg, WA 98926

Place

Founded in 1891, the university consists of four divisions: the President' Division, Business and Financial Affairs, Operations, and Academic and Student Life (ASL). **Annual LGBT Event Highlights:** National Coming Out Day (October), Transgender Day of Remembrance (November), Freedom to Marry (February), Ally Trainings (ongoing), Guess the Straight Panels (ongoing), The Power of One: LGBT Leadership Conference (April), Pride Week (May). **LGBT Resource center/office:** Diversity Education Center (LGBT Student Services, 400 E University Way, Ellensburg, WA **98926**).

Hebeler Hall

Notable queer alumni and faculty:

Hebeler Hall, 907 N Wildcat Way, Ellensburg, WA **98926**, is named to honor **Amanda Hebeler** (1890-1969), who played an integral role in the teacher training programs at CWU in its early decades. Hebeler directed the Washington State Normal School's student teaching program from 1924 to 1956, and was a professor of education from 1935 until her retirement in 1960. Hebeler was born in Maple Grove Township, MI. She graduated from Michigan State Normal School (now known as Eastern Michigan University) in 1916 and taught in the Wolverine State for several years. In 1922, she decided to further her education and enrolled in the Teacher's College at Columbia University in New York City, earning a BS in 1924. While working at WSNS, she also continued her studies at the Teacher's College, receiving her MA in 1927. By the early 1930s, it had become clear that Edison Hall (no longer standing), home of the student teaching programs, was no longer adequate and Hebeler began working with the school's administration on plans for a new education building. In 1937, WSNS was granted the authority to issue four-year degrees and was renamed Central Washington College of Education. Additionally, that year the federal Public Works Administration and the Washington State Legislature appropriated fund to build a new teacher training laboratory building to replace Edison Hall. The new structure, originally called the College Elementary School, was completed in 1939. It would continue to be used as a teaching lab school until 1982, when the state decided to close such instructional facilities for cost reasons. The new building incorporated design ideas suggested by Hebeler, based on her years of experience in the classroom. It also boasted stained glass windows and fireplace tiles (depicting ancient printing processes and children's book characters) created by CWCE art professor Sarah Spurgeon and her students. Fireplace tiles in the Kindergarten classroom depicting Mother Goose characters were crafted by another CWCE art professor, Reino Randall. Three years after her retirement, the College Elementary School was renamed to honor Hebeler. She continued living in Ellensburg until her death in 1969. Hebeler Hall, which is now home of College of Humanities and Arts programs, has an architectural style that has been described as Neo-Classical Revival with Modern influence. It was designed with ten classroom suites that originally housed a nursery, Kindergarten, and grades one through six. The floorplan of two-story Hebeler is L-shaped and it has a brick and stone exterior with interior concrete walls. In the mid-80s, the structure was substantially remodeled to modernize it and make it more useful for instructional purposes. An elevator was added in 1985 and electrical wiring was replaced in the mid-90s.

Dorothy Dean (1901-1987) was a Central Washington University professor emeritus. Dean taught chemistry at Central Washington University from 1928 until she retired in 1968. During her tenure she was advisor to pre-dental and pre-medical students, many of whom went on to the U. of Wash. med. or dental school. Dorothy Dean was born in Neosho, MO, the daughter of Herbert Day Dean (1858–1946) and May L. Johnson (1865–1961). She was a graduate of Montana State University and received her master's degree from the University of Chicago. She did graduate work at Columbia University and the University of Michigan and was a National Science Foundation grantee in 1958 and 1980. Dean taught chemistry at Central from 1928 until she retired in 1968. Dean Hall, 1200 D St, Ellensburg, WA **98926**, a science building constructed on the Ellenaburg campus in 1968 was named for Dean. She was also an early recipient of the CWU alumni award and was listed in Who's Who of American Women. She was a member of the American Assoc. of U. Professors, Amer. Assoc. of U. Women, Amer. Chemical Soc., Sigma Xi, Phi Kappa Phi, Phi Upsilon Omicron, Retired Teachers Assoc., Washington State Education Assoc.-of which she was a past president, Memorial Hospital Guild in Ellensburg, Orthopedic Hospital Guild in Olympia and both the Ellensburg and Lacey chapters of PEO.

Sarah Spurgeon outside the home that she designed and decorated with her life partner, Amanda Hebeler, circa 1960.

House: Sarah Spurgeon (1903-1985) moved to Ellensburg, WA, from Iowa in 1939 and joined the art department at the college the same year. She took a hiatus from her work at Central Washington College of Education during WWII when she went to work for Boeing as an artist. Following the war, she returned to Ellensburg and continued as a professor until her retirement in 1971. At first she taught at the University of Iowa for four years. During her time there she exhibited her oil paintings in national and regional exhitions including the Corcoran Gallery, the Kansas City Art Institute, and the Joslyn Museum in Omaha, Nebraska as well as winning several regional awards. In 1933, Spurgeon attended the Chicago World's Fair, A Century of Progress International Exposition. It was there that she first saw the paintings of Thomas Hart Benton, whose work she admired and was later influenced by, especially in the use of tempera as an artistic medium. Her work was noticed by famed Iowa artist Grant Wood, and he hired her to assist him, along with other talented young artists, to create a series of murals for the Iowa State University library in Ames, Iowa, in 1934. The murals were commissioned under the Civil Works Administration as part of President Roosevelt's emergency employment New Deal programs. She also modeled for a few of the female figures in the murals. As she recalled, All the boys put on jeans and I had an apron made out of old-fashioned dark blue calico... Most of the people on the project were men. In fact I don't recall another woman besides myself being there in Iowa City. In 1935, Spurgeon was hired to teach English at Buena Vista College in Storm Lake, Iowa. The school was only eighteen miles from her parents' home and both were suffering, from serious health problems that concerned her. At the time, the school had no art department and she endeavored to start one. She became the only faculty member of the department and struggled to establish it, even doing some of the construction work for making the gallery into a space for exhibiting art. Since there were no funds available from the school, she used her own money to purchase basic art supplies for the students. In 1939, Spurgeon moved to Ellensburg, WA, to accept a position in the Art Department of Central Washington College of Education (now University). Around this time she began using Sarah as her given name, although she never legally changed it. In 1942 she took a two-and-a-half-year leave of absence to work for the Boeing Company as a production illustrator on the B-17 and B-29 aircrafts. She had attempted to join the military to serve in the war but was rejected. In Seattle she joined Women Painters of Washington and became involved in their exhibitions and lectures. After the war, she returned to Ellensburg and resumed her position at the college. Sometime in the 1940s Spurgeon met fellow CWCE professor Amanda K. Hebeler, who had joined the faculty in 1924. Hebeler had earned her BS and MS degrees from Columbia University, with graduate study at Yale and the University of Southern California. Director of the College Elementary School from 1929 until 1956, she was actively involved in numerous educational and cultural organizations in the region. She was professor of education from 1935 until her retirement as professor emeritus in 1960. In 1963 the school was renamed the Amanda Hebeler Elementary School (later named the Washington Center for Early Childhood Education). The school was closed in the spring of 1981. Today, Hebeler Hall at the university is named in her honor. Spurgeon and Hebeler lived on E Eighth Av, Ellensburg, WA **98926** (between C Street and N Wildcat Way). Her life partner, Amanda, passed away in 1969, and Spurgeon retired in 1971. A final tribute came in 1978 when Central Washington University celebrated the dedication of the Sarah Spurgeon Gallery (400 E University Way, Ellensburg, WA **98926**) with an exhibit featuring fifty-five of her former students. Her last years were plagued with poor health, and she relied on former students and friends to assist her, especially the prominent regional artists Jane Orleman and her husband, Richard C. Elliott. Spurgeon passed away in October 1985, surrounded by loved ones and in the arms of her intimate friend, jewelry artist Ramona Solberg, who lived at 802 C St, Ellensburg, WA **98926**.

Purser Place, the barn behind Spurgeon and Hebeler's house they rented to students. The second floor housed Spurgeon's library.

Other non-queer residents: William Orville Douglas (1898-1980), Prairie House (Prairie House Ln, Goose Prairie, WA **98937**), from 1964 to 1980.

Oldest Bar in the State: The Brick Saloon, 100 W Pennsylvania Ave, Roslyn, WA **98941**. There is some controversy about who can claim the title of oldest bar in the state, but The Brick Saloon in Roslyn dates back to 1889 and features a 100-year-old bar, its own basement jail cell, and a 23-foot running water spittoon still operating from the Brick's first days in operation.

Store: In one of the northernmost corners of the continental US, the Thorp Fruit & Antique Mall, 220 Gladmar Rd, Thorp, WA **98946**, started out as a roadside fruit stand. Now, it's a huge shopping complex; its most distinctive feature is the larger-than-life red lettering that can be seen a mile off. Inside you'll find a seasonal selection of fruit and veg, as well as racks of Pacific Northwest wine, goods from their own private label, locally-made ice cream, and all sorts of pickles and sauces. As the name suggests, there are plenty of antiques to rifle through, too. Named among the Most charming general stores in every US state, 2018, by Love Food.

National Park: In 1954, Sarah Spurgeon (1903-1985) painted a large modernist mural for the Ginkgo Petrified Forest Museum now known as Ginkgo Petrified Forest Interpretive Center (630 Ginkgo Ave, Vantage, WA **98950**), on the Columbia River. She designed and executed the twenty-foot-wide interior mural, while architect Lionel Pries designed the exterior decorations at the entrance to the building. The petrified forest was discovered in 1931 by a fellow CWCE faculty member, geologist George F. Beck, whom she later memorialized in a portrait now in the university's collection. Spurgeon's mural and decorative work for the Ginkgo Petrified Forest Museum have been destroyed.

99000

| Restaurant/Bar: | Ben & Jerry's, 100 N Hayford Rd, Airway Heights, WA **99001** |

| Accommodation: Located just 10 minutes west of downtown Spokane, Northern Quest Resort & Casino (100 N Hayford Rd, Airway Heights, WA **99001**) welcomes visitors with a contemporary urban | setting and 250 luxurious guest rooms and suites. Part of World Rainbow Hotels (WRH), Lesbian and Gay Welcoming Hotels. |

99100

| Restaurant/bar: | Rico's, 200 E Main, Pullman, WA **99163**, included in the 1984 Gayellow Pages. |

School: Washington State University (370 Lighty Student Services, P.O. Box 641067, Pullman, WA **99164**) has been named among the 100 Best Campuses for LGBT Students by The Advocate College Guide for LGBT Students, 2006. It is a public research university. Founded in 1890, WSU is one of the oldest land-grant universities in the American West and features programs in a broad range of academic disciplines. The Holland Library and Student Union T-Rooms have been included in the Damron Address Book from 1977 to 1980. Annual LGBT Event Highlights: LGBT Brown Bag Discussions (monthly, Fall/Spring), LGBT Knitting Circle (monthly, Fall/Spring), Drag Show (monthly, Fall/Spring), Welcome Back BBQ (August), Pride Week (October), National Coming Out Day (October 11), National Day of Transgender Remembrance (November), Family Thanksgiving (November), World AIDS Day (December 1), National Freedom to Marry Day (February), National Day of Silence (March/April), Week of Dignity (March/April), Lavender Graduation (April) LGBT Resource center/office: Gender Identity/Expression and Sexual Orientation Resource Center (P.O. Box 641430, Smith Gym 303, Pullman, WA **99164**).

99200

Spokane

Spokane, WA, has been named among the Gayest Cities in America by The Advocate, 2013
Spokane, WA, has been named among the Queerest City in America by The Advocate, 2015
Spokane, WA, has been named among the Queerest City in America by The Advocate, 2016

House: Vachel Lindsay (1879–1931) lived at 2318 W Pacific Ave, Spokane, WA **99201**, from 1925 to 1928.

Historic District: Bus Depot, 221 W 1st Ave, Spokane, WA **99201**, included in the from 1972 to 1980.

LGBTQ friendly bookstore:

Curious Book Store, 327 W 2nd Ave, Spokane, WA **99201**, included in the Damron Address Book from 1978 to 1979.

Happy's Adult Book Store, 45 W Main Ave, Spokane, WA **99201**, included in the Damron Address Book from 1978 to 1980.

Payless Books & Arcade, 329 W 2nd Ave, Spokane, WA **99201**, included in the Damron Address Book from 1978 to 1980.

The Arcade, 311 W Riverside Ave, Spokane, WA **99201**, included in the Damron Address Book in 1980.

Montvale Hotel

Accommodation: *A Lovely Boutique Hotel.* LGBTQ friendly

Address: 1005 W 1st Ave., Spokane, WA, 99201
National Register of Historic Places: 98000369, 1998

Montvale Hotel

Place

The Montvale Hotel is a boutique hotel in Spokane. Originally built in 1899 as an SRO (Single Room Occupancy Hotel), the Montvale Hotel also served Spokane as an apartment building, a brothel, and as a youth hostel during Expo '74 and then was abandoned for 30 years. It was restored and re-opened in January 2005 as a 36-room boutique hotel, becoming one of Spokane's premier hotels with The Davenport Hotel and the Hotel Lusso. On August 25, 2015, it was announced that the Montvale Hotel had been acquired by Jerry Dicker's Ruby Hospitality. With the demolition of the Pennington Wing at the Davenport Hotel, the Montvale gained the distinction as Spokane's oldest hotel. Kilmer and Son's Hardware was located on buildings' main floor for over 60 years. Kilmer once employed Henry J. Kaiser, the American industrialist who became known as the father of modern American shipbuilding. Currently located in the same building as the Montvale Hotel is Scratch Restaurant and is located on the street level of the building.

The Davenport Hotel

Address: 10 S Post St, Spokane, WA 99201
National Register of Historic Places: 75001874, 1975

The Historic Davenport, Autograph Collection

Place

The Davenport Hotel was commissioned by a group of Spokane businessmen, and named after Louis Davenport, its first proprietor and overseer of the project. Architect Kirtland Cutter designed the building in 1914. The Davenport Hotel was the first hotel in the US with air conditioning, a central vacuum system, pipe organ, and dividing doors in the ballrooms. It is also the place at which the first Crab Louis (named after Louis Davenport) was created and served. In 1924 Vachel Lindsay (1879–1931) moved to Spokane, where he lived in room 1129 of the Davenport Hotel until 1929. On May 19, 1925, at age 45, he married 23-year-old Elizabeth Connor. The new pressure to support his considerably younger wife escalated as she bore him daughter Susan Doniphan Lindsay in May 1926 and son Nicholas Cave Lindsay in September 1927. Desperate for money, Lindsay undertook an exhausting string of readings throughout the East and Midwest from October 1928 through March 1929.

Restaurant/Bar:
Baby Bar (827 W 1st Ave, Spokane, WA **99201**), gay bar. Neko Case, a member of the Canadian indie rock group The New Pornographers called Baby Bar the best bar in America.

Ben & Jerry's, 808 W Main Ave Cafes, On 3 Space 10, Spokane, WA **99201**
Billy Tipton (1914-1989) was an American jazz musician and bandleader. He is also notable for the postmortem discovery that, although he

lived his adult life as a man, he was assigned female at birth. Born in Oklahoma City, OK, Tipton grew up in Kansas City, MO, where he was raised by an aunt after his mother died. He subsequently rarely saw his father, G. W. Tipton, a pilot. As a high-school student, Tipton went by the nickname Tippy and became interested in music, especially jazz, studying piano and saxophone. He returned to Oklahoma for his final year of high school and joined the school band there. As Tipton began a more serious music career, he adopted his father's nickname, Billy, and more actively worked to pass as male by binding his breasts and padding his pants. At first, Tipton only presented as male in performance, but by 1940 was living as a man in private life as well. Two of Tipton's female cousins, with whom Tipton maintained contact over the years, were the only persons known to be privy to Tipton's assigned sex. In 1958 Tipton settled in Spokane, and the Billy Tipton Trio became the house band at the downtown nightclub Allen's Café (412 W Riverside Ave, Spokane, WA **99201**), The gayest spot in town. Early in his career, lived with a woman named Non Earl Harrell, in a relationship that other musicians thought of as lesbian. The relationship ended in 1942. Tipton's next relationship, with a singer known only as June, lasted for several years. For seven years, Tipton lived with Betty Cox, who was 19 when they became involved. Cox remembered Tipton as the most fantastic love of my life. Tipton kept the secret of his extrinsic sexual characteristics from Betty by inventing a story of having been in a serious car accident resulting in damaged genitals and broken ribs, and that it was necessary to bind the damaged chest to protect it. From then on, this was what he would tell the women in his life. In 1960, Tipton ended his relationship with Cox to settle down with nightclub dancer and stripper Kitty Kelly (later known as Kitty Oakes), who was known professionally as The Irish Venus. They adopted three sons, John, Scott, and William. Because of the couple's ongoing arguments over how they should raise the boys, Tipton left Kitty in the late 1970s, moved into a mobile home with their sons (two of their sons had run away from home after being physically abused by Kitty), and resumed an old relationship with

a woman named Maryann. He remained there, living in poverty, until his death. In an attempt to keep the secret, Kitty arranged for his body to be cremated, but later after financial offers from the media, Kitty and one of their sons went public with the story. The first newspaper article was published the day after Tipton's funeral and it was quickly picked up by wire services. Stories about Tipton appeared in a variety of papers including tabloids such as National Enquirer and Star, as well as more reputable papers such as New York Magazine and The Seattle Times. Tipton's family even made talk show appearances.

Carriage House at Otis Hotel, 110 S Madison St, Spokane, WA **99201**, included in the Damron Address Book from 1978 to 1980.

The Casbah, 919 W Sprague Ave, Spokane, WA **99201**, included in the 1963 and 1966 Lavender Baedeker. Included in the 1964 Directory. Included in the 1965 Guild Guide. Included in the Damron Address Book from 1965 to 1970. Later Dorothy's Tavern, included in the Damron Address Book from 1971 to 1974. Later Other Side, included in the Damron Address Book from 1975 to 1976.

First Emperor's Club, 425 W 1st Ave, Spokane, WA **99201**, included in the Damron Address Book in 1979. Sonya's Magic Inn, included in the Damron Address Book from 1977 to 1978.

Jack's Nite Hawk, 330 W Riverside Ave, Spokane, WA **99201**, included in the Damron Address Book from 1972 to 1980.

Main Door, 309 W Main Ave, Spokane, WA **99201**, included in the Damron Address Book in 1980.

nYne Bar & Bistro (232 W Sprague Ave, Spokane, WA **99201**), lesbian owned, one of the city's gay bars.

Saddle Tavern, 927 W 1st Ave, Spokane, WA **99201**, included in the Damron Address Book from 1968 to 1971.

Show Boat, 1201 W 1st Ave, Spokane, WA **99201**, included in the Damron Address Book from 1976 to 1978.

Upper Level, 301 W Main Ave, Spokane, WA **99201**, included in the Damron Address Book in 1980.

Wild Sage Bistro, 916 W 2nd Ave, Spokane, WA **99201**

Accommodation:
Muzzy Mansion B&B (1506 W Mission Ave, Spokane, WA **99201**), LGBTQ owned.

Parson's Hotel, 108 S Jefferson St, Spokane, WA **99201**, included in the Damron Address Book from 1976 to 1977.

School: Brent Hartinger (born 1971) is an American author, playwright, and screenwriter, best known for his novels about gay teenagers. Hartinger was born in 1971 in Washington State and grew up in Tacoma. He earned a bachelor's degree from Gonzaga University (502 E Boone Ave, Spokane, WA **99202**), and studied for a masters in psychology at Western Washington University. Gonzaga University is a private Roman Catholic university in Spokane, WA. Founded in 1887 by the Society of Jesus, it is one of 28 member institutions of the Association of Jesuit Colleges and Universities. It is named for the young Jesuit St Aloysius Gonzaga. The campus houses 105 buildings on 152 acres (62 ha) of grassland along the Spokane River, in a residential setting one-half-mile (0.8 km) from downtown Spokane.

LGBTQ friendly bookstore: Adult Book Store, 1820 E Sprague Ave, Spokane, WA **99202**, included in the Damron Address Book from 1978 to 1980.

Club: Sauna Baths, 217 N Division St, Spokane, WA **99202**, included in the Damron Address Book in 1972.

Other non-queer residents: Harry Lillis (Bing) Crosby (1903-1977), 508 E Sharp Ave, Spokane, WA **99202**, from 1913 to 1925.

Restaurant/Bar:	
The Blind Buck, 204 N Division St, Spokane, WA **99202**, one of Spokane's hottest gay bars.	Disco 425, 425 E 1st Ave, Spokane, WA **99202**, included in the Damron Address Book in 1980.

House:

Hannes Bok, pseudonym for Wayne Francis Woodard (1914–1964), was an American artist and illustrator, as well as an amateur astrologer and writer of fantasy fiction and poetry. He painted nearly 150 covers for various science fiction, fantasy, and detective fiction magazines, as well as contributing hundreds of black and white interior illustrations. Bok's work graced the pages of calendars and early fanzines, as well as dust jackets from specialty book publishers like Arkham House, Llewellyn, Shasta Publishers, and Fantasy Press. His paintings achieved a luminous quality through the use of an arduous glazing process, which was learned from his mentor, Maxfield Parrish. Bok shared one of the inaugural 1953 Hugo Awards for science fiction achievement (best Cover Artist). Today, Bok is best known for his cover art which appeared on various pulp and science fiction magazines, such as Weird Tales, Famous Fantastic Mysteries, Other Worlds, Super Science Stories, Imagination, Fantasy Fiction, Planet Stories, If, Castle of Frankenstein and The Magazine of Fantasy & Science Fiction. Hannes or Hans Bok was a precocious talent in Seatlle and one of the youngest of the regional WPA artists. Although active in Seattle only intermittently during the 1930s, he met and befriended some of the successful gay artists in the region, as well as sympathetic straight talents like artist Fay Chong, who remained a lifelong friend. Bok lived at 1417 E 16th Ave, Spokane, WA **99203**. Bok, Thomas Handforth, and Richard Bennett were among several North-west gay artists who gained fame as illustrators. However, Bok found his niche in science fiction, becoming one of the country's finest and most influential illustrators in that genre. He moved to New York for career opportunities, and although he became successful in his field, he could never lift himself out of poverty. He died of a heart attack at age 49, purpotedly the result of improper nutrition and starvation.

Guy Anderson (1906–1998) was an American artist known primarily for his oil painting who lived most of his life in the Puget Sound region of the US. In the late 1930s he lived at 1628 W Tenth Ave, Spokane, WA **99204**. The Lavender Palette: Gay

Culture and the Art of Washington State at the Cascadia Museum in Edmonds was a packed art show and a powerful history lesson. Museum curator David F. Martin put together artwork by dozens of gay men and women who often, just a few short decades ago, had to hide who they were in order to express themselves artistically. Perhaps the saddest story illustrated in the exhibit is that of Lionel Pries, the head of the University of Washington architecture department in the 1920s and a first-class watercolorist. Arrested for sodomy in a Seattle Police Department sting, Pries lost his job and everything, Martin said. To commemorate a three-way they had with artist Lionel Pries in the 1930s, Morris Graves and Guy Anderson made a two-sided watercolor — Graves' nude study of Anderson on one side, Anderson's study of Graves on the other.

Park: Manito Park, 1702 S Grand Blvd, Spokane, WA **99203**, included in the Damron Address Book from 1972 to 1980.

Restaurant/Bar:	Red Lobster, 4703 N Division St, Spokane, WA **99207**
Accommodation:	Marianna Stoltz House B&B (427 E Indiana Ave, Spokane, WA **99207**), LGBTQ friendly.

Queer Architects: Waikiki (now Bozarth Mansion and Retreat Center, 12415 N Fairwood Dr, Spokane, WA **99218**), Amanda and Jay P. Graves Residence, Interior Design by Elsie De Wolfe. The Bozarth Mansion and Retreat Center was originally known as Waikiki. The mansion, which was designed by famed architect Kirkland K. Cutter, was constructed at a cost of approximately $100,000 in 1911-1913. The famed Olmstead Brothers of Boston designed the gardens and underground water system and the interiors were by Elsie de Wolfe, America's first well-known decorator. The home was built for J.P. Graves, whose father, John James Graves, was one of Spokane's early-day mining and railroad tycoons. J.P. Graves was the builder and president of the Inland Empire Traction Lines, one of Spokane's street car companies. However, one of Mr. Graves' principal businesses was his famous, 1,000 acre cattle and dairy ranch, Waikiki, on which the mansion was constructed. Waikiki Ranch is said to have had the largest herd of thoroughbred Jersey Cattle in the Pacific Coast region. The dairy was very well known throughout the world and breeding stock were shipped as far away as China. In 1936, the mansion and remaining ranch property was sold to Mr. & Mrs. Charles E. Marr for $175,000. The Graves, who apparently also owned a home on Upper Terrace on Spokane's South Hill, moved to Pasadena, California. In 1983, Waikiki was renamed the Bozarth Mansion and Retreat Center in honor of Horace and Christine Bozarth who gave a substantial gift to renovate the mansion.

99300

Park:
Sacajawea State Park, 2503 Sacajawea Park Rd, Pasco, WA **99301**, included in the Damron Address Book in 1980.
Columbia River Park, Sacajawea, Heritage Trail, Kennewick, WA **99336**, included in the Damron Address Book from 1978 to 1980.

Restaurant/Bar:	Red Lobster, 1120 N Columbia Center Blvd, Kennewick, WA **99336**

School: Whitman College (515 Boyer Ave, Walla Walla, WA **99362**) has been named among the 100 Best Campuses for LGBT Students by The Advocate College Guide for LGBT Students, 2006. It is a private liberal arts college. Founded as a seminary by a territorial legislative charter in 1859, the school became a four-year degree-granting institution in 1882. **Annual LGBT Event Highlights:** Homecoming Celebration with LGBT Alumni (Fall), Same-Sex Hand-Holding Day (Fall), Bisexuality Awareness Day (October), National Coming Out Day (October), Queer Prom/Rainbow Rage (October), World AIDS Day (December), Dragweek and Dragfest (April), National Day of Silence Observance (April), Matthew Shepard Lecture Series (Fall/Spring), David Nord Award for Gay and Lesbian Studies (Spring). **LGBT Resource center/office:** Intercultural Center (Whitman College, 345 Boyer Ave, Walla Walla, WA **99362**).

Park: Pioneer Park, 940 E Alder St, Walla Walla, WA **99362**, included in the Damron Address Book from 1977 to 1980.

Attractions: The Whitman Mission National Historic Site (328 Whitman Mission Rd, Walla Walla, WA **99362**) tells the story of the murder of the Whitman family (Dr. Marcus Whitman, his wife Narcissa Whitman, and 11 others) in 1847 by a group of Native Americans. The Whitmans were missionaries known for helping establish the Oregon Trail; many saw the murders as a protective measure against the spread of measles to the native people. Among the 50 most popular historic sites in America, 2022.

Accommodation:
CarltAnn House B&B (1004 Alvarado Terrace, Walla Walla, WA **99362**), gay owned. Restored 1906 historic home of Walla Walla. Close to Whitman College and a 15 minute walk to downtown where you will find dozens of wine tasting rooms, interesting shops, and many fine restaurants. Shady patio and beautiful trees and gardens.

Books by Elisa Rolle

- **Days of Love: Celebrating LGBT History One Story at a Time**
- **The world of Gene Marshall and Friends: A Collector's Guide**
- **Queer Places: Retracing the Steps of LGBTQ people around the World**: Africa and Oceania
- **Queer Places: Retracing the Steps of LGBTQ people around the World**: South and Central America
- **Queer Places: Retracing the Steps of LGBTQ people around the World**: Asia
- **Queer Places: Retracing the Steps of LGBTQ people around the World**: Canada
- **Queer Places: Retracing the Steps of LGBTQ people around the World**: Eastern Europe (Armenia, Austria, Belarus, Bosnia and Herzegovina, Bulgaria, Crimea, Croatia, Czechia, Estonia, Georgia, Hungary, Latvia, Lithuania, Macedonia, Moldova, Poland, Romania, Russia, Serbia, Slovakia, Turkey, Ukraine)
- **Queer Places: Retracing the Steps of LGBTQ people around the World**: France
- **Queer Places: Retracing the Steps of LGBTQ people around the World**: Paris
- **Queer Places: Retracing the Steps of LGBTQ people around the World**: Ireland
- **Queer Places: Retracing the Steps of LGBTQ people around the World**: Italy Center (Lazio, Umbria, Sardegna, Toscana)
- **Queer Places: Retracing the Steps of LGBTQ people around the World**: Italy North (Piemonte, Valle d'Aosta, Liguria, Lombardia, Veneto, Friuli Venezia Giulia, Trentino-Alto Adige, Emilia Romagna)
- **Queer Places: Retracing the Steps of LGBTQ people around the World**: Italy South (Marche, Abruzzo, Puglia, Basilicata, Campania, Molise, Calabria, Sicilia)
- **Queer Places: Retracing the Steps of LGBTQ people around the World**: Netherlands
- **Queer Places: Retracing the Steps of LGBTQ people around the World**: Scandinavia (Denmark, Finland, Iceland, Norway, Sweden)
- **Queer Places: Retracing the Steps of LGBTQ people around the World**: Southern Europe (Albania, Andorra, Cyprus, Gibraltar, Greece, Malta, Montenegro, Portugal, Slovenia, Spain)
- **Queer Places: Retracing the Steps of LGBTQ people around the World**: Western Europe (Belgium, Germany, Liechtenstein, Luxembourg, Switzerland)
- **Queer Places: Retracing the Steps of LGBTQ people around the World**: United Kingdom (London – West and West Central)
- **Queer Places: Retracing the Steps of LGBTQ people around the World**: United Kingdom (London - South East and South West)
- **Queer Places: Retracing the Steps of LGBTQ people around the World**: United Kingdom (Greater London and London - East, East Central, North and North West)
- **Queer Places: Retracing the Steps of LGBTQ people around the World**: United Kingdom (East Midlands)
- **Queer Places: Retracing the Steps of LGBTQ people around the World**: United Kingdom (East of England)
- **Queer Places: Retracing the Steps of LGBTQ people around the World**: United Kingdom (North East and North West England, Scotland, and Northen Ireland)
- **Queer Places: Retracing the Steps of LGBTQ people around the World**: United Kingdom (South East England: Sussex, Hampshire, Isle of Wight, Kent)
- **Queer Places: Retracing the Steps of LGBTQ people around the World**: United Kingdom (South East England: Berkshire, Buckinghamshire, Oxfordshire, Surrey)
- **Queer Places: Retracing the Steps of LGBTQ people around the World**: United Kingdom (South West and Islands)
- **Queer Places: Retracing the Steps of LGBTQ people around the World**: United Kingdom (Wales)
- **Queer Places: Retracing the Steps of LGBTQ people around the World**: United Kingdom (West Midlands and Yorkshire and the Humber)
- **Queer Places: Retracing the Steps of LGBTQ people around the World**: United States of America – Central Time Zone (Alabama, Louisiana, Mississippi, Tennessee)
- **Queer Places: Retracing the Steps of LGBTQ people around the World**: United States of America – Central Time Zone (Arkansas, Kansas, Missouri, Oklahoma, Texas)

References

A

- Ackroyd, Peter. Queer City: Gay London from the Romans to the Present Day
- Aldrich, Robert. The Seduction of the Mediterranean: Homosexual Writing, Art and Fantasy
- Aldrich, Robert, Wotherspoon, Garry. Who's Who in Gay and Lesbian History Vol.1: From Antiquity to the Mid-Twentieth Century
- Alessandro Borghese - 4 ristoranti
- Anderson, J. Seth. LGBT Salt Lake (Images of Modern America)
- Andrews, Nancy. Family: A Portrait of Gay and Lesbian America
- Anesko, Michael. Henry James and Queer Filiation
- Atkins, Gary. Gay Seattle: Stories of Exile and Belonging
- Austin, Jill, Brier, Jennifer. Out in Chicago: LGBT History at the Crossroads
- Avery, Simon, Graham, Katherine M. Sex, Time and Place: Queer Histories of London, c.1850 to the Present
- Axel, Madsen. Stanwyck

B

- Bach, Steven. Marlene Dietrich: Life and Legend
- Baim, Tracy. Out and Proud in Chicago: An Overview of the City's Gay Community
- Balint, Valerie. A Guide to Historic Artists' Home and Studios
- Banner, Lois W. Intertwined Lives: Margaret Mead, Ruth Benedict, and Their Circle
- Barlow, Clare. Queer British Art 1861-1967
- Barnet, Andrea. All-Night Party: The Women of Bohemian Greenwich Village and Harlem, 1913-1930
- Bartlett, Neil. Who Was That Man?: A Present for Mr. Oscar Wilde (The Masks Series)
- Baxter, John. Chronicles of Old Paris: Exploring the Historic City of Light (Chronicles Series)
- Beachy, Robert. Gay Berlin: Birthplace of a Modern Identity
- Beemyn, Brett. Creating a Place For Ourselves: Lesbian, Gay, and Bisexual Community Histories
- Beemyn, Genny. A Queer Capital: A History of Gay Life in Washington D.C.
- Bell, Barbara. Just Take Your Frock Off: A Lesbian Life
- Bell, David, Valentine, Gill. Mapping Desire: Geog Sexuality
- Benshoff, Harry M. Queer Images A History of Gay and Lesbian Film in America
- Benstock, Shari. Women of the Left Bank: Paris, 1900 – 1940
- Bérubé, Allan, D'Emilio, John, Freedman, Estelle B. Coming Out Under Fire The History of Gay Men and Women in World War II
- Betsky, Aaron. Queer Space: Architecture and Same-Sex Desire
- Binheim, Max. Women of the West: A Series of Biographical Sketches of Living Eminent Women in the Eleven Western States of the United States of America
- Biro, Jordan. Uncommon Knowledge: A History of Queer New Mexico 1920s-1980s
- Black, Cheryl. The Women of Provincetown, 1915–1922
- Boag, Peter. Re-Dressing America's Frontier Past
- Boag, Peter. Same-Sex Affairs: Constructing and Controlling Homosexuality in the Pacific Northwest
- Boswell, John. Christianity, Social Tolerance, and Homosexuality: Gay People in Western Europe from the Beginning of the Christian Era to the Fourteenth Century
- Boswell, John. Same-Sex Unions in Premodern Europe
- Boucai, Michael. Glorious Precedents When Gay Marriage Was Radical
- Bourne, Stephen. Fighting Proud: The Untold Story of the Gay Men Who Served in Two World Wars
- Bowers, Scotty. Full Service: My Adventures in Hollywood and the Secret Sex Lives of the Stars Kindle Edition

- Boyd, Nan Alamilla. Wide-Open Town: A History of Queer San Francisco to 1965
- Bragg, Lynn. More than Petticoats: Remarkable Washington Women, 2nd (More than Petticoats Series)
- Bram, Christopher. Eminent Outlaws: The Gay Writers Who Changed America
- Brawley, Steven Louis. Gay and Lesbian St. Louis (Images of America)
- Bray, Alan. The Friend
- Bret, David. Greta Garbo: A Divine Star
- Brett, Philip, Wood, Elizabeth et al. Queering the Pitch
- Bronski, Michael. A Queer History of the United States
- Bronski, Michael. Pulp Friction: Uncovering the Golden Age of Gay Male Pulps
- Brown, Jessica. Expatriate Gardens in Tuscany: Planting Ideas of Nationality
- Brown, Ricardo J. The Evening Crowd at Kirmser's: A Gay Life in the 1940s
- Bruno Barbieri - 4 hotel
- Bryans, Robin. The Dust Has Never Settled

C

- Callahan, Dan. Barbara Stanwyck: The Miracle Woman
- Campbell, Katie. Paradise of exiles: the Anglo-Florentine garden
- Capó, Julio, Jr. Welcome to Fairyland: Queer Miami before 1940
- Carey, Allison Elise. Domesticity and the modernist aesthetic : F.T. Marinetti, Djuna Barnes, and Gertrude Stein
- Carpenter, Humphrey. The Brideshead Generation: Evelyn Waugh and His Friends
- Chadwick, Whitney. Amazons in the Drawing Room: The Art of Romaine Brooks
- Champagne, John. Italian Masculinity as Queer: An Immoderate Proposal
- Chauncey, George. Gay New York: Gender, Urban Culture, and the Making of the Gay Male World, 1890-1940 Kindle Edition
- Chenault, Wesley. Gay and Lesbian Atlanta (Images of Modern America)
- Cherry, Deborah. Beyond the Frame: Feminism and Visual Culture, Britain 1850 -1900
- Cinema Treasures, Your guide to movie theaters
- Clay, Catherine. British Women Writers 1914-1945: Professional Work and Friendship
- Cocks, H.G. Nameless Offences: Homosexual Desire in the 19th Century
- Coffield, Darren. Tales from the Colony Room: Soho's Lost Bohemia
- Collis, Rose. Portraits to the Wall: Historic Lesbian Lives Unveiled (Gender Studies: Bloomsbury Academic Collections)
- Cook, Matt. London and the Culture of Homosexuality, 1885-1914
- Cook, Matt. Queer Domesticities: Homosexuality and Home Life in Twentieth-Century London (Genders and Sexualities in History)
- Cook, Matt. The Inverted City: London and the Constitution of Homosexuality, 1885-1914
- Cook, Matt, Bauer, Heike. Queer 1950s: Rethinking Sexuality in the Postwar Years
- Cook, Matt, Evans, Jennifer V. Queer cities, queer cultures : Europe since 1945
- Cook, Matt, Mills, Robert, Trumbach, Randolph, Cocks, Harry. A Gay History of Britain Love and Sex Between Men Since the Middle Ages
- Crase, Douglas. Both: A Portrait in Two Parts
- Crase, Douglas. Ruperti Imagines: A Portrait of Rupert Barneby
- Crain, Caleb. American Sympathy: Men, Friendship, and Literature in the New Nation
- Crawford, Elizabeth. The Women's Suffrage Movement: A Reference Guide 1866-1928 (Women's and Gender History)
- Crompton, Louis. Homosexuality and Civilization
- Curtis, Cathy. Restless Ambition: Grace Hartigan, Painter

D

- Dabakis, Melissa. A Sisterhood of Sculptors: American Artists in Nineteenth-Century Rome
- Dall'Orto, Giovanni, Basili, Massimo. Italia arcobaleno: Luoghi, personaggi e itinerari storico culturali LGBT
- David, Hugh. On Queer Street: Social History of British Homosexuality, 1895-1995
- Dawson, John "Gene" E. Farm Boy, City Girl: From Gene to Miss Gina
- de Acosta, Mercedes. Here Lies The Heart
- de la Croix, St. Sukie. Chicago Whispers: A History of LGBT Chicago before Stonewall
- Deschamps, David, Singer, Bennett L. LGBTQ stats lesbian, gay, bisexual, transgender, and queer people by the numbers
- Dick, Bernard F. Claudette Colbert She Walked in Beauty
- Dietrich, Marlene. Marlene
- Doan, Laura L. Fashioning Sapphism: the origins of a modern English lesbian culture
- Dowling, Linda. Hellenism and Homosexuality in Victorian Oxford
- Duberman, Martin, Vicinus, Martha, Chauncey, George. Hidden from History: Reclaiming the Gay and Lesbian Past
- Duncan, Stephen Riley. The Rebel Cafe: America's Nightclub Underground and the Public Sphere, 1934-1963
- Dynes, Wayne R. Encyclopedia of Homosexuality: Volume I and II

E

- Eastman, John. Who Lived Where: A Biographical Guide to Homes and Museums
- Edwards, Elizabeth. Women in Teacher Training Colleges, 1900-1960: A Culture of Femininity (Women's and Gender History)
- Ehrenstein, David. Open Secret - Gay Hollywood 1928 - 1998
- Ellenzweig, Allen. George Platt Lynes: The Daring Eye
- Elliman, Michael, Roll, Frederick. Pink Flaque Guide to London Copertina
- Elliott, Clinton. Hidden: The Intimate Lives of Gay Men Past and Present
- Emerson, Maureen. Riviera Dreaming: Love and War on the Côte d'Azur

F

- Faderman, Lillian. Odd Girls and Twilight Lovers: A History of Lesbian Life in Twentieth-Century America
- Faderman, Lillian. Surpassing the Love of Men: Romantic Friendship and Love Between Women from the Renaissance to the Present
- Falby, Alison. Between the Pigeonholes: Gerald Heard, 1889-1971
- Fellows, Will. A Passion to Preserve: Gay Men As Keepers of Culture
- Fellows, Will. Farm Boys: Lives of Gay Men from the Rural Midwest
- Fellows, Will, Branson, Helen P. Gay Bar: The Fabulous, True Story of a Daring Woman and Her Boys in the 1950s
- Ferentinos, Susan. Interpreting LGBT History at Museums and Historic Sites (Interpreting History Book 4)
- Ferguson, Kathy E. Emma Goldman Political Thinking in the Streets
- Field, Edward. The Man Who Would Marry Susan Sontag And Other Intimate Literary Portraits of the Bohemian Era
- Fleming, E.J. Hollywood Death and Scandal Sites: Seventeen Driving Tours with Directions and the Full Story
- Fleming, E.J. Paul Bern: The Life and Famous Death of the Mgm Director and Husband of Harlow
- Ford, Charles H. and Littlejohn, Jeffrey L. LGBT Hampton Roads (Images of Modern America)
- Frances, Hilary. Our Job Is to Free Women: The Sexual Politics of Four Edwardian Feminists from c. 1910 to c. 1935
- Frank, Barney. Improper Bostonians: Lesbian and Gay History from the Puritans to Playland

- Frankel, Noralee, Dye, Nancy S. Gender, Class, Race, and Reform in the Progressive Era
- Franzen, Trisha. Spinsters and Lesbians: Independent Womanhood in the United States (The Cutting Edge: Lesbian Life and Literature Series Book 6)
- Frederickson, Kristen, Webb, Sarah E. Singular Women: Writing the Artist
- Furman, Adam Nathaniel, Mardell, Joshua. Queer Spaces: An Atlas of LGBTQ+ Places and Stories

G

- Gerard, Alice. Palisades and Snedes Landing: The Twentieth Century
- Giard, Robert. Particular Voices: Portraits of Gay and Lesbian Writers
- Gleichen, Helena. Contacts And Contrasts
- Gordon, Phillip. Gay Faulkner: Uncovering a Homosexual Presence in Yoknapatawpha and Beyond
- Gough, Cal. Gay and Lesbian Library Service
- Graves, Donna J., Watson, Shayne E. Citywide Historic Context Statement for LGBTQ History in San Francisco
- Green, Martin Burgess. The Mount Vernon Street Warrens: A Boston Story, 1860-1910
- Grey, Antony. Quest for Justice: Towards Homosexual Emancipation
- Griffin, Gabriele. Who's Who in Lesbian and Gay Writing
- Gunn, Drewey Wayne. For the Gay Stage: A Guide to 456 Plays, Aristophanes to Peter Gill
- Gunn, Drewey Wayne. Gay American Novels, 1870-1970: A Reader's Guide
- Gunn, Drewey Wayne. Gay Novels of Britain, Ireland and the Commonwealth, 1881-1981: A Reader's Guide
- Gurganus, Allan. Preservation News

H

- Haggerty, George E. Men in Love: Masculinity and Sexuality in the Eighettnth Century
- Hagius, Hugh. Swasarnt Nerf's Gay Guides for 1949
- Hallett, Nicky. Lesbian Lives: Identity and Auto/biography in the Twentieth Century
- Hamer, Emily. Britannia's Glory: A History of Twentieth-Century Lesbians
- Harbin, Billy J. The Gay & Lesbian Theatrical Legacy: A Biographical Dictionary of Major Figures in american Stage History in the Pre-Stonewall Era
- Harris, Leonard, Molesworth, Charles. Alain L. Locke: Biography of a Philosopher
- Haslam, Nicholas. Redeeming Features: A Memoir
- Henry, Frances H.I. Love, Sex, and the Noose: The Emotions of Sodomy in 18th Century England
- Hession, Jane King, Quigley, Tim. John H. Howe, Architect: From Taliesin Apprentice to Master of Organic Design
- Higgs, David. Queer Sites: Gay Urban Histories Since 1600
- Hinman, Ida. The Washington Sketch Book: A Society Souvenir
- Hinrichs, Donald W. Montreal's Gay Village: The Story of a Unique Urban Neighborhood Through the Sociological Lens
- Horak, Laura. Girls Will Be Boys: Cross-Dressed Women, Lesbians, and American Cinema, 1908-1934
- Houlbrook, Matt. Queer London: Perils and Pleasures in the Sexual Metropolis, 1918-1957 (Chicago Series on Sexuality, History, and Society)
- Howard, John. Carryin' on in the Lesbian and Gay South
- Howard, John. Men Like That: A Southern Queer History
- Howe, Kathleen, LaFrank, Kathleen. Historic Context Statement for LGBT History in New York City
- Howgate, Sara. David Hockney: Portraits
- Hunter, John Francis. The Gay Insider: A Hunter's Guide to New York and a Thesaurus of Phallic Lore

I

- Irwin, Inez Haynes. Heterodoxy to Marie
- Isherwood, Christopher. Diaries: 1939-1960

- Isherwood, Christopher. Liberation, diaries. Volume three : 1970-1983
- Isherwood, Christopher. Lost Years: A Memoir 1945 - 1951
- Isherwood, Christopher, Bachardy, Don. The Animals: Love Letters Between Christopher Isherwood and Don Bachardy

J

- Jennings, Rebecca. A Lesbian History of Britain: Love and Sex Between Women Since 1500
- Jorgensen, Jay. Edith Head: The Fifty-Year Career of Hollywood's Greatest Costume Designer
- Jorgensen, Jay, Scoggins, Donald L. Creating the Illusion: A Fashionable History of Hollywood Costume Designers

K

- Kagan, Jérôme. Eugene MacCown, démon des Années folles
- Kaiser, Charles. The Gay Metropolis: The Landmark History of Gay Life in America since World War II
- Kaplan, Morris B. Sodom on the Thames: Sex, Love, and Scandal in Wilde Times
- Karlin, Rick, De La Croix, St Sukie. Last Call Chicago: A History of 1001 LGBTQ-Friendly Taverns, Haunts & Hangouts
- Karson, Robin S. Fletcher Steele, Landscape Architect: An Account of the Gardenmakers Life, 1885-1971
- Katz, Jonathan Ned. Love Stories: Sex Between Men Before Homosexuality
- Kelley, Louise Parker. LGBT Baltimore (Images of Modern America)
- Kennedy, Elizabeth Lapovsky, Davis, Madeline D. Boots of Leather, Slippers of Gold: The History of a Lesbian Community
- Kennerley, David. Getting In: NYC Club Flyers from the Gay 1990s
- Kester, Norman G. Liberating Minds: The Stories and Professional Lives of Gay, Lesbian, and Bisexual Librarians and Their Advocates
- Kiedrowski, Thomas. Andy Warhol's New York City: Four Walks, Uptown to Downtown
- Knight, Carlo. La torre di Clavel
- Kreisel, Martha. American Women Photographers: A Selected and Annotated Bibliography

L

- Larivière, Michel. Dictionnaire historique des homosexuel-le-s célèbres
- Larivière, Michel. Femmes d'homosexuels célèbres
- Larivière, Michel. Les amours masculines de nos grands hommes: Homosexuels et bisexuels célèbres
- Laurie, Alison J. Lady-Husbands and Kamp Ladies: Pre-1970 Lesbian Life in Aotearoa/New Zealand
- Leddick, David. Intimate Companions: A Triography of George Platt Lynes, Paul Cadmus, Lincoln Kirstein, and Their Circle
- Lee, Laura. The Mysterious Mr. Schwabe
- Lee, Laura. Wilde Nights and Robber Barons
- Leonard, John William. Woman's Who's Who of America: A Biographical Dictionary of Contemporary Women of the United States and Canada
- Lerman, Leo. The Grand Surprise: The Journals of Leo Lerman
- Levin, Amy K. Gender, Sexuality and Museums: A Routledge Reader
- Levin, Sue. In the Pink: The Making of Successful Gay- and Lesbian-Owned Businesses
- Lewis, Brian. British Queer History: New Approaches and Perspectives
- Lipsky, William. Gay and Lesbian San Francisco (Images of Modern America)
- Lobenthal, Joel – Tallulah! The Life and Times of a Leading Lady
- Loescher, Ermanus. Rome and its neighborhood visited in eight days
- Lopez, Russ. The Hub of the Gay Universe: An LGBTQ History of Boston, Provincetown, and Beyond
- Lubenow, W.C. The Cambridge Apostles, 1820–1914: Liberalism, Imagination, and Friendship in British Intellectual and Professional Life
- Lyons, Louis S. Who's Who Among the Women of California

- Madsen, Axel. The Sewing Circle: Hollywood's Greatest Secret—Female Stars Who Loved Other Women
- Manion, Jen. Female Husbands: A Trans History
- Mann, Richard G. United Kingdom I: The Middle Ages through the Nineteenth Century
- Mann, Richard G. United Kingdom II: 1900 to the Present
- Mann, William J. Behind the Screen: How Gays and Lesbians Shaped Hollywood, 1910-1969
- Mann, William J. Gay Pride: A Celebration Of All Things Gay And Lesbian
- Mann, William J. Kate: The Woman Who Was Hepburn
- Marbury, Elisabeth. My Crystal Ball
- Marcocci, Giuseppe. Matrimoni Omosessuali nella Roma del tardo Cinquecento: su un passo del "Journal" di Montaigne
- Marcus, Eric. Making Gay History: The Half Century Fight for Lesbian and Gay Equal Rights
- Marcus, Sharon. Between Women: Friendship, Desire, and Marriage in Victorian England
- Marschak, Beth. Lesbian and Gay Richmond (Images of Modern America)
- Martin, David F. The Lavender Palette: Gay Culture and the Art of Washington State
- Martinac, Paula. The Queerest Places: A National Guide to Gay and Lesbian Historic Sites
- Matador Network: https://matadornetwork.com/
- Matthews, Peter. Who's Buried Where in London (Shire Library Book 770)
- McBride, Dennis. LGBTQ Las Vegas (Images of Modern America)
- McCourt, James. Queer Street: Rise and Fall of an American Culture 1947-1985
- McFadden, Margaret H. Golden Cables of Sympathy: The Transatlantic Sources of Nineteenth-Century Feminism
- McGarry, Molly, Wasserman, Fred. Becoming Visible : An Illustrated History of Lesbian and Gay Life in Twentieth-Century America
- McKayle, Donald. Transcending Boundaries, My Dancing Life
- McLaren, Angus. The Trials of Masculinity: Policing Sexual Boundaries, 1870-1930
- McMahon, Lucia. Mere Equals: The Paradox of Educated Women in the Early American Republic
- McManus, Fabrizzio. Homosexuality, Homophobia, and Biomedical Sciences
- Middleton, Judith. A History of Women's Lives in Hove and Portslade
- Miescher, Stephan F., Mitchell, Michele, Shibusawa, Naoko - Gender, Imperialism and Global Exchanges
- Miller, Neil. In Search of Gay America: Women and Men in a Time of Change
- Mims, La Shonda Candace. Drastic Dykes and Accidental Activists: Lesbians, Identity, and the New South
- Minton, Henry L. Departing from Deviance: A History of Homosexual Rights and Emancipatory Science in America
- Mitchell, Charlotte. Women students at UCL in the early 1880s
- Mizner, Addison. Florida Architecture of Addison Mizner (Dover Architecture)
- Money, James. Capri: Island of Pleasure
- Monsiváis, Carlos. Los gays en México: la fundación, la ampliación, la consolidación del ghetto
- Moreira, Luciana. Living Lesbian Relationships in Madrid: Queering Life and Families in Times of Straight Living Fossils
- Moreno, Barry. Homes of Hollywood Stars (Postcard History Series)
- Moschetti, Carole Olive. Conjugal Wrongs Don't Make Rights: International Feminist Activism, Child Marriage and Sexual Relativism
- Muzzy, Frank. Gay And Lesbian Washington, D.C. (Images of Modern America)
- Myers, John Brown. Tracking the Marvelous: A Life in the New York Art World

N

- Newton, Esther. Cherry Grove, Fire Island: Sixty Years in America's First Gay and Lesbian Town
- Nicholson, Virginia. Singled Out: How Two Million Women Survived without Men After the First World War
- Nickels, Thom. Gay and Lesbian Philadelphia (Images of America)
- NYC LGBT Historic Sites Project, a project of the Partner Program of the Fund for the City of New York, a 501(c)(3) nonprofit organization

O

- Oakley, Ann. Women, Peace and Welfare
- Oram, Alison, Turnbull, Annmarie. The Lesbian History Sourcebook: Love and Sex Between Women in Britain from 1780–1970

P

- Parker, John. Who's Who in the Theatre: A Biographical Record of the Contemporary Stage
- Peiss, Kathy. Passion and Power: Sexuality in History
- Pemble, John. The Mediterranean Passion: Victorians and Edwardians in the South
- Petry, Michael. Hidden Histories: 20th Century Male Same Sex Lovers In The Visual Arts
- Pini, Andrea. Quando eravamo froci. Gli omosessuali nell'Italia della dolce vita (La cultura)
- Plant, Richard. The Pink Triangle: The Nazi War Against Homosexuals
- Potvin, John. Bachelors of a Different Sort: Queer Aesthetics, Material Culture and the Modern Interior in Britain
- Potvin, John. Material and Visual Cultures Beyond Male Bonding, 1870–1914: Bodies, Boundaries and Intimacy
- Price, Lucien. Immortal Youth: A Study in the Will to Create
- Price, Steven M. Trousdale Estates: Midcentury to Modern in Beverly Hills

Q

- Queer Happened Here (@queer_happened_here), Instagram
- Quinn, Carolyn. Mama Rose's Turn: The True Story of America's Most Notorious Stage Mother

R

- Rahtz, Sebastian. The Protestant Cemetery Catalogue
- Rebellato, Dan. 1956 and All That: The making of modern British drama
- Reed, John Shelton. Dixie Bohemia: A French Quarter Circle in the 1920s (Walter Lynwood Fleming Lectures in Southern History)
- Rennison, Nick. Bohemian London
- Rettenmund, Matthew, Barnes, Patrick, et al. Two Hearts Desire: Gay Couples on their Love
- Richards, Dell. Lesbian Lists
- Rieder, Ines, Voigt, Diana. The Story of Sidonie C, Freud's famous case of female homosexuality
- Riva, Maria. Marlene Dietrich: The Life
- Robb, Graham. Strangers: Homosexual Love in the Nineteenth Century
- Robinson, Jane. Ladies Can't Climb Ladders: The Pioneering Adventures of the First Professional Women
- Rocke, Michael. Forbidden Friendships: Homosexuality and Male Culture in Renaissance Florence (Studies in the History of Sexuality)
- Roden, Frederick S. Same Sex Desire in Victorian Religious Culture
- Rodger, Gillian M. Just One of the Boys: Female-to-Male Cross-Dressing on the American Variety Stage (Music in American Life)
- Rodriguez, Suzanne. Wild Heart: A Life: Natalie Clifford Barney and the Decadence of Literary Paris
- Rohan, Timothy M. The Architecture of Paul Rudolph
- Rorem, Ned. The Paris Diary & The New York Diary, 1951–1961
- Rossini, Gill. Same Sex Love, 1700–1957: A History and Research Guide

- Rothblum, Esther D. Boston Marriages: Romantic but Asexual Relationships Among Contemporary Lesbians
- Rowse, A.L. Homosexuals in History - a Study of Ambivalence in Society, Literature and the Arts
- Rupp, Leila J. A Desired Past: A Short History of Same-Sex Love in America
- Rupp, Leila J. Sapphistries: A Global History of Love between Women
- Rupp, Leila J., Freeman, Susan K. Understanding and Teaching U.S. Lesbian, Gay, Bisexual, and Transgender History
- Russell, Ina. Jeb and Dash: A Diary of Gay Life, 1918-1945
- Rydstrom, Jens. Odd Couples: A History of Gay Marriage in Scandinavia
- Rydström Jens, Mustola, Kati. Criminally Queer: Homosexuality and Criminal Law in Scandinavia 1842–1999

S

- Schanke, Robert A. Passing Performances: Queer Readings of Leading Players in American Theater History
- Schnadelbach, R. Terry. Hidden Lives / Secret Gardens: The Florentine Villas Gamberaia, La Pietra and I Tatti
- Schneck, Ken, McClelland, Shane. LGBTQ Columbus (Images of Modern America)
- Schneck, Ken. LGBTQ Cleveland (Images of Modern America)
- Schoppmann, Claudia. Sprung ins Nichts: Überlebensstrategien lesbischer Jüdinnen in NS-Deutschland
- Schwarz, Judith. Radical feminists of Heterodoxy
- Scott, Mary Wingfield. Winkie
- Scupham-Bilton, Tony. Mayflower 400 Queer Bloodlines
- Sedgwick, Eve Kosofsky. Between Men English Literature and Male Homosexual Desire
- Sears, Clare. Arresting Dress: Cross-Dressing, Law, and Fascination in Nineteenth-Century San Francisco
- Sears, James T. Rebels, Rubyfruit, and Rhinestones: Queering Space in the Stonewall South
- Seth, Koven. Slumming: Sexual and Social Politics in Victorian London
- Shand-Tucci, Douglass. Boston Bohemia, 1881-1900: Ralph Adams Cram--Life and Architecture
- Shand-Tucci, Douglass. The Crimson Letter: Harvard, Homosexuality, and the Shaping of American Culture
- Shayne, Alan, Sunshine, Norman. Double life a love story from Broadway to Hollywood
- Shernoff, Michael. Gay Widowers: Life After the Death of a Partner
- Sinnott, Megan J. Toms and Dees : transgender identity and female same-sex relationships in Thailand
- Skidmore, Emily. Exceptional Queerness: Defining the Boundaries of Normative US Citizenship, 1876-1936
- Skidmore, Emily. True Sex: The Lives of Trans Men at the Turn of the Twentieth Century
- Slide, Anthony. Inside Hollywood Fan Magazine
- Slide, Anthony. Lost Gay Novels: A Reference Guide to Fifty Works from the First Half of the Twentieth Century
- Slide, Anthony. On Actors and Acting
- Soares, André. Beyond Paradise: The Life of Ramon Novarro
- Sonnentag, Stefanie. Spaziergänge durch das literarische Capri: Spaziergänge durch das Capri und Neapel der Literaten und Künstler
- Souhami, Diana. No Modernism Without Lesbians
- Spagnoli, Lorenzo. Franklin D. Israel. La creazione del disordine
- Spoto, Donald. Blue Angel: The Life of Marlene Dietrich
- Spoto, Donald. Possessed: The Life of Joan Crawford
- Springate, Megan E. LGBTQ America: A Theme Study of Lesbian, Gay, Bisexual, Transgender, and Queer History

- Stern, Keith. Queers in History: The Comprehensive Encyclopedia of Historical Gays, Lesbians and Bisexuals
- Stewart-Winter, Timothy. Queer Clout : Chicago and the Rise of Gay Politics
- Stoneley, Peter. A Queer History of the Ballet
- Streitmatter, Rodger. Outlaw Marriages: The Hidden Histories of Fifteen Extraordinary Same-Sex Couples
- Stryker, Susan. Transgender History: The Roots of Today's Revolution
- Summers, Ken. Queer Hauntings: True Tales of Gay & Lesbian Ghosts
- Syme, Alison. A Touch of Blossom: John Singer Sargent and the Queer Flora of Fin-De-Siecle

T

- Takach, Michail, Schwamb, Don. LGBT Milwaukee (Images of Modern America)
- Tamagne, Florence. A History of Homosexuality in Europe: Berlin, London, Paris, 1919-1939, Volume I & II
- Thellung di Coutelary, Francesca. Il medico di Istanbul
- Thompson, Brock. The Un-Natural State: Arkansas and the Queer South
- Tiemeyer, Phil. Plane Queer: Labor, Sexuality, and AIDS in the History of Male Flight Attendants
- Tippins, Sherill. February House: The Story of W. H. Auden, Carson McCullers, Jane and Paul Bowles, Benjamin Britten, and Gypsy Rose Lee, Under One Roof in Brooklyn
- Turner, Mark. Backward Glances: Cruising Queer Streets in London and New York

V

- Vale, Allison. A Woman Lived Here: Alternative Blue Plaques, Remembering London's Remarkable Women
- van Gelder, Lindsy, Brandt, Pamela Robin. Are You Two Together?: Gay and Lesbian Travel Guide to Europe

W

- Wagner, Laurie, Rausser, Stephanie, Collier, David. Living Happily Ever After: Couples Talk About Lasting Love
- Wagner, R. Richard. Coming Out, Moving Forward: Wisconsin's Recent Gay History
- Wagner, R. Richard. We've Been Here All Along: Wisconsin's Early Gay History
- Wagner, R. Richard. Wisconsin, LGBT History Timeline
- Wallace, David. A City Comes Out: How Celebrities Made Palm Springs a Gay and Lesbian Paradise
- Wallace, Kevin. Liam O'Gallagher: Every Exit is an Entry
- Ward, Katie. Building an Identity Despite Discrimination: A Linguistic Analysis of the Lived Experiences of Gender Variant People in North East England
- Weissberger, L. Arnold. Famous Faces: A Photograph Album of Personal Reminiscences
- Wharton, Edith, Codman, Ogden Jr. The Decoration of Houses
- Whisnant, Clayton. Queer Identities and Politics in Germany: A History, 1880–1945
- White, Edmund. States of Desire Revisited: Travels in Gay America
- Wilcox, Melissa M. Queer Women and Religious Individualism
- Willard, Frances E., Livermore, Mary A. A Women of the Century: Leading American Women in All Walks of Life
- Willett, Graham, Bailey, Angela, Jones, Timothy W., Rood, Sarah. A History of LGBTIQ+ Victoria in 100 Places and Objects
- Williams, James S. Jean Cocteau
- Wilson, Scott. Resting Places: The Burial Sites of More Than 14,000 Famous Persons
- Windmeyer, Shane L. The Advocate College Guide for Lgbt Students
- Witt, Lynn, Thomas, Sherry, et al. Out in All Directions: A Treasury of Gay and Lesbian America
- Woods, Gregory. Homintern: How Gay Culture Liberated the Modern World
- Wotherspoon, Garry. Gay Sydney: A History

Y

- Yoch, James J. Landscaping the American Dream: The Gardens and Film Sets of Florence Yoch : 1890-1972

Z

- Zikratyy, Yuriy. Cross-Class Escape and the Erotics of Proletarian Masculinity in Thomas Painter's Sexual Record and Visual Archive
- Zimmer, Dieter E. What Happened to Sergey Nabokov
- Zollo, Paul. Hollywood Remembered: An Oral History of Its Golden Age
- Zultanksi, Steven. Honestly

Milton Keynes UK
Ingram Content Group UK Ltd.
UKHW050807201123
432900UK00011B/286